Small and Interr
Urban Cent

DATE DUE	
JUL 0 3 1993	

Other Development Studies titles available:

Development as Social Transformation
Transforming the World Economy?
Protectionism and Industrial Decline

Small and Intermediate Urban Centres:

Their Rôle in Regional and National Development in the Third World

edited by
Jorge E. Hardoy and David Satterthwaite

WESTVIEW PRESS
Boulder, Colorado
in association with the United Nations University

Published in 1986 in the United States by
WESTVIEW PRESS
Frederick A. Praeger, Publisher
5500 Central Avenue
Boulder, Colorado 80301

LC 86-50446 (Westview)
ISBN 0-8133-0404-0 (Westview)

Printed in Great Britain.

Contents

List of Tables

List of Maps

About the Contributors

Babiker A. Abdalla is a lecturer at the Department of Geography, University of Khartoum and coordinator of a project on Indicators of Environmental Change and Desertification in Kordofan Province sponsored by the Institute of Environmental Studies, Khartoum University and Clark University, USA. Recent publications include 'Demographic and Spatial Growth Patterns of Gezira Settlements' (co-author with S.A.El Arifi), Chapter 3 in *The Role of Intermediate and Small Centres in the Development of Gezira, Sudan,* IIED/SGAHS, London/Khartoum, 1986.

Tade Akin Aina is currently senior lecturer in the Department of Sociology, University of Lagos. With a degree in Sociology from Lagos University, a masters from the London School of Economics and a doctorate from the University of Sussex (UK), he has been a member of the University of Lagos Human Settlements Study Group since 1980. His recent publications include *Popular Settlements in Metropolitan Lagos* (co-authored with David Aradeon), Lagos University, 1986.

David Aradeon teaches architectural design and currently heads the Department of Architecture at the University of Lagos, Nigeria. He also directs the research team at this University which has collaborated with IIED since 1977. A graduate of the School of Architecture, Columbia University, USA, he was awarded the NIAE Paris Travelling Prize Award for the best architectural design thesis project. Between 1968 and 1971 he travelled widely in North and West Africa on Ford and Farfield foundation grants, studying human settlements, and the 1977 Festac Exhibition on African Architectural Technology which resulted from his work during these years is now part of the Museum of African Culture in Lagos. Since 1976, he has published several research papers on the problems of human settlements in Africa.

B. S. Bhooshan is a consultant, completing his doctorate at the Institute of Development Studies, Mysore University, India. With a degree in Architecture from Kerala University and a masters in City and Regional Planning from Madras University, his recent publications include: *Towards Alternative Settlement Strategies* (ed.), Heritage Books, India, 1980, and *The Development Experience of Nepal,* Concept Publishing, India, 1979.

Omer M. A. El Agraa is currently Dean of the Graduate College and a Professor at the Department of Architecture, University of Khartoum. He also set up and directs the Sudanese Group for Assessment of Human Settlements at Khartoum University which has collaborated with IIED since 1977. With a degree in Architecture from Khartoum University and a doctorate in Building Science from the University of Liverpool, UK, he also chairs the Council on Scientific and Technological Research of the Sudanese National Council of Research and chairs the committee set up by the Minister of Construction and Public Works to revise physical planning, land and municipal laws in the light of new devolution laws. He was head of the building committee for the New Khartoum international airport project 1981–83 and has been head of the Dar Fur regional university physical planning and architectural project since 1983. Among his recent publications are *Human Settlements in Arab Countries Vol. I,* 1980, *Vol. II,* 1986 and Arabic Version of *Volume I,* 1986, co-author with Adil M. Ahmad, Khartoum University Press; *The Role of Intermediate and Small Centres in the Development of Gezira, Sudan* (co-editor with Ian Haywood and author of five chapters), IIED/SGAHS, London/Khartoum, 1986; and *Popular Settlements in Khartoum* (co-author with Adil M. Ahmad, Ian Haywood and Osman El Kheir), SGAHS, Khartoum, 1985.

Salih A. El Arifi is at the Department of Geography, University of Khartoum and a member of the Sudanese Group for Assessment of Human Settlements. His recent publications include 'Demographic and Spatial Growth Patterns of Gezira

Settlements' (co-author with B.A.A. Rahman), Chapter 3 in *The Role of Intermediate and Small Centres in the Development of Gezira, Sudan,* op. cit. and 'Nature and Rate of Urbanization in the Sudan' in *Urbanization and Urban Life in the Sudan,* Valdo Pons (ed.), University of Khartoum and Hull, 1980.

Ali Mohamed El Hassan is at the Department of Economics, Gezira Univesity, Sudan, and a member of the Sudanese Group for Assessment of Human Settlements. His recent publications include 'Production Relations in the Gezira Scheme', Chapter 5 in *The Role of Intermediate and Small Centres in the Development of Gezira, Sudan,* op. cit.

Mohamed Osman El Sammani is a lecturer at the University of Khartoum and, since 1982, has been a member of the Sudanese Group for Assessment of Human Settlements. Recent publications include, 'Gaps in the Water Provision Map of the Sudan', *Sudan Notes and Records,* Vol. LIX, No. 59; 'The Impact of Water Sources on Eco-systems', *Sudan Notes and Records,* Vol. LIX, No. 61; and 'Some Environmental Developments and Related Implications in Gezira', Chapter 6 of *The Role of Intermediate and Small Centres in the Development of Gezira, Sudan,* op. cit.

Jorge E. Hardoy is Director of the Human Settlements Programme, International Institute for Environment and Development and Senior Fellow, Centro de Estudios Urbanos y Regionales (Buenos Aires). At present, he is also President of the National Commission for Historical Monuments of Argentina and a member of the advisory board of the Argentinian National Research Council (CONICET). Qualifying as an architect from Buenos Aires University, with a masters degree in City and Regional Planning and a doctorate from Harvard University, he is a former Senior Research Fellow of the International Development Research Centre of Canada. He is also a former President of the Inter-American Planning Society and has twice been a Guggenheim Fellow. Recent books include *El Impacto de la urbanizacion en los centros historicos de America Latina* (co-authored with Mario R. dos Santos), published by UNESCO/UNDP in Lima, 1983; *Shelter: Need and Response* (co-authored with David Satterthwaite), published by John Wiley and Sons, 1981; *Politicas Agarias y politicas urbanas en America Latina,* IDRC, Bogota, 1981; and *Shelter Provision in Developing Countries* (with A.L. Mabogunje and R.P. Misra), John Wiley and Sons, 1978. He is also author of two books and many articles on urbanization in Precolumbian cities and editor of a series of volumes on Latin American urban history.

Ian Haywood is a planning consultant and was Professor of Planning at Khartoum University's Department of Architecture between 1979 and 1985. With a masters degree in Urban Design and Regional Planning from Edinburgh University, he is a member both of the Royal Institute of British Architects and of the Royal Town Planning Institute. Recent publications include *The Management of Human Settlements in Hot Dry Climates,* UNESCO, 1984; 'City Profile — Khartoum', *Cities,* Vol. II, No. 2, August 1985; and 'Housing in Denmark' in Martin Wynn (ed.), *Housing in Europe,* Croom Helm, 1983.

Mabel Manzanal is a researcher with the Centro de Estudios Urbanos y Regionales (CEUR) in Buenos Aires, Argentina and a member of the National Research Council (CONICET) of Argentina. With a degree in business administration from the University of Buenos Aires and a masters degree in Economics from the University of Santiago, Chile, her most recent publications include *Agro, Industria y Ciudad en la Patagonia Norte,* Ediciones CEUR, Buenos Aires, 1983, and 'Lo aparente y lo real en la estrategia de desarrollo economico en la provincia de Rio Negro, 1958–64', *Revista Interamericana de Planificacion,* Vol. XIV, No. 53, March 1980.

H. N. Misra is a Senior Fellow of the International Institute for Development Research, Allahabad, India, and Reader in the Department of Geography, Allahabad University. With both a masters degree and a doctorate in Geography from Allahabad University, he received a Fulbright Fellowship in 1976–77. Among his recent publications are *Urban System of a Developing Economy*, IIDR, 1984; *Rural Geography* (ed.), Heritage Press, New Delhi, 1985; and 'Poverty, Economic Stagnation and Disease in Uttar Pradesh; A Case Study' in J. S. Tulchin (ed.), *Habitat, Health & Development*, Rienner, USA, 1986.

Hassan Mohamed Salih is at the Department of Social Studies, Khartoum University. With a masters degree in Social Anthropology from Khartoum University and a doctorate in Social Anthropology from Hull University, UK, his recent publications include 'The Evolving Socio-Economic Role of Gezira and some of its Towns' (co-author with Omer M.A. El Agraa), Chapter 4 in *The Role of Intermediate and Small Centres in the Development of Gezira, Sudan*, op. cit., and 'A Preview of Human Settlements in Gezira' (co-author with Omer M.A. El Agraa, Adil M. Ahmad, S.S. Hassan and Ian Haywood) in *Towards Alternative Settlement Strategies*, op. cit. *Strategies*, op. cit.

David Satterthwaite is a researcher with the Human Settlements Programme, International Institute for Environment and Development, and a working associate of the Development Planning Unit, University College, London. He was rapporteur of the United Nations' Expert Group Meeting on Small and Intermediate Urban Centres in November, 1984 and has helped organise a three month training programme on this subject for the staff of Third World governments and international agencies at the Development Planning Unit. With a degree in History and Ancient History from Bristol University and a diploma in Development Planning from University College, London, his recent publications include *Shelter: Need and Response* (co-author with Jorge Hardoy), John Wiley and Sons, 1981; a chapter on 'Third World Cities and the Environment of Poverty' (co-author with Jorge Hardoy) in R. Repetto (ed.), *The Global Possible*, Yale University Press, 1985; a chapter on 'Preventive Planning' in J.S. Tulchin (ed.), *Habitat, Health and Development*, Rienner, USA 1986 and a contribution to *The Gaia Atlas of Planet Management* edited by Norman Myers, Pan, 1985.

Joe U. Umo is Associate Professor of Economics at the University of Lagos, Nigeria. With a doctorate in Economics from Indiana University, USA, his most recent books are *Economics: an African Perspective*, Collins, 1985, and *Modern Micro-Economic Analysis in African Context*, Peacock Publishers, Lagos, 1985.

Cesar A. Vapnarsky is currently a researcher with the Centro de Estudios Urbanos y Regionales in Buenos Aires, Argentina and a member of the National Research Council (CONICET) of Argentina. Graduating as an architect from the National University of Buenos Aires, a Doctorate in Sociology from Cornell Univesity (USA) and a former Guggenheim Fellow, he has specialized in urbanization problems and is author of articles and research papers published in specialized journals and anthologies in Argentina, Italy, the United States and other nations. His recent books include *La Poblacion Urbana Argentina en 1970 y 1960*, CEUR, Buenos Aires, 1979, and *Pueblos del Norte de la Patagonia 1779-1957*, Editorial de la Patagonia, General Roca, Argentina, 1983.

Preface

This book is the result of contributions, help and support from numerous people and several agencies. We are particularly grateful to the Swedish Agency for Research Cooperation with Developing Countries, the Swedish Council for Building Research and the United Nations Centre for Human Settlements (Habitat) for funding the work on which this volume is based – and doing so before the subject had come to be regarded as important and relevant. Within these agencies, special thanks is due to Olle Edqvist, Pietro Garau, Bruce Hyland, Bob and Ingrid Munro and Arcot Ramachandran. We are also grateful to our friends and colleagues in IIED's Human Settlements Programme who have worked with us on this subject – Jane Bicknell, Silvia Blitzer, Ana Maria Cabrera, Maria Graciela Caputo and Julio Davila. Julio Davila deserves special thanks for his help in refining and editing the final text; so too do Jane Bicknell and Ana Maria Cabrera for patiently putting up with endless last minute changes to the text.

Special mention must also be made of all the members of the collaborating teams:

Mabel Manzanal and Cesar Vapnarsky, Centro de Estudios Urbanos y Regionales (Centre for Urban and Regional Studies, CEUR, Buenos Aires, Argentina);

Babiker A. Abdalla, Omer El Agraa, Salih El Arifi, Ali Mohamed El Hassan, Mohamed El Sammani, Ian Haywood and Hassan Mohamed Salih from the Sudanese Group for Assessment of Human Settlements, University of Khartoum, the Sudan;

B. S. Bhooshan (Institute of Development Studies, Mysore, India) and H.N. Misra and R.P. Misra (International Institute for Development Research, Allahabad, India); and

David Aradeon, Tade Akin Aina, Ajato Gandonu, Siyanbola Tomori and Joe Umo (Human Settlements Unit, Faculty of Environmental Design, Lagos University, Nigeria).

Within these, special thanks should go to David Aradeon, Shashi Bhooshan, Omer El Agraa, Harikesh Misra and Cesar Vapnarsky as the people responsible for organizing each of the five regional studies on which most of this book is based.

Finally, our grateful thanks to Liz Mills for her comments on Chapters 7 and 8, to the International NGO Division, Canadian International Development Agency (and especially Ronald Leger) for the support given to the work of our programme over the last eight years and to the publishers, Hodder and Stoughton (especially to

Philip Walters and Fiona Wray) for putting up with our continual delays in finalizing the manuscript and in striving so hard to produce this book at as low a cost as possible.

Jorge E. Hardoy and David Satterthwaite
Human Settlements Programme
International Institute for Environment and Development

Introduction

This book summarises the findings and presents conclusions from the first phase of a collaborative research programme on the present and potential role of small and intermediate urban centres in the development process. The main body of this first phase consisted of five regional studies (two in India, one each in the Sudan, Argentina and Nigeria) which examined how social, economic and political forces mould and shape urban systems over time and thus contribute to (or constrain) the development of small and intermediate urban centres. Chapter 1 discusses the rationale for the research, the interest of governments and international agencies in the subject and some definitional questions, while Chapters 2–6 are summaries of the regional studies. Chapter 7 is a survey of published material on factors which affect the development of small and intermediate urban centres, while Chapter 8 surveys government policies and their links with small and intermediate urban centres. Chapter 7 is thus more of a review of empirical studies while Chapter 8 reviews literature which deals with the influences that government policies, actions or expenditures have (or could have) on small and intermediate urban centres. Chapter 9 draws some tentative conclusions.

Organisation of the research

The research was undertaken by the Human Settlements Programme of the International Institute for Environment and Development (IIED) in collaboration with five Third World institutions: the Centro de Estudios Urbanos y Regionales (Centre for Urban and Regional Studies) in Buenos Aires, Argentina; the Institute of Development Studies, University of Mysore, India; the Human Settlements Unit, Faculty of Environmental Design, Lagos University, Nigeria; the International Institute for Development Research, Allahabad, India; and the Sudanese Group for Assessment of Human Settlements, Khartoum University, the Sudan.

Each of these institutions has been involved in a collaborative programme of research and training which dates back to 1977, when IIED's Human Settlements Programme was founded. Apart from collaborative research on small and intermediate urban centres, this network of institutions has also collaborated in undertaking a series of assessments of Third World nations' housing, land and settlement policies, in studies of how low income 'popular settlements' form and develop in major Third World cities, and in studies of the links between health and the habitat of lower income groups. This book also draws on work undertaken by IIED's Human Settlements Programme in collaboration with Agence Cooperation et Amenagement and the Organization for Overseas Scientific and Technical Research (ORSTOM) in France, undertaken at the request of the European Commission's Directorate General for Development on 'Secondary Towns in Africa: their role and functions in National and Regional Development'. Under IIED's direction, national reports were prepared on Tanzania (by Deborah Bryceson of St Antony's College Oxford), on the Sudan (by Ian Simpson from the University of Leeds' School of Economic Studies) and on Nigeria (by Anthony O'Connor of the Department of Geography, University College, London). In addition, a report of the Gezira Region in the Sudan was undertaken by Ian Simpson and the Sudanese Group for Assessment of Human Settlements, Khartoum University. Finally, this book draws on discussions and work undertaken with the United Nations Centre for Human Settlements (Habitat) in Nairobi, Kenya.

Support for the research on small and intermediate urban centres was received from the Swedish Agency for Research Cooperation with Developing Countries, the Swedish Council for Building Research and the United Nations Centre for Human Settlements (Habitat).

Research focus

The research chose to look at the growth and development of urban systems in two regions in India, and one each in Nigeria, Argentina and the Sudan. If one wants to study an urban system, boundaries have to be defined within which the research is to concentrate. The choice of boundaries is recognised as being largely arbitrary in that they cannot define closed systems.[1] Social, economic and political forces acting across the boundaries used to delimit any urban system are obviously likely to have major impacts. Not surprisingly, this was found to be the case in each of the five regional studies, even in the North Indian region where largely subsistence level agriculture still provides the livelihood for most of the population. But the research concentrated on the development of urban systems within the chosen boundaries over time and the impact of social, economic and political forces internal to the defined region. Where social, economic or political forces which influenced the regions' urban system but came from outside the region were much in evidence, these were noted and are discussed in Chapter 8. Because of limited funds for the research, however, the decision was made to leave a detailed analysis of these to a second research phase. The need for a second research phase to complement work completed is certainly suggested by the findings from the first phase. Chapter 8 also includes a more general discussion, drawing from both the regional studies and the literature reviewed in Chapter 7 on the influence of government structure and of national governments' macro-economic and pricing policies and sectoral plans on the development of small and intermediate urban centres.

Choice of regions

Each Third World institution selected a region for research in consultation with IIED. Pilot studies were undertaken in four of the chosen regions in 1980 to test their suitability for detailed research.[2] In 1981, the International Institute for Development Research in Allahabad was invited to join this research programme, both because of its interest in the subject and because the region it chose to study had major differences with the region selected by the Institute of Development Studies, which was also in India.[3]

When choosing regions, a balance was sought in terms of size and population between those regions with a wide range of settlements and urban centres yet regions small enough to allow detailed analysis. One of the weaknesses evident in published papers on small and intermediate urban centres has been that they were either done at a level of aggregation which allowed no detailed study of individual urban centres within the system, or they concentrated only on one urban centre. For instance, as an interest in small and intermediate urban centres (or secondary cities) has developed, some studies have been undertaken for entire nations or, at best, large regions. In none of these studies does one find much detailed analysis at the level of small urban centres and of their interaction with surrounding areas. In published papers dealing with a nation, continent or indeed the entire Third World, there is a tendency to generalise about town or secondary city characteristics based on population size, as if all urban centres within particular population size classifications had identical characteristics with regard to economic base and specialisation, growth trends and prospects for further development. Such aggregate studies do not allow the analysis of, for instance, the relationship between trends in individual urban centres' population growth or economic structure and their interactions with different ecological areas, productive systems, land tenure relations and connections with major metropolitan areas.

Since resources available for the collaborative research did not permit much primary data collection and analysis, the chosen regions could not be totally different from regions for which census data and other official government data were available. Since the research never sought to find urban systems which could be examined in isolation from the wider regional, national and international context, more pragmatic criteria could be used to choose regions. The first criterion was the need for a diversity of urban centres in terms of population size and economic base and at least one with around 100,000 inhabitants. The second was regions for which there was relatively good data. The third was regions accessible to the researchers, so that gaps in existing data could be filled by some primary data collection and by frequent visits to the regions to talk to informants there. Prior knowledge of the region on the part of the researchers involved was also considered an advantage. This clearly limited the choice to areas close to the institution involved in the research. But this still meant considerable diversity in the ecological and economic base of the five regions in that the network of collaborating institutions was formed to ensure considerable cultural and geographic diversity, hence the original invitation to institutions from sub-Saharan Africa, Asia, Latin America and the Arab world to collaborate with IIED's Human Settlements Programme.

The regional studies

Chapters 2–6 contain summaries of the regional studies. Since these are only relatively short summaries of longer reports which run to 100,000 or more words, inevitably they lack much of the detail contained in the original reports. To keep this book to a readable length, they also give no physical, social or economic background information on the nations within which the study regions are located, except where this is of direct relevance to the subject under study.

The summaries of the regional studies, like the reports from which they are drawn, are not uniform in the type and quantity of data they present. This is for two reasons. First, the quality and quantity of secondary data varied greatly from region to region. For instance, for the region in Nigeria, official data on something as fundamental as population for urban centres, regions and districts is not available (or trustworthy) for more than two dates: 1952 and 1963. There is also little official economic and social data for this region. Thus, the level of detail in, say, population growth in urban centres since 1900 and in the sophistication in analysing urban trends and in seeing how they interact with social, economic and political changes, is very different from, say, the two Indian regions and the Argentinian region where more reliable census data (or estimates) are available.

The second reason is the agreed orientation of the research and the professional make-up of each team. The subject of the research is sufficiently broad that researchers from many disciplines can bring relevant experience and insights to it. From the onset, each team felt that this was collaborative research, not comparative research. The distinction is important. Comparative research implies a carefully structured research methodology common to each research effort. This is impossible, given the differences in the regions and in the data available for those regions. But comparative research would also impose a constraint on teams made up of people with different backgrounds and skills. Thus, the decision was made that each team would concentrate on common themes and questions, but each could approach the research on these themes and questions, based on their previous experiences and on available data. The purpose of the work was never to compare five regions but to understand the forces which moulded and shaped each of their economic bases and urban systems.

From five such studies in very disparate regions and from other published empirical work, it is possible to suggest some tentative findings of more general relevance and this is what we seek to do in Chapters 8 and 9. In examining factors which underpin the economic growth or stagnation of small and intermediate urban centres in each of the five regions, it is possible to suggest those which are unique to each region and those which have a wider relevance. We hope that these might provide a basis for policy makers to better understand the possibilities of alternative investment patterns and policies.

In addition, by summarising the findings from regional studies, we hope to provide material for use by universities, research groups and national or international institutions and to stimulate them to undertake further work on this subject. We hope that our work will encourage new case studies which can help develop a better body of knowledge and widen the understanding of small and intermediate urban centres' present and potential role in development and of the need for a more detailed empirical understanding of how urban systems form and develop as a prerequisite for developing national or regional settlement (or spatial) policies. Our regional studies are presented as a contribution to this, and we recognise their limitations. We did not have the time or the resources to investigate each of the regions as thoroughly as we would have liked. Indeed, as Chapter 8 outlines, our work raises additional questions which deserve further research.

Review of the literature

The review of published literature relevant to the subject of this volume draws on annotated bibliographies produced by IIED's Human Settlements Programme. Annotated bibliographies have been published covering the whole of the Third World (in English) and for Latin America (in Spanish)[4]. Relevant papers for inclusion in these annotated bibliographies were drawn from a literature search through the issues of 50 journals published since 1970, and selected readers. The journals were selected because of their interest in human settlement issues or wider issues which included human settlements. Journals published in Africa, Asia, Latin America, North America and Western Europe were included and they are listed in the Appendix (page 412). Certain papers published in these journals prior to 1970 and certain other publications which contained material of particular relevance to the subject of this book were also included. The review concentrated on material published in Spanish and English, although some material published in French and Portuguese was also included. Chapters 7 and 8 are intended both as guides to published literature of relevance to small and intermediate urban centres in the Third World and as commentaries on what the literature has to say.

Notes

1 There may still be areas or regions in the Third World which are sufficiently isolated for their economy or population to have no interaction with higher levels of government or economic forces located outside their boundaries, but this is certainly not the case in any of the five study regions. If such areas or regions do exist, they are certainly exceptional cases and are unlikely to encompass more than a tiny fraction of the Third World's population.
2 The results of the pilot studies were published under the title *Towards Alternative Settlements Strategies,* edited by B. S. Bhooshan and produced by Heritage, India (1980).
3 An important reason for the choice of a second region in India was to show the differences between two regions within the same nation. The five regions chosen for detailed study were never intended to be 'typical' of that nation since the very concept of a 'typical' region within a nation has very limited validity.
4 Bicknell, J., Blitzer, S., Davila, J., Hardoy, J. E. and Satterthwaite, D., *Small and Intermediate Urban Centres: Their Role in Third World Development: An Annotated Bibliography* (Human Settlements Programme, International Institute for Environment and Development, London, 1985) and Blitzer, S., Caputo, M. G., Hardoy, J. E. and Satterthwaite, D., *Las Ciudades Intermedias y Pequenas en America Latina: Una Bibliografia Comentada* (Ediciones CEUR, Buenos Aires, 1983).

1

Why Small and Intermediate Urban Centres?

Jorge E. Hardoy and David Satterthwaite

Purpose of the research

Our work on small and intermediate urban centres has two main aims. The first is to undertake research to provide a better understanding of how economic, social and political forces act to shape or mould urban systems over time, and their impact on social and economic development in such centres and their surrounding areas. The second is to provide a better understanding of the rationale and of the costs and benefits of various kinds of government intervention which seek to stimulate development in such centres and their wider regions. The research undertaken to date on which this volume is based concentrates on the first aim, although Chapter 8 discusses the issues raised by this research which are relevant to the second. We hope that a second phase of research can concentrate on the second aim, but building on the findings of the first phase.

Our interest in this subject arises from our concern to explore alternatives to processes which concentrate the comparatively high productivity and high income jobs, savings and investments in one (or a few) cities within each nation. It also arises from a concern to try to better understand how the performance of regional economies can be improved and how a more equitable spread of the benefits of development can be promoted in terms of increasing the proportion of people with both access to basic social and physical services (for instance piped water, improved sanitation, health care services and education) and an adequate, stable livelihood. Virtually all national government policies and policy advice given to Third World governments related to small and intermediate urban centres claim to have such economic and social objectives. But as the discussion in Chapter 8 suggests, there seems to be a considerable gap between the explicit aims of actual or proposed policies and their likely effects.

Thus, this volume (and the further research we hope to undertake in a second phase) seek to clarify what kinds of government policies on small and intermediate urban centres could increase the proportion of the national population with access to publicly provided social and physical services and with a more adequate and stable livelihood. In doing so, it will also consider the costs of such policies to the national economy; clearly a special policy on small and intermediate urban centres which adversely affects national production is likely to lessen a government's ability to fund public services and to ensure more poor households obtain adequate livelihoods. This volume will also consider the extent to which special government policies on small and intermediate urban centres might contribute to other commonly stated spatial aims – such as slowing migration to major cities (or metropolitan areas) or existing concentrations of industry, or improving service provision to rural populations, or achieving 'better regional balance'.[1]

The question whether spatial policies – including those on small and intermediate urban centres – can actually achieve such social and economic objectives is of considerable relevance given many Third World governments' apparent concern for the failure of past or current development policies, and plans to spread social and economic benefits more widely. This concern is evident in the increasing number of national plans which include elaborate spatial policies that are justified because these are meant to promote a wider distribution of social and economic benefits. An assessment of trends over the last 30 years demonstrates why a concern with such questions of distribution is valid. Although most Third World nations made considerable progress in this period, at least until the mid-Seventies, in expanding and developing their economies, very few successfully spread the benefits of this development. This lack of success can be seen in social terms by the fact that the benefits have been concentrated in a small group of relatively high income people while the poorest 20 to 40 per cent of the population often hardly benefited at all (and may indeed have become poorer).

But this lack of success can also be seen in spatial terms. Most of the urban population living outside the major cities or metropolitan areas also benefited little.[2] And in most nations, the vast majority of the agricultural population (on whose purchasing power the economies of most small urban centres largely depend) also benefited little. This is seen in large and often widening disparities in production between the more urbanised regions (which include the major cities) and regions which are more backward in economic terms. There is no shortage of policy advice for Third World governments. The review of published work in Chapters 7 and 8 shows the large volume of material advising governments as to what should be done, but there was certainly no agreement as to what can and should be done. Alonso's criticism of location theory made in 1968, in which he stated that it is characterised by an abundance of opinion but a paucity of facts (Alonso, 1968) could equally be applied to the range of policy advice given to governments on small and intermediate urban centres.

The paucity of fact is demonstrated by the lack of Third World based studies on how urban systems grow and develop, and the influence of social, economic and political forces on this process. The lack of empirical work was one of the most startling results of our review of published literature. Yet without a more detailed and geographically defined understanding of the dynamics behind present settlement or urban trends, it is difficult to see how realistic policy advice can be given to governments intent on changing them.

For instance, in suggesting how urban growth can be stimulated in smaller urban centres, papers giving policy recommendations rarely consider factors which our regional studies suggest are of considerable importance. For example, the links between the structure of land ownership or tenure and local urban centres' population growth and economic structure are rarely considered. Yet this structure influences both the size and the nature of demand for urban based production and consumption oriented goods and services. Another example is the nature of local agricultural production. Certain cash crops can produce a very high return per hectare and provide a relatively dense agricultural population with a high income. Certain crops can also stimulate many ancillary activities related to production, commercialisation or processing which are best located in urban centres nearby. By contrast, activities such as animal husbandry provide less support for urban-based economic activities, and can only provide incomes for a far less concentrated labour force. And of course, farming which is dominated by agricultural production largely for farming households' own consumption provides virtually no support for urban based economic activities.

Then there is the form that the organisation for input provision, credit, collection of crops, marketing and sale takes; this too affects the type and scale of support for local urban development. Thus, the kind of agricultural production and the mix of crops produced, the extent to which production is for sale and the extent to which farmers are able to obtain high yields and good prices, and the organisation for input provision, marketing and sale can all have a major bearing on local urban centres' growth and development.

Another example of a factor often given little attention in policy recommendations is a nation's political structure in terms of subnational levels of government powers, responsibilities and fiscal bases and the effect this has on the economic base of the urban centres where different levels of government are located. The importance of such factors was evident in the regional studies, as will be described in detail later. Yet, very few of the 150 or so papers and publications reviewed in Chapters 7 and 8 gave them much attention.

Certain aspects of the influence of social, economic and political forces on Third World urban systems have attracted the interest of researchers. One is the historical role of large cities and metropolitan areas, especially the role of major colonial cities as centres of political and administrative power and of economic control in terms of managing the export of raw materials and the import and sale of colonial powers' own products. The economic, political and administrative primacy of certain cities in independent nations (usually national capitals) has also been studied. So too have the links which these have with cities first developed under colonial rule. The links such primate cities have with the world economic system have also received some attention.

There are also a few detailed historical studies of certain urban centres other than primate cities or major metropolitan centres. But detailed studies of Third World nations' or regions' urban systems, of their evolution and development over time and of their complex interaction with social, economic and political forces both from within and from outside this system, are very rare.

The lack of detailed research is all the more puzzling when one recalls that the present spatial distribution of urban population in most Third World nations is rooted in past trends, especially in the colonial past when practically all the major national and regional centres were founded. Of course, where ancient civilisations once flourished, the distribution of national and regional centres and of comparatively densely populated rural areas was a major influence on the colonial settlement patterns; the colonial powers needed a labour force. In the relatively low population density lands in Latin America, in much of Africa south of the Sahara and in many Asian regions, the location of present urban centres was usually powerfully influenced by the urban system (or proto-system) developed by the colonial powers. Even where there was a pre-colonial urban system or series of urban centres onto which the colonial system was grafted, usually the colonial government's economic orientations and administrative structures profoundly modified this. In many nations, after independence, formerly unoccupied territories were settled which gave rise to new urban centres. For instance, in Latin America, Patagonia, southern Chile, eastern Ecuador and southern Venezuela were first settled in the second half of the nineteenth century, while parts of Amazonia have been settled more recently.

An initiative to revive an interest in the process by which national and regional spaces are transformed over time, and the influence of different national and international social, economic and political forces would probably confirm the powerful influence of past actions on present trends; this was apparent in each of our case studies. It might also confirm another finding from the case studies which is that major changes in a region's economy (and where relevant, urban centres and urban system) almost always arise from (or are much influenced by) forces exogenous to the region. Exceptions to this, which also need further investigation, might include the changes in regions' or nations' economy and urban system brought about by sudden political change.

But the purpose of our research is not just a clarification of this topic based only on five relatively small Third World regions. It is also to help clarify why many Third World governments' attempts to modify settlement trends have met with so little success both in achieving the desired spatial objectives and in reaching a wider section of their population with improved living conditions. While there seems to be a growing consensus among governments and international agencies that something must be done to change present urban or settlement patterns and trends, there is a relatively poor understanding of, for instance, how public action can steer urban growth and development away from the major cities, of the very real limitations faced by governments in market or mixed economies in being able to do so, of what measures must be taken to stimulate the growth and development of small and intermediate urban centres, of the costs and benefits of doing so, and of who benefits from the proposed measures.

Attempts by Third World governments to divert urban growth and development to 'growth poles', 'growth centres', 'growth axes' and 'new towns' have met with relatively little success in terms of spreading the benefits of development to those previously bypassed. Such schemes have generally involved considerable expense (both in terms of capital investment and of scarce managerial and technical skills). And they have been based on tools, techniques and research devised for, and done in countries (mainly the 'North'), whose problems and possibilities bear little resemblance to the problems most Third World nations are facing.

What seems to be lacking is a clear understanding of the 'settlement' or 'urban' component of government policies to spread economic and social benefits to lower income groups and of the needed role of government at local, state (or provincial) and national level. There is a need to understand the interplay and strength of private interests, both within nations and impinging on them from the international economy, in shaping the spatial distribution of development. There is a need to understand the 'urban' component of rural and agricultural development strategies. Finally, there is a need to clarify what actions can modify settlement trends and the forces which are major causes of those trends. We hope the findings from our research will help to throw light on these issues since each is relevant to the already stated two main aims of our work. Perhaps not surprisingly, most of our conclusions on mechanisms to stimulate the growth and development of small and intermediate urban centres relate far more to modifying the social, economic and political forces which seem to be the major causes of existing spatial trends and not spatial mechanisms such as diverting investment to 'growth centres' or 'new towns'.

Why focus on small and intermediate urban centres?

Despite the attention given by researchers to large cities and metropolitan areas, most of the Third World's inhabitants live outside urban centres with 100,000 or more inhabitants. According to United Nations' estimates for 1980, almost four-fifths of the Third World's population lived outside urban centres of 100,000 or more inhabitants, while in Africa and Asia, more than three-quarters lived outside settlements of 20,000 or more inhabitants.

It is not only the predominance of Third World inhabitants living outside what might be termed large urban centres which prompted our interest in small and intermediate urban centres. There appear to be at least five reasons why Third World governments might usefully consider the present and the potential role of small and intermediate urban centres in their social and economic development plans—although, of course, the relevance of each of these reasons will vary greatly from nation to nation (or indeed region to region).

The first is the fact that it is small or intermediate urban centres which are the urban centres with which most rural people and rural enterprises interact.[3] Yet the role that such centres can play in supporting social and economic development within rural areas – providing rural populations with access to, for example, schools and health care centres, being the location for, for instance, agricultural extension services, irrigation offices and agro-industries linked to local products – is rarely given sufficient attention. Nor is sufficient attention given to the need for publicly funded transport and communications infrastructures within and between small and intermediate urban centres and between these centres and rural areas. Yet all these aspects are usually essential 'urban' components of any successful rural development programme.

What we choose to call small and intermediate urban centres remain the least studied and perhaps the least understood elements within national and regional urban systems. But since the purpose of the research was never to study any particular category of settlement (however defined) in isolation, this meant the study of small and intermediate urban centres both in relation to rural population (and the economic base of their livelihood), and in relation to larger centres such as major cities and metropolitan areas. As with the definition of regions, the definition of 'small' and 'intermediate' urban centres is only to provide a focus and convenient delimitation for our research.

The reason for undertaking research on small and intermediate urban centres was not only because the needs of the people living in or around them has been given insufficient attention — both in terms of their needs for services and facilities, such as piped water supplies, provision for the hygienic disposal of human wastes, public transport, education and health care services and for measures to strengthen the basis for their livelihood.

A second reason relates to their political role. Sub-national and sub-regional levels of government administration are usually located in small and intermediate urban centres. It is through such centres that the needs and priorities of sub-national and sub-regional populations should be channelled to influence policies and resource allocations at higher levels of government. If a government's power and resources are highly centralised, such centres are deprived of their political role as the places through which local demands are articulated. Over-centralisation of government power and resources often ensures that central governments are over-burdened and deprives lower levels of government located in small and intermediate urban centres of the power and resources they need to address local problems and local development needs. Political centralisation will tend to be reflected in urban centralisation, that is in a national urban system dominated by the national capital.

In addition, governments can arrive at a better understanding of real development possibilities and development constraints through a better understanding of existing circumstances and current trends in small and intermediate urban centres and their surrounding areas, and through an appreciation of the unique characteristics of each centre and its links with its surrounds and the wider regional and national economy and urban system. Such an understanding allows a more realistic assessment of local skills and local resources. The failure (or only partial success) of so many attempts by governments to stimulate urban development away from larger cities (or their wider regions) is frequently due to a poor understanding of local circumstances, local needs and local possibilities in the urban centres which are meant to serve as growth centres.

A third reason why small and intermediate urban centres deserve special attention in many Third World nations is because certain of these centres will (or could) play an important part in many national government priorities. For instance, national goals such as increasing agricultural production or productivity or replacing food imports with local production imply a need for increased investment in infrastructure, services and facilities within or serving certain small and intermediate urban centres and their surrounds. Yet even when national plans include such goals, the actual spatial distribution of public investments and the spatial biases implicit or explicit in national policies frequently do not mesh with stated policy objectives. Chapter 8 includes a discussion of how the spatial biases inherent in macro-economic and pricing policies, and the sectoral distribution of public investment frequently help concentrate productive investment in the largest city, even when government plans are explicit about seeking to steer such investment away from that city. Furthermore, the type and location of public investments in infrastructure may bear little relation to explicit spatial goals or, indeed, encourage a spatial pattern of urban development almost exactly opposite to such goals.

A fourth reason why small and intermediate urban centres deserve special consideration, which applies to Third World nations or regions with a relatively low level of urbanisation, is that long-term policies can lessen the tendency towards what can be judged to be undesirable concentrations of industries, services and government officials in a few (or just one or two) urban centres. Carefully formulated and implemented plans for small and intermediate urban centres and the removal (or lessening) of spatial biases in macro-economic policies, sectoral plans and government structures which both inhibit such centres' development and do not serve social and economic development goals, can over time profoundly affect the spatial distribution of development within an evolving urban system.

In predominantly agrarian economies, increases in food production for the domestic market, in the production and processing of export crops and in public service provision can and should imply less centralised patterns of urbanisation than those evident in most parts of the Third World today.

A fifth reason why many Third World governments might usefully consider a special policy on small and intermediate urban centres relates to such centres' potential role in managing urban expansion within large city regions. But this will probably only have relevance for relatively few Third World governments in that this is part of an 'urban growth management' policy for large cities or metropolitan centres where there is a good social and economic rationale for supporting productive investment in certain nearby small or intermediate urban centres. This is not part of a strategy to encourage urban and industrial development in backward regions; indeed, it may help concentrate economic activities in core regions.

Each of the five reasons which have been outlined has relevance for many Third World nations although, as noted earlier, the relevance of each one can only be assessed on a nation by nation basis. For instance, as Chapter 8 discusses, support for productive investment in certain small and intermediate urban centres close to large urban centres is unlikely to serve social and economic development in most of the less populous and less urbanised Third World nations. Then there are other reasons for explicit policies for certain small and intermediate urban centres which have less general relevance when talking about 'Third World nations' in general but which may have great relevance to a few nations or regions. For instance, special programmes for selected small and intermediate urban centres and their regions may be needed to help address problems in areas subject to recurring natural disasters or in areas where there is rapid colonisation of new land or to consolidate population in border regions. But here, as in all special programmes for small and intermediate urban centres, the justification is based on the role each individual urban centre can play in social and economic development relative to specific local, regional or national goals and based on the unique range of skills, resources, links with the surrounding area, links with the wider regional and national economy and constraints on development which are particular to each urban centre. As Chapter 8 will describe in more detail, this is very different from the form that many governments' policies on small and intermediate urban centres have taken in the past. It also differs significantly from the policies recommended by many researchers and policy advice specialists.

The interest of governments and international agencies in this subject

Over the last ten years, Third World governments and international agencies have shown a growing interest in arriving at a better understanding of the spatial dimension of national development policy and, within this, of the present and potential role of small and intermediate urban centres (or secondary cities) as possible foci for public investment and public programmes.

This interest can be seen in the Recommendations for National Action unanimously approved by 132 governments at the United Nations Conference on Human Settlements (Habitat) in Vancouver in May-June 1976. These Recommendations point to the urgent need for every government to establish 'a national policy on human settlements, embodying the distribution of population and related economic and social activities over the national territory' (Recommendation A.1) as 'an integral part of any national economic and social development policy' (A.2), with the aim of improving 'the conditions of human settlements, particularly by promoting a more equitable distribution of the benefits of development among regions and by making such benefits and public services equally accessible to all groups' (A.4).

This interest can also be seen in the decision of the United Nations Inter-Governmental Commission on Human Settlements[4] to choose 'planning and management of human settlements, with emphasis on small and intermediate towns and local growth points' as the topic for a special theme paper and for discussion at their Eighth Session in 1985. The research on which this book is based is intended as a contribution to this discussion.

In the last ten years, many Third World governments have become more involved in seeking to guide the location of economic development and in giving more consideration to the spatial distribution of social and economic investments. There is growing acknowledgement that market forces operating both within and from outside national boundaries cannot by themselves promote economic and social development in the poorer and more backward regions and cannot solve many of the settlement problems confronting both national and local governments. The prevailing pattern of industrial and agricultural development which market forces and past government policies have produced are recognised as one of the root causes of rapid urban growth in certain urban centres and, very often, of economic stagnation and lack of basic service provision in less urbanised regions and rural areas. Chapter 8 includes a review of some Third World governments' recent plans and programmes associated with small and intermediate urban centres and a discussion as to their effectiveness in promoting social and economic development.

Certain international aid agencies have also become more interested in this subject, including the World Bank Group, the United Nations Development Programme, the European Development Fund, the US Agency for International Development's Office of Housing and Urban Programs and the Inter-American Development Bank. The extent to which certain multilateral aid agencies' lending to settlement projects has been concentrated in large cities (as opposed to small and intermediate urban centres) will be discussed in Chapter 8.

Definition of rural and urban

Definitions as to what is meant by 'rural', 'urban', 'small and intermediate urban centre', 'town', 'urban system' and 'urbanisation' will have to be made, before presenting the summaries of the regional studies. These will be accompanied by some discussion as to how and why these were arrived at.

The distinction between 'rural' and 'urban' population is perhaps the most controversial since there is no agreement among researchers or governments as to a satisfactory division between the two. There is some agreement that a distinction between the two is useful both because it helps distinguish between the homeplace of those working in agriculture and those working in non-agricultural activities, and helps distinguish between populations with or without immediate access to retail stores, services and facilities which are normally considered to be characteristic of 'urban areas'.

Population thresholds are commonly used, so that once a nucleated settlement grows beyond this threshold, it becomes 'urban'. Even assuming that each nation can arrive at some population threshold for settlements below which most of the population of the settlements work in agriculture, this threshold will be very different for different nations and regions. For instance, in India, many settlements with 2,000-5,000 inhabitants have a high proportion of households working in agriculture whereas in most Western nations and in some Third World regions, settlements with less than 1,000 inhabitants often have a low proportion. Indeed, in many areas in the West, and some in the Third World, a high proportion of the inhabitants living in settlements of less than a few hundred inhabitants do not work in agriculture.

Most national censuses use population thresholds to distinguish between 'rural' and 'urban' settlements. But the chosen thresholds vary enormously from nation to nation.[5] They can be as low as 1,000 inhabitants (or indeed, in a few nations, as low as a few hundred); alternatively they can be as high as 10,000 or more, although most generally fall into the 2,000-5,000 inhabitant range. Many other national definitions are not based on population thresholds. In some, 'urban settlements' are those which serve as centres for local government; everyone living outside these is said to be 'rural'. In others, more sophisticated criteria are used which combine population thresholds or settlements' role as local government headquarters with thresholds for the proportion of working-age population employed in non-agricultural activities, or thresholds for population density or some other characteristic thought to be typical of an 'urban' centre.

Some governments define their urban population as those living in 'townships' or 'municipalities' or other forms of administrative area within which a certain proportion of the population live in one or more nucleated settlements which are said to have urban characteristics. Although many books and papers including official documents from agencies such as the United Nations and the World Bank present international comparisons as to different nations' urbanisation levels or rates of urban population growth, these are clearly of very limited validity given that the criteria used to distinguish between 'urban' and 'rural' population is so different from nation to nation. And as if this, in itself, did not present researchers with enough problems, national criteria for making this rural/urban distinction often change in successive censuses.

For this book, given the data available in each of the regional studies, a common population threshold in all the regional studies had to be used to distinguish between 'rural' and 'urban' settlements, since detailed statistical information on other characteristics for all nucleated settlements was not available. We recognise that this is unsatisfactory, and that in fact, within most populated regions, there is a continuum of settlements ranked by population size, going from isolated households through small and large villages to nucleated settlements with much larger populations. Within this continuum, we chose to describe settlements with 5,000 or more inhabitants as 'urban centres' and those with less than 5,000 inhabitants as 'rural'.[6]

Theoretically, such arbitrary cut-off points are known to be unsatisfactory. Many settlements with less than 5,000 inhabitants in the Argentinian region have larger concentrations of trading and commercial enterprises and higher order goods and services available than more populous urban centres in the Indian regions—largely because much of the population in or close to these Argentinian settlements have much higher disposable incomes. But data is not available on the size or diversity of every settlement's economic base. In each region, the data suggests that population size in nucleated settlements does correlate with increasing volumes of non-agricultural goods production and retail trade, increasing importance in terms of administrative status and budget, and increasing availability of higher order goods and services. A lower limit of 5,000 population for the Nigerian, Sudanese and Argentinian studies seemed the best compromise—and, incidentally, this was the figure also chosen by recent Indian, Sudanese and Nigerian censuses, although it was also qualified with criteria other than population size.

The term 'town' is used to refer to settlements regarded as 'urban' by national governments for that point in time, which did not have a population of 5,000 or more inhabitants.

The term 'urban system' is used to mean a set of independent urban centres within a defined area and their interactions; in most instances it is used to refer to the set of independent urban centres within the five study regions (after Bourne and Simmons, 1978). Our study of urban systems within the five study regions is made somewhat less complex than many studies of urban systems within more urbanised nations or regions since most urban centres are too small in size and population and in the kinds of economic activities they encompass to have developed into city-regions. Secondary and tertiary economic activities are overwhelmingly concentrated within urban centres' boundaries. So, too, is their workforce. Where there are exceptions to this–for instance, from people commuting daily to work in certain urban centres or farmers living in urban centres and working in rural areas or some economic activities intimately linked to a particular urban centre but located outside its boundary–these are noted. The Argentinian case study also includes some discussion of how the core area of the study region which contains eight urban centres within a 700 square kilometre area can be said to function as a metropolitan centre, even though it did not evolve from the development of a single city.

The term 'urbanisation' is only used to describe the process by which an increasing proportion of the population of a defined area or region or nation comes to live within settlements defined as 'urban centres'.

Definition of small and intermediate urban centres

The decision to study what we term small and intermediate urban centres and their interactions both with larger and with smaller settlements brings with it the need to distinguish 'small' and 'intermediate' urban centres from larger and smaller settlements. A review of the literature found no agreement among governments or researchers as to how such urban centres should be defined. Perhaps the considerable variation in what different governments and researchers understand by such terms helps explain the lack of clarity which has characterised much of the work on this subject to date. But the validity of a discussion about the present and potential role of these two categories of urban centres in government development strategies largely depends on whether useful and valid categories can be defined.

If the purpose of the research is to consider urban centres' present or potential role in government strategies, then the definitions should be based on thresholds relating to scales and diversities of economic activities, public services and contributions to national or regional production and thus should be particular to each nation or region, and would change over time. Then it would be possible to define 'small' and 'intermediate' urban centres in relation to their roles within particular regions or nations. But the data base does not exist for this. Even if it did, it might obscure important rural-urban links. For instance, perhaps the value of production within an urban centre would not be separated from that derived from agriculture in the case of an agro-processing industry which uses local crops as raw materials. In the Third World, very rarely is the data base sufficiently sophisticated to allow such a separation.

Indeed, the only statistical information which exists about most of the urban centres in the five study regions is population. But it has already been noted that the use of some population threshold to distinguish between different classes of settlements has grave limitations since it implies that settlements with comparable populations have other characteristics in common. As Chapters 2 to 6 will show, urban centres within the same region with comparable population sizes can have very large differences in the type of employment and economic base.

However, when combining data on population and on the type and scale of economic activities, social services and facilities in urban centres for each of the study regions, a population threshold of 20,000 inhabitants was found to be useful in distinguishing between different scales and types of contribution to national and regional development. For instance, in each of the study regions, urban centres with 20,000 or more inhabitants have generally enjoyed a higher administrative status, better road and/or rail links with the wider regional or national economy, a larger population in surroundings areas which relied on it to provide goods and services and a lower proportion of the labour force working in agriculture, compared to what we term small urban centres with between 5,000 and 20,000 inhabitants. Urban centres with 20,000 or more inhabitants contained most of the manufacturing activities within each region; and all had more diversified economic bases than most of those in their region with less than 20,000 inhabitants—although with one prominent exception.[7]

However, a single, universally valid population threshold to distinguish between 'intermediate' and 'larger' urban centres cannot be justified. In each of the nations within which the study regions are located, there are qualitative and quantitative differences between the concentration of productive activities and public services in, say, urban centres with 20,000-100,000 inhabitants and those with more than 500,000 inhabitants. But if just one population threshold distinguished between 'intermediate' and 'large' urban centres for all five study regions, it would obscure rather than clarify these qualitative and quantitative differences.

Thus, the distinction between 'intermediate' and 'large' urban centres is based on our judgements as to the scale and type of their contribution to national production and trade and regional service provision, and therefore was done separately for each of the study regions. For the North Indian and Sudanese region, no urban centre was judged to have developed beyond an 'intermediate urban centre' although one in each region–Wad Medani in the Sudan and Rae Bareli in North India–have recently acquired functions which could allow their development beyond 'intermediate' urban centre category in the near future.

Within the South India study region, Bangalore Metropolitan Area has clearly developed far beyond intermediate urban centre status both in terms of its contribution to national (and regional) production, and in terms of its concentration of higher order public and private enterprises serving the population in a large region. All but one of the other urban centres in this study region fall without too much difficulty into the 'small' and 'intermediate' urban centre categories. But one does not. Mysore urban centre cannot be said to compare with Bangalore Metropolitan Area in terms of contribution to national production or public and private sector service provision to a wider regional population. Indeed, many of the enterprises providing higher order services used by the inhabitants of Mysore urban centre are based in Bangalore. Mysore has also recently begun attracting industries as a satellite of Bangalore. But Mysore, with close to 500,000 inhabitants, is qualitatively and quantitatively in another class to other urban centres within the region with more than 20,000 inhabitants, in terms of contribution to regional production and public and private sector service provision. Within a country such as India with a large population and a large and well developed urban system–despite a relatively low level of urbanisation–Mysore city's contribution to national production and total service provision is 'intermediate'. But within its own region, it might be judged to be more than 'intermediate'. However, for the purpose of this book, Mysore is classified as an 'intermediate' urban centre.

The Nigerian study region has only 'small and intermediate urban centres' although the urban system and economic base of the entire study region is much influenced by the fact that Nigeria's largest urban centre, Lagos, is close to the study region's border and indeed in recent years, has grown into the study region. The Argentinian study region also has only 'small and intermediate urban centres' although Chapter 2 discusses how a cluster of small and intermediate urban centres concentrated within an area of 700 square kilometres has come to include sufficient productive activities and contain a sufficiently large and diverse range of private and public services for a wider region that collectively these urban centres might be judged to be a 'large city' or 'metropolis'.

In summary, then, small urban centres are nucleated settlements with between 5,000 and 20,000 inhabitants. Intermediate urban centres are nucleated settlements with 20,000 or more inhabitants; they are judged not to make a substantial contribution to national production and to providing services for more than the population living close by. We recognise that the definition for the upper limit of an 'intermediate urban centre' is not precise; for instance, it raises questions as to 'what is or is not a substanial contribution to national production' and when is a region and its population 'more than living close by'. But the five case studies presented here should clarify this, for each of the regions.

We hope that this work will encourage further research on this subject and suggest that definitions for different categories of urban centre must be based on those appropriate to the region or nation being studied and not necessarily the ones used here. A specific and more universal upper threshold to distinguish between 'intermediate' and 'large' urban centres might be more easily understandable. But the phenomenal diversity in the type and scale of economic activities and services–and in the distribution through the urban system–makes such a threshold of little use in distinguishing different urban centres' present and potential roles within governments' development strategies. And as will be discussed in some detail in Chapter 8, some Third World nations have such a small and undiversified non-agricultural economic base and such a low proportion of their national populations living and working in urban centres that only the national capital might be regarded as having developed beyond the 'intermediate urban centre' category.

Notes

1 Regional balance is usually measured by the scale of the differences between regions' per capita GDP; government policies which seem to contribute toward lessening these differences are said to have helped improve 'regional balance'. Chapter 8 includes a discussion of the possible conflict between improving this 'regional balance' and increasing the proportion of the population with more adequate and stable livelihoods.
2 This is not meant to imply that the majority of the inhabitants of cities and metropolitan areas benefited, but it was generally within these cities and metropolitan areas that most of the high productivity and high paying jobs became concentrated. Both public and private investment in enterprises were usually concentrated here, as were a high proportion of public investments in infrastructure and services.
3 In effect, most of the Third World's population which has some interaction with urban centres, either lives in or depends on small or intermediate urban centres for access to goods, services and markets.
4 This is the governing body of the United Nations Centre for Human Settlements (Habitat) which is the UN Agency specialising in housing and human settlements issues.
5 UN statistical documents on urban growth in the world's nations usually list urban definitions used by different nations; see for instance 'Estimates and Projections of Urban, Rural and City Populations, 1950–2025, the 1980 Assessment', Department of International Economic and Social Affairs, United Nations, New York, 1982.
6 In the regional studies in South and North India, there are some settlements with 5,000 or more inhabitants which are not officially recognised as urban centres so there is virtually no data available about them. Thus, these could not be considered as small urban centres in the regional studies. However, the 1981 census definition for what constitutes an urban centre ensures that their exclusion could not affect the research findings in any significant way since they house such a small proportion of each region's population and contain a small proportion of each region's non-agricultural activities.

   The 1981 census definition in India included all 'statutory towns' and all other places with 5,000 or more inhabitants, 75 per cent or more of their male working population engaged in non-agricultural activities and a density of at least 400 persons per square kilometre. There are relatively few 'statutory towns' with less than 5,000 inhabitants; only 0.5 per cent of India's urban population lived in towns with less than 5,000 inhabitants. In each of the Indian regions, it would have proved possible to exclude 'statutory towns' with less than 5,000 inhabitants from the analysis, but it would not have been possible to include settlements with more than 5,000 inhabitants which did not meet the employment and density criteria to be elevated to the status of an urban centre. Little data is available on these 'large villages'. Thus, we chose to follow India's census definitions as the lower limit for small centres. In the North India region, five of the 18 officially recognised urban centres in the 1981 census had less than 5,000 inhabitants; the least populous of these had 3,857 on the data.

7 The urban centre of Cutral Co-Plaza Huincul in the Argentinian region had 33,850 inhabitants in 1980 but its economic base was essentially sustained by the. exploitation of just one natural resource—oil (and associated gas). While certain manufacturing and commercial enterprises have sprung up to meet local demand, the urban centre's economic base could not be called diversified and its population is likely to fall rapidly when, in the near future, oil and gas in and around it begin to run down.

References

Alonso, William, 'Urban and regional balances in economic development', *Economic Development and Cultural Change,* 17/1, October, 1968, p. 4.

Bourne, L. S. and Simmons, J. W., Introduction to *Systems of Cities,* Oxford University Press, 1978.

2

The Development of the Upper Valley of the Rio Negro and its Periphery Within the Comahue Region, Argentina

Mabel Manzanal and Cesar A. Vapnarsky

Background

The Comahue region as defined here encompasses 310,700 square kilometres in Northern Patagonia, Argentina. It consists of the provinces of Neuquen and Rio Negro and Patagones County in Buenos Aires Province, as shown in Map 2.1.Very low rainfall ensures that intensive agriculture and population concentrations only exist where alternative water sources are available. Thus, most of the Comahue's population is concentrated in a few areas in river valleys where irrigation has been developed or in settlements which serve the exploitation of oil, natural gas or minerals. For much of the Comahue, like the rest of Patagonia, low density sheep-rearing is the only way in which the cool, dry and windswept plateaus are exploited.[1]

This chapter describes the development of the economic core and main population concentration in the Comahue, the Upper Valley of Rio Negro and Neuquen from 1879 to 1980. This Valley's development was only possible because of the ready availability, year round, of river water. Covering some 700 square kilometres, it is an intensively cultivated, irrigated strip of land which runs alongside the Negro River's Upper Valley and the Limay and Neuquen Rivers' lower valleys.[2] The valleys' widths vary from between 3 and 12 km and their combined lengths total less than 180 km.

As the figures in Table 2.1 show, this sub-region (which will be referred to throughout this book as 'the Upper Valley') contained 47 per cent of the Comahue Region's population in 1980, on less than a quarter of one per cent of its land area. This chapter concentrates on the Upper Valley's development within the context

Map 2.1 *The Upper Valley of the Rio Negro and Neuquen and its periphery within the Comahue and Argentina*

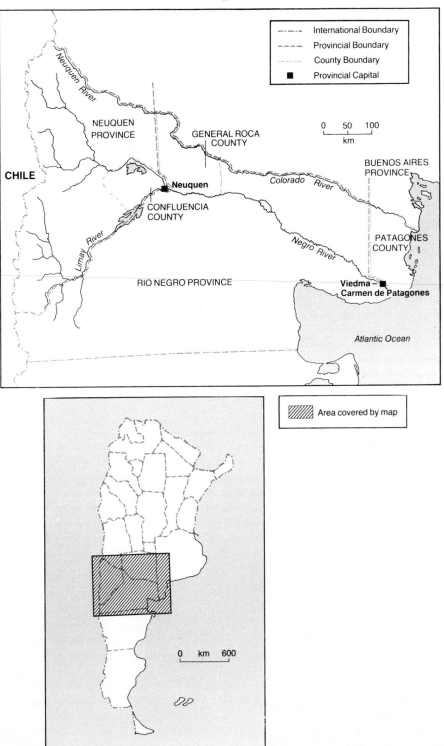

Table 2.1 *Background statistics*[a]

	Area (km²)	Population (1980)
Argentina (continental)	2.8 million	27,862,800
Patagonia	800,250	1,056,250
Comahue region	310,700	650,150
Upper Valley of Rio Negro and Neuquen	c. 700	304,950[b]
Upper Valley's Periphery	c. 25,000	54,850

Upper Valley of Rio Negro and Neuquen

	1910	1930	1950	1960	1970	1980
Population	7,000	27,000	81,150	129,150	195,600	304,950[b]
Population in small urban centres (5,000-19,999)	—	—	28,300	54,600	33,750	64,600
Number of small urban centres	—	—	3	5	3	5
Population in intermediate urban centres (20,000 or more)	—	—	—	22,500	96,500	175,600
Number of intermediate urban centres	—	—	—	1	3	3

The Upper Valley's Periphery

	1950	1960	1970	1980
Population	11,250	18,750	37,100	54,850
Population in small urban centres (5,000-19,999)	9,450	15,550	5,300	13,250
Number of small urban centres	1	1	1	1
Population in intermediate urban centres (20,000 or more)	—	—	23,850	34,000
Number of intermediate urban centres	—	—	—	—

Notes: a—Population figures rounded to 50 inhabitants.

b—This population figure refers only to the set of 16 adjacent municipalities (municipios) which exist today. Their boundaries are illustrated in Map 2.5. It does not include two municipalities which emerged as cultivated areas after around 1965 beyond the north-western and eastern extremes of the Y-shaped Upper Valley, and whose combined populations reached 1,750 inhabitants in 1980 but were only 50 in 1950, 500 in 1960 and 600 in 1970. These two areas are outside the two counties taken here as study areas: General Roca in Rio Negro Province and Confluencia in Neuquen Province. Detailed data was only available for the 16 municipalities over time but since these two cultivated areas were settled only relatively recently, their exclusion has no effect on the historical account while their relatively low population means that their exclusion has little effect on the economic and demographic analysis.

of the Comahue region. A second sub-region which adjoins the north and west of the Upper Valley will be referred to as 'the Upper Valley's Periphery'. This sub-region extends over more than 25,000 square kilometres and includes some of Argentina's richest oil and gas fields. In the Upper Valley's Periphery, 86 per cent of the population lived in two urban centres associated with oil and natural gas exploitation in 1980, because of a lack of water and soil resources to allow the kind of irrigated farming which developed in the Upper Valley. The Upper Valley and its Periphery together cover two counties: General Roca county in Rio Negro Province; and Confluencia county in Neuquen Province.[3]

Development up to 1957

1879-1903 Colonisation of the Upper Valley

As Table 2.1 suggests,the Upper Valley's population growth has been very rapid for virtually all of the twentieth century. The Valley was only settled after 1879 when the threat of Indian attacks was removed by military expeditions. The nomadic Indians had been expelled from the area surrounding Buenos Aires from the 1930s but had prevented permanent settlement beyond a very slowly advancing 'frontier' by subjecting the white population living on the fringes of Argentina's core region to frequent attacks. By the 1870s, increasing demand for food in Europe encouraged the development of an economy based on agricultural exports. Thus, the elite in power, the merchants living in the city of Buenos Aires and the large landowners in Buenos Aires Province, had to deal with 'the Indian menace' since this inhibited the expansion of land under cultivation.

In 1879, General Julio A. Roca[4] commanded a military expedition into the southern and western Pampa (to the north-east of the study region, which became the main livestock raising area in Argentina) and Northern Patagonia. In that same year, Patagonia became fully incorporated into the territory under the jurisdiction of the Argentine government. Roca's expedition was followed by three more until by 1885 the Indians were no longer a threat to white settlers.

The Upper Valley's first settlement was founded as a town and fortress by one of Roca's officers when his troops arrived there in 1879, and was named 'Fuerte General Roca'. No other town existed until the turn of the century. In 1882, an agricultural colony of 42,000 hectares was created, also called General Roca (see Map 2.2), with a fortress and town at its centre. At this point in the river valley, the strip of fertile soil exists only to the north of the river. Within this new colony, land was sold or given free by the government to individuals in relatively small parcels and under certain legal conditions designed to prevent this land's appropriation by absentee landlords. Such measures were not used to dispose of land in other parts of the newly conquered territories so other areas within the Upper Valley were not so protected.[5]

No agricultural production was possible without irrigation, so by 1886, a rather precarious irrigation canal had been constructed which drew water from the junction of the Limay and Neuquen Rivers and ran parallel to the Negro River. But initially, the area under irrigation grew very slowly; by 1900 there were no more than 1,300 irrigated hectares, all close to General Roca town. The town also received some economic support since it became a service centre for a vast area around it, where increasingly sheep were being raised. Sheep herds were being moved south from the Pampa since cattle raising was becoming the staple there.

Map 2.2 *The Agricultural Colonies and sub-areas which developed in the Upper Valley, 1882–1957*

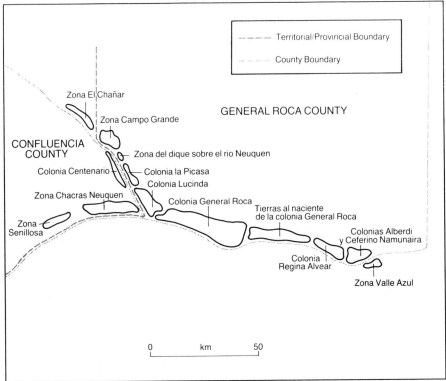

General Roca agricultural colony's economic prosperity depended heavily on the presence of troops in need of a permanent supply of basic goods and services. Some sheep, cattle and horse raising was supplemented by arable farming, mostly cereals and fodder for local consumption. The expansion and intensification of farming was impossible without a larger market for local produce (which local demand could not provide) and without more secure irrigation infrastructure, including controls against floods. Access to a larger market was provided when the railway arrived in 1899, while the problem of irrigation infrastructure and flood control was solved when a dam and a modern irrigation system were built between 1910 and 1932.

The need for flood control was demonstrated by a flood in 1899 which caused considerable damage to General Roca town and the cultivated lands around it. The acting commander of the military post ordered the transfer of the town to a parcel of land nearby, owned by the army, which was at a higher altitude.

The railway arrived in the Upper Valley in the same year as the flood. The reason the government constructed the railway was not to support agricultural development in the Upper Valley but to allow the rapid movement of troops to the Argentina-Chile border to the

Map 2.3 *The Comahue region: the development of the railway*

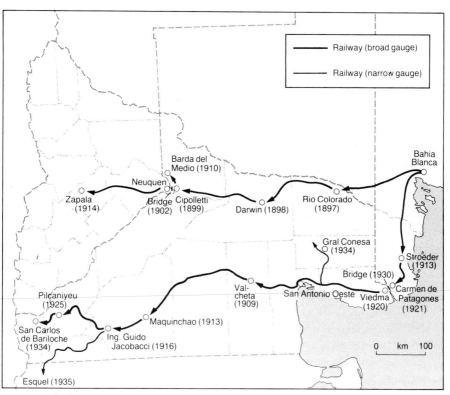

west of the Upper Valley. By 1895, a conflict with Chile over the international boundary threatened to develop into a war. A private British company, Ferrocarril Sud, built the railway, reaching the Upper Valley from Bahia Blanca,[6] a distance of some 500 km, in just three years. This company was paid by being granted exemption from all national taxes both for this new railway and for the railway network that the company was developing over the rich Southern Pampa and through being allowed to import all the goods needed to construct and run the railway system without paying import taxes. According to Ortiz (1946), the British company well knew the potential of the Upper Valley and other areas in or close to the railway for commercial agriculture. The company judged correctly that the new railway linking the Upper Valley to Bahia Blanca and Buenos Aires would prove very profitable; the tax and import duty concessions were merely an added bonus. When the conflict with Chile was resolved in 1903, the military post in General Roca was abandoned. Thus the town had to face the damage of the 1899 flood and the loss of its major market for local produce, the soldiers. However, the arrival of the railway had opened up the possibility for local produce to reach markets outside the Upper Valley and the Comahue.

In 1903, there was practically no population outside the town and agricultural colony of General Roca. The colony's population had grown from 829 to 1,390 inhabitants between 1886 and 1895, but fell after the flood and grew to 1,449 in 1901.[7] Two very small spontaneous settlements had developed by 1903, facing each other across the Neuquen River; these were on sites which later developed as the intermediate urban centres of Neuquen and Cipolletti. The railway reached Cipolletti in 1899 and, with the construction of a bridge across the river, Neuquen in 1902 (see Map 2.3). In 1903, the second agricultural colony in the Upper Valley, Colonia Lucinda, was founded to the west of General Roca, with Cipolletti at its centre. In 1904, the town of Neuquen with its new railway station was designated capital of the Territory of Neuquen. This designation as capital of a national territory and its confirmation as capital of a province when Neuquen territory became Neuquen Province in 1957 was to prove of great significance to its development and to its importance relative to other urban centres within the Upper Valley. Thus by 1905, there were three towns in the Upper Valley, each of them on the new railway, and a total population of around 3,000. The role that immigrants played in colonising the Upper Valley can be gauged by the fact that 17 per cent of the Upper Valley's population in 1886 and 26 per cent in 1901 were foreign-born.

1904-1913: Early agricultural developments and transition to the Alfalfa Cycle

By 1913, the Upper Valley's population had grown to around 11,000. The period 1904–1913 coincided with the most rapid population growth in Argentina's history and ten years of uninterrupted prosperity. In the Upper Valley, it saw both successful and unsuccessful attempts to found and develop agricultural colonies. Colonia Lucinda and the new town of Cipolletti within it, was developed by an army general after he purchased 5,000 hectares from the government and constructed a main canal and other irrigation works. After reserving several large tracts for himself, some relatives and the contractors who built the irrigation system, he sold parcels of land to those new arrivals with sufficient capital to afford them. He also donated land for the town of Cipolletti.

In 1907, the national government laid down a policy to stimulate agricultural production in the Upper Valley. Public land was sold at a very low price, provided that the purchasers formed a co-operative association to construct and maintain irrigation works; each member had to contribute 20 times the amount they paid for the land in stock. This policy sought to ensure that land was acquired by people who would farm it themselves (ie not absentee landlords) but who had the capital to invest in irrigating and developing the land. In

1907 an irrigation co-operative for General Roca was formed which repaired and widened the existing system and brought several thousand more hectares under irrigation. Many of those who bought land were relatively rich people from outside the region (for instance, from the Province of Buenos Aires, or from the Provinces of San Juan and Mendoza which at that time already had a tradition of irrigation developments), and they often bought land from smaller farmers who sold or abandoned their lands after the 1899 flood. Some became absentee landowners although most put their newly acquired land into cultivation under the supervision of managers. It was not uncommon for absentee owners to build summer houses and spend part of the year on their farms. Other new landowners came to live permanently in the Upper Valley. For instance, the main leader in the irrigation co-operative formed in 1907 founded a new town, Allen, to serve some of the new land brought under irrigation between General Roca and Cipolletti.

Alfalfa became the dominant crop while the plantation of vineyards and wine production was also important. Other initiatives developed colonies to the east of General Roca, including Colonia Rusa largely developed by Russian Jews, Colonia Cervantes by Spanish immigrants and Colonia Francesa where the main stockholders were French. Each of these new colonies encountered substantial difficulties. For instance, in Colonia Cervantes, poor administration[8] and difficulties inherent in clearing and levelling the land led to the Spanish farmers leaving the area. The land was abandoned in the Twenties and only after 1940 was it subdivided and put back into production. It was then that a small settlement, Cervantes, developed within it. Colonia Francesa also collapsed since the irrigation system never worked satisfactorily. Like that of Colonia Cervantes, it was based on pumping water from the Negro River. A small town, Ingeniero Luis A. Huergo, had emerged there by 1914 but it was almost depopulated by 1920 and only after that began a slow recovery.

The land around the new town and railway station of Neuquen was also developed for irrigated agriculture. Most of the land in the lower Limay River belonged to four large absentee landowners and one had managed to purchase (or at least control) most of the arable land around Neuquen town. He gave land to the government for streets within the new town's plotted area and 20 per cent of the plots. The rest he retained as a speculative investment. From 1911, arable land near the town was subdivided and sold in small plots to poor farmers who paid for it through long-term monthly instalments. In contrast to farmers elsewhere in the Upper Valley, these were in effect peasants who cultivated crops mainly for their own consumption—with only a small surplus sold. Irrigation was provided by the state from a canal parallel to the Limay River but the cost of pumped irrigation water was more than could be recovered from the farmers. Only in 1927 with a new, modern gravity irrigation system did this part of the Upper Valley acquire similar characteristics to other more prosperous areas. Thus, the town of Neuquen developed slowly. Only its role as the headquarters of the Territory of Neuquen underpinned its development. Since surrounding farmers lacked much disposable income and did not produce much for sale, it did not grow as an agricultural market and service centre.

To the west of these three colonies, a physician from Buenos Aires, Dr Plottier, moved to the Upper Valley and irrigated an area of land he owned and cultivated it with success. By the Forties, this large estate was subdivided and sold in small and medium size farms; only then did the town of Plottier emerge.

1914–1929: The Alfalfa Cycle and construction of the dam

Between 1910 and 1916, the government financed the construction of a dam on the Neuquen River[9] from which water for irrigation was withdrawn to a natural empty basin nearby which became Lake Pellegrini. The Argentine National Department for Irrigation (Direccion Nacional de Irrigacion) prepared the plan for the new irrigation system, essentially consisting of a main canal from the dam to the eastern end of the Upper Valley from which branches were drawn off. The railway company, Ferrocarril Sud, was contracted to construct the canals but at cost price. The advantage to the company in doing so was the boost the new irrigation system would provide for commercial crop production and thus for the company's business, since it owned the only economic means of transport out of the Upper Valley.

To transport the materials for building the dam, the railway company built a 30 km line running from Cipolletti along the eastern side of the Neuquen River valley. The dam's construction gave rise to a small town, known today as Barda del Medio, which was almost exclusively inhabited by workers and technicians for the irrigation system. In 1911, a subsidiary of the railway company purchased a large tract of land between Cipolletti and Barda del Medio which included some 3,000 hectares of arable land. Two years later, these became a new agricultural colony, Colonia la Picasa with the new town of Cinco Saltos as its centre.

The railway company's interest was not in farming the land but in encouraging crop production for export out of the region to increase business for the railway. It therefore sold small parcels of land and encouraged farmers to grow cash crops. It was here that modern fruit growing practices began, which later became the Upper Valley's main economic activity.

At this time, fruit-growing was essentially only for local consumption. Alfalfa had rapidly become the Upper Valley's staple crop since it was easy and cheap to grow and local soil and climatic conditions allowed four crops a year. Alfalfa also helped prepare the soil for perennial crops; being a legume, it contains nitrogen fixing bacteria in its roots and helps build up nitrogen levels in the soil. There was a good level of demand for this crop in Europe. Meanwhile, the whole irrigation system came under the control of the government. By 1921, the main canal in the Rio Negro portion of the Upper Valley extended from the dam down to Colonia Francesa; privately owned and developed canals became secondary branches in the irrigation system and a system of irrigation charges was worked out for farmers who took water from the canals. As the main canal was extended further east, it allowed further expansion to the irrigated area. The new irrigation system allowed water distribution by gravity which greatly reduced the costs for those areas which had previously relied on water pumped from one of the rivers.

In 1921, a new colony, Colonia Centenario, was founded on the other side of the Neuquen River from Colonia La Picasa and the town of Cinco Saltos, and the town of Centenario developed within it. In 1924, another new agricultural colony, Colonia Regina, was formed, based on Italian capital. Several thousand hectares were purchased from one of the few large remaining landowners in the Upper Valley's eastern end. Thirteen hundred hectares were immediately brought under cultivation and Italian immigrants were provided with 5–15 hectare plots of excellent land, a house and tools. Long-term mortgages from the National Mortgage Bank of Argentina helped underpin this colony's rapid settlement. Rapid growth and development of agriculture here helped turn the town of Villa Regina which developed within it into one of the most important urban centres in the Upper Valley within 20 years, despite various financial difficulties faced by the company.

During the alfalfa cycle, nearly half the cultivable land in the Upper Valley was put into cultivation. The cultivated area grew from 5,000 hectares in 1910 to more than 30,000 by 1930. The only large cultivable holdings which still remained unused were east of Colonia Regina and north of the Neuquen River dam. Elsewhere, only marginal land near the riverbank or near the barda (which marked the limit of fertile land) did not receive irrigation water. By 1922, alfalfa cultivation had extended over 20,000 hectares; it remained at around this level up to 1951. But the volume of alfalfa marketed outside the Upper Valley reached its peak in 1928. During the Thirties, it fell to one-third of its peak (as fruit became the Upper Valley's major product) and after 1951 to less than one-tenth of its peak. Alfalfa cultivation was usually replaced by fruit trees since once the initial investment is made in such perennial crops, the returns are much higher. Although alfalfa continued to be cultivated and today can be seen on lands just opened for cultivation, lands where fruit orchards and vineyards are to be replaced or on land whose soil quality has been depleted, after 1930 it came to be grown largely for local consumption, especially for fodder for horses whose numbers greatly increased until they were replaced by tractors after World War II.

By 1930, there had been an important change in landholding sizes as most of the cultivated land was in relatively small irrigated farms cultivated by their owners. During the transition to the alfalfa cycle (1904-1913), landholdings of 20-100 hectares or over 100 hectares had dominated the already irrigated portions of the Upper Valley. Outside the irrigated areas, which at this point were restricted to portions of Colonia General Roca and Colonia Lucinda, a few parcels remained in public ownership. In the extremes of the Upper Valley, much of the land was held in privately owned tracts of thousands of hectares which were neither irrigated nor cultivated. Some were part of even larger holdings which extended into the northern Patagonic plateau. These were not sub-divided until much later when the fruit-growing cycle was well advanced.

During the alfalfa cycle, 1914-1929, as the area under irrigation grew, the increasing value of land still not cultivated encouraged large land-owners to subdivide and sell medium or small parcels. At this time, access to farmland in the Pampa was becoming increasingly difficult and some tenant farmers from the Pampa looked to the Upper Valley as an attractive alternative.

Thus, the state's investment in flood control and irrigation came to enrich those who had earlier acquired large tracts of land. Another reason for the predominance of landowners as farmers was the long-term investment needed to grow more remunerative crops such as fruit, which made farming less attractive as a speculative investment producing quick returns for absentee landlords. Owner occupied farms remained the norm.[10]

Although a lack of population censuses between 1920[11] and 1947 inhibits accurate figures for the Upper Valley's population growth, estimates suggest that total population grew from around 11,000 in 1913 to 27,100 in 1930. The Upper Valley's population grew very slowly between 1913 and 1920; the First World War essentially halted immigration into Argentina, and immigrants had played an important role in boosting the Upper Valley's population growth. The 1914 census revealed that more than half the Upper Valley's population was foreign-born with 29 per cent from Spain, 7 per cent from Italy, 7 per cent from other European countries and around 7 per cent from Chile. Many poor, unqualified workers from Chile came to the Upper Valley in search of employment.

The Fruit Cycle: 1930-1957

Although fruit trees planted by some of the first farmers for their own consumption showed how Upper Valley soil and climate were well suited for fruit production, commercial fruit production was inhibited by the high cost and long lead time needed to establish large orchards. It takes many years for fruit trees to grow to the point where they produce a good crop. This ties up the capital invested in the land and in raising the trees for a long period with no return. There are also annual costs for fertilizers, since perennial crops do not allow crop rotation to help maintain soil fertility and expensive measures are needed to protect trees from frost, disease and pests. Together with the labour input needed to care for the trees before they produce a crop, this represents a very considerable investment before the farmer sees any returns. Finally, commercial fruit production in the Upper Valley demanded irrigation and only between 1910 and 1930 was a modern, gravity-fed irrigation system installed.

The national government's response to the Great Crash of 1929 and the prolonged world recession that followed was, like many other Latin American governments, to encourage import substitution. Although import substitution is commonly associated with industrial development, the Argentine Government also encouraged the cultivation of some crops including some fruits; it also took measures to cut the production of other crops and of certain processed products. For instance, to protect the economies of the provinces of San Juan and Mendoza, the main wine-producing areas in Argentina (to the north of the study region), severe controls were imposed on vineyards elsewhere. This had an impact on the Upper Valley where the area under vines had grown rapidly from almost nil in 1907 to over 9,000 hectares in 1933. Controls such as higher taxes on new vineyards were an important factor in the decline in the area under vineyards in the Upper Valley to less than 7,000 hectares during the Forties, although it increased to over 12,000 by 1960.

The railway company played a major role in fostering fruit production. By the Thirties, in La Pampa, the construction of a paved road network and the growing numbers of lorries meant severe competition for this company's railway business there. So it sought to maximise its returns in goods and in areas like the Upper Valley where railway transport would remain important. Even before 1930, the company had begun to foster fruit-growing in the Upper Valley and it rapidly increased this role by coming to control the whole process of packing, marketing and transporting Upper Valley fruit produce.

As early as 1918, the company established an agricultural station close to Cinco Saltos to select crops best suited to local climate and soil and to domestic and foreign markets. Although many crops and crop varieties were tried, certain varieties of apples and pears were found to be most suitable. The company published a number of booklets for farmers on modern agricultural practices. It also collected detailed economic, agricultural and demographic data on the farmers; indeed, this rendered the work of a state-owned agricultural station established in 1912 near General Roca almost useless for many years. The company also analysed the relative advantages of different potential markets in the northern hemisphere.

In 1928, the company founded a subsidiary company, Argentine Fruit Distributors, in association with other British owned railway companies. This subsidiary constructed fruit packing plants in the railway yards of Cinco Saltos, Cipolletti and Allen and in one of General Roca's two stations. Later, a fifth plant was built in Villa Regina. The agricultural station was put under this subsidiary's supervision. Before these fruit packing plants were built, the relatively low amount of fruit produced for sale was packed without any standardisation regarding quality of product or size of box and with inadequate provision for protecting the fruit. Now a modern packing system was introduced with lorries transporting fruit from farms to packing plants. Once carefully packed, they were sent by railway to Buenos Aires from where they were either exported or sold in the wholesale food market.

Argentine Fruit Distributors came to market most of the produce it packed and to undertake around 70 per cent of the Upper Valley's packing. It also introduced a form of payment to farmers which, with minor variations, still exists today. The farmer receives an advance payment but does not know the return his fruit crop will produce until the company has sold it. Of course, this is a considerable advantage for the company and a considerable disadvantage for the producer. The railway company also benefited from owning the only economic form of transport for taking fruit to major markets. The tariffs for fruit transportation were carefully set so that it was hardly cheaper to send produce to the port of Bahia Blanca rather than to Buenos Aires, despite the fact that the journey to Bahia Blanca is less than half the 1,200 or so kilometres to Buenos Aires. These tariffs therefore encouraged the use of the railway company's offices, port facilities and cold storage plants which were concentrated in Buenos Aires.

The area under fruit trees increased rapidly from 1930 as Figure 2.1 shows. On average, about half the annual crop of apples was exported and half went to the domestic market. The Upper Valley became Argentina's major apple and pear producer for export; estimates suggest that more than 85 per cent of the apples and pears exported by Argentina between 1934 and 1967 were from the Upper Valley. Figure 2.1 also shows the general trend towards increased production, although the Second World War caused a serious collapse in sales to Europe. The figure for 1946 was helped by a bilateral treaty with Brazil which allowed the export of Argentinian apples and pears in return for Brazilian grapefruit and oranges obtaining access to the Argentine market. The poor year in 1948 reflects problems which came from the nationalisation of the railway company and its subsidiary Argentine Fruit Distributors. Their reorganisation

Figure 2.1 *Growth in area under cultivation, area under fruit trees and exports*

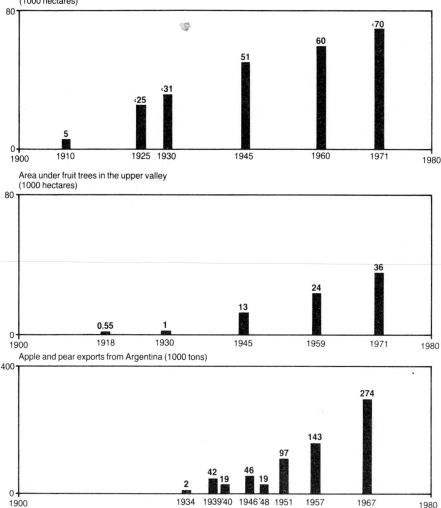

Area under cultivation in the upper valley
(1000 hectares)

Area under fruit trees in the upper valley
(1000 hectares)

Apple and pear exports from Argentina (1000 tons)

meant a drop in the customary efficiency with regard to packing, marketing and transporting the fruit. After nationalisation, fruit packing and marketing increasingly came to be undertaken by farmers' co-operatives and private firms.

Although a detailed description of the growth in cold storage, processing and manufacturing associated with increasing fruit production and of the vertical integration of fruit production belongs to a later section, since it was after 1957 that most of this took place, the first signs of such development were evident by 1957. For instance, vertical integration with a single company undertaking or controlling many (or all) the stages from the fruit's cultivation to fruit products' final sale had begun in a modest way after the Second World War. Before the War, some firms operating in Buenos Aires' wholesale food market began to undertake small scale fruit exports. After the War, they took advantage of the loss in efficiency in the now nationalised Argentine Fruit Distributors and set up their own packing plants.

However, the extension of their activities into buying their own farms, making wooden boxes for packing fruit and controlling transport of the produce out of the Upper Valley by motor trucks was most evident after 1957, as is described on page 57. The rapid growth of cold storage facilities which allowed the packing and transport of the rapidly growing volume of apples and pears to be spread over a longer period also took place after 1957. But again, the first signs of this were evident earlier; the first cold storage plant was constructed in 1945. However, in 1957, total cold storage capacity did not exceed 10,000 tons when total production was over 200,000 tons.

Similarly, by 1957, a core of industrial activities had already developed in the Upper Valley linked to fruit, tomato and wine production. This core later grew rapidly, especially after 1965. By 1930, there were three new agricultural processing industries in addition to winemaking which had begun as early as 1907. Two alfalfa mills had been set up in the town of Ingeniero Luis A. Huergo with the output exported; they contributed to the town's prosperity in an area which continued to depend on alfalfa growing for many years, although the mills were dismantled a few years after the Second World War. Tomato extract factories were built by an Italian entrepreneur first in Villa Regina, then in Allen, and these helped encourage tomato production. Industries preparing dried fruits were also set up, using fruit unsuitable for fresh consumption. New industries also emerged from backward linkages with agriculture, including the fabrication of wooden boxes (which utilised wood from locally grown poplar trees)[12] and of tools and machines needed for handling fruit. By the Fifties, some of these tools and machines were also being sold outside the Upper Valley. During the Forties, a large chemical factory was built in Cinco Saltos which utilised locally extracted minerals in producing various biocides for local crop protection. Some of these new industries diversified; for instance, tomato extract plants began to make cider, preserves and other products derived from locally produced fruits.

Thus, by 1957 a considerable volume of industrial production had developed, most of which was intimately linked to the production or export of local agricultural produce. It is possible to talk of a transition from fruit production to agro-industry as the dominant economic activity. This was a change which took place between 1947 and 1967. To allow a comparison between economic developments and changes in the urban system, 1957 will be taken as the end of the fruit-growing cycle and the beginning of the agro-industrial cycle,[13] even if 1967 is a more important year in terms of the full development of the agro-industrial cycle since this is when cold storage capacity had been expanded enormously and when the transport of fruit produce rapidly transferred from railway to road.

In this transition, three events had important effects on the Upper Valley's development: the nationalisation of the railway and its subsidiary (the major fruit packer) in 1947, which has already been mentioned; a change in political organisation in 1957; and higher tariffs for railway transport which encouraged the switch of fruit transport from railway to road in 1967. In 1957 elected provincial authorities assumed responsibility for the government of the new provinces of Neuquen and of Rio Negro which encompass most of the Comahue region. Up to 1955 , these provinces had been 'national territories' with their governors appointed by and their budgets coming from the Federal government. The citizens of national territories did not have representatives in the national Congress and did not participate in national Presidential elections. As an electorate, only those living in municipalities had a role when they elected their municipal governments.[14] The boundaries of national territories had been defined in 1884 at which time the Upper Valley had less than 2,000 inhabitants. These boundaries were not changed when the territories became provinces, even though such boundaries had come to cut through the Upper Valley's large population concentration.

As Map 2.1 shows, part of the Upper Valley is in Rio Negro Province while the other part is in Neuquen Province. The territorial capitals became provincial capitals. For Neuquen Province, the retention of Neuquen as the provincial capital could be justified since it was (and remains) the province's largest and most important urban centre. The retention of Viedma as the provincial capital of Rio Negro Province was more controversial. Viedma had been the largest and most important urban centre in Rio Negro territory in the late nineteenth and early twentieth centuries, before the Upper Valley became an important concentration of people and economic activities. But developments in the first half of the twentieth century saw Rio Negro territory's economic staple move from sheep rearing (which Viedma grew to serve) to cash crop exports in which the Upper Valley was predominant. This meant that General Roca county with such rapidly developing urban centres as General Roca, Cipolletti, Villa Regina, Cinco Saltos and Allen were subservient to the provincial capital Viedma, some 500 km away.[15] Given the strong centralist tradition in Argentina where central (Federal) and provincial governments tend to concentrate their investments in and around their capital city, the designation of Neuquen and Viedma as provincial capitals was to have important long-term effects on the development of the urban

Map 2.4 *Urban centres in the Comahue region*

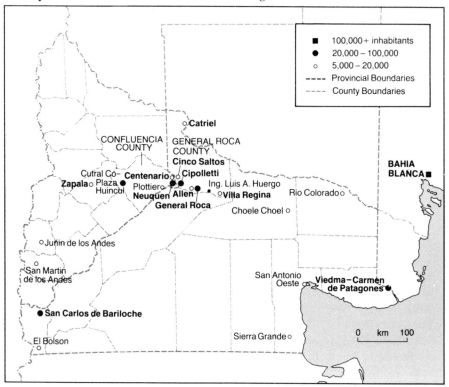

system in both the Upper Valley and in the wider Comahue. While Neuquen city received a disproportionate share of the provincial public investment relative to its share in housing Neuquen province's population, General Roca County and the urban centres within it received a disproportionately low level relative to their share in housing more than half Rio Negro Province's population and concentrating well over half its economic activity.

Population changes in the Upper Valley and its urban system: 1910-1960

Table 2.2 shows the rapid population growth that the Upper Valley experienced between 1910 and 1960, which essentially coincides with what have been described as the alfalfa cycle (1914-1930) and the fruit growing cycle (1930-1957). It also shows population growth in different categories of urban centres (defined by population size)[16] and other population categories.

Censuses and other sources of data available for the Upper Valley in the first half of the twentieth century allow the disaggregation of population into various categories shown in Table 2.2. Since the

Table 2.2   *Population Growth in the Upper Valley, 1910–1960*

Population Categories	1919	1920	1930	1940	1950	1960
Total population	7,000	13,750	27,100	41,800	81,150	129,150
Dispersed population[a]	3,300	4,600	14,600	22,300	38,450	41,250
Agglomerated population[a]	3,700	9,150	12,500	19,500	42,700	87,900
Population in 5,000 + urban centres[b]	—	—	—	5,100	28,300	77,100
Population in 20,000 + urban centres[c]	—	—	—	—	—	22,500
Population in largest urban centre	1,500 (Neuquen)	3,350 (Roca)	4,100 (Roca)	5,100 (Neuquen)	12,850 (Neuquen)	22,500 (Neuquen)

Notes: a—Agglomerated population is defined as the population living in habitation clusters with at least 50 inhabitants; each agglomeration may consist of a single, continuous built-up area, or of more than one, provided the distance between the edges of contiguous built-up areas is no more than 1 km. For the Upper Valley, dispersed population is assumed to be all the population apart from agglomerated population.

   b—For this book, this is the same as the population in small and intermediate urban centres.

   c—For this book, this is the same as the population in intermediate urban centres.

Source: Estimates based on national censuses of 1914, 1947 and 1960; territorial censuses of 1912 and 1920; a population count made in 1942 by Argentina, Obras Sanitarias de la Nacion; data drawn from commercial guides of 1924, 1929, 1947 and 1951; and yearly counts of dispersed population made by Argentina Direccion Nacional de Irrigacion, and the Ferrocarril Sud company between 1927 and 1936.

Upper Valley only began to have permanent settlements in the late nineteenth and early twentieth centuries, it is not possible to talk of an 'urban population' in the Upper Valley until around 1940, if we only consider nucleated settlements with 5,000 or more inhabitants as 'urban'. Since the two main interests of this book are firstly, population dynamics for settlements which today exceed 5,000 and 20,000 inhabitants and secondly, the economic, social and political forces which underly these dynamics, it is important to examine population growth in urban centres (and the factors which underpinned this growth) before they exceeded 5,000 and 20,000 inhabitants.

Thus, Table 2.3 gives population figures for all today's urban centres for each decade between 1910 and 1980 and also includes all settlements whose population had exceeded 2,000 inhabitants by 1980. Map 2.4 shows their location. Table 2.4 gives annual average growth rates by decade between 1910 and 1960 for all today's urban centres and for total, dispersed and agglomerated population. The distinction between 'agglomerated' and 'dispersed' population is useful in that this essentially distinguishes between population living on individual farms and population living in nucleated settlements with 50 or more inhabitants.[17]

Links between socio-economic and political changes and changes in the Upper Valley's urban system, 1910-1960.

This section will divide this fifty year period into two. To take 1910-1930 first, figures in Tables 2.2 and 2.4 show how total population growth was very rapid. Given annual average population growth rates of 7.0 per cent for both decades, net imigration must have played the dominant role; population growth from natural increase was less than 2.5 per cent per year at that time.

Immigration played a major part in this; we noted earlier how the 1914 census showed that more than half the Upper Valley's population was foreign born. European immigration into Argentina effectively ceased in 1930, which helps explain the sudden down-turn in population growth rate during the Thirties. It is also worth noting that if one takes the period 1910 to 1930, growth rates for total population and for dispersed population were higher than for agglomerated population and for any of the towns. This suggests that the settlement of households on farms was particularly important in this period, since there are very few possibilities other than farming by which households can derive a living outside towns or agglomerations.

During the Alfalfa Cycle, 1914-1930, General Roca, Neuquen, Cipolletti and Allen contained most of the Upper Valley's service and retail enterprises. As Table 2.3 indicates, these were the only Upper Valley settlements to have more than 1,000 inhabitants in 1920 and 1930. To examine the factors which help explain the dominance of these four towns and of the other smaller settlements listed in Table 2.3 for 1920 or 1930, it is worth dividing the functions and activities concentrated in these settlements into those serving the Upper Valley and those with a more localised range. Unless otherwise stated, the following description refers to what existed in 1925.

As capital of the national territory of Neuquen, Neuquen town was the seat of national and territorial government agencies. Some of the national agencies located there also had jurisdiction over the part of the Upper Valley which was in the neighbouring Rio Negro territory. Since 1904, it had been the seat of Neuquen territory's governor and his small staff and the territory's police chief, jail and first instance judge. It was also the seat of a mail district, a roads and bridges district and a military district.[18] In 1905, the Banco de la Nacion (Argentina's main bank) moved its branch from General Roca to Neuquen, despite the fact that it had only been established

Table 2.3 *Population of Upper Valley settlements whose population exceeded 2,000 by 1980*

	1910	1920	1930	1940	1950	1960	1970	1980
1. Neuquen	1,500	2,050	3,000	4,550	12,850	22,500	43,000	90,800
2. General Roca	1,200	3,350	4,100	5,100	9,800	18,250	29,350	44,050
3. Cipolletti	1,000	1,550	1,800	2,400	5,650	13,700	24,150	40,750
4. Villa Regina	—	—	500	1,900	3,050	8,250	13,300	18,550
5. Cinco Saltos	—	150	300	800	2,400	7,900	11,100	15,100
6. Allen	—	1,400	1,600	2,100	3,650	6,500	9,350	14,050
7. Centenario	—	—	—	350	1,350	2,350	4,900	9,600
8. Plottier	—	—	—	50	100	900	2,600	7,300
9. Ingeniero Luis A. Huergo	—	—	500	1,200	1,450	1,850	2,300	3,450

Sources: Our estimates based on national censuses of 1914, 1947, 1960, 1970 and 1980, territorial censuses of 1912 and 1920 and a population count of 1942 made by Argentina, Obras Sanitarias de la Nacion, plus data contained in commercial guides of 1924, 1929, 1947 and 1951.

Table 2.4   *Annual average population growth rates in the Upper Valley*

	1910– 1920	1920– 1930	1930– 1940	1940– 1950	1950– 1960
Total population	7.0	7.0	4.4	6.8	4.8
Dispersed population	3.4	12.2	4.3	5.6	0.7
Agglomerated population	9.5	3.2	4.5	8.1	7.5
Towns					
Neuquen	3.2	3.9	4.3	9.8	5.8
General Roca	10.8	2.0	2.2	6.8	6.4
Cipolletti	4.5	1.5	2.9	8.9	9.3
Villa Regina	—	—	14.2	4.8	10.5
Cinco Saltos	—	a	a	a	12.7
Allen	—	1.3	2.8	5.7	5.9
Centenario	—	—	—	a	5.7
Plottier	—	—	—	a	24.6

Source: Derived from Tables 2.2 and 2.3.

Note: a—Not computed because, since the town did not have 500 inhab-
    itants by the first date, the increase during the following decade
    was very quick only because of the arrival of initial settlers.

in General Roca the previous year. This remained the only bank in
the Upper Valley up to 1920. In 1923, the National Mortgage Bank
set up a branch in Neuquen, and this remains the only branch in the
Upper Valley. The Upper Valley's only foreign consulates, those of
Spain and Chile, came to Neuquen (the Chilean consulate had moved
to Neuquen from General Roca in 1904). However, as Table 2.3
shows, Neuquen's population remained below that of General Roca
in 1920 and 1930. Commercial agriculture had developed very little
around Neuquen town. In the absence of a road bridge linking it to
the Rio Negro portion of the Upper Valley (a road bridge was not
completed until 1937), it remained relatively isolated from the rapidly
expanding economic core of the Upper Valley which at this time was
based on alfalfa production and export.

    Despite losing certain important offices to Neuquen, after Neuquen
became capital of a territory, General Roca remained the largest and
commercially the most important town in the Upper Valley throughout the Twenties. Some functions of more than local scope were also
in General Roca. For instance, its police supervisor had jurisdiction
over the whole west of the territory of Rio Negro. In 1920, the Banco
de la Nacion once again opened a branch there. In that same year,
a private bank, Banco de Rio Negro and Neuquen, opened there;
its stockholders were landowners, farmers and merchants from all
over the Upper Valley. General Roca also had two important private
boarding schools which drew pupils from the wider region. And

nearby, the headquarters of the irrigation works for the Rio Negro portion of the Upper Valley were being built.

Cipolletti and Allen also had some services of more than local scope; for instance, in Cipolletti, there was a meteorological station and the administrative offices for that part of the irrigation works already in service. In Allen there was the office of the general supervisor of primary education for the Upper Valley and, from 1925, the only hospital which served the whole Upper Valley. While the offices of the railway company were (and still are) in Neuquen, its agricultural station remained in Cinco Saltos. Thus by the Twenties, various higher level services were distributed among the larger towns in the Upper Valley, and not concentrated in the kind of hierarchic pattern postulated by central place theory.

General Roca, Neuquen, Cipolletti and Allen each contained concentrations of enterprises and functions which served more restricted areas of demand. General Roca was certainly the leading town in terms of trade and manufacturing. But in all four, there was an official who was both 'judge of the peace' (dealing with minor disputes) and in charge of the registry of births, deaths and marriages, a post office, a police station and three or four primary schools. By 1925, each had several voluntary associations, mostly formed by immigrant groups as self help or sports associations. Two weekly journals were published in General Roca while a weekly journal and daily newspaper were published in Neuquen, although these only printed local news. National and international news arrived after a 2-3 day delay on the railway from Bahia Blanca or Buenos Aires. Modest hotels and restaurants existed in all four towns. With regard to industry, as noted earlier, by 1930 there were two alfalfa mills in Ingeniero Luis A. Huergo and a tomato extract factory in Allen, in addition to the gypsum factory in General Roca.

Wholesale trade did not exist until after 1930 and most retail trade was through general stores which stocked a wide range of goods. Many of these represented important business houses from Bahia Blanca and Buenos Aires. Specialised stores were slowly appearing, especially in General Roca. Each of the four towns had one or more physicians and two drug stores. Despite a population of only 500 in 1930, Ingeniero Luis A. Huergo also had a physician and a drug store. Allen and General Roca had dentists. Only in Neuquen and General Roca were there public notaries. At this point, there were no architects or engineers (except for those working on irrigation). Only in General Roca were there buildings along a main commercial street stretching a few blocks which gave the impression of an urban atmosphere; in the other three towns, the commercial street faced the railroad yard so commercial buildings were only on one side of the street. Most other buildings were very spread out; indeed in Neuquen, entire downtown blocks remained vacant. There were very few two-storey buildings and none of three storeys. In all four towns, modest local power-plants supplied electricity to town houses as well as public lighting in a few corners. After 1916, a few blocks in Neuquen received piped water supplies but in the rest of the town and in the other three towns, water was supplied by water carts or pumped directly from the smallest irrigation canals which ran alongside the town streets. Such water had to be filtered and boiled to eliminate health risks.

Telephones had been installed in the four largest towns by 1913 and in 1916, these were linked together. But the system was only local in scope; long-distance calls could not be made until the Forties. The system's central office was in General Roca. This system allowed increased interaction between the towns (and the farms of those rich enough to be able to afford to pay for a line) at a time when personal transport between the towns was uncomfortable and time consuming. From 1916, a local train ran daily between Neuquen and the eastern extreme of the Upper Valley. In 1922, a similar service began between Neuquen and the Neuquen dam. New stations were opened with the average distance between stations of seven kilometres, so these were accessible to most people living on farms within half an hour's journey by horse-cart (the most common mode of personal transport at that time). From 1920, the number of automobiles (overwhelmingly Model T Fords) increased considerably. The town of Neuquen could only be reached from General Roca, Cipolletti, Allen and other settlements in the Rio Negro portion of the Upper Valley by railway or ferry. Some professionals had two offices, one in the town where they lived and another in a town to be visited once or twice a week. The fact that marriages between people from different towns were not uncommon suggests that there was a social network of personal linkages which covered the whole Upper Valley. Commuting between towns was impossible since trains were too infrequent to allow daily round trips.

Buenos Aires and Bahia Blanca were the two urban centres outside the Upper Valley with which there were strong economic links. Passenger and freight transport between them depended on the railway. Trains covered the 1,250 kilometres between Neuquen and Buenos Aires in 28 hours, four times a week. Salesmen used to come regularly from Bahia Blanca or Buenos Aires and spend one or two days in each Upper Valley town. The Upper Valley also developed economic links with the south of Rio Negro territory and the interior of Neuquen territory. By 1925, motor trucks were rapidly replacing horse-carts in bringing wool to Upper Valley railway stations and carrying back supplies to remote settlements and households.

The development of the larger towns in the Upper Valley by 1930 can be linked to agricultural developments. General Roca's rapid growth, at least up to the early Twenties, can be linked to the fact that it was serving the first intensively cultivated agricultural colony. Cipolletti and Allen had grown to serve the other earliest agricultural colonies on which intensive irrigated crop production developed successfully. No towns of comparable size had developed in the three agricultural colonisation attempts east of General Roca but as noted earlier, none of these had proved successful. Indeed, the town of Ingeniero Luis A. Huergo linked to Colonia Francesa which had emerged in 1914 was almost depopulated by 1920. By 1920, Barda del Medio had emerged as the Upper Valley's fifth largest population concentration, but this was due to the fact that it housed people working on the dam and irrigation works. This did not provide a growing economic base, so its population hardly grew at all from the 650 inhabitants it had in 1920.

Taking the period 1930-1960, Tables 2.2 and 2.4 show that total population growth was still rapid, although less so than between 1910 and 1930. Migration flows from other parts of Argentina and from Chile became more important, as the flow of European immigrants essentially ceased in 1930 and only resumed in a smaller and more short-lived wave in the first few years after the Second World War. Many in-migrants were drawn from the rest of the national territories of Rio Negro and Neuquen which became net out-migration areas. In addition, many people (especially those from the middle class) moved from Buenos Aires or the Pampas.

It is interesting to note in Table 2.4 that agglomerated population grew more rapidly than total population while dispersed population grew more slowly between 1930 and 1960. Indeed, by the Fifties, dispersed population was hardly growing at all, despite a continuance of rapid population growth for the Upper Valley. Once most of the arable land had been put into cultivation and cultivation had shifted from alfalfa to more intensive crops, agriculture's ability to sustain increased labour absorption declined. Up to the late Forties, the increasing area of intensively cultivated land was reflected in the rapid growth of dispersed population; once this began to slow its growth, so too did the growth of dispersed population. Furthermore, once the road network improved, many farmers began to live in towns and commute to their farms, and this is one of the reasons for the very rapid increase in agglomerated population after 1940. Indeed, it was during the fruit cycle that the number of dispersed population was overtaken by the number of those living in agglomerations, while towards the end of the fruit-growing cycle, the population in small urban centres (ie of 5,000 or more inhabitants) also surpassed the total for dispersed population.

After the territories of Rio Negro and of Neuquen became provinces in 1957, the Upper Valley over time became divided into 16 municipalities: 13 in Rio Negro Province; and three in Neuquen Province (see Map 2.5). Thus, municipalities replaced agricultural colonies as areal units in censuses. Each municipality generally had one existing town as its nucleus which had developed as the service centre when the agricultural colony had formed. Squatter settlements also developed but some were too far from the main towns to be considered part of them.

However, during the Fruit Cycle, the urban system was not complex. Three municipal headquarters, Neuquen (also a provincial headquarters), General Roca and Cipolletti, had more than 10,000 inhabitants by the end of the Cycle. Three others had more than 5,000 inhabitants; Villa Regina, Cinco Saltos and Allen. All other settlements with more than 400 inhabitants with one exception[19] were municipality headquarters.

In examining the location of functions or economic activities in 1950, Neuquen, General Roca and Cipolletti contained most that were of more than local scope. Neuquen had received the largest amount of publicly funded functions. It became Northern Patagonia's main military garrison, so in 1941, the headquarters of one of the Argentine army's six divisions was transferred there from Bahia Blanca. This had a considerable effect since it increased demand for many goods and services. Officers and their families moved to Neuquen (or its surrounds), and some draftees or recruits who spent time there also decided to stay. Besides, the barracks, administrative buildings and houses for army officers had to be constructed. By the early Forties, Neuquen and General Roca were the only Upper Valley towns to have educational establishments beyond primary school level, so these establishments attracted students from other settlements. In 1950, the Upper Valley's first radio station opened in Neuquen.

For General Roca, 1934 was an important year since it was in that year that one of the only two first instance judges in Rio Negro moved there from Viedma. By becoming a seat for a first instance judge and headquarters for a judicial district, General Roca had more attorneys at law in 1950 than either Viedma or Neuquen, the two territorial capitals. Between 1934 and 1950, branches of national agencies such as the Ministry of Finance (especially tax revenue offices), the Ministry of Agriculture (especially those concerned with public land administration, forestry control and wine regulation) and the Ministry of Labour were opened there. Some of these had jurisdiction over the Neuquen portion of the Upper Valley too. Finally, when the construction of the main irrigation system in the Rio Negro portion of the Upper Valley was almost completed by 1930, the central administrative offices moved from Cipolletti to General Roca. From 1942, General Roca had three secondary schools. In 1946 its weekly journal, *El Tribuno*, became the Upper Valley's only daily.[20]

By 1950, General Roca also had almost all the Upper Valley's voluntary associations including charity institutions of regional scope (which kept homes for orphans and old people), labour unions and professional associations, and the Chamber of Agriculture, Commerce and Industry to which firms from the whole Upper Valley belonged. Later, similar chambers developed in other towns with the scope of that in General Roca restricted to its immediate area.

After Neuquen and General Roca, Cipolletti had a greater number of activities and functions of more than local scope than other towns. From 1947, it contained the regional branch of the National Water and Electric Energy Authority which managed a modern thermal power station in Allen and later came to manage hydro-electric plants built at various points along the main irrigation canal. It remained the seat of the meteorological station and by 1950 had some regional offices of the Ministry of Agriculture. Allen, Villa Regina and Cinco Saltos contained some services covering the whole Upper Valley including the old regional hospital and the Federation of Associations of Fruit Producers in Allen.

The eight largest towns were all administrative centres for their own irrigation districts. Except for Neuquen and Centenario districts (which were to the west of the Neuquen River), the rest were subservient to the central office in General Roca. This was a common pattern with the eight towns having some lower level offices under the direction of higher level offices in Neuquen, General Roca or Cipolletti. For example, local branches of a private bank with headquarters in General Roca had branches in Cipolletti and Villa Regina, while various offices of the Ministry of Agriculture were under the direction of central offices in General Roca and Cipolletti. Thus, in 1950 no town had within it a high proportion of the functions or services of regional scope and all towns depended to some extent on services in Neuquen, General Roca or Cipolletti.

For functions of local scope, only Neuquen, General Roca and Allen had elected local government by 1925. By 1950, there were also autonomous municipalities in Cipolletti, Villa Regina and Cinco Saltos, although not yet in Ingeniero Luis A. Huergo and Centenario. In these latter two towns, as in many smaller settlements, there was a limited form of local government ('comision de fomento') directly appointed by the territory's governor.

By 1950, each of the eight largest towns had a judge of the peace, a registry of births, deaths and marriages, a post office, a police station, several public schools, some kind of public health centre, doctors, dentists and drug stores. The three largest, Neuquen, General Roca and Cipolletti, had private clinics and specialist doctors. No new banks had come to the Upper Valley since 1925 but the Banco de Rio Negro y Neuquen had opened branches in Cipolletti and Villa Regina and was to do so in the near future in most of the other main towns. Various voluntary associations of local scope were evident in each town. Among these were so-called 'social clubs' as meeting places for the elite, associations for various sports (soccer was the most important) and cooperative associations of farmers who owned packing plants and wineries. All eight towns had one or two cinemas and had hotels, restaurants and side-walk coffee houses.

Apart from General Roca's daily newspaper which had news for the whole Comahue region, weekly newspapers were abundant: four in General Roca and one or two in four other towns, although these weekly newspapers had disappeared by 1957 with competition from national newspapers, radio and television. General Roca remained the pre-eminent commercial town. Within it were agents from important business houses of Buenos Aires and Bahia Blanca including insurance companies and wholesale distributors for a wide range of goods, although there were few wholesale stores in any town. Bahia Blanca remained the main wholesale centre for the Upper Valley and in many other respects Bahia Blanca was the metropolitan centre on which the population and the enterprises in the Upper Valley relied. General stores remained common although many specialist stores had developed, with most of these concentrated in General Roca. Some fulfilled demand for the whole Upper Valley, for instance selling fruit packing materials. Others show the more sophisticated and complex demand for higher order goods and services such as optometrists, gun-shops and shops selling glass for windows. A few nationwide chain stores had opened branches in the Upper Valley, mostly in Neuquen. Agricultural processing industries were distributed among various towns, although Cipolletti was becoming the main centre for agro-industry.

However, the physical environment had not improved much from that described earlier for 1925. Except for Neuquen's downtown area which had piped water supplies, drinking water continued to be pumped into water tanks in each house from the smallest canals in the irrigation system which ran underneath the principal streets. There were no sewage systems. Although a rich source of natural gas existed in the nearby oilfield of Plaza Huincul to the west of Neuquen, no gas pipeline was built to supply the Upper Valley. Although electricity supplies were soon to become abundant with the construction of hydro-electric plants on the main irrigation canals, at this time there were only tiny local thermal power plants plus one modern one in Allen. Certain towns, notably General Roca (but also Neuquen) were exposed during the winter to torrential run-off from the northern plateaus which damaged buildings and put thick deposits of sediment on streets. In the absence of any urban planning policy, new developments in and around the original layouts took place in a haphazard fashion. There were still no architects and most buildings continued to be planned and built by lay technicians. By 1950, only five architect-designed buildings existed in the whole Upper Valley. In this, the government provided no lead, since all new public buildings built in the Upper Valley were designed in Buenos Aires with no consideration for local environmental characteristics. Most public offices still oper-ated in poorly adapted, rented, old buildings, since public investment in national territories was very small.

After Neuquen and Rio Negro became provinces, the quality of public architecture slowly improved. Before 1955, there seems to have been only one three-storey building (in Allen). As built-up areas expanded, the humble adobe brick houses tended to disappear from the central areas but reappeared on peripheral plots. The lower income groups lived in squatter settlements of very poor quality. Tiny squatter settlements also began to emerge at some distance from towns, inhabited by unqualified, landless agricultural workers. Some grew in size from the late Fifties onwards; one, Barrio Mosconi in General Roca Municipality, even became a town in its own right by the Seventies.

The growth in the number of telephones was slow: from 430 in 1929 to 1,508 in 1951 and then a decrease to 1,462 in 1961. By 1951, all but Centenario among the eight largest towns were connected to the telephone system. It is interesting to note that the number of telephones in General Roca and in surrounding farms was 573 com-pared to 235 for Neuquen and 217 for Cipolletti. The other towns had between 100 and 150. Around 1950, it became possible to com-municate by telephone to Buenos Aires and other important Argen-tine cities, after the construction of a radio station in General Roca.

In 1950, the railway remained the most important transport mode linking the Upper Valley with the outside. Trains ran every day to Bahia Blanca and Buenos Aires, but the journey time had not been cut from that existing in 1925. A regular air service had opened in 1947, with flights twice a week in an aeroplane with 13 passengers. By 1950, motor trucks were growing in importance, even if trains were preferred for transporting commodities in and out of the area. Although not paved, the road network had much improved since 1930.

Buses or motor cars were the most common mode of inter-town or local transport in the Upper Valley. Local trains had stopped in 1935 and been replaced by slow and uncomfortable buses. There were no express buses. The main bus line, serving the area between Neuquen and Villa Regina, had been acquired by the railway company (a fact that was only discovered when the railway was nationalised in 1947). Neither the company nor the government paid much attention to improving public transport. Although the horse-drawn cart had almost disappeared by 1950 and the number of cars per head was one of the highest in the country, poor public transport especially hindered the mobility of the poor, the old and young and women (very few women drove a car at this time). Commuting was only possible if one had a car. This not only greatly restricted people's access to services of regional scope but also prevented the expansion and improvement of higher order services which a population the size and wealth of that in the Upper Valley should have been able to support. One example is in higher education. Many relatively well off families continued to send their children away to school in Bahia Blanca, Buenos Aires or La Plata because of dubious quality secondary schools in the Upper Valley. Those lacking a car found that their employment opportunities were very limited. In fact, one way of defining social stratification could have been by car ownership, since people's accessibility to services and facilities and to employment opportunities was so greatly enhanced with a car.

Towards the end of the Fruit Cycle, 1930-57, another sub-region, what was defined earlier as the Upper Valley's periphery, had developed to the point where it began to affect the Upper Valley's economy and urban system. To the west of Neuquen town, in the middle of an arid plateau, oil exploitation had begun in 1918. A state-owned company had been given a tract whose centre was the railway station, Plaza Huincul. Here, a town developed as the residence for oil workers and technicians. The company made great efforts to provide them with a comfortable environment including piped water supply, retail stores and services and vegetation in the streets. No person was allowed to live here without the company's permission.

After 1930, during a time of widespread national unemployment, people looking for work in the oil industry came to the area and built a miserable shanty town just across the western boundary of the land reserved for Plaza Huincul. This new settlement, then known as 'Dangerous Quarter', grew rapidly. After lobbying by prominent people from Plaza Huincul, this settlement obtained official recognition in 1933. In 1936, a local government was created, appointed by the territorial governor.

The shanty town was renamed Cutral Co. and by 1936 had more than 2,000 inhabitants; Plaza Huincul probably had around the same number. By 1950, the population of both, in a single agglomeration, had reached 8,000 and grew to 12,000 in 1960. Most lived in Cutral Co. since the company prevented Plaza Huincul from growing beyond a few thousand. Lack of water and a lack of trees to shield Cutral Co. from the strong western winds made conditions very poor. It was not unusual for a sand dune to build up overnight blocking the entrance to the houses, most of which were built of adobe bricks. Windows were kept very small to minimise sand and dust intrusion. Streets were not paved until the mid-Sixties and it was even later that piped water was supplied.

The twin town's only economic base was (and remains today) petroleum extraction. Up to 1962, the petroleum was exported from the region by railway; in 1962 a pipeline replaced the railway. Except for a small refinery producing for local demands, hardly any industrial development took place on the basis of the oil extraction. An active retail trade developed in response to rising local demand and building quality improved. The serious physical environmental problems were not overcome. However, in the future, since the twin town's entire economic and employment base derives from petroleum extraction, with the diminution and eventual exhaustion of deposits there, the entire urban settlement is likely to decline and even to disappear.

By 1957, Cutral Co-Plaza Huincul was the only settlement in the Upper Valley's periphery, apart from a small poor pastoral colony, Catriel, on the Colorado River bank, north of the Upper Valley. Catriel had been founded around the turn of the century and only had a few hundred inhabitants by 1957. A description of its development, as oil was discovered nearby, is included on page 61. So too is the increasing interaction between the economy and the population of those living in the urban centres in the Upper Valley's periphery and major urban centres in the Upper Valley. Only during the Sixties did such an interaction develop on a significant scale.

Economic changes during the Agro-Industrial Cycle: 1957–1980

The period 1957-1980 which we call the agro-industrial cycle included the largest expansion in the Upper Valley's economy. During this period, virtually all cultivable land came to be cultivated with an increasing proportion devoted to intensive production of apples and pears. Once the initial investments have been made, these give the highest return per hectare. Annual average production of apples and pears grew more than threefold in this period. But serious problems became evident in the late Seventies as traditional markets for locally grown crops became less certain and as an over-valued Argentinian peso meant lower returns for farmers. In addition, many farmers with relatively small land-holdings had few possibilities of increasing production; there was little or no new cultivable land and they had already achieved very high yields. Furthermore, their dependence on larger, vertically integrated firms for packing, processing and marketing their produce had increased.

During this same period, industrial production grew and diversified, much of it due to forward and backward linkages with fruit production. Increasing technical concentration (through which production rose much faster than employment) and vertical integration (whereby certain enterprises came to own a larger and more diverse set of activities) were evident. Details about these economic changes are given in sub-sections on agriculture, manufacturing and trade and services. As noted earlier, the transition from what was termed the Fruit Cycle to the Agro-Industrial Cycle took place between 1947 and 1967. Within this twenty-year transition, there are various key dates. The first is the sudden drop in the area devoted to alfalfa in 1952. Apple production began to grow rapidly around 1960. In 1967, as is described in more detail later, there was a rapid switch from rail to road for the transport of fruit and fruit products out of the Upper Valley. The period of rapid economic expansion lasted until the late Seventies, based on increasing fruit production and the most important characteristic of this period, as the title given to this period implies, was the growth in industrial activities intimately linked to fruit production and processing. Then there was a crisis in the Upper Valley's economy beginning in the late Seventies which was associated with factors such as a contraction in the domestic market for Upper Valley produce, the high value of the Argentinian peso against foreign currencies (which lessened export earnings) and a reduction in import duties.

Agricultural production in the Upper Valley

As Table 2.5 shows, apple and pear production had come to dominate production in the Upper Valley by 1969, while tomato, grape and alfalfa production declined in importance during the Sixties. Neither animal raising nor cereal production was of importance. Apple production continued to increase after 1969; annual average production was around 150,000 tons during the Fifties, 300,000 during the late Sixties and close to half a million after 1976. Although the trend in pear production from 1960 to 1980 was not as rapid as Table 2.5 suggests, since 1960 was a particularly poor year and 1969 an exceptional year, average annual pear production during the Seventies substantially exceeded those of the previous 20 years.[21] And it was in the Rio Negro portion of the Upper Valley that more than 80 per cent of total agricultural production value originated.

To study differences in agricultural production within the Upper Valley, statistics are only available for the irrigation districts. Although irrigation district boundaries are not identical to municipality boundaries (for which other statistical data such as population is available), irrigation districts do cover one or more whole municipalities as shown in Maps 2.5 and 2.6, so broad comparisons can be made between agricultural production (based on irrigation district data) and population data (based on municipalities).

By the end of the Fruit Cycle in 1957, the eight largest towns in the Upper Valley including six with 5,000 or more inhabitants were the chief towns within the irrigation districts. Table 2.6 shows changes in cultivated area and in the proportion of this area devoted to the dominant crops for 1958 and 1978. By 1978, virtually all cultivable land was cultivated—and cultivated land area is essentially the same

Table 2.5   *Upper Valley gross agricultural production value for five main crops, 1960 and 1969*

| Crop | Gross production value[a] | | | |
| | 1960 | | 1969 | |
	Thousands of pesos	%	Thousands of pesos	%
Apple	9,856	44.6	16,742	65.8
Grape	4,423	20.0	1,873	7.4
Tomato	3,997	18.1	1,722	6.8
Alfalfa (fodder)	1,791	8.1	529	2.0
Pear	1,201	5.4	3,028	11.9
Others	826	3.8	1,552	6.1
Total	22,094	100.0	25,446	100.0

NB The five crops are those which, ranked according to production value in 1960, represented in that year more than 95 per cent of the Upper Valley's gross agricultural production value.

Note: a—Constant values of 1960, calculated on the basis of Argentina, Banco Central, Gerencia de Investigaciones Economicas, *Sistemas de cuentas del producto e ingreso de la Argentina* (Buenos Aires, 1975), Vol. II.

Source: Derived from data supplied in Floreal Forni *et al.*, unpublished materials of the project *Estructura ocupacional del sector agropecuario argentino, 1914–1969* (Buenos Aires: CEIL-CONICET, 1979).

as irrigated area, since intensive cultivation is impossible without irrigation.

Both before and during the Agro-Industrial Cycle, there were important differences in, for instance, crop specialisation, crop yields and size of land holdings between irrigation districts, and these had important influences on urban development within each district. For instance, Cinco Saltos, Cipolletti and Centenario to the west were the first to specialise in apple and pear production and retained this specialisation. They had among the highest yields per hectare for apples and pears and the highest number of small-holdings and smallest average size holdings. Going west to east, specialisation in apple production decreases with the proportion of land devoted to alfalfa generally increasing; the average size of land holdings also tends to increase going west to east.

Trends in the mix of crops grown within each irrigation district have been influenced by their different colonisation histories. The earliest successful agricultural colonies and those which first received the benefit of the modern gravity-fed irrigation system were usually those which first came to specialise in fruit production. Cinco Saltos's early specialisation in fruit was also encouraged by the presence there

Map 2.5 *The Upper Valley: municipality boundaries around 1970*

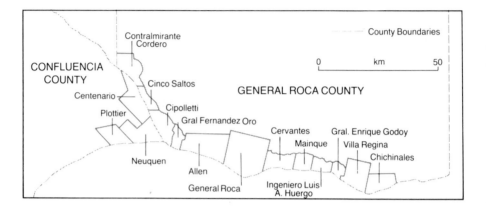

Map 2.6 *The Upper Valley: irrigation districts (this includes district-equivalents and newly developed agricultural areas outside districts)*

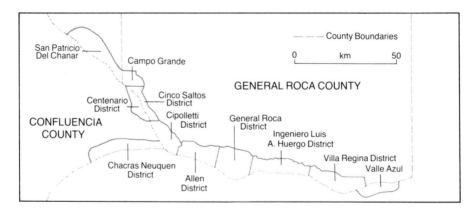

of some British farmers and the British railway company's agricultural station which sought to stimulate fruit production to bring more business for the railway.

By contrast, further to the east, alfalfa remained the most widely grown crop in Ingeniero Luis A. Huergo. It was within this district that two early agricultural colonies (Cervantes and Francesa) failed, so that by the Twenties, much of their land had been abandoned. It was connected to the modern irrigation system later than districts to its west. Since alfalfa is a crop typically used to prepare soil for more intensive crops, it is no surprise to see alfalfa retaining its importance in this district, long after its importance in most other districts had greatly diminished. But between 1958 and 1978, as Table 2.6 shows, the increasing importance of fruit trees and vineyards became evident at the expense of alfalfa. Ingeniero Luis A. Huergo's land was found to be well suited to grapevine cultivation which is why it came to have one of the highest proportions of cultivated area devoted to vineyards of any irrigation district.

The proportions of cultivated area devoted to the different crops usually change relatively slowly; it is more costly and more difficult to change the areas devoted to perennial crops in response to short-term price fluctuations than it is for cereals or other annual crops. Because of longer lead times and of the high investment needed to make major changes—in response to longer term price changes or technological changes—government support is needed, especially for small and medium farmers who lack the resources to allow major changes in their mix of perennial crops.

Different crops also have different implications for the stimulation of other productive activities in the Upper Valley. Apple production has more forward and backward linkages to industrial, commercial and service activities within the Upper Valley than other crops. As will be discussed in more detail later, there is a higher degree of urban-based economic activity in those municipalities with the largest or most intensive apple cultivation. In making such comparisons, note must be taken of total area under cultivation. For instance, even though there is a far lower proportion of cultivated area in General Roca devoted to fruit than in, say Cinco Saltos or Colonia Centenario, the cultivated area under apples in General Roca was larger than in the two other irrigation districts in 1978.

In examining the type of land tenure that existed for farms and of trends in the size of land-holdings during the Seventies, two important facts emerged. The first is that most holdings were still being farmed by their owners, as had been the norm in the first half of the century and not by tenants or managers for absentee landowners. The second is that there are no clear trends towards further subdivision of land holdings among the smallest landholders but some evidence of subdivision among larger holdings. This raises two ques-

Table 2.6 Cultivated areas and percentage devoted to most important crops for Upper Valley irrigation districts, 1958 and 1978[a]

Irrigation Districts	Cultivated area (hectares)		% to Apples		% to Vineyards		% to Alfalfa (fodder)		% to Pears		% to Tomatoes		% to Alfalfa (pasture)	
	1958	1978	1958	1978	1958	1978	1958	1978	1958	1978	1958	1978	1958	1978
General Roca County														
Cinco Saltos	2,954	3,516	75	71	3	3	7	1	11	10	—	—	—	1
Cipolletti	6,555	7,333	49	52	24	17	3	2	12	12	—	—	3	—
Allen	8,272	9,769	28	33	33	32	18	2	12	17	—	1	6	4
General Roca	13,353	13,818	12	32	30	23	24	7	4	10	3	2	15	3
Ingeniero Luis A. Huergo	6,810	11,837	8	24	25	30	36	13	3	6	18	4	—	—
Villa Regina	15,014	15,113	20	50	11	11	25	4	5	18	11	4	—	—
Confluencia County														
Chacras Neuquen	4,068	6,175	23	33	14	15	37	17	7	6	—	—	2	8
Colonia Centenario	3,127	3,355	60	74	5	1	11	2	3	4	—	—	—	—

NB If crops were ranked by proportion of cultivated area they covered, in 1978 this would be: apples, vineyards, alfalfa fodder, pear, tomato and alfalfa (pasture). Other crops such as barley, alfalfa (seed), corn, potatoes, peaches, hops and forest and tree nurseries covered one or more per cent of cultivated areas in one or both of the years shown in some irrigation districts but they never covered more than 7 per cent of the cultivated area for any particular irrigation district for one year and they usually covered less than 1 or only 1 or 2. The number of cultivated hectares does not coincide exactly with the number of hectares under cultivation since some double cropping is practised.

Note: a—The years 1958 and 1978 refer to the growing seasons of 1958–59 and 1978–79.

Source: Drawn from Argentina, Ministerio de Economia, Secretaria de Estado de Energia y Mineria, Agua y Energia Electrica, Intendencia Regional Zona V, *Memoria Anuales*.

tions. The first relates to the extent to which vertical integration which is evident in manufacturing and trade also includes the ownership or control of agricultural land. The second is the extent to which small independent farmers who own their own holding are actually obtaining an adequate living. Linked to these is the question of the extent of 'minifundia' ie landholdings too small to adequately sustain the farming household and whether their numbers seem to be increasing over time.

In looking at the size of agricultural holdings for the whole Upper Valley, roughly two-thirds were between 1 and 10 hectares and a quarter between 10 and 20 (see Table 2.7). The number of holdings above 100 hectares is very low and these only covered a small proportion of the land. A rough guide as to the minimum lot size needed to provide an adequate living (ie below which it becomes a minifundium) is around 6-8 hectares for apple trees and 10 hectares for tomatoes or vines.[22] Up to the late Seventies, a farm of 20-30 hectares was reckoned to provide a good living, provided the initial investment had been made to allow intensive cultivation. It should also be noted that with an intensively cultivated irrigated landholding, the scale economies on the farm achieved by extending the cultivated area beyond 30-40 hectares are insignificant.

In looking at trends over time in land-holding sizes, the number between 1 and 5 hectares did increase considerably in the transition from the Fruit Cycle to the Agro-Industrial Cycle; these had represented 22 per cent of total farms in the early Forties and had reached around a third of all farms during the Seventies. Looking at farm-holding sizes for the different irrigation districts, the districts specialising most in apples tended to have the highest number of holdings of 1 to 5 hectares; Centenario, Cinco Saltos and Cipolletti which had the highest proportion of cultivated area devoted to apples in 1969 and 1979 had among the highest proportion of holdings of this size for both dates. But this does not necessarily imply that all or even most of these were minifundia; average apple yields per hectare were particularly high in Centenario and Cipolletti so that some holdings of less than 5 hectares could adequately support the farm household.

Moving east, Allen, General Roca, Ingeniero Luis A. Huergo and Villa Regina have a much lower incidence of 1 to 5 hectare holdings. A similar spatial pattern going west to east, is evident if one considers the average size of all land-holdings and in 1979 this was 5 hectares for Cinco Saltos, 7 for Cipolletti, Centenario and Neuquen and 10-11 for Allen, General Roca, Ingeniero Luis A. Huergo and Villa Regina. Land-holdings' average size did not change significantly during the Seventies. The increase in the number of holdings evident in Table 2.7 was generally from the subdivision of 10-30 hectare holdings due to inheritance. And there was no noticeable difference in trends over time for a decrease in average size of land-holdings in the different irrigation districts.

Table 2.7 *Agricultural holding sizes in the Upper Valley, 1969–1979*

Size of holding (hectares)	1969				1979			
	Number	%	Hectares	%	Number	%	Hectares	%
1 to 5	2,304	35	7,491	11	2,480	34	8,310	12
5 to 10	2,233	33	16,143	23	2,526	35	18,026	26
10 to 20	1,636	24	21,747	31	1,719	24	22,630	33
20 to 30	339	5	8,251	11	314	4	7,664	11
30 to 50	165	2	6,810	10	149	2	6,050	9
50 to 100	89	1	7,089	10	65	1	5,099	7
100+	13	0	2,663	4	9	0	1,606	2
Totals	6,779	100	70,194	100	7,262	100	69,385	100

NB Holdings of less than one hectare have been excluded since they are not considered as true units of agricultural exploitation. In 1969, there were 592 holdings of less than one hectare which covered 278 hectares. In the percentage columns, if the figure did not reach 1, it is expressed as 0.

Source: elaboration of statistics from Argentina, Ministerio de Economia Secretaria de Estado de Energia y Mineria, Agua y Energia Electrica, Gerencia de Riego, Intendencia Regional Zona V, *Memorias anuales.*

Some studies have suggested that two trends were evident—one of economic concentration, due to a process of vertical integration whereby large enterprises involved in packing, marketing and processing also become major landowners, and another of increasing land-holding subdivision. But there is insufficient information to check that there is increasing concentration of land-holdings under vertically integrated firms although, as will be described in the next sub-section, such vertical integration is evident in other economic activities associated with agricultural production. An increasing control of economic activities by large firms need not imply increasing concentration of land-holdings under their ownership; control can be achieved by their control of commercial and industrial activities which take place after produce leaves the farms. Similarly, existing data does not necessarily imply an increase in the number of minifundia, and since it is ambiguous, no definite conclusions can be drawn.[23]

However, it is clear that farmers relying solely on relatively small holdings are facing serious difficulties. The problem is most evident in the districts of Centenario, Cipolletti and Cinco Saltos where specialisation and reliance on intensive crops is most evident and holdings are smallest. There is less possibility for increasing farm incomes, especially since there is little possibility of extending the area under cultivation. It is in these three districts where yields are already high and crop cultivation is most intensive so there is less possibility of increasing farm incomes. If they are increasingly dependent on larger, vertically oriented firms for packing, processing and marketing their produce, these farmers are relatively powerless to further develop their income derived from farming.

Manufacturing

In 1974, the municipalities of General Roca, Cipolletti and Cinco Saltos contained most of the large industrial enterprises. Of the 19 which employed more than 75 people in the Upper Valley, General Roca had six, Cippolletti four and Cinco Saltos three. Villa Regina and Neuquen each had two while Centenario and Plottier each had one. Since much of the data on manufacturing is only available at the level of county or province, then General Roca County (in Rio Negro Province) and Confluencia County (in Neuquen Province) will be considered separately.

Figures for 1963 for General Roca County confirm the dominant role of the municipalities of General Roca, Cipolletti and Cinco Saltos, which was also apparent in 1974 statistics for the whole Upper Valley. Each of these three contained a fifth or more of the county's total manufacturing production value while the three together accounted for around 70 per cent. In terms of number of plants and of people employed, General Roca and Cipolletti were the most important, followed by Villa Regina, then Cinco Saltos, then Allen. These five municipalities out of a total of 12 in the county accounted for more than 85 per cent of the number of plants, people employed and total production value. Thus, as is the case for intensive agricultural production, it is the areas settled first, the western-most municipalities, where industrial activities are spatially concentrated.

Table 2.8 shows the number of plants and of people employed in the dominant manufacturing sectors in General Roca county for 1963 and 1973. In both these years, wine industries and the elaboration and conservation of fruit and vegetables were the most important in terms of production value. In terms of employment, they were also among the most important for both years, although in 1963 industries producing paper and cardboard packages and in 1974 sawmills and other activities associated with wood processing were major employers too. The figures in Table 2.8 also show that there was a dramatic increase in production value (more than 120 per cent at constant prices) but the number of plants did not change and the number of people employed only increased a little. This process whereby total production rises far faster than number of plants and people employed is an example of *technical concentration*. Thus, between 1963 and 1973 production per plant and per employee rose for all but one of the different activities listed in Table 2.8.[24] The growth in production per plant and per employee was particularly noticeable for the two important industries in terms of production value: wine industries; and fruit and vegetable elaboration and conservation.

The links between agriculture and industry are obvious, although the categories used in the censuses reproduced in Table 2.8 understate their extent. For instance, package and cold storage plants are class-

Table 2.8   *The most important industrial branches in General Roca County, 1963 and 1973/4*

Activities (categories according to 1974 code)	Plants				Personnel employed				Production value[a]			
	1974		1963		1973		1963		1973[b]		1963	
	Number	%	Number	%	Number	%	Number	%	Thousand pesos	%	Thousand pesos	%
Wine industries	110	16	155	19	653	9	1,063	15	17,435	32	5,445	22
Elaboration and conservation of fruit and vegetables	22	3	30	4	832	10	1,905	27	9,757	18	4,688	19
Sawmills, wood shaving workshops, and other workshops where wood is processed	78	12	49	6	2,012	26	127	2	1,846	3	196	1
Elaboration of non-metal mineral products not classified in other branches	44	7	20	2	502	6	103	1	1,797	3	316	2
Production of wood and straw packages	24	4	52	6	647	8	1,313	18	1,462	3	2,116	8
Production of paper and cardboard packages	4	1	7	1	167	2	81	1	1,103	2	1,036	4
Residual branch	50	8	n.a.	n.a.	1,193	15	n.a.	n.a.	13,205	25	n.a.	n.a.
Subtotal	332	51	n.a.	n.a.	6,096	76	n.a.	n.a.	46,515	88	n.a.	n.a.
Total	660	100	661	100	8,018	100	6,662	100	53,284	100	23,740	100

NB For more details about this subject and about the problems and distortions in this table as a result of available data, reference should be made to Vapnarsky and Manzanal, 1982.

Source: Based on unpublished listings from the national economic censuses of 1963 and 1974 (provisional results).

Notes: a—Constant 1960 pesos.
         b—Although the census was in 1974, the data on production value was for 1973.

ified under commerce and services and these are totally linked to agricultural produce. Cider production is included under 'wine industry'. A substantial proportion of the production from sawmills is associated with the production of fruit-packaging. Half or more of manufacturing production value and of people employed in manufacturing were involved in industries intimately linked to fruit production while many others have important but less direct links.

One important manufacturing industry whose links to agricultural production cannot be seen in Table 2.8 is the factory in Cinco Saltos with over 400 employees and a very high production value. Among its products are fertilisers and biocides used in agriculture. At least three factors help explain its location in Cinco Saltos. The first is proximity to a source of cheap electricity; the factory obtains its power from a hydro-electric station it built on the main irrigation canal. The second is proximity to raw materials; it extracts certain minerals from the bardas of the valley close by. But the third is the fact that location within Cinco Saltos gives it easy access to the large and concentrated market of farmers who need its products. Its location in Cinco Saltos not only gives it easy access to farmers in that municipality but also to those in all 15 other municipalities in the Upper Valley.[25]

As well as what we termed *technical concentration*, another process, *vertical integration,* is evident in manufacturing. This is the process by which one enterprise comes to own a larger and more diverse set of activities. This trend cannot be quantified since the categories used in censuses do not allow its detection. But various case studies have shown its importance. To give one example, a packaging plant, Cascada S.A., began as a packaging plant in 1957 and gradually expanded and extended its activities so that by 1973 it owned over 400 cultivated hectares in the Upper Valley and in two other valley areas downriver, two fruit concentrate and juice production units in Cipolletti and General Roca municipalities, sawmills in General Roca and in the Middle Valley, and mechanised packaging and cold storage plants in Cipolletti.

The portion of the Upper Valley in Confluencia County evidently contains less manufacturing activity than the portion in General Roca County.[26] Even in 1974, when Confluencia County's statistics for total industrial production value were enlarged by oil production from Cutral Co-Plaza Huincul (which is outside the Upper Valley), Confluencia County's industrial production value was less than half that of General Roca County. In 1963, when oil production was much less, it had been less than a third. One should recall that Confluencia County has approximately one-sixth of the cultivated area in the Upper Valley (the rest is in General Roca County), and that a high proportion of General Roca County's manufacturing activities are directly or indirectly related to agricultural production.

Drawing from field-work and from information sources other than censuses, industrial activity linked to local agricultural produce in Confluencia County seem to be concentrated not in Neuquen, the largest urban centre, but Plottier and Centenario, two adjacent municipalities which seem increasingly to be becoming industrial and residential suburbs of Neuquen. The most important packaging plants, (including cold storage plants), wineries, box factories and dried fruit production plants are in these two municipalities. As in General Roca County, the trend towards technical concentration (ie total production value growing faster than number of plants and employees) is evident. Industrial activities with more tenuous (or no) direct links with Upper Valley agricultural production such as 'elaboration of bakery products', 'cattle slaughter', capital goods, 'elaboration of non-metal mineral products' and consumer goods seem to be more heavily concentrated in Neuquen municipality, although data does not exist to allow more precision as to their location, number of employees and production value. But the lack of manufacturing plants linked to local agricultural produce in Neuquen municipality is not surprising, given its lack of cultivated land area compared to most other municipalities. Nor is the concentration of other manufacturing activities there surprising, given its role as the largest population concentration and urban centre with the highest administrative status (a provincial capital) within the Upper Valley.

Trade and services

Existing data allows us to describe the spatial distribution of these activities and trends over time within all the Upper Valley municipalities. In 1963, the major centres of trade and service employment were the same as those for manufacturing, as is shown in Table 2.9. Among the municipalities in the Upper Valley, General Roca was dominant in terms of number of establishments, people employed and sales, followed by Neuquen and Cipolletti. These three and Villa Regina, Cinco Saltos and Allen contained 85 per cent or more of all establishments, people employed and sales. The most important subsectors were 'food and beverages', 'general stores', 'car-sales' and 'clothing'. Unfortunately, 1974 economic census data was too aggregated to allow comments on the distribution of such activities within the Upper Valley.

The marketing of agricultural produce is the Upper Valley's most important commercial activity; we should recall that up to 1947 this was virtually monopolised by a subsidiary of the British owned railway company. After the railway's nationalisation in 1947, this subsidary lost its traditional efficiency and some enterprises with sufficient financial resources took advantage of the financial difficulties faced by farmers and assumed an increasing role in marketing. Some were

Table 2.9 Distribution of industry and commerce in the Upper Valley in 1963, 1971 and 1974

Municipalities	Manufacturing[a]			Commerce			% Cold storage Plants in Comahue 1971 (approx.)	Large industries in 1974[b]
	% of plants	% people employed	% prodn. value	% of centres	% people employed	% sales		
General Roca	25	20	21	21	27	33	15	6
Cipolletti	19	28	21	15	16	19	25	4
Villa Regina	18	15	10	12	5	8	12	2
Cinco Saltos	15	12	27	9	8	6	15	3
Allen	8	12	9	9	8	6	12	—
Contralmirante Cordero	2	2	1	3	2	1	—	—
Ingeniero Luis A. Huergo	2	2	2	3	2	2	—	—
Other five municipalities	9	9	8	4	5	1	—	—
Total for General Roca County	—	—	—	76	73	76	—	—
Neuquen	—	—	—	19	22	21	4	2
Centenario	—	—	—	4	4	2	9	1
Plottier	—	—	—	1	1	1	—	1
Total for Confluencia County	—	—	—	24	27	24	—	—

Notes: a—Figures only available for General Roca County
b—Those with more than 75 persons employed

Sources: Manufacturing and commerce figures derived from data in 1963 economic census published in Provincia de Rio Negro Secretaria Tecnica de la Gobernion. *Indices municipales*, Viedma. 1963. Confluencia County figures from unpublished 1963 census documents. Data on cold storage plants from unpublished records of Ministerio de Agricultura y Ganaderia, Direccion General de Produccion y Fomento Agricola, Direccion de Frutas y Horalizas, Departamento de Interior y Fiscalizacion. Data on large industries from unpublished tables of 1974 economic census.

formed by associations of Upper Valley producers; others came from Buenos Aires or Bahia Blanca. Whatever their origin, many expanded and diversified their operations beyond marketing to reach a high degree of vertical integration and thus control the entire process from fruit production to packaging and processing to final sale in domestic and foreign markets. There are also independent producers who sell their produce to a wholesaler, collector or integrated enterprise. In 1973-4, 70 per cent of the agricultural producers in General Roca County were independent while 20 per cent were members of marketing cooperatives, 6 per cent owned their own packaging plant and 4 per cent were integrated enterprises. However, the role of integrated enterprises was much higher when one looks at the total volume of fresh apples and pears produced, since integrated enterprises were responsible for 20 per cent. Most of the larger enterprises which export fresh fruit from Argentina have operations in the Upper Valley. The growth and development of Cascada S.A. was described earlier. Another example is Valle de Oro S.A. which was formed by an association of 21 fruit growers to market and export members' produce and grew to own a large packaging and classification plant, a cold storage plant, 100 hectares of fruit trees, a fleet of cold storage trucks and establishments outside the Upper Valley. Integrated enterprises' plants in the Upper Valley are concentrated in those municipalities with the greatest concentration of industries. For instance, integrated enterprises own a high proportion of cold storage capacity; nearly all of the 75 or so cold storage plants in the entire Comahue region in 1971 were in the Upper Valley; 19 were in Cipolletti, 11 each in Cinco Saltos and General Roca, 9 each in Allen and Villa Regina, 7 in Centenario and 3 in Neuquen.

With increasing vertical integration, the small independent farmers tend to get squeezed out. They cannot organise the marketing of their produce outside the region by themselves. And such farmers only know the final price their crops obtain after they have been sold by the intermediary who undertakes the marketing. Thus, it is the farmer, not the intermediaries, who bear most of the risk. The costs of the complex marketing process from fruit classification, packaging, storage and transport to final marketing with all the intermediaries involved are also very high. And it is the independent farmers who usually operate on the smallest farms and thus face the most difficulty in raising capital needed to further intensify production. The power of the integrated enterprises is not so much in the amount of land they farm or the crops they grow but in their control of the commercial and industrial activities after the farmgate. Independent farmers and cooperatives usually have no choice but to use these.

Developments in the Upper Valley periphery

We noted in an earlier section the emergence of Cutral Co-Plaza Huincul as an important urban centre which had developed around oil exploitation. This urban centre, within Confluencia County, had 15,550 inhabitants in 1960. Its population grew rapidly, in line with expanding oil production, to reach 33,850 in 1980. A second urban centre, Catriel, emerged and developed rapidly during the Agro-Industrial Cycle, on the northern border of General Roca County. Oil was discovered there in 1959 and began to be fully exploited in the mid-Sixties. Since 1962, pipelines have been constructed to transport oil and gas from the fields around these two urban centres out of the region, mostly to Bahia Blanca and Buenos Aires. In neither of these urban centres have economic activities developed much, other than those based on oil and gas extraction. Predictions suggest that if 1977 production levels remain constant, petroleum reserves in General Roca County will be exhausted within 20 years and those within Confluencia County may be exhausted sooner. Cutral Co-Plaza Huincul may survive as an urban centre as long as oil and gas are exploited in the wider region since it contains the regional headquarters of Yacimientos Petroliferos Fiscales (YPF), the government company in charge of oil exploitation and the homes of many workers and technicians involved in oil and gas exploitation. But the possibilities of a stronger and more diversified economic base developing are being eroded by the trend for many activities linked to oil exploitation to move to Neuquen urban centre. Catriel is even more vulnerable, although the fact that YPF decentralised some of its administrative offices to Catriel in 1974, rather than organising most activities there from Cutral Co-Plaza Huincul, helped foster some economic and population growth. Since Catriel is in a river valley, perhaps there is some possibility of developing agriculture there.

The 1963 census revealed that in Cutral Co-Plaza Huincul, there were 26 manufacturing plants employing a total of more than 200 people, the most important being the petroleum refinery with 115 employees. Apart from this refinery, the others were small scale (none employed more than 10 persons) and were mostly craft and small-scale activities to meet local demand. For an urban centre with over 16,000 people on that date, this is hardly a strong manufacturing base. In Catriel, on this same date there were only 9 manufacturing plants employing a total of 34 people. This low level is not surprising given that oil exploitation at Catriel was at a very low level at that time.

As Catriel's population expanded in the Sixties and Seventies to a total of 13,250 by 1980, more establishments appeared, especially for trade and services. Very little manufacturing developed. In Cutral Co-Plaza Huincul, by the early Seventies there were around 120 manufacturing plants covering a wide range of activities. None had

more than 10 persons except for a few directly linked to oil production. Catriel's economic growth was inhibited by a housing shortage there and the fact that many of those who worked in the oilfields
close by did not live there. For instance, in 1976, out of the 800
persons employed by YPF in or close to Catriel, more than 400 still
commuted by air from their homes in Neuquen or Plaza Huincul.
This suggests that most of their consumer expenditures were made
outside Catriel, although their income derived from activities based
there.

Only a few other settlements with a significant concentration of
population developed in the Upper Valley's Periphery. The most
important was Villa El Chocon which arose in the late Sixties as the
home of the workforce associated with the construction of a large
dam. Total population probably surpassed 5,000 during the early
Seventies but once the dam was built, its population fell to more
modest levels (1,100 in 1980) as it only retained the workforce associated with running the dam and the trade and service establishments
their demand would support. This cycle of very rapid population
growth in response to a short-lived economic activity and then decline
is likely to happen in other places as several large and important
infrastructure works are being constructed or are planned in the
Comahue. For the period that their construction activities peak,
clearly their workforce's demand for goods and services influences
the area. Since several settlements of this type have arisen and fallen
in the last 15-20 years, and others are likely to arise in the future,
their combined impact over time makes up an almost permanent
contribution to the area's economic growth.[27]

Development of the urban system in the Upper Valley during the Agro-Industrial Cycle, 1957–1980

Population growth in the Upper Valley and Comahue

Population growth in the Upper Valley for the period 1950-1980 was
much more rapid than that for the rest of the Comahue region and
for Argentina as a whole. While population growth rates in the Upper
Valley in the decades between 1950 and 1980 did not sustain figures
comparable to some earlier decades,[28] annual average growth rates
of between 4.2 per cent and 4.8 per cent nonetheless indicate rapid
sustained population growth.

In the rest of the Comahue region, population growth rate for the
Fifties was well below the rate of natural increase. There was a
considerable loss in population through net out-migration. During
the Sixties, annual average growth at 2.3 per cent was close to the

rate of natural increase while during the Seventies, at 3.7 per cent, it was well above, indicating net in-migration. The enormous gap between population growth rates in the Upper Valley compared to those in the rest of the Comahue region, apparent for many decades, narrowed in the Seventies.

Rapid population growth in the Upper Valley during the Fifties coincides with the peak of the fruit cycle and much of its transition to the agro-industrial cycle, and also to the time when the national territories of Neuquen and Rio Negro became provinces. In contrast, during this decade, the economy of the rest of the Comahue hardly grew at all. The rapid growth in oil production in the Upper Valley's periphery only began during the late Fifties. Thus, it is not surprising to find that during this decade, annual average growth rates for all today's urban centres in the Upper Valley ranged from 5.7 to 12.6 per cent. During the Fifties, Upper Valley urban centres were increasingly linked by paved roads. With this increasing inter-connection between the major population concentrations there, it became feasible for many enterprises to set up in the Upper Valley serving more than just the local population. It was during the Fifties that the urban system within the Upper Valley acquired services which previously had only been available from enterprises in Bahia Blanca or Buenos Aires.

During the Sixties, there was some slackening in the rate of population growth in the Upper Valley and a considerable increase in that for the rest of the Comahue, although the Upper Valley's population still grew a lot more rapidly than that in the rest of the Comahue. As will be discussed in more detail later, during the Sixties a consolidation of the urban system became evident in the Upper Valley. The change in population growth rates in the rest of the Comahue were largely due to three developments there: the growth in oil exploitation in the Upper Valley's periphery, the development of tourism in the lakes and mountains sub-region to the south-west of the Upper Valley, and substantial public investment in and around Viedma, the capital of Rio Negro Province. However, for much of the Comahue including the northern and central Andean sub-regions in Neuquen Province and the southern plateaus in Rio Negro Province, the economy stagnated and population growth was well below the regional average.

During the Seventies, annual average growth rates for population in the Upper Valley were a little above that for the Sixties, while for the rest of the Comahue, there was again a noticeable increase. But once again, economic developments and above average demographic growth in the Comahue outside the Upper Valley was restricted to a few small areas. The construction of large hydro-works on the Limay and Neuquen Rivers, the rapid population growth in Sierra Grande, close to the Atlantic coast as the infrastructure was constructed to allow the exploitation of iron ore deposits (the population has since declined to the level needed only to extract the iron ore), and rapid growth in San Carlos de Bariloche and San Martin de los Andes as tourist centres are three examples. For much of the Comahue, the economy remained stagnant.

Population distribution within the Upper Valley

Table 2.10 gives figures for population growth between 1950-1980 for the most important municipalities in the Upper Valley and totals for those in the counties of Confluencia and of General Roca and for the Upper Valley as a whole. In terms of population distribution among the 15 municipalities, the growing role of the three municipalities in Confluencia County is particularly noticeable; they included little more than a quarter of the Upper Valley's population in 1950 while by 1980 the proportion had risen to close to two-fifths. While the population in the municipalities in General Roca County grew by some 36 per cent during the Seventies, the population in the municipalities in Confluencia county grew by more than 98 per cent.

This relatively sudden increase in Upper Valley population concentration in the part which is in Confluencia County (and especially that in Neuquen Municipality) is particularly interesting in that relative population-size among municipalities (and their major urban centres) had not changed much between 1920 and 1960 despite rapid changes in the Upper Valley including very rapid total population growth, different waves of colonisation, rapid expansion of area under irrigation, development of an economy based on fruit-growing and the development of agro-industries. Since 1960, the distribution of population within the Upper Valley has undergone a significant change with Neuquen Municipality increasing its share of Upper Valley population from less than 20 per cent to more than 30 per cent. The proportion living in each of the more populated municipalities in General Roca County fell, as shown in Table 2.10, with the exception of Cipolletti whose share in Upper Valley population remained constant.

To look more closely at this change in the population distribution, the population will be divided into two categories: 'agglomerated' (those living in nucleated settlements with 50 or more inhabitants) and 'dispersed' (which for the Upper Valley is everyone but agglomerated population). The figures in Table 2.10 show that it is not changes in the numbers of dispersed population that contribute to Neuquen municipality's increasing share in the Upper Valley's total population. Indeed, Neuquen municipality had less than 2,000 people living as 'dispersed population' in 1980; substantially less than General Roca, Cipolletti, Villa Regina and Allen which had between 4,000

Table 2.10 *Upper Valley: Population in municipalities and proportion in agglomerations 1950–1980 for General Roca and Confluencia Counties*

Municipalities	Total Population				Annual Average Growth Rates			Percentage Agglomerated			
	1950	1960	1970	1980	1950–1960	1960–1970	1970–1980	1950	1960	1970	1980
General Roca	16,400	25,050	37,400	52,650	4.3	4.1	3.5	61	75	83	88
Cipolletti	12,150	20,350	31,050	48,300	5.3	4.3	4.5	46	69	79	87
Villa Regina	5,300	11,200	17,550	23,150	7.8	4.6	2.8	58	75	78	83
Allen	8,650	11,400	14,800	19,650	2.8	2.6	2.8	42	57	63	72
Cinco Saltos	4,600	10,200	13,500	17,150	8.3	2.8	2.4	52	77	82	88
Ingeniero Luis A. Huergo	3,100	3,400	3,950	5,100	1.0	1.4	2.7	47	54	58	68
Seven other municipalities	9,500	14,150	18,250	22,700	4.1	2.6	2.2	17	25	32	42
Total for General Roca County	59,700	95,400	136,150	188,350	4.8	3.6	3.3	47	65	72	79
Neuquen	16,000	25,150	45,400	92,050	4.6	6.1	7.3	80	89	95	98
Centenario	4,100	6,550	9,250	14,900	4.7	3.5	4.9	36	44	61	78
Plottier	1,350	2,050	4,900	9,750	4.0	9.1	7.1	8	45	53	82
Total for Confluencia County	21,450	33,750	59,550	116,700	4.6	5.8	7.0	67	78	86	94
Total for Upper Valley	81,150	129,150	195,600	304,950	4.8	4.2	4.5	53	68	77	85

Source: Derived from National Population Censuses 1947, 1960, 1970 and 1980.

and 7,000. While 47 per cent of the Upper Valley's population had been in this 'dispersed' category in 1950, in 1980, it had fallen to 15 per cent.

When looking at the 16 municipalities, there is no relation between total population and dispersed population. Available data suggests a relation between the quantity of arable land within a municipality and the dispersed population. General Roca, Cipolletti, Villa Regina, Allen and Centenario have the largest areas of cultivated land and in 1980 had the largest numbers of dispersed population. Neuquen, Cinco Saltos and Plottier have much smaller numbers of dispersed population. When looking at trends in the numbers of dispersed population over time within each municipality, it seems that the number grows to reach a certain saturation point, then it stabilises and perhaps later declines a little. This saturation point coincides with the full sub-division and intensive cultivation of arable land there. Table 2.10 suggests that by 1950, General Roca, Cipolletti, Allen and Cinco Saltos had reached this saturation point. In Villa Regina and other less populous municipalities not shown on Table 2.10, dispersed population grew considerably during the Fifties and, although slower, also in the Sixties. In all these, dispersed population grew as the area under cultivation expanded or as already cultivated lands were subdivided.

Neuquen Municipality is again unusual in that it was the only municipality where the number of dispersed population decreased rapidly between 1950 and 1980, even though between 1960 and 1980 its total population growth was particularly rapid. This is attributable to the decrease in cultivated area as agricultural land was being converted to urban uses. The 'dispersed population' category seems to approximate to 'population deriving a living from agricultural activities', although there are farmers and agricultural workers who live in 'agglomerations' and a number of people working in 'agglomerations' but living outside them. Thus, Neuquen Municipality's increasing share in Upper Valley population is not due to a growth in agricultural area. Nor is it likely to be due to a growing agricultural population. Indeed, it has probably experienced higher declines in both of these since 1950 than most or all other municipalities.

Population growth trends in agglomerations, in urban centres and in individual urban centres are very different from those for 'dispersed' population between 1950 and 1980. While dispersed population grew very little between 1950 and 1980, total population grew almost four-fold, while agglomerated population grew more than six-fold and urban population grew more than eight-fold. It is interesting to note that the growth in agglomerated population was particularly rapid in the three municipalities in Confluencia County: Neuquen, Centenario and Plottier. In 1950, these municipalities had contained only

31.5 per cent of the Upper Valley's agglomerated population; by 1980 they contained 42.4 per cent.

Table 2.11 shows the rapidly increasing proportion of Upper Valley population living in urban centres with rapid urbanisation evident for each of the three decades. All urban centres also sustained annual average growth rates for each of these decades of 3.1 per cent or more while all achieved much higher rates for one or more of these decades. By 1980, nearly 93 per cent of the Upper Valley's agglomerated population lived in the eight urban centres.

The growth rates of Neuquen urban centre are particularly noticeable for two reasons. The first is that it was the only urban centre among the five largest where population growth rates increased rather than decreased, decade by decade between 1950 and 1980. Secondly, its population more than doubled in one decade (between 1970 and 1980). While there are many instances of this happening for relatively small urban centres, especially when some natural resource begins to be exploited nearby (as in Catriel in the Sixties), it is far less common to see such rapid population growth in larger and more consolidated urban centres and is unprecedented in the history of Argentina. Neuquen urban centre came to contain more than 30 per cent of the entire Upper Valley's population by 1980, compared to less than 20 per cent in 1950. The three urban centres in Confluencia County, Neuquen, Centenario and Plottier had the three highest annual average population growth rates of any urban centre in the Upper Valley during the Sixties and the Seventies.

However, despite the fact that the portion of the Upper Valley in Confluencia County considerably increased its share of the Upper Valley's agglomerated and urban population, there were no major changes in the urban centres' rank, if defined by population size. Neuquen began and ended the period as the most populous urban centre. Neither of the other two urban centres in Confluencia County had populations which grew sufficiently to displace one of the five urban centres in General Roca County as the next five largest Upper Valley urban centres. The most noticeable change was not in rank size but in relative size between the largest and the rest. From 1910 until well into the Sixties, Neuquen, General Roca and Cipolletti had had populations of comparable size; this was no longer the case in 1980 when Neuquen had more than twice the population of either of the other two.

In comparing the contribution of net in-migration to natural increase for the agglomerations in Confluencia and General Roca Counties, a major change in trends became evident during the Seventies. Although reliable figures are not available for natural population growth rates for the Fifties and Sixties, annual average population growth rates well above, say 3 per cent clearly suggest net in-migration as a major contributor. An annual average popu-

Table 2.11 *Population of Upper Valley settlements whose population exceeded 2,000 by 1980 and annual average population growth rates, 1950–1980*

Agglomeration	Population				Annual Average Population Growth (%)		
	1950	1960	1970	1980	1950–60	1960–70	1970–80
Total population	81,150 (100.0)	129,150 (100.0)	195,600 (100.0)	304,950 (100.0)			
Neuquen	12,850	22,500	43,000	90,800	5.8	6.7	7.8
General Roca	9,800	18,250	29,350	44,050	6.4	4.9	4.1
Cipolletti	5,650	13,700	24,150	40,750	9.3	5.8	5.4
Villa Regina	3,050	8,250	13,300	18,550	10.5	4.9	3.4
Cinco Saltos	2,400	7,900	11,100	15,100	12.6	3.5	3.1
Allen	3,650	6,500	9,350	14,050	6.0	3.7	4.1
Centenario	1,350	2,350	4,900	9,600	5.7	7.7	7.0
Plottier	100	900	2,600	7,300	c	11.0	9.0
Ingeniero Luis A. Huergo[a]	1,450	1,850	2,300	3,450	2.4	2.2	4.1
Population in urban centres[b]	28,300	77,100	130,250	240,200			
Percentage in urban centres	34.9	59.7	66.6	78.8			

Notes: a—Not included in the category of urban centre.
b—Defined as population in settlements of 5,000 or more inhabitants.
c—Since this decade coincides with Plottier's emergence as a significant population concentration, any figure for population growth rate would appear misleading in relation to the others.

Source: Derived from data drawn from national population censuses of 1947, 1960, 1970 and 1980.

lation growth rate for the Fifties of 5.7 per cent, or more as shown in Table 2.11, was sustained by all the Upper Valley's current urban centres while four sustained figures of 9 per cent or more. Unless part of the increase in population is due to changes in boundaries between 1950 and 1960, and there is no evidence of this, net in-migration was clearly the main contributor to population growth in what are now the Upper Valley's urban centres. It was also obviously the major factor for some during the Sixties and Seventies and an important factor for most. Taking all agglomerations in that portion of the Upper Valley in General Roca County, one can estimate that there was net in-migration of around 20,000 persons per decade for the Fifties, Sixties and Seventies. For agglomerations in the portion of the Upper Valley in Confluencia County, net in-migration was around 10,000 during the Fifties, less than 7,000 in the Sixties and more than 30,000 during the Seventies. And the urban centre within General Roca County where net in-migration contributed most to total population growth was Cipolletti.

Links between demographic change and social, economic and political developments in the Upper Valley, 1950-1980

Although a lack of data on the distribution of manufacturing, trade and commerce employment among the different municipalities for the years other than 1963 makes an accurate analysis of trends over time impossible, it seems that the economic and political dynamics underlying rapid urban growth in Confluencia County (with the urban centres of Neuquen, Centenario and Plottier) are very different in this period to those underlying the less rapid urban growth in General Roca County (with the urban centres of General Roca, Cipolletti, Villa Regina, Cinco Saltos and Allen).

The figures in Table 2.9 for the distribution of non-agricultural economic activities within the Upper Valley show their concentration in General Roca County. If the urban centres in this County are ranked according to population size in 1960 and in 1970, this corresponds to the quantity of productive activities located within them. For instance, the urban centre General Roca, the largest in the county for the whole period 1950-1980, had much the largest commerce and trade sector in 1963, the second largest concentration of cold storage plants in 1971 and the second largest workforce employed in manufacturing and manufacturing production value in 1963. In the 1974 census, it had the highest number of large industries[29] in the Upper Valley, including by far the largest, Aserradero del Valle (sawmills), with more than 1,000 employees. The irrigation district of General Roca is likely to have had the highest total production value of any irrigation district within the Upper Valley for the whole period.[30] Similarly, Cipolletti, the second largest urban centre in General Roca

County for the whole period, had the second largest commerce and trade sector and the largest number of people employed in manufacturing in 1963.

In 1974, it had the second highest number of large industries in the Upper Valley (4 out of 19). It also had the largest number of cold storage plants in 1971. Total production value in the irrigation district of Cipolletti was also among the highest of any irrigation district for the whole period 1950-1980. Villa Regina, the third largest urban centre in General Roca County, had the third largest commerce and trade sector and manufacturing labour force in 1963 and the fourth largest number of cold storage plants in 1971. The irrigation district of Villa Regina also had the largest cultivated area. But land in this irrigation district began to be intensively cultivated much later than in the districts of General Roca and Cipolletti.

Thus, total production value from Villa Regina district is likely to have been substantially lower than that of these other two irrigation districts, at least until relatively recently.

Similarly, the ranks of Cinco Saltos and Allen as fourth and fifth largest urban centres in General Roca County broadly correspond to their share in the county's manufacturing, trade and commerce in 1963 and share of cold storage plants in 1971. Cinco Saltos had the highest manufacturing production value of any municipality in the county in 1963, but this was due to the very high production value per employee produced by one chemical factory and it shared fourth place with Allen in terms of size of workforce employed in manufacturing. The irrigation district of Cinco Saltos also had by far the smallest cultivated area, but probably had the highest production value per hectare of any municipality. It had more cultivated area devoted to apples and pears in 1958 than both General Roca and Ingeniero Luis A. Huergo, despite the fact that it had a much smaller cultivated area.

It is interesting to consider why no urban centre of 5,000 or more inhabitants had emerged in the irrigation district of Ingeniero Luis A. Huergo by 1980. But this was the irrigation district which was the last to bring all its cultivable land under cultivation and the last to turn this land to crops such as apples and pears which give the highest returns per hectare. In effect, it remained within an Alfalfa Cycle while other districts had developed through the Fruit Cycle to the Agro-Industrial Cycle. In both 1958 and 1978, it had the lowest proportion of cultivated land devoted to apples and pears and the highest devoted to alfalfa for fodder. It also had the lowest yields per hectare for apples and pears in 1978. A combination of late development, relatively low total agricultural production (despite the third largest cultivated area) and proximity to General Roca urban centre, the largest centre for commerce and trade, help explain why the town of Ingeniero Luis A. Huergo had not exceeded 5,000 inhabitants by 1980 and its very low population growth rate during the Fifties and Sixties. The more rapid population growth rate during the Seventies reflects the change in the cultivated lands around it to more intensive production.

Thus, in General Roca County, the key factors underpinning population growth in urban centres seem to be first, location in irrigation districts which first developed intensive cultivation and second, location in irrigation districts with the highest total production value. The urban centres, ranked by population size, correspond to the distribution among them of productive activities located there (a high proportion of which are linked to agricultural production) and to the demand for goods and services generated by those who make a living, directly or indirectly, from agricultural production, packing, processing and marketing.

It also seems that the peak in urban centres' population growth rates broadly corresponds to the decades when the switch is being made in the agricultural lands around them to intensive agricultural production. The urban centres in General Roca County grew because enterprises located there to provide goods and services for the agricultural population around them and for agricultural activities. Their location on the railway and central location on roads ensured they also emerged as centres for storing, processing and transporting agricultural produce. And the largest urban centres also developed as they came to contain higher order goods and services which met demand for an area larger than their local agricultural population. The urban centres which developed first were those which came to contain most of these higher order goods and services since these tended to be the urban centres closest to the demand for such higher order activities, when this demand first developed to the point when it could support new activities located there.

In Confluencia County, this link between agricultural and urban development is far less obvious. The largest urban centre in the Upper Valley, Neuquen, is not in an irrigation district with among the highest total agricultural production value. Indeed, in 1978, the cultivated area in Neuquen irrigation district was the lowest of all eight irrigation districts in the Upper Valley and yields per hectare were among the lowest. In that same year, Colonia Centenario irrigation district had the second smallest, although yields per hectare were among the highest.

Neuquen Municipality had far fewer cold storage plants in 1971 than Cipolletti, General Roca, Cinco Saltos, Villa Regina, Allen and Centenario. And, as noted earlier, urban centres in Confluencia County had only a small proportion of the Upper Valley's manufacturing industries linked to agricultural production in 1963. While in the Fifties it was urban centres in General Roca County which had the most rapid population growth,[31] in the Sixties and Seventies it was Neuquen and Plottier in Confluencia County. Clearly, the forces underlying population growth in the three urban centres in Confluencia County, Neuquen, Centenario and Plottier, are not comparable to those underlying population growth in urban centres in General Roca County.

The reason for particularly rapid population growth during the Seventies in Neuquen urban centre, in the other urban centres within the Upper Valley in Confluencia County and in Cipolletti seems to be the growing dominance of the urban centre of Neuquen as the main employment concentration within the Upper Valley. And, as noted earlier, this is not employment related to the Upper Valley's main products—agricultural crops or goods or services linked to their production. The municipalities closest to the urban centre of Neuquen seem to be developing as residential and industrial suburbs, even if the built-up area of each is still separate. Studies of commuting patterns found that 17.5 per cent of the population in the municipalities of Plottier and Centenario in 1979 worked in Neuquen Municipality. In 1982, 12 per cent of Cipolletti's labour force worked in Neuquen while the proportion for more distant urban centres within General Roca County such as Cinco Saltos (5 per cent), Allen (3 per cent) and General Roca (1 per cent) were much lower. This suggests a gradient in which the proportion of the labour force living in municipalities other than Neuquen increases with 'accessibility' to Neuquen. This helps explain the rapid population growth evident during the Seventies in Plottier, Centenario and Cipolletti, relative to other Upper Valley urban centres. Thus, the question which has to be addressed is why Neuquen urban centre became the main employment centre and rapidly increased its role as such a centre during the Seventies. As data presented already shows, the role of industries associated with the Upper Valley's main products for sale outside the region (apples and pears) has been minimal in Neuquen urban centre compared to other urban centres. The role of demand coming from the agricultural population around Neuquen in stimulating its economic development is also minimal, compared to other Upper Valley urban centres.

The reason why Neuquen came to dominate the Upper Valley's urban system seems to derive from its role as the urban centre with the highest administrative rank, since it is the capital of a province. Successive provincial governments in both Neuquen and Rio Negro (with the capital at Viedma, 500 km from the Upper Valley) have tended to concentrate public and promote private investment in their provincial capitals. Not only have the number of offices associated with provincial government multiplied much more rapidly in Neuquen than in, say, Cipolletti and General Roca, but so too have national government offices which have jurisdiction over the whole of the Upper Valley and beyond. It is almost a bureaucratic convention in

Argentina to concentrate such national offices in provincial capitals. Even public offices and enterprises which first set up in Cipolletti or General Roca began to move their headquarters to Neuquen. For instance, the management office of the public telephone company, originally set up in 1913 in General Roca, moved to Neuquen in 1978. Similarly, many of the offices and enterprises associated with oil and gas production within the wider region—including such production in the Upper Valley's periphery—also established offices in Neuquen. Workshops associated with the construction of the hydro-electric complex at El Chocon-Cerros Colorados set up in Neuquen. An increasing number of government officers, military personnel, workers and technicians thus became concentrated in Neuquen. Executives of enterprises from Buenos Aires related to such activities who have to visit the Upper Valley arrive by air. And since the Upper Valley's only major airport developed close to Neuquen, it is here that the hotels, restaurants and other service activities associated with airports developed. While the University of the Comahue was set up with various departments spread around the Upper Valley, most are concentrated in Neuquen. No doubt one of the reasons that Centenario, Plottier and Cipolletti have come to house a significant proportion of Neuquen's labour force is due to the rapid rise in land prices as a result of Neuquen's rapid economic development and population growth.

The urban centres in General Roca County are tending to lose their role as centres providing goods or services for an area wider than their surrounding agricultural population. For instance, the private regional bank founded in General Roca in 1920 closed in 1978 and General Roca has lost its role as the main centre for financial services within the Upper Valley. Thus, there are relatively strong empirical grounds for stating that public policies are playing a major role in increasing Neuquen urban centre's dominance within the Upper Valley. This is a major change which has important consequences for future developments within the Upper Valley.

One particularly interesting characteristic of the Upper Valley's development has been, at least up to 1970, no emergence of a single dominant urban centre despite rapid population growth (including rapid net in-migration) and rapid urbanisation over 70 years. Despite the fact that the Upper Valley only covers some 700 square kilometres, various separate urban centres grew and developed as enterprises grew within each to provide the population and the economic activities in their hinterland with goods and services. And as enterprises providing higher order goods and services developed which could only be supported by demand larger than that in any one urban centre's hinterland, these did not concentrate in any one urban centre.

By 1980, the Upper Valley with a population exceeding 300,000 within 700 square kilometres contained a range of higher order goods and services which are commonly associated with a regional metropolitan centre. But the higher order goods and services are not concentrated within one or even two core cities. In effect, the distribution of population and of economic activities does not resemble the classic core plus suburbs pattern. The early development of urban centres to serve a prosperous agricultural population and support intensive agricultural production around them has facilitated this. The multi-nucleated urban system within the Upper Valley thus can be regarded as a regional metropolitan area; certainly, in terms of concentration of population, of higher order goods and services and of contribution to national production, the Upper Valley can be regarded as one of Argentina's metropolitan areas, even if its urban population is distributed within eight urban centres including three with more than 40,000 inhabitants.

Bahia Blanca's role as the metropolitan centre serving the Upper Valley which had been evident in wholesale trade, secondary and later higher education, newspaper publishing and distribution and specialist medical services has increasingly been displaced by enterprises within the Upper Valley. These enterprises providing higher order goods and services are not concentrated in Neuquen, the largest urban centre. For instance, the Upper Valley's only daily newspaper—and incidentally one whch is read throughout the Comahue—is published in General Roca. The Upper Valley's only purpose-built (and best organised) library is in Cipolletti. Until its recent closure, the only independent cinema showing a wide range of films was in Centenario. The private X-ray clinic in Cipolletti is one of the best equipped in Argentina. Until relatively recently, General Roca, not Neuquen, was the urban centre with the widest range of shops. This dispersion of functions serving the whole Upper Valley's population between different urban centres gives the Upper Valley the character of a 'dispersed city' (Burton, 1963). There are only nine zones in all of Argentina having a higher population than the Upper Valley in less than 700 square km and all are either within single agglomerations such as Greater Buenos Aires or in 'twin cities' such as Resistencia and Corrientes.

But this pattern by which various urban centres contain enterprises or facilities serving a wider population than that in their immediate hinterland is changing with this change especially evident since 1970. And the main factor underpinning this change has been the concentration of public investment and public offices within Neuquen urban centre. Thus, it is possible for the national government and the provincial governments of Neuquen and Rio Negro to consider whether the present and planned distribution of public offices and enterprises and of public investments in infrastructure and services are making best use of the poly-nucleated urban system which emerged in the Upper Valley and which present public policies and investments are helping to change. There are, at present, diseconomies which result from very rapid population growth of Neuquen's urban centre—including its rapid physical growth over valuable irrigated farmland, traffic congestion due to the increasing concentration of higher order goods and services there and of inter-regional traffic passing through it, the rapid rise in house prices as a result of rapid rises in land prices, uncontrolled urban sprawl producing a pattern and density of development, for which it is unnecessarily expensive to provide infrastructure and a rising backlog in the number of dwellings requiring water and sewers.

Clearly, some of these should be addressed by measures relating only to that urban centre—such as an urban land policy which discourages the present under-utilisation of land or indeed land being left vacant, within the built-up area. Although the subject would require more detailed study than that undertaken in research to date, an efficient and appropriate public transport system and a consideration as to different distributions of public offices and services among the Upper Valley's urban centres might lessen the diseconomies mentioned above without necessarily damaging the Upper Valley's economic base or the population's access to such offices and services. It could also help strengthen and diversify the economies of some of the urban centres in General Roca County, since these have become more dependent on the performance of the Upper Valley's agriculture than before, as Neuquen has attracted much of the productive investment and public sector jobs in recent years.

The economies of the urban centres in General Roca County are particularly vulnerable since, in 1979, various factors caused a crisis in the sale and/or export of Upper Valley products. An efficient public transport system would improve the accessibility of the various urban centres (and smaller settlements) to the Upper Valley population living in other municipalities and could strengthen the existing pattern whereby various higher order goods and services supported by demand from the whole Upper Valley are located not just in one urban centre but distributed among several of them.

The present system of inter-urban and indeed intra-urban public transport is very poor. As in the period up to 1950, those who do not own cars have a much more restricted access to employment, retail stores and services. The railway track linking all the urban centres already exists, although its potential to serve as a regular, cheap and efficient mode of inter-urban transport and the effects such a service would have on population distribution within the urban system have not been considered.

Finally, there is the issue of the whole Upper Valley's future development within Argentina. The Upper Valley has been facing a crisis since around 1978 when prices for its fruit exports began to fall. Part of the crisis was certainly linked to the policy of the then Military government to keep the Argentine peso's value high against foreign currencies. This reduced returns to the Upper Valley farmers and affected all those whose living was directly or indirectly derived from or linked to agricultural production for export. During the second half of the Seventies, beginning with the *coup d'etat* in 1976, credit was much more expensive so farmers could not resort to credit to help them over one or two poor years. The interest of the (then) government in helping Upper Valley farmers to overcome their problems is best illustrated by the suggestion of one senior government official that they should plant wheat. Wheat could only provide farmers with less than one twentieth of the return per hectare of fruit and would also imply that farmers would have to write off the high, long-term investment in growing and protecting fruit trees and find the money to clear their orchards.

Other factors external to the Upper Valley also had serious consequences. Some relate to the export market. Demand for Argentinian fruit from Europe and Brazil was declining. Fruit production was rising in Brazil and in the European Economic Community and quotas imposed by the EEC were beginning to restrict Argentinian produce's access. In addition, increasing apple production in Chile was competing with Argentina for foreign markets. Others are linked to a weaker internal market; Upper Valley producers had long sold a substantial proportion of their produce to the internal market athough the relative weight of the Argentine market compared to export varied considerably; during the Seventies, the domestic market accounted for around 40 per cent of sales. But with the economic crisis within Argentina, demand for Upper Valley products was not sustained.

Although the research to date has not studied in detail the impacts and influences of public sector policies, private actions and international influences on developments within the Upper Valley, these are factors of considerable importance in understanding possibilities of just arriving at a more diversified economic base than one or two crops. The research planned on this is described on page xii.

Sources

This chapter is based on research undertaken by Dr Cesar Vapnarsky and Dr Mabel Manzanal in the Centro de Estudios Urbanos y Regionales in Buenos Aires, Argentina. To date, the research has resulted in two books: Vapnarsky, Cesar, (1983), *Pueblos del Norte de la Patagonia 1779-1957,* Editorial de la Patagonia, Fuerte General Roca, and Manzanal, Mabel (1983), *Agro, Industria y Ciudad en la Patagonia Norte,* Ediciones CEUR. These are available from CEUR, Piso 7, Cuerpo A, Avenida Corrientes 2835, (1193) Buenos Aires, Argentina.

The two references made in the text of this chapter to other works were: Burton, Ian (1963), 'A Restatement of the dispersed city hypothesis', *Annals of the Association of American Geographers*, Volume 5, No 3, September, pp 285-289. Ortiz, Ricardo M. (1946), *El Ferrocarril en la Economia Argentina*, Editorial Problemas, Buenos Aires.

Notes

1 The north-west corner of the Comahue region is the only important exception to this.

2 In Patagonian rivers, the valley's floor typically rises in a gentle slope perpendicular to the river, until the area of fertile soil ends abruptly at the border of a plateau where a wall (known as a 'barda') forms. In most instances, the barda runs close to the river on one side and leaves the whole valley bottom on the other. The lower valley of the Limay River and the upper valley of the Negro River are on the north-eastern and northern banks respectively. The lower valley of the Neuquen River is an exception and the fertile land extends on both sides of the river.

3 Two municipalities have emerged outside these countries' boundaries but they have been excluded from this analysis. See footnote to Table 2.1, p. 31.

4 General Julio A. Roca was later elected President of Argentina for two periods: between 1880 and 1886, and between 1898 and 1904.

5 Up to 1903, much of the land in the conquered territories had been purchased by absentee owners as speculative investments. Between 1886 and 1903, a few individuals had acquired large land holdings in the Upper Valley, outside Colonia General Roca.

6 The railway between Buenos Aires and Bahia Blanca had already been built as part of the network to serve the Southern Pampa.

7 These figures do not include the military population which had included four regiments in 1900.

8 Vicente Blasco Ibanez, a well-known Spanish novelist sought to organise this, bringing peasants from Spain to farm the land. His success as a writer well-known outside Spain dates from the time after he returned to Spain, when this venture collapsed.

9 The town Cipolletti is named after an Italian engineer, Cesar Cipolletti, who had been commissioned by the Argentinian government to study the possibility of using the Negro and Colorado Rivers for navigation and irrigation and for controlling floods. His report was submitted in 1899, but having been summoned by the Government in 1908 to supervise such work, he died and another Italian engineer, Severini, took over.

10 In 1969, only eight per cent of the farms in General Roca County were worked by tenants; by way of comparison, the figure for Buenos Aires Province in this same year was 27 per cent.

11 Although there were no national population censuses between 1914 and 1947, fortunately, censuses were undertaken in national territories in 1912 and 1920.

12 Poplars were planted in great quantity in rows surrounding fruit plantations to protect the fruit trees from the strong western winds.

13 Obviously, it is impossible to assign this transition to one particular year. Economic trends which show the increasing importance of agro-industry to the Upper Valley's economy, in comparison to fruit production, take place over many years with no single year being totally satisfactory as the year of transition. The same is true in assigning a year for the transition from the alfalfa cycle to the fruit-growing cycle, but specific years are assigned to the beginning and end of these cycles to allow a discussion of the links between economic trends and demographic trends.

14 Although by law any town with more than 1,000 inhabitants was able to have an elected municipal government, such governments were not formed in many towns whose population had exceeded that threshold. Cipolletti had 1,000 inhabitants by 1910 but did not have a municipal government until the late Forties when there were well above 4,000 inhabitants in the town and over 10,000 within municipal boundaries (since these included population in the arable lands surrounding the town).

15 There was a lively debate about whether the new capital of the new Province of Rio Negro should be Viedma, General Roca or Choele Chole (which is roughly halfway between Viedma and General Roca).

16 On page xii in the Introduction there is a discussion on how unsatisfactory it is to arbitrarily choose a population threshold for nucleated settlements above which they are 'urban' and below which they are 'rural'. But in the absence of social and economic data about all settlements for different points in time, we have little alternative to population thresholds.

17 There is another useful population category called 'scattered population' which is people living in households so far from one another that they have no daily interaction either with each other or with those living in agglomerations of 50 or more inhabitants. For vast areas in the wider Comahue region, most of the population would fall into this category, although none do in the Upper Valley.

18 An administrative role, not a garrison of troops.

19 The exception was Barda el Medio which housed staff for the dam.

20 This disappeared in 1963 after a weekly journal, *Rio Negro,* became the main daily newspaper and the only one of regional scope in Northern Patagonia.

21 Figures in Table 2.5 for grape production are not representative of trends between 1960 and the late Seventies since low prices in 1968 affected production in 1969. Better prices after 1969 encouraged increased production in the Seventies, so grape production retained its role as the third most valuable Upper Valley crop.

22 This can at best be only a rough guide in that this minimum size depends on factors such as the soil's productive capacity, the efficiency with which the land is cultivated and the technology adopted.

23 Since data only exists on trends in land-holding size and not on individual's or companies' total land holdings, it is not possible to draw unambiguous conclusions about the process of land ownership concentration or on the number of minifundia. Many farmers own more than one land holding. Thus, there may be more landownership concentration

than that implied by the figures for numbers of land holdings. Similarly the number of families with insufficient land to support their needs could be over-stated. There are farmers who own small farms but work them as a part-time activity and have jobs in urban areas, which means that the number of small land holdings is not the same as the number of farming households with inadequate incomes.

24 The only exception was in the production of wood and straw packages where production per person employed at constant prices did not rise between 1963 and 1973. However, a change in the activities included in this category was made in the 1974 national economic census, so an exact comparison between 1963 and 1973 figures is not possible.

25 A substantial proportion of its products are also sold outside the Upper Valley and indeed outside the Comahue region.

26 When turning to Confluencia County in Neuquen Province it is difficult to separate activities relating to the Upper Valley from those relating to the Upper Valley's periphery, since statistics only exist for the whole county. By 1980, 24 per cent of the county's population lived outside its portion of the Upper Valley. Virtually all of these were in Cutral Co-Plaza Huincul. Unlike data from General Roca county, data on manufacturing was not disaggregated into municipalities. However, because economic activities in the portion of Confluencia county outside the Upper Valley (ie in the Upper Valley's periphery) are so distinct from those of the Upper Valley, some disaggregation is possible. Land-extensive sheep and goat rearing, oil and gas extraction and certain activities linked to large infrastructure projects such as large dams and a heavy-water plant are the only significant economic activities taking place in the Upper Valley's periphery.

27 Examples since 1970 include Cerros Colorados and Planicie Banderita (both hydro-electric developments) and Arroyitos (a hydro-electric and heavy-water plant).

28 Annual average population growth rates for the Upper Valley were 7.0 per cent between 1910 and 1930.

29 Those with more than 75 employed persons.

30 Villa Regina irrigation district had a larger cultivated area but less intensive production; although no figures for each irrigation district's total production value are available, it is possible to infer from Table 2.6 that General Roca irrigation district had the highest total production value.

31 Plottier's annual average growth rate during the Fifties is an exception, but only during the Fifties did Plottier emerge as a significant population concentration, growing from 100 inhabitants to 900 inhabitants.

3

The Gezira Region, The Sudan

Omer M. A. El Agraa, Ian Haywood, Salih El Arifi, Babiker A. Abdalla, Mohamed O. El Sammani, Ali Mohamed El Hassan, Hassan Mohamed Salih

Background

The study region is the Gezira Irrigated Scheme and its Managil Extension which encompasses some 8,800 square kilometres. Located on the Gezira Plain, the triangular area between the Blue and White Niles south of Greater Khartoum (the Sudan's capital and largest city), it covers around one-third of the area of Gezira Province, one of the Sudan's 18 provinces.[1] Average altitude is around 400 metres above sea level and the Gezira is very flat with a gentle slope from south to north and from east to west, a fact of great importance to the development of gravity irrigation there. There is little variation in climate across the region; the climate is hot and dry for most of the year although hot and humid during the rainy season (July-October). The alkaline clay soil is suitable for the annual cultivation of crops, if sufficient water is available. Average annual rainfall is 250-500 mm, although rainfall is erratic and cannot be relied on for commercial farming. Thus, only when a steady water supply was guaranteed through an extensive network of irrigation canals with water drawn from the Blue Nile was widespread intensive agriculture made possible. Virtually the entire study region is now under irrigated cultivation.

Developments up to 1955

Historical background before the Gezira Scheme

Before the beginning of the Irrigation Scheme in 1925, most of the region's inhabitants were nomadic or semi-nomadic. To the north,

Map 3.1   *The Gezira region and its location within Gezira Province and the Sudan*

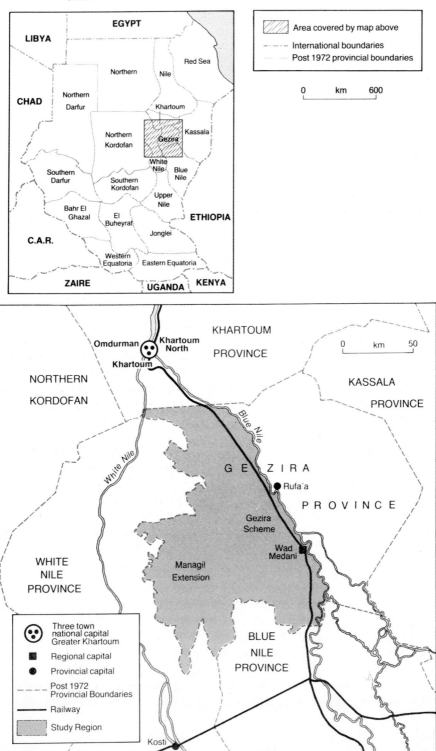

Table 3.1   *Background statistics*

	Area (km²)	*Population (1983)*
The Sudan	2,505,813	n.a.
Gezira Province	25,304	1,997,155
The Study Region	8,800	1,712,584

The Study Region: The Gezira irrigated scheme and the Managil Extension

	1955/6	*1964/5*	*1973*	*1983*
Urban population[a] according to the Sudan's criteria	67,758	109,217	193,338	295,220
Population in small urban centres (5,000–19,999 inhabitants)	6,983	36,607	58,575	109,886
Number of small urban centres	1	5	6	12
Population in intermediate urban centres (20,000 or more inhabitants)	50,171	66,358	107,150	177,155
Number of intermediate urban centres	1	1	1	2

Notes: a—Some of the urban population for 1955/6, 1964/5, 1973 and 1983 included settlements which had less than 5,000 inhabitants. For instance, in the 1973 census, settlements of administrative and/ or commercial importance or with populations of 5,000 or more inhabitants were defined as urban centres. In 1973, there were 7 settlements counted as 'urban' each with less than 5,000 inhabitants and with a total population of 27,610. In 1983, there were two urban centres with less than 5,000 inhabitants and a total population of 8,179.

Source: First Population Census of the Sudan, 1955/56, Population and Housing Surveys, 1964/65, Second Population Census, 1973, Third Population Census, 1983, Preliminary Results.

rainfall was too scarce and irregular to support permanent settlements, except for those located by the Blue or White Niles; a settled agricultural population had developed along the Blue Nile. Crops were grown on islands and river banks after the annual floods receded, with the cultivated area usually extended by irrigation using traditional water wheels. The emergence of settled cultivators along the river led to the development of private land ownership, the land usually being owned by tribal and religious leaders or merchants. Abundant water supplies and the relative ease of transport along the river had supported the development of some permanent market centres. One was El Messellamiya which had its importance further enhanced when it was designated the administrative centre for the northern part of the region in the late nineteenth century. Other permanent settlements developed as commercial or administrative centres such as Wad Medani and Arbaji. Wad Medani was designated the provincial capital by the colonial government and its importance was further enhanced when it became a railway station on the line built to link Khartoum to Sennar, and to Kosti on the White Nile. Tayiba developed as a religious centre. These and other permanent settlements were connected by caravan routes to other Sudanese and foreign towns.

The central plains, well away from perennial rivers, supported seasonal encampments. Those who used them had strong links with settlements along the Nile for trade and for grazing along the river front during the dry season (November to June). Around late June, when there had usually been adequate rainfall to replenish seasonal water sources in the central plains and to moisten the soil for cultivation, families and their herds would move to seasonal encampments or other sites on which crops could be raised. Unlike the private land ownership which developed for settled cultivators, here land ownership remained largely communal; individuals obtained permanent usufructuary rights in cultivable tracts while the rest belonged to the tribe (or a section of it) and was commonly used by all as pasture. The location of seasonal encampments was usually determined by sites which had good drainage conditions and water supplies. Quick maturing dura (sorghum) was grown as the subsistence staple food. Livestock were also important to the subsistence base, especially camels, sheep and goats. Once the crops had been harvested, the population would move back to places with assured water supplies for the dry season. Thus there were few permanent settlements on the central plain, although some existed around wells. In the south, annual average rainfall is higher (it averages over 400 mm per year) but still insufficient for commercial crops. The soil is also difficult to farm with handtools and thus the land was left as pasture for nomads' livestock.

Before the start of the Gezira Scheme, some cotton was grown on the central plains, especially in what later became the Managil Extension. Most of the cotton was produced for local use and spun and woven into a rough cloth. Only a small proportion of the cotton was taken for sale in the permanent market centres. The same was true for surpluses of food crops. According to official records, there was only one urban centre of any size in 1925 when the Gezira Scheme began: Wad Medani with an estimated 30,000 inhabitants.

By the beginning of the twentieth century, the Sudan was essentially ruled by Britain. In 1820/21, Muhammad Ali, Viceroy of Egypt under the Ottoman Turks, sent an army to conquer the Sudan. Khartoum was chosen as the administrative capital and by 1881 Egyptian influence had been extended over most of the territory which now makes up the Sudan. Ismail Pasha who became Viceroy of Egypt in 1863 had sought to extend the area under Egypt's control and to attract

European capital and expertise in developing his empire's economy. Under his rule, one sees the increasing introduction of European Christians in the Sudan to help develop and extend the area under Egyptian rule and to control the slave trade. But in 1879, Ismail Pasha was forced into exile as Egypt was unable to repay its debts and an International Commission was appointed by European powers to oversee Egyptian finances. Then in 1882, Britain occupied Egypt after an army was sent to suppress a nationalist uprising.

In the Sudan an uprising developed between 1880 and 1885 led by the Mahdi and his followers who sought to reassert the Muslim faith. The uprising also drew support from the powerful vested interests in the slave trade and from those who opposed a foreign government and its taxation. By 1885, the Mahdists had gained control over a considerable area of the Sudan and after the Mahdi died in 1885, his successor brought most of the Sudan into a single nation.

The Sudan was invaded, once again, by an Anglo-Egyptian army in 1897-8. The French who had opposed Britain's occupation of Egypt had sent an expedition to construct a dam on the White Nile well to the south of the study region. If they had succeeded in restricting water flow, this would have had serious consequences on Egyptian agriculture.[2] The Anglo-Egyptian army consolidated its control of the Sudan and under an agreement signed in 1899, the Sudan became an Anglo-Egyptian Condominium with sovereignty shared between the two nations. But in reality, the British dominated the Condominium from its inception.

With no obvious sources of exploitable minerals, the Condominium government was interested in the possibility of encouraging cash crops for export. Existing exports were very limited in quantity and diversity; subsistence production was the rule for the vast majority of the population. And irrigation was needed, but it had to be developed without adversely affecting Egyptian agriculture's water needs. In Egypt, increasing the area of perennial irrigation needed for cotton or other cash crops was seriously constrained by the Nile's flow, outside its flood season. So any measure to utilise the waters of the Nile and its tributaries in the Sudan had first to be sanctioned in Cairo.[3]

The Development of cotton production

Investigations in the Sudan showed that the Gezira Plain was well suited to irrigated agriculture. Water could be drawn from the Blue Nile to irrigate the plain since the plain's flatness and its gentle slope permitted water distribution through gravity. Sparse vegetation meant no heavy costs in land clearance. And by the early twentieth century, the need for new sources of cotton for British mills was recognised and demand for the longer and finer cotton was rising.[4] Increasing foreign competition was forcing British mills to produce finer cloths which demanded the use of long staple cotton for whose cultivation the Gezira seemed well-suited.

The results obtained by a private syndicate, the Sudanese Experimental Plantations Syndicate in growing cotton at Zeidab (on the Atbara river 290 km north-west of Khartoum) appeared promising after a few years' operation. Meanwhile, between 1900 and 1910, the extension of the railway linked Khartoum and then Wad Medani and Sennar to the new port on the Red Sea, Port Sudan. This made possible the transport of cash crops such as cotton to ports for export.

A test pumping station was opened by the Government at Tayiba in 1911 (see Map 3.2) on land rented from local landowners, and after a good crop in the first year, extended to 2000 feddans[5] (840 hectares) in the second year. The Sudan Plantations Syndicate[6] had been invited to manage it, on a fee basis, and apply its experience drawn from the Zeidab Scheme. At Zeidab, the Syndicate levied fixed charges per hectare for land and water. This and the early experience with a similar system at Tayiba did not produce sufficient return for the Syndicate. So the basic structure of a partnership between Government, the Syndicate and tenants was worked out for the planned irrigation developments. This arrangement then provided the basis for the development of the Gezira Scheme.

The government was to rent or purchase the land to be irrigated from the native owners (a fixed price was set for both renting and buying) and be responsible for bringing water to the land through the construction and maintenance of the main works and canals. With a loan guaranteed by the British government, the Sudanese government was to construct a dam at Sennar and the major canals. Successive land laws and ordinances were issued by the government during the first three decades of the twentieth century to gain control over the land. Ownership rights to land had to be registered before the scheme commenced, but the government then either purchased the land or paid a nominal rent for it. Although land ownership was not nationalised, in effect the state became the only landlord. If landowners did not sell their land to the government, they had to rent it. The main compensation for existing landowners was not the rent they received but the rights to a tenancy within the scheme. The size of tenancies was initially fixed at 30 feddans (12.6 hectares). Landowners were allowed to take up tenancies but only for an area which they themselves could cultivate. Large landowners were allowed to allocate up to four tenancies to other family members; the aim being to prevent the development of large absentee landlords.

The Syndicate was to act as a Government agent in allocating holdings to tenancies and in directing and supervising their cultivation. Profits from cotton produced on each holding were to be divided between the government (35 per cent), the Syndicate (25 per cent) and the tenant (40 per cent).[7] This was known as the Joint Account System and remained in force, with only minor modifications, until 1980. In 1914, the Syndicate built another pilot pumping station at Barakat, some 20 km south of Tayiba. The First World War (1914-18) delayed the construction of the dam at Sennar until 1925. This delay allowed the government to make arrangements to rent or purchase all the land within the area to be irrigated. Before the completion of the dam and the beginning of the Gezira Scheme proper in 1925, 19,500 feddans (8,190 hectares) were brought under irrigated cultivation from new pumps at Hag Abdulla in 1921-2 with a further 30,000 (12,600 hectares) in 1923-4 with a new pumping station at Wad el Nau. An agreement in 1919 stipulated that the Syndicate should retain the concession to manage the Scheme for 10 years after at least 50,000 feddans (21,000 hectares) were under irrigation, with the right of renewal for a further four years if the Syndicate's performance was judged to be satisfactory. The agreement also stated that the Syndicate would be responsible for making loans to the tenants to pay for needed inputs, implements and other costs.

Map 3.2 shows how irrigated area expanded from 300,000 feddans (126,000 hectares) in 1926 to 682,000 (286,440 hectares) in 1931. The Nile Waters Agreement with Egypt in 1929 allowed the withdrawal of sufficient water from the Blue Nile to irrigate a gross area of 1,000,000 feddans (420,000 hectares) in the Gezira. Tenants were allocated three 10 feddan (4.2 hectare) plots: one for cotton; one split between lubia (a leguminous fodder crop) and dura (a form of sorghum which was the traditional subsistence food); and one left fallow. The size of the tenancy was meant to be such that the tenant household could provide most of the work for its own holding, although extra labour would have to be hired to help harvest the cotton. Tenants lived in villages scattered throughout the Scheme since they had to be close to their fields. The area under cotton grew to 131,292 feddans (55,143 hectares) by 1928-9 and by then, cotton had become the Sudan's major export, accounting for around 70 per cent of all export earnings.

The relative shares of net proceeds from cotton sales were renegotiated in 1926. The government found that their share of proceeds was not producing an adequate return, once their costs had been paid. Furthermore, it was in their interest to extend the area under irrigation since the marginal costs of doing so were much less than the initial costs per hectare. Government's share in net proceeds from cotton sales thus gradually rose between 1926 and 1930 to reach 40 per cent, with that of the Syndicate falling from 25 to 20 per cent. In return, the Syndicate's concession was extended to 1950.

Problems with two diseases, one a bacterial disease known as black-arm, the other a virus known as leafcurl, meant very low average cotton yields in many of the early years. One of several methods tried

Map 3.2 *The expansion of the Gezira Scheme over time*

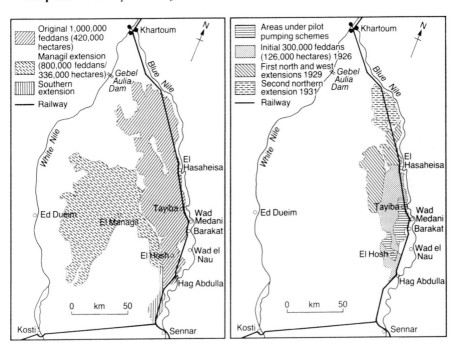

to combat these diseases was changes in crop rotation. By 1932, a complex 8 year rotation was tried and then kept with the area left fallow doubled and the tenancies increased to 40 feddans (16.8 hectares). One quarter of the tenancy was planted with cotton with one eighth each to lubia and dura. Although there were major annual fluctuations in cotton yield, they remained well above the very low yielding years of 1930-31 and 1932-33.

A second problem was the low prices obtained for the cotton on the world market. Before the Gezira Scheme was developed, the assumption was that around 15 English old pennies per pound weight would be obtained for the cotton. Prices obtained for the cotton grown in the last year of the pilot schemes, 1924-25, and for the first four crops from the Gezira Scheme were between 16 and 20 pennies. But in 1929-30 it fell to 8 pennies and a year later to 6 pennies. It varied year by year but remained below 11 pennies every year until 1946 (see Table 3.2 over for more details).

For the tenant, this meant four years of high average profits from 1925-1929, then a slump between 1930 and 1934 when little or no profit was made, then a slow general trend of improving profit up to 1945 although, as Table 3.2 shows, with considerable yearly variations. A Tenants Reserve Fund was set up in the Thirties to repay bad debts from the depression years, to give security for loans to

Table 3.2 *Cotton yields and returns 1925–1950*

	Average yield			Average profit per tenancy (£ sterling)
	kantars/ feddan	kg/hectare	Price[a]	
1925–6	4.8	1634	18.0	67
1927	4.7	1600	18.0	84
1928	3.3	1124	19.7	58
1929	3.6	1226	18.4	55
1930	2.3	783	7.9	nil
1931	1.4	477	6.4	nil
1932	4.1	1396	8.5	12
1933	1.9	647	8.1	nil
1935–39 (average)	4.4	1498	7.4	16
1940–44	3.9	1328	9.5	24
1945	4.9	1668	10.6	54
1946	3.4	1158	10.3	49
1947	4.0	1362	19.2	96
1948	3.4	1158	38.5	204
1949	4.3	1464	38.5	221
1950	4.6	1566	41.3	281

Note: a—Price is expressed in English old pennies per pound weight; one should recall that at this time there were 240 pence to £1 sterling. This column of figures has not been converted into new pence (ie with 100 pence per £1 sterling) per kilogram, since its only purpose is to show the large annual fluctuations in price.
Source: Gaitskell (1959)

tenants and to provide an equalisation fund to boost profits in bad years. Gaitskell comments that in these years of adversity with most of the decisions relating to land cultivation pre-determined by the Syndicate, 'the tenants seemed to have precious little liberty or economic advantage. They seemed little more than labourers in their own land, cogs in a cotton production machine' (p. 203). Despite the difficulties faced by the tenants, the scheme still gave profits to the Syndicate and met the government's expenses, including the amortisation of the capital costs.

From the mid-Forties, some major changes became evident. One was the recovery in cotton prices on the world market. Although still subject to major annual fluctuations, this meant higher profits per tenancy from 1945, especially for the years 1948, 1949 and 1950. The government had begun to recognise how Sudanese opinion was not being consulted. In 1942, the Graduates' Congress[8] presented a memorandum to the government with a list of demands, including the right to self determination in the national government after the Second World War, the end of the Syndicate's concession in the Gezira and increased 'Sudanisation'. Although the memorandum was rejected, in 1944 the Government notified the Syndicate that its concession would not be renewed after 1950, and a tenants' strike in

1946 meant a refusal to plant cotton until money was drawn from the Reserve Fund and paid to the tenants. In 1950, a new Sudan Gezira Board took over the management of the Scheme. It too received 20 per cent of the profits from the cotton crop while the government and the tenants each received 40 per cent.

Population and urban centres

Information about population growth and the development of an urban system in the Gezira Scheme for the first thirty years of its operation is very scarce. Estimates taken in 1912 suggest population of some 136,000 persons in the study region—in the districts of Wad Medani, El Messellamiya, El Kamlin and El Managil. In 1912 Wad Medani was noted as a town of some 16,000 inhabitants.

The only settlements considered as towns at the beginning of the Scheme in 1925 were Wad Medani with some 30,000 inhabitants, El Hasaheisa with 1,500 and El Kamlin with 1,000. Thus, Wad Medani appears as the only settlement with a sufficient concentration of population to be regarded as an important urban centre. Under Anglo-Egyptian Condominium rule, Wad Medani was the only settlement in the study region with the rank of a provincial headquarters; it was the capital of Blue Nile province. In addition to housing the provincial administration, its satellite settlement, Barakat, became the management centre of the Gezira Scheme. It was also the major railway station on the railway line and the flow of goods between Khartoum to the north and Kosti and El Obeid to the west also pass through Wad Medani. The Gezira Agricultural Research Station was located just to the west of Wad Medani.

A lack of statistics make it impossible to give more details as to changes in the urban system in the study region for the first quarter of the twentieth century. Two settlements other than Wad Medani, El Hasaheisa and El Kamlin were referred to as towns in this period and obviously contained some functions commonly associated with urban centres.

The first was Arbaji which had been established as an administrative centre, centuries before the Turko-Egyptian, Mahdist and Anglo-Egyptian governments. It lost importance when the Anglo-Egyptian Condominium government transferred the administrative activities located at Arbaji to El Messellamiya. El Messellamiya had been an important commercial centre long before the Condominium government was set up. It was the main centre in the region for the slave trade and for trade in other commodities and its commercial links stretched up to Egypt. El Messellamiya, in turn, lost importance after the administrative functions it housed were transferred to El Hasaheisa. El Messellamiya had begun to lose its commercial dominance when the railway was built from Khartoum down to Wad Medani

Map 3.3 *Major settlements in or close to the Gezira study region*

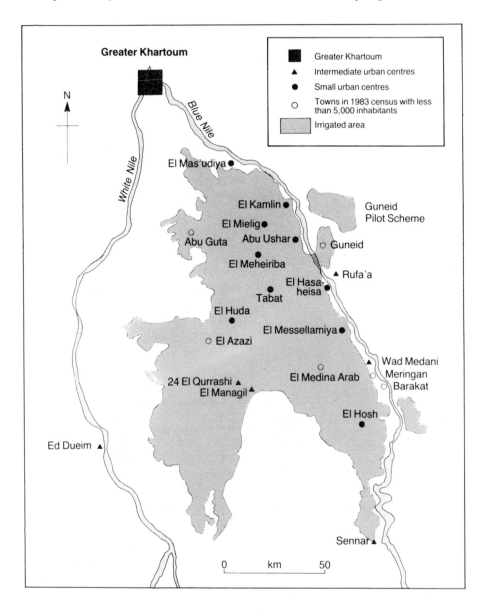

and Sennar. Merchants in El Messellamiya had opposed the railway coming to their town, one reason being the possibility it gave for slaves to escape and another, the control that the colonial government could impose on their activities. Nearby El Hasaheisa was therefore chosen as the railway station in that part of the line.

El Hasaheisa did not have a long history as a permanent settlement. Settled initially by pastoralists migrating from around Khartoum during the first decade of the twentieth century, it rapidly developed as an important sorghum market, once the railway arrived there. The sorghum market was closed with the development of the Gezira Scheme but with the transfer of administrative offices from El Messellamiya in 1927, the construction of cotton ginning factories there in 1928 and the various other activities which developed there linked to the Gezira Scheme (including a river port through which building materials were brought), it grew to become the study region's second largest urban centre by 1955.

Socio-economic developments 1955-1983

Major changes were made to the Gezira Scheme in the period 1955-1983. First, the area under irrigation was almost doubled and new cash crops and a more intensive use of land were promoted in an attempt to increase total production and tenants' incomes. Secondly, the Joint Account System which had been in force since 1925 was replaced by a new system in 1981 whereby tenants pay land and water charges, instead of giving the Government and the Gezira Board a share of the proceeds from cotton production. Each of these will be described in more detail, since each has an important bearing on the growth and development of the urban system. In addition, developments in industry, transport, education, health services and social structure are described.

Extension, intensification and diversification

In 1957, work began on the Managil Extension to the west of the existing irrigated area. This added 800,000 feddans (336,000 hectares) to the 1 million feddans (420,000 hectares) which the original Scheme had reached by 1952. This extension was made possible by a new agreement with Egypt on an increased water withdrawal from the Blue Nile which allowed the construction of a new dam at Roseires. Tenancies in the new extension were 15 feddans (6.3 hectares), less than half the size of those in the Gezira Scheme, which allowed a greater number of tenancies and thus a more dense agricultural population. Initially, similar crops were grown—cotton, dura and lubia. Since an increasing amount of hired labour was being used in the 40 feddan (16.8 hectare) Gezira tenancies, the smaller Managil tenancies were

Table 3.3 *Area under cotton and average yields for selected years 1925–*
1980

Crop year	Area under cotton		Average yield, seed cotton Kantar/	
	feddans	hectares	feddan	kg/hectare
1925/6	80,031	33,613	4.8	1,634
1929	131,292	55,143	3.6	1,226
1940	206,880	86,890	3.8	1,294
1950	206,737	86,830	4.6	1,566
1970/71	603,277	253,376	5.5	1,873
1970/71– 1974/5 average	603,889	253,633	4.8	1,634
1975/76– 1979/80 average	490,526	206,021	3.3	1,124
1980/81	501,120	210,470	2.1	715

NB Figures prior to 1950 are given for selected years by way of comparison;
more details of yearly variations in area planted and yields are given
in Table 3.2.
Source: Gaitskell (1959) and SGB (1981) *Statistical Bulletin* No 2, Barakat,
March.

meant to be of a size which allowed most of the labour input to be
undertaken by the tenant household; the smaller size also allowed
more tenancies. Production relations through the Joint Account System remained the same.

Between 1950 and 1983, the number of tenant-cultivators rose from
around 21,000 to around 101,000.[9] Total population rose more slowly
since average tenancy size fell, both because of the sub-division of
the 40 feddan (16.8 hectare) tenancies in the original Gezira Scheme
and because of the smaller tenancies introduced in the Managil Extension. Fieldwork in three villages in 1978/79 in Central Gezira (where
the 40 feddan tenancy was still the standard) found that 46 per cent
of the tenancies were half the size of the standard tenancy while 5
per cent were larger than the standard.[10]

Cotton production grew rapidly between the early Fifties and 1970/
71. Total cotton production in 1970/71 was more than three times
that in 1950 when in both years, yields per unit area were unusually
high. But as the figures in Table 3.3 show, increased production owed
far more to an increase in the area under cotton cultivation (which
virtually tripled) than it did to increases in yields. But during the
Seventies, first one sees a substantial decrease in yields and then, in
the second half of the decade, a decrease in area under cotton. By
1980/81, total cotton production in a year of very low yield was
actually little more than in 1950 even though the area under cotton
had more than doubled.

Under pressure from the Tenants' Union, new cash crops and a
more intensive crop production system were introduced during the

Table 3.4 *Fluctuations in tenants' income from cotton proceeds 1950–1962*

Season	Average share of cotton proceeds per tenant in Sudanese Pounds
1950-51	716.9
1951-52	246.6
1952-53	176.0
1953-54	218.6
1954-55	174.9
1955-56	241.0
1956-57	289.0
1957-58	28.8
1959-60	166.1
1960-61	62.8
1961-62	104.5
1962-63	98.2
Average (13 years—1951/63);	204.7
Average (12 years—1952/63):	162.1

Source: Ali, K.E. (1982), *The Politics of Agrarian Relations,* unpublished MSc thesis, The Hague.

Seventies. The average income received per tenancy showed little sign of increase in the early Fifties, apart from a bumper year in 1950-51, and by the late Fifties had declined as is shown in Table 3.4. Furthermore, since data does not exist to turn the figures in Table 3.4 into Sudanese pounds of constant purchasing power, with rising costs and a rising cost of living, the average return each tenant received in the late Fifties was well below that of, say, the period 1948-1957.

The area under cotton in a standard tenancy remained the same in both Gezira and Managil tenancies (ie 10 feddans, 4.2 hectares in a standard Gezira tenancy and 5 feddans, 2.1 hectares in a Managil tenancy). The area under fallow was halved with wheat introduced for one quarter of the tenancy and dura and/or groundnuts grown in the other quarter. The legume, lubia was removed from the rotation in the Seventies as it is a host crop for cotton pests. Thus, virtually no fodder crops are grown. Attempts to grow rice were abandoned. And some tenants began to grow vegetables. But one should recall that cropping patterns for each tenancy were still controlled by the Gezira Board. The management maintained a strict control over the main production activities, crop rotation, inputs and timing of operations.

Table 3.5 shows the increasing importance given to wheat and groundnuts and the disappearance of lubia. It also shows the large fluctuations, year by year in the proportion of planted area devoted to any one crop. Indeed, in certain years, the area under wheat exceeded that under cotton. Wheat and groundnuts also came to provide an important part of tenants' incomes. In 1959/60, 82 per

Table 3.5 *Area under different crops for selected years (thousand of hectares)*

	1968/69	1975/76	1976/77	1978/79	1979/80	1981/82
Cotton	249	166	210	210	227	183
Wheat	69	238	212	209	158	112
Dura	135	143	148	144	113	144
Groundnuts	66	178	105	91	112	111
Rice	—	5	5	2	4	0
Lubia	53	0.6	0.3	0	0	0
Vegetables	16	10	13	11	14	18
Total	593	742	693	667	628	568

NB Sums of columns may differ slightly from totals owing to rounding of
figures and to very small areas being devoted to other crops.
Source: Records of Sudan Gezira Board.

cent of tenants' incomes came from cotton with 15 per cent from
dura. In 1971/2, only 55 per cent came from cotton with wheat
providing 28 per cent and groundnuts 11 per cent.

The whole structure of labour input into tenancies had also
changed. In the early years of the Scheme, tenant households had to
do most of the work although labour was hired to help harvest the
cotton and sometimes for weeding. By the early Seventies, most of
the labour input into tenancies was provided by hired labour which
lived in the locality so the Scheme supported a large population of
permanently settled agricultural labourers in addition to the seasonal
migrants who came for the cotton harvest. Studies in the 1971/72
season showed that only 39 per cent of the labour input was provided
by the tenant with a further 12 per cent by family. Twenty-three per
cent was provided by permanent wage labourers and 22 per cent by
migrant labourers. On average each tenancy supported more than
four local wage-earners.

A study in the mid-Seventies showed that reliance on hired labour
was highest for groundnuts where it provided 71 per cent of the
labour input. For wheat it was 50 per cent and for cotton and dura,
28 per cent. Many tenants are no longer directly involved in agricultural work. A high proportion of Gezira tenants have share-cropping arrangements with resident labourers in their groundnut plots.
There is also evidence of share-cropping for sorghum and even in
some instances for cotton. One estimate suggested that share-cropping
is practised on 60 per cent of tenancies. Furthermore, many tenants
prefer to hire labour to undertake most of the work on the tenancy
while they undertake another full or part time job. Fieldwork in 3
villages in Central Division (Gezira Scheme) found that only 36 per
cent of tenants had no other employment, as is shown in Table 3.6.

Fieldwork in the mid-Seventies in another village found that from
120 heads of households, only half had tenancies. Of the other 60,
40 had jobs in Khartoum or Wad Medani, 10 were working in Saudi

Table 3.6   *Additional occupations undertaken by tenants in three rural settlements*

Additional occupation	Number of tenants involved	% of tenants in settlements
None	67	36
Clerical employment	49	26
Skilled labour	28	15
Unskilled labour	26	14
Medical services	7	4
Shopkeeping	6	3
Policemen	4	2
Total	187	100

Source: Fieldwork

Arabia or other Gulf States and 10 were employed in non-agricultural work within the village. Although, officially, tenancy leases have to be renewed annually, such renewals are automatic and evictions are virtually unknown. When a tenant dies, the tenancy usually goes to the tenant's heir or in some cases his widow which helps explain why 12-15 per cent of tenants are female.

The introduction of new crops and more intensive production made tenants' annual cycle of irrigation water needs more complex. There was an overlap in the water requirements for the different crops. By 1976, the competition for irrigation water for the different crops was being acknowledged as one of the new problems facing the Scheme. The new crop rotations also showed up the difference between the priorities of the Gezira Board and the tenants. The Gezira Board's main interest was in cotton production. This provided the bulk of their income and was of great importance to the national economy. For the tenant, however, cotton production was harder work and often produced poor returns. Shortages and delays in obtaining imported inputs because their supply was constrained by a serious balance of payments problem hindered attempts to increase yields. Average yields per unit area during the late Seventies were very low and indeed, in 1980-81, were less than half that achieved in each of the first three years of the Scheme from 1925-1927. It is worth recalling that an average yield of 5 kantars per feddan was assumed when calculations about the viability of the proposed Gezira Scheme were being made in the early twentieth century. Only in three years between 1970 and 1981 was this yield achieved. In one block, in 1980/81, only 52 out of 1,198 tenants received a net profit from their cotton crop. In addition, there was evidence of soil deterioration in some parts of the Scheme including infestation of weeds, declining dura yields, soil becoming compacted and developing a hard surface (which does not allow water to percolate), water logging and increasing salinity.

These factors help explain why tenants often give more attention to other crops even if they cannot decide on the allocation of land to different crops. Dura is important because it remains the household's staple food. It also requires less labour input, compared to groundnuts, and provides straw for animal fodder and for constructing the temporary huts for the hired labour needed to pick the cotton. Groundnut production has the advantage of giving farmers an early return (it is harvested seven months before cotton or wheat) and since its sale is under the control of the tenant, loans from merchants are more easy to obtain. But groundnuts, too, suffer from large annual price fluctuations. Vegetable production seems to be profitable and a preferred choice since many tenants apply for permission to grow vegetables on their tenancies. But production is limited because of irrigation water shortages in the summer when they are grown. The marketing of surplus dura and of groundnuts and vegetables is essentially the responsibility of the tenant.

Wheat is popular with many tenants since it requires relatively little labour input. But both management and tenants agree that it is expensive to produce and yields are very low (typically 1.4 tons per hectare in the Gezira Scheme). Official prices are also low, although better prices can be obtained on the black market. But the Government has been encouraging its production to reduce the import bill. Thus, overall, yields per hectare have never been particularly high, although detailed information about yields for crops other than cotton are not available. It is also worth noting that there is a considerable variation in crop yields within the Scheme. In the 1982/83 season, in the Managil Extension, the average cotton yield was 4.3 kantars per feddan (1,450 kgs per hectare) with the average being below 4 kantars for some of the 46 blocks in this extension and above 6 in others. There are also variations in yields among the 900 or so tenant farmers within each block.

Livestock have remained an important component of farming in the study region, although they no longer play such a central role as they did before the Irrigation Scheme was developed. Total livestock population has increased very considerably since the first two decades of this century, although the number of animals per family has fallen. A recent estimate suggested that there were around 400,000 cows, 1,400,000 sheep, 1,100,000 goats and 150,000 donkeys, horses and camels. However, accurate figures are impossible to give in that the total number of livestock increases considerably after the cotton harvest as animals are brought in to graze on old cotton stalks, before these are pulled up. In addition, the migrants who come every year to harvest the cotton bring their own animals with them. The availability of permanent sources of drinking water, of grazing on fallow fields and on canal edges, and of crop residues which serve as animal fodder (especially from dura and cotton) helps explain the relatively high density of livestock, although it is perhaps surprising that their numbers seem to have been maintained, despite the removal of lubia, the fodder crop, from the crop rotation. Goats are kept by nearly all families while most cattle are raised by tenants and other relatively rich households. The importance of sheep has declined in recent years, due mainly to the expansion of mechanised rain-fed cultivation on fringe areas of the Irrigation Scheme; this has reduced the land under natural pasture on which sheep used to depend for part of the year.

Livestock in a Gezira village are usually cared for by professional herdsmen, each of whom will care for the animals of more than one tenant. Their services are particularly needed from December to February when most of the land is under crops. As the area left fallow decreased with crop intensification, with grass in natural grazing areas now cut and sold, and with herdsmen and straw becoming more expensive, livestock rearing is under pressure.

Production relations

There was no substantial change in the Joint Account System when the Sudan Gezira Board replaced the Syndicate as the manager of the Gezira Scheme in 1950. It also changed little with Independence in 1956 and with the construction of the Managil Extension. The principle of a three-way division of the proceeds from cotton sales between national government, management and tenants remained in force up to 1980/81.

However, over time, the tenants' share increased while that of management decreased. Between 1957 and 1971, tenants' share grew from 40 to 49 per cent.[11] Central government's share increased to 42 per cent in 1957 but had fallen to 36 per cent by 1964. Management's share fell to 10 per cent in 1957. Small shares of the proceeds were allocated to two new sources; a Social Development Fund which received 2 per cent in the Fifties and Sixties (rising to 3 per cent in 1970) while local government within the region received 2 per cent from 1957. In addition, certain costs originally borne by the tenants were transferred to the joint account including the costs of seeds and picking.

During the late Sixties and Seventies, it became increasingly clear that the Gezira Scheme and Managil Extension were not producing results which satisfied tenants, government or management. For the tenants, declining crop yields and rising production costs meant inadequate returns. For instance, the cost of fertilizers and crop protection for cotton rose nearly threefold between 1970/71 and 1978/79. For the government, the contribution from its share in the proceeds from cotton sales was falling as yields declined and as no new land was brought under cotton cultivation. National government's returns from the Scheme fell from LS15 million in 1977/78 to around LS5 million in 1980/81.[12] The Gezira Board suffered not only from the fact that cotton proceeds were falling but also from the fact that it only received 10 per cent of net proceeds, compared to the 20 per cent that the Syndicate had received before nationalisation. Its share of net proceeds from cotton sale no longer covered its costs. Only 55 per cent of its administrative expenses were covered in 1978/9 with this per centage falling to 37 per cent in 1979/80 and 17 per cent in 1980/81. Indeed, central government made a net loss overall since it had to pay for this deficit. The deficit of LS6.7 million in 1980/81 was more than the LS5.0 million it had received from its share of cotton proceeds.

The Joint Account System was abolished in 1980 with Land and Water Charges replacing it in 1981/82. Under this system, tenants pay fixed charges per unit area for the different crops grown, the charge per unit area being based on the different crops' water needs and administration and management costs. Thus, the fact that a hectare of cotton demands a much higher input of irrigation water than, say, wheat or groundnuts, means that the tenant has to pay a higher charge for a hectare of cotton. Similarly, charges per hectare for wheat and groundnuts are substantially higher than for dura which has relatively low irrigation costs. But a hectare of cotton should produce a substantially higher return than a hectare of groundnuts or wheat. Thus, the Gezira Board's income is no longer dependent on a small share of the net proceeds from cotton sales. And tenants' payments for their land and water are no longer drawn only from cotton production, as had been the case under the Joint Account System.

The hope is that Land and Water Charges will help stimulate production, especially of cotton, and better serve the interest of both the tenants and the government. Cotton prices are announced as picking commences, so tenants know the return they will receive per unit weight of cotton harvested. In addition, a World Bank sponsored rehabilitation scheme is underway. The rehabilitation scheme is to cover the Gezira Scheme and Managil Extension, as well as other cotton schemes (such as the Rahad Scheme), and includes the purchase of new tractors and irrigation pumps, and rolling stock for the Gezira light railway. The EEC is also supporting increased production through the increased supply of fertiliser.

By drawing government and management costs and revenues from all crops with charges for each crop based on administration and management costs, the disincentive to cotton production and the implicit subsidy to other crops is removed. The hope is that this will better serve the national interest in terms of boosting cotton production and exports (and thus increasing much needed foreign earnings) and, at the same time, with the rehabilitation scheme, boosting tenants' incomes. Calculations in 1979 suggested that returns for cotton per unit area and per unit of irrigation water should be substantially higher than for other cash crops such as groundnuts, wheat and rice. In addition, cotton should produce the highest foreign exchange earnings per unit of domestic resources with wheat producing the lowest. The idea of replacing the Joint Account System with land and water charges had been recommended by a series of missions and working parties in reports dating back to 1965.

Land and Water Charges will also (in theory) provide the Government and the Gezira Board with a fixed, predetermined income. However, fixed charges levied per unit area mean that tenants bear more of the risks. Under the Joint Account System, if cotton yields were low or cotton prices low (or both, as was often the case), the burden was shared by government, management and tenants alike. And in other government-managed irrigated schemes where Land and Water Charges have been in force, there have been considerable difficulties in levying charges, especially for crops other than cotton. Furthermore, with each rise in inflation or management costs, land and water charges should be increased to guarantee cost recovery, although regular revision of such charges may involve lengthy and difficult negotiations with tenants. The charges set in 1981 have been raised by 30 per cent for 1983/84 although it is not certain whether such charges can continually be raised to keep pace with inflation; the Gezira Tenants Union will obviously oppose this.

Thus, the success of the new system will depend on the extent to which high crop yields can be achieved through the successful implementation of the Rehabilitation Scheme. Projections for the sixth year of Land and Water Charges suggest a net return for a typical cotton tenancy of between 1500 and 1600 Sudanese pounds compared to 308 Sudanese pounds which was the average net tenant income for the last four years of the Joint Account System and around 370 Sudanese pounds for the first year of Land and Water Charges. Average cotton yields have increased since the start of the Rehabilitation Scheme and the replacement of the Joint Account System with Land and Water charges. Cotton yields per hectare for 1982/83 and 1983/84 were more than twice that achieved in the very poor year of 1980/81 (4.7 and 4.9 kantars per feddan compared to 2.1 in 1980/81) but still below the 6.7 figure achieved in 1956/57. An increasing use of fertilisers and insecticides and the introduction of medium staple cotton[13] should allow average yields to continue to rise. However, even a relatively small drop in yield below those projected would drastically cut tenant incomes.[14] There is also the problem that standard Land and Water charges will discriminate against tenancies on less fertile land or those less favourably placed with regard to water availability. Indeed, tenancies located on poorer land may simply be abandoned.

Industry and transport

In 1955, thirty years after the Gezira Scheme was begun, the only industry of any significance was cotton ginning. Ginning industries developed at Meringan and Barakat (both close to Wad Medani) and at El Hasaheisa. After the Second World War, the development of import substitution industries was encouraged in the Sudan and today there are a number of factories manufacturing consumer goods such as cigarettes, shoes, beer, air coolers and furniture. The government both constructed and operated industrial plants and encouraged private investment through tax incentives and through controlling or taxing imports, but most industrial units were set up in Greater Khartoum. In 1977, out of a total of 822 industrial enterprises in the Sudan, 547 were reported as being in Greater Khartoum with only 43 in the study region.

Wad Medani contained 30 of these 43 units and they included five vegetable oil mills, three textile, three footwear and three macaroni/vermicelli factories, two soap and two metal furniture factories, and a flour mill, tannery and tobacco/cigarette, ice, mineral water and cutlery factory. Among the largest industrial plants are a spinning and weaving company (2,500 employees) and a textile company (1,100 employees). The Meringan industrial area, close by, has five of the study region's 12 cotton ginning plants and a large oil crushing mill with 210 employees. About 10 km to the north of Wad Medani is a government-owned tannery with around 420 employees. Wad Medani also has numerous small-scale workshops and plants.

El Hasaheisa had six of the 43 industrial units (including ginning, textile, oil and soap factories) while El Kamlin, El Messellamiya, Mi'elig, El Managil and 24 El Quarrashi had one each. Around 12,000 people are employed in the cotton ginneries at Meringan, Barakat and El Hasaheisa, although 8,000-9,000 of these are contract workers employed for 5-6 months a year.

In the last few years, there are signs of a rapid increase in industrial investment in the study region although figures on total production or employment generation are not available. New industries related to agricultural or animal products are most in evidence; examples include a milk processing plant at Barakat and several oil and soap industries based on cotton seeds or groundnuts in El Managil and El Hasaheisa. El Managil also has factories for groundnut shelling and for macaroni fabrication and a wheat flour mill while El Hasaheisa has sweet industries in addition to its cotton ginning, textile and oil mill industries. A government-owned textile factory, built by China in El Hasaheisa, employs 1,787 workers and 200 technicians. There are also signs of industrial development in or close to El Masudiya, on the northern border of the region, close to Khartoum.

Recent industrial developments around El Gadid el Thawra and Bagir which are very close to this town help explain its rapid population growth between 1973 and 1983. However, only in Wad Medani and El Hasaheisa do industries contribute significantly to urban centres' employment base.

As noted on page 83, only through the construction of railways linking Wad Medani and El Hasaheisa to Khartoum and then to Port Sudan did the Gezira Scheme's aim of growing cotton for export become feasible. In 1955, this railway remained by far the most important transport mode linking the region with the outside while a light railway built within the study region by the Sudan Plantations Syndicate transported the cotton from collection centres (block head-quarters) to the ginning factories and distributed agricultural inputs.

Since 1955, the study region's roadlinks with the rest of the Sudan have been much improved. A paved highway from Khartoum to Wad Medani was completed in 1969. In 1977, a bridge across the Blue Nile just north of Wad Medani was completed. This opened a road connection linking the region to major towns such as Gedaref and Kassala to the east and, eventually, to Port Sudan. The highway from Khartoum to Wad Medani was extended to Sennar and then from Sennar to Kosti, another major town which is on the White Nile close to the study region's south-west corner. This highway was only completed in 1984. These highways link the Gezira Scheme and its Managil Extension with many of the Sudan's other large irrigation schemes such as the Kenana sugar project which has developed close to the White Nile opposite Kosti and the Rahad Irrigation Project whose northern limit comes close to Wad Medani but to the east of the Blue Nile. Bus services between urban centres on this road are frequent. The railway line from Khartoum to Sennar runs close to the road and is of diminishing importance for passengers and freight.

By contrast, the region's internal road system is still poor. There are only a few seasonal roads constructed by the Government and some branch roads built by villagers. The network of irrigation canals and the fact that the 'black cotton soils' readily retain water, inhibit road construction. In the dry season, seasonal roads are adequate since the soil bakes hard. The Gezira's narrow gauge railway cannot cope with more than the distribution of seeds, fertilisers and other inputs for cotton to block headquarters and the collection of cotton for the ginning factories. Automobiles, pick-ups, buses and lorries increasingly link villages and markets. Lorries have to be used to transport groundnuts and wheat because the light railway's capacity is already over-strained by cotton. Donkeys are still important, although their use is restricted to inter-village and village-tenancy movement. Horse-drawn carts are also used, with their range extend-ing to transporting goods between villages, market centres and urban centres. They are also used to carry seeds and fertilisers from block headquarters to the tenancies and they have replaced camels as the means for transporting cotton from tenancies to collection centres.

Health, education and social facilities

In 1950, when the Irrigation Scheme was nationalised, there were only two hospitals (one each at Wad Medani and Abu Ushar). Only 45 per cent of adult males and virtually no adult females were found to be literate (Gaitskell, 1959). The first government-funded secondary school to serve the region was only built in 1946; this was a boys' secondary school built at Hantoub across the Blue Nile from Wad Medani with an annual intake of 160 pupils. The new canals, irrigated fields and reservoirs introduced or exacerbated health problems. They provided favourable breeding grounds for the snail host of the parasitic worm which causes schistosomiasis (also called bilharzia) and various attempts to control it up to 1953 had met with little success. Although malaria had been present before the irrigation scheme (unlike schistosomiasis), the long dry season had kept it in check and gave time for the infected population to recover. But the water in the new canals and irrigated fields allowed the disease vector, the anopheline mosquito, to survive throughout the year, and malaria became endemic.

Considerable progress has been made since 1950 in expanding educational and health facilities, although substantial health problems still remain. New schools received support from three sources: the national Ministry of Education, the Social Development Department of the Gezira Board and private initiatives. In 1977/78, 66.2 per cent of children went to primary school while 15.7 per cent went to higher secondary schools. Around a fifth of pupils at boys' academic higher secondary schools and around three-fifths of pupils at girls' academic higher secondary schools were at private schools. Such schools had played a more prominent role in the late Thirties and Forties when a lack of publicly funded educational facilities caused a number of private primary and intermediate schools to be set up. Apart from the academic higher secondary schools, there are three technical colleges, an agricultural college and a teachers' college. And a university opened in Wad Medani in the late Seventies.

There has been a comparable expansion of hospitals and health centres, the number of hospitals growing from two to 19 between 1956 and 1981. There was also a rapid expansion in the number of health centres, dispensaries and dressing first aid stations especially since 1970. The Gezira Board's Social Development Department has supported the construction of dressing stations, dispensaries or health centres in villages and small towns and the provision of safer water supplies. Around three-quarters of the larger registered villages are reported to have water supply systems while most of the smaller villages still rely on water drawn from irrigation canals, with all the health risks that this implies. In places which are not geologically suited to deep bores, water has to be drawn from irrigation canals. Water is normally drawn from a relatively large canal (from where water supply is secure all year). Where provision has been made to provide safe water, the canal water is filtered and pumped into a water tower. Because such facilities are built by major canals, they are often at some distance from villages. Pipes have been run to some villages, paid for by their inhabitants, sometimes with help from the Social Development Department. Shortages of fuel to power the pumps, lack of spare parts and poor filter maintenance limit their effectiveness. So too does the fact that many villages have not been connected to them. The long walk from the village to collect water encourages water collection from unprotected water sources closer to hand. Water sources drawn from tubewells in those parts of the region with water-yielding aquifers can suffer comparable problems of fuel shortages and pump breakdowns. Then there are still many settlements lacking any form of protected water source; this is particularly the case in the labour camps. There are also health hazards from biocide residues in irrigation water which become concentrated higher up the food chain.[16] Despite this expansion of protected water supplies and health facilities, the incidence of diseases like schistosomiasis, malaria, dysentery and typhoid remained high when their incidence was last measured during the Sixties and in 1970.

Some 116,000 cases of malaria are reported annually, and these are estimated to represent one-third of the total. Schistosomiasis is endemic; a report published in 1975 noted that 60 per cent of seven-year-olds were infected.[17] Typhoid and dysentery remain major problems too, although the incidence of dysentery has decreased in recent years, due largely to more hygienic practices spread by health education. The serious health problems in the study region led to the establishment of a Blue Nile Health Project in 1979 run by the Sudan government and the World Health Organisation. This seeks to greatly reduce the incidence of schistosomiasis, malaria and diarrhoeal diseases in the Gezira and Managil, and in the Rahad Scheme to the east of the study region. One of its goals is to supply 80 per cent of the population of Gezira with safe water. Up to the early Fifties, most social facilities were concentrated in the few, larger urban centres. Over the last 20-30 years, their number has increased while their concentration in larger urban centres has probably lessened. In 1981, a total of 589 social clubs, 630 mosques, 93 beer houses and 4,905 television sets were reported to be in settlements in the Gezira.[18]

Table 3.7   *Average net incomes of tenants and of staff at the Sudan Gezira Board*

(1) Tenants	Sudanese Pounds
Average under Joint Account System 1970/71–1980/81	258
Average under Joint Account System 1976/77–1980/81	308
Expected income in year 1 after rehabilitation scheme (1981/82)	371-374
Expected income in year 6 after rehabilitation scheme	1,517-1,609
(2) SGB staff in 1981	
Unskilled labour (including office boys, guards and messengers)	600
Skilled labour (including carpenters and electricians)	1,625
Clerks and storekeepers	2,070
Field staff (including inspectors and engineers)	2,668

Social structure

In a sample village in the early Fifties, four broad social groups could be distinguished: the more prosperous tenants with whole or half tenancies and the principal village shopkeepers; the bulk of half tenancies, tradesmen and craftsmen; casual labourers and herdsmen; and seasonal migrants.

A sample village in the mid-Seventies revealed a similar structure with administrators, rich tenants, merchants, lorry owners, money-lenders and other entrepreneurs being the richest followed by poorer tenants (essentially those who depended only on the income from their tenancy); and then various categories of labourers. Among the labourers, there are the share-croppers (typically people from the Western Sudan who may have been living in the Gezira Scheme for many years or even born there but have been unable to obtain a tenancy), labourers who are also permanent residents and labourers who only come for the cotton harvest each year. There are substantial numbers of people of Nigerian descent, although in most areas they are share-croppers or labourers and not tenants. The suggestion that a tenant-household which relied only on income from production on the tenancy was usually not so well-off is supported by figures for average income earned by tenants during the Seventies. As Table 3.7 shows, it was not only the inspectors, engineers, clerks and store-keepers who had much higher net incomes than tenants in 1981 but also skilled and unskilled labour working for the Gezira Board. If the rehabilitation scheme projections shown in Table 3.7 prove to be realistic, then net incomes for tenants will rise very substantially.

The three broad categories in the rural social structure – tenants, share-croppers plus resident labourers, and migrant labourers – can be seen in rural area's settlement system. The main villages are primarily tenant villages. Resident labourers and share-croppers usually live in more or less permanent labour villages or camps and these are generally more congested and have lower standards of housing and amenities. Labourers' camps are often considered as part of nearby villages although they are usually physically separate from them. In addition to the labourers' camps, there are also the temporary camps set up to house seasonal migrants who come to harvest cotton. An estimate in 1980 suggested that there were around 710 labourers' camps with 170,000 inhabitants and over 1,000 tenants' base villages with 597,000 inhabitants. In 1973/4, out of a total of 542,000 persons engaged in the cotton picking season, 139,000 were tenants and family members, 57,000 were resident labourers, 9,000 were casual labourers and 336,000 were 'imported' labourers, most of whom would have come just for the season. In more recent years, the number of such seasonal migrants has probably fallen to between 150,000 and 200,000. Usually, family groups come and a high proportion of the migrants are from agricultural households in the rainland areas.

Development of the urban system 1925–1983

Population distribution

Preliminary figures from a census undertaken in February 1983 suggest that there were 1,714,705 people living in the study region with 295,220 living in towns[19] and 1,419,485 living in rural areas. No figures are available for the study region's population in 1973 but for the whole Central Region, within which the study region is located, average annual population growth rates between 1973 and 1983 are officially estimated at 2.5 per cent; lower than the national average of 2.8 per cent. This implies that over the 10-year period, there may have been net out-migration from the three provinces which make up the Central Region (one should recall that the study region contains most of the population of the most populous of the three provinces within the Central Region). But certainly natural increase rather than migration seems to be the major contributor to population growth in the Central Region and to the study region located within it.[20]

In examining the urban centres listed in Table 3.8, in terms of population size, there seems to be three obvious categories. Wad Medani is in a class of its own in terms of population size. El Managil and 24 El Qurrashi are intermediate urban centres by our definition. There are also grounds for believing that El Hasaheisa's population exceeds 20,000 and that the 1983 census figure represents an underenumeration (see page 114 for more details). After these three urban centres come ten small urban centres with between 5,000 and 9,000

Table 3.8   *Population growth of urban centres in or close to study region, 1925–1983*

Urban Centres	1925	1955/56	1964/65	1973	1983
(a) *In the study region*					
Wad Medani	30,000	50,171	66,350	106,415	141,065
El Managil	—	—	6,722	15,223	36,090
24 El Qurrashi	—	—	—	4,393	21,666
El Hasaheisa	1,500	6,933	12,315	18,747	18,328
El Kamlin	1,000	4,456	6,770	6,690	8,732
El Huda	—	—	5,277	5,288	7,945
Abu Ushar	—	—	—	7,590	7,689
El Masudiya	—	—	—	5,037	7,303
El Meheiriba	—	—	—	3,022	7,016
El Hosh	—	—	3,150	3,290	6,885
Tabat	—	—	—	4,891	6,815
El Cremet	—	—	—	—	6,235
El Messellamiya	—	3,228	5,523	4,628	5,978
El Mielig	—	—	—	3,491	5,294
Wad Ellebieh[a]	—	—	—	—	4,098
El Medina Arab[a]	—	—	3,102	3,895	4,081
(b) Close to the study region					
Greater Khartoum	—	253,600	438,900	799,800	—
Kosti	—	22,700	37,900	60,000	—
Duiem	—	12,300	15,900	26,800	—
Sennar el Medina	—	8,626	18,270	28,546	—
Rufa'a	—	9,505	15,228	15,228	20,750

Note: a—These were classified as towns by the 1983 Sudanese census but because their population was under 5,000, they are not in the category of 'small urban centre'.

Source: First Population Census 1955/56; Housing Surveys 1964/65; Preliminary Results of the Second Census 1973; Preliminary Results of the Third Census 1983.

inhabitants. For settlements with less than 5,000 inhabitants, most fall into the category either of a small village with 100-500 inhabitants or a large village with 500-1,000 inhabitants.

However, before proceeding with an attempt to link demographic change in the urban system (shown by changes in urban centres' populations and sex ratios) to economic, political or social developments, a word should be said about the statistical base. First, only preliminary census figures for 1983 were available. Secondly, demographic trends suggested by successive census data did not, on occasion, match local informants' perceptions. Examples of the possible under-enumeration of Wad Medani and El Hasaheisa are discussed later. Thirdly, local and regional government boundaries have changed considerably during the Seventies which means that the comparison of population data for successive censuses is often impos-

Table 3.9 *Population distribution among Area Councils in 1983*

Area Council	Total popn. 1983	% in towns	%in small & intermediate urban centres	Names of towns[a]
North Gezira	344,235	13.3	13.3	El Hasaheisa El Messellamiya El Meheiriba Abu Ushar, Tabat
Bahri El Gezira	202,005	10.6	10.6	El Kamlin El Mielig El Masudiya
West Gezira	401,177	13.6	12.5	El Managil El Huda El Cremet Wad Ellebieh
South Gezira	313,285	3.5	2.2	El Hosh El Medina Arab
24 El Qurrashi	166,229	13.0	13.0	24 El Qurrashi
Central Gezira	287,774	49.0	49.0	Wad Medani
Study Region	1,714,705	17.2	16.7	—

Note: a—All but El Medina Arab and Wad Ellebieh had more than 5,000 inhabitants in 1983; see Table 3.8 for more details.
Source: Preliminary Census Results, 1983.

sible. For instance, sub-provincial administrative areas were different in the 1973 and 1983 censuses; Table 3.9 gives population distribution in the six area councils which make up the study region, for 1983. Finally, with regard to figures for the population of urban centres, we suspect that, at least in certain instances, figures for urban centres' population do not reflect the population living in the agglomeration but population within boundaries which no longer accurately delimit the urban centres' built-up area.

The preliminary 1983 census figures differ greatly from those for 1980 given in the Gezira Village Guide and Directory. This Directory gives population estimates for every settlement in the study region with the exception of Wad Medani, El Managil and El Hasaheisa. These estimates were obtained from local authorities. Combining figures from this Directory and estimates for the populations of the three excluded urban centres puts the study region's population in 1980 at 2,050,732 (compared to the 1983 preliminary census figure of 1,714,705) while the population in small and intermediate urban centres was 820,545 (compared to the figure of 287,041 derived from the preliminary 1983 census figures). The Directory suggested that there were 77 urban centres in the study region (ie settlements with

5,000 or more inhabitants) compared to the 13 listed in the 1983 census. Fifty-five of these 77 urban centres had populations estimated at between 5,000 and 10,000 inhabitants. Finally, the Directory suggested that the population of Abu Ushar, El Kamlin, El Masudiya and El Meheiriba in 1980 was two or more times that suggested by preliminary results from the 1983 census.

Some degree of uncertainty in the population in different settlements is inevitable. One reason is the substantial seasonal migration of cotton pickers who journey in and out of the study region. Furthermore, for the Directory, many population estimates were rounded off to the nearest 1,000 and since local authorities did not have access to reliable counts, they may have pitched estimates on the high side or included some of the population in the settlement's hinterland since these population figures have been used for the allocation of sugar and other scarce commodities. Fieldwork within the study region suggests that the preliminary 1983 census figures are closer to reality.

The administrative hierarchy—and its relation to the urban system

The study region has had two distinct administration hierarchies since the Gezira Irrigation Scheme began: regional and local government; and the management of the Scheme itself. Although a description of the present structure of government and Gezira Board administration and their evolution over time might seem somewhat divorced from our concern with the development of the urban system, changes in these administrative structures have had a profound influence on developments within the study region's urban system.

As we noted earlier, Wad Medani is capital of one of the six regions into which the Sudan was divided in 1980. As capital of the Central Region, Wad Medani has a governor and deputy governor, regional ministers and a directly elected People's Regional Assembly. Regional governments have the power to raise both direct and indirect rates. The Central Region includes White Nile, Gezira and Blue Nile Provinces and encompasses more than a quarter of the national population and a high proportion of the nation's intensively farmed irrigated area. Quite apart from the Gezira Scheme and its Managil Extension, the Central Region also includes the Kenana Sugar Scheme and the northern part of the Rahad Scheme.

Below the regional government, there is a four-stage local government hierarchy; province, area, rural/town, and village/neighbourhood. With regard to the level of province, one should recall that the study region makes up about one-third of Gezira Province and contains most of its population. Wad Medani had been Gezira Province's capital before the new regional governments were formed, but its designation as capital of Central Region meant that Rufa'a became capital of Gezira Province. Rufa'a is just outside the study region on the east bank of the Blue Nile opposite El Hasaheisa (see Map 3.3).

The level below the province is the area. The study region is divided into six area councils: North Gezira (capital El Hasaheisa), Bahri El Gezira (capital El Kamlin), West Gezira (capital El Managil), South Gezira (capital El Hosh), 24 El Qurrashi (capital 24 El Qurrashi) and Central Gezira (capital Wad Medani). Area councils are important local government units which work under the supervision of the Provincial Commissioner.

The third level in the Central Region's government hierarchy, rural or town councils, have limited functions and powers delegated to them from area council level. Thus, an area council based at, say, El Hasaheisa or El Managil will supervise the activities of town and rural councils within their areas. Finally, below town and rural councils there are village and neighbourhood level councils. As will be examined in more detail later, there is a strong correlation between urban centres' rank defined by population size, and the administrative rank of urban centres defined by their role as centres for regional, provincial, area or town/rural governments.

It seems that it is the regional and the area levels of government which have the most power and the strongest funding base. The Central Region's government provides the entire funding for the provincial administrations and most of that for the area, town and rural councils. Town and rural councils do raise some revenue (for instance through market taxes and fees and house taxes) but these fall far short of their total expenditure. Thus, they depend on funding coming from regional government.

But Central Region's government is in turn heavily dependent on national government. In 1983/84, this level of government's recurrent expenditure was over LS110 million while its direct revenue was LS25 Million. This imbalance is likely to be lessened somewhat in 1984/85 when revenues derived from various taxes will be allocated directly to the regional governments. But more than half the regional governments' funding is still likely to come from central government.

The provincial administration appears to play a very minor role. Gezira Province's administration is based at Rufa'a and its annual budget was said to be of the order of only LS22,000 with its major role being that of inspecting and reporting on the activities of area councils.

Apart from the town council of Wad Medani, where 46 per cent of its expenditure was raised locally, other town councils are heavily dependent on the Central Region's government to cover their expenditure. Despite the decentralisation, national government still retains a lot of power. All major development projects which involve foreign funding agencies are dealt with by national government. The regional government's development budget in 1982/83 was relatively small (LS8.5 million budgeted of which LS7.9 million was paid out) and this was entirely financed by national government.

Then the irrigation scheme has its own administrative hierarchy which is quite distinct from that of local government. Its headquarters are in Barakat near Wad Medani. Irrigated areas are divided into divisions which are in turn divided into blocks. By 1980, there were 14 divisions and 107 blocks. Each block has a headquarters with an office, a warehouse for fertilisers and other supplies and staff housing. These headquarters are often sited outside the villages, especially in the original Gezira Scheme area. Block headquarters are located on the light Gezira railway.

Since the whole Irrigated Scheme is a national project, it comes under the authority of the Ministry of Agriculture (based in Khartoum, the national capital) and the Ministry of Irrigation (in Wad Medani) which is responsible for managing the Scheme.

Central places and their links with the urban system

A study of the location and concentration of retail stores and social, administrative and commercial services[21] showed that urban centres fall into three distinct categories. Their concentration in Wad Medani put it in a category of its own. This was hardly surprising, given the fact that its population in 1983 was more than four times that of the next largest urban centre. Wad Medani is the dominant administrative, commercial, industrial and financial centre in the study region.

Wad Medani's role as the most important administrative centre in the region was established at the beginning of the twentieth century when, under the Anglo-Egyptian Condominium Government it was designated capital of Blue Nile Province. Prior to this it had been the main Egyptian base in the Sudan after the Turco-Egyptian occupation in 1821, before the base was moved to Khartoum in 1833. As noted earlier, it became the capital of Gezira Province with the subdivision of the Sudan's nine provinces into 18 in 1971/72. Then it became capital of Central Region (with the capital of Gezira Province moving to Rufa'a) in 1980. The concentration of provincial and, more recently, regional government offices in Wad Medani and national government's initiatives to decentralise responsibilities and funds to sub-national levels of government between 1973 and 1983 have certainly played a major role in under-pinning its population growth. Firstly, this has meant a growing body of public officials with comparatively high and stable salaries who live in and around Wad Medani. The national Ministry of Irrigation is also located in Wad Medani and not in Khartoum, the national capital.[22]

Secondly, the expanding government apparatus and number of public employees inevitably creates or expands the demand for goods and services, a proportion of which is met by local firms. Thirdly, the fact that Wad Medani has been the dominant centre of government in the region for over 70 years has also meant that it became the chosen centre for publicly funded higher order services. The two most prominent examples are the region's only university and its largest hospital with 747 beds. Wad Medani also contains several other higher education institutions which attract students from the wider region.

Fourthly, the fact that Wad Medani was the most important administrative centre meant that it was favoured when inter-regional railways and roads were constructed. These four factors demonstrate the importance of government policies in influencing and shaping urban system's developments. The concentration of private sector manufacturing and of commercial and financial enterprises in Wad Medani has been powerfully influenced by the direct and indirect effects of its increasing concentration of publicly funded government administrators and services and by its location on major transport routes.

Wad Medani's role within the growth and development of the Irrigation Scheme was also important to its development. The Gezira Scheme's headquarters are in Barakat, a few kilometres away. The Gezira Agricultural Research station opened nearby in 1918. As noted earlier, cotton ginning industries developed at Meringan which is between Barakat and Wad Medani and Wad Medani has become the region's most important industrial centre.

Occupational data from the 1973 census gives some idea of the relative importance of the various activities in terms of employment. Community, social and personal services accounted for 26.8 per cent of the labour force with 15.5 per cent in wholesale and retail trade, 13.6 per cent in primary production, 10.9 per cent in electricity and water, 10.2 per cent in manufacturing, 8.0 per cent in transport and storage and 7.4 per cent in construction. Although it is rarely entirely clear which activities fit into which category, the high proportion of the workforce in community, social and personal service presumably reflects the concentration of government staff and health and educational facilities while, as noted earlier, the high proportion in electricity and water is presumably due to the location of the national Ministry of Irrigation there. The proportion working in wholesaling and retailing is no doubt boosted by the fact that Wad Medani is an important livestock market. Many animals brought from the West are sold in Wad Medani after a period of finishing on concentrated feed on plots on the outskirts of the town.

The proportion working in manufacturing appears low, although some of the labour force commutes daily from surrounding villages.

Table 3.10   *Annual average population growth rates for small and interme-diate urban centres*

Urban Centre	Annual Average 1955/56–1964/65	Population growth rate % 1964/65–1973	1973–83
Wad Medani	3.2	5.4	2.9
El Managil	—	9.5	9.0
24 El Qurrashi	—	—	17.3
El Hasaheisa	6.6	4.8	−0.2
El Kamlin	4.8	−0.1	2.7
El Huda	—	0.02	4.2
Abu Ushar	—	—	0.1
El Masudiya	—	—	3.8
El Meheiriba	—	—	8.8
El Hosh	—	0.5	7.3
Tabat	—	—	3.4
El Cremet	—	—	—
El Messellamiya	6.1	−1.9	2.6
El Mielig	—	—	4.3

Source: Derived from figures in Table 3.8.

The labour force in the textile factories in particular is drawn from surrounding villages with buses being sent daily to collect the workers. A significant proportion are women; for example 60 per cent of the workforce of the Wad Medani Textile Company, which employs 1,100 people, are women.

In addition to the administrative, transport and communications, commercial, financial, educational and industrial roles played by establishments within it which serve the whole region, Wad Medani also serves as a centre for wholesale and retail trade, higher education and administration for an area smaller than the whole study region with the extent of its influence being limited by comparable zones of influence from other major urban centres: Khartoum to the North, Sennar to the South and and El Managil to the West. In addition to its role as a regional capital, it is also the headquarters of the Western Area Council, one of the six area councils which cover the study region. Thus, it is surprising to find that its annual average population growth rate fell from 4.6 per cent between 1955/56 and 1973 to 2.9 per cent between 1973 and 1983. An estimate for 1980 had put its population at 163,774, much higher than the 1983 census figure of 141,065. This former figure would imply an annual average growth rate of 6.0 per cent between 1973 and 1980. Various local informants, questioned during a visit to Wad Medani in May 1984, suggested that the population was still growing rapidly and it may be that the 1983 census figure did not reflect the size of the agglomeration since it did not include population growth outside boundaries which no longer define the urban centre's built-up area.

Only El Hasaheisa and El Managil fall into the second category of urban centre in terms of location and concentration of retail stores and of social, administrative, professional and commercial services. Each of these urban centres contains a broad range of such services, although they lack the multiplicity and concentration of such services and of retail activities evident in Wad Medani. In terms of administrative rank, both are area council headquarters while within the Irrigation Scheme, El Managil is the main urban centre within the Managil Extension.

El Managil was no more than a village in 1958 when the Managil Extension was being developed. Its population grew in step with its increasing administrative and commercial importance; from 6,722 inhabitants in 1964/65 to 36,090 in 1983. As the headquarters of West Gezira Area Council (within which there are four town and seven rural councils) and the major centre of administration for the Managil Extension, it has become the seat of the various government departments and thus the home for a large group of government employees whose growth in numbers has stimulated the construction of offices and housing and the demand for goods and services. In 1956, it was the site of a market two days a week; by 1980 it had 240 permanent shops and nearly three times as many stalls. In the last ten years, it has gained two banks, a cinema and four factories. It has also become a centre for automobile repairs. Its growth has been further enhanced by the concentration of publicly funded health and education services there, including two higher secondary schools and a 106-bed hospital. Its population growth which averaged nine per cent or more a year between 1964/65 and 1983, mostly reflects its growing role as an administrative and market centre. It serves as an agricultural market and retail centre for areas beyond the study region, such as to the south outside the irrigated area where there is rainfed sorghum cultivation and livestock grazing. It is an important market centre for groundnuts and there are a number of decorticating plants close to the market area. There is limited industrial development; total employment in industrial plants such as the oil crushing mills, pasta factories, automated bakeries and furniture factory is unlikely to exceed 1,000 in 1984, although some new industrial plants are planned. As in many other urban centres, there are numerous small workshops. There are regular daily bus services to Wad Medani and to Khartoum over the unpaved tracks and many local services. No 1973 data on occupations were given in the census.

With regard to the 1983 census figures of 36,090 inhabitants, local informants suggest that this is likely to be more accurate than that for Wad Medani, although town council officials believed that by May 1984, El Managil's population had exceeded 40,000 which implies some under-enumeration in the 1983 census.

El Hasaheisa has a longer history than El Managil as an urban centre. It was originally established in 1908 by pastoralists looking for water and pasture. The construction of the Khartoum-Wad Medani railway through El Hasaheisa soon afterwards, its site on the Blue Nile and its strategic location with respect to rainfed dura production meant it developed as the major market for marketed dura, before the development of the irrigation scheme. The dura market declined as the Gezira Irrigated Scheme developed, but in 1927, the Anglo-Egyptian Condominium Government transferred the administrative headquarters of the northern part of the Gezira from El Messellamiya to El Hasaheisa. A cotton ginning factory was established in 1928. Thus, perhaps more than any other factor, it was El Hasaheisa's location on the new railway which allowed its development as a market and centre for cotton ginning and which made it an obvious choice as an administrative centre. In 1950, a ferry-boat service across the Blue Nile enhanced El Hasaheisa's role as it became the point of entry into the region for thousands of seasonal workers who came to work on the Gezira Scheme. The introduction of electric power in 1959 led to the growth of a light industrial area while the construction of the Khartoum-Wad Medani highway in 1969 made El Hasaheisa more accessible as a centre for retail trade to settlements on or close to this road.

El Hasaheisa was a district headquarters prior to the changes in local government structure in the mid-Seventies, while in the 1983 census, it is the headquarters of the North Gezira Area Council with jurisdiction over five town and seven rural councils. In terms of public services and facilities, El Hasaheisa has permanent branches of the Sudanese Savings Bank and the Bank of Khartoum. An industrial school, a teacher training college and four other higher secondary education institutions have been set up in El Hasaheisa since the early Seventies; it also contains nine secondary and 11 primary schools. The study region's third largest hospital (with 138 beds) was established there in the early Sixties. There are also three courts and a police station, a cinema and a soccer stadium and, as noted earlier, seven ginning factories, a textile mill with around 2,000 employees (although many of these come from surrounding villages and from Rufa'a) and various other industries and workshops. With regard to retail trade, a survey in 1980 counted 419 shops and 553 kiosks.

The 1983 census figure for El Hasaheisa's population presents even more of a puzzle than that for Wad Medani, for it implies that El Hasaheisa's total population declined slightly between 1973 and 1983. Local informants find this difficult to believe. El Mustafa (1983) in a doctoral thesis based on a study of El Hasaheisa quotes a 1978 population of 30,112 inhabitants obtained from the northern Gezira statistics office at El Hasaheisa council. In May 1984, the town council estimated the population to be around 22,000. The Gezira Guide and Handbook quotes a 1980 estimate at 27,278. Although there is no evidence of El Hasaheisa actually losing population between 1973 and 1983, it seems that its importance within the study region's urban system may have declined. Its grain and livestock markets are said to have diminished in importance, with those of Wad Medani, 40 km to the south on the main road, gaining importance. In addition, it has been suggested that Rufa'a, an urban centre, which is outside the study region and is linked to El Hasaheisa by a six km road and a ferry across the Blue Nile, is drawing urban activities away from it. Rufa'a's population 20,750 according to the 1983 census. However, it seems that Rufa'a serves primarily as an independent centre with activities located there serving the eastern districts of Gezira Province (ie outside the study region). Like El Hasaheisa, it also had a medium size hospital (148 beds), two bank branches, a cinema, and many schools.

Occupational data from the 1973 census showed that 32.9 per cent of El Hasaheisa's labour force worked in primary production (virtually all in agriculture), with 25.2 per cent in manufacturing, 15.6 per cent in community, social and personal services, 7.9 per cent in wholesale and retail trade, 6.3 per cent in transport and storage, 3.4 per cent in construction and 2.3 per cent in electricity and water. Thus, compared to Wad Medani, there is a much higher proportion of the labour force working in agriculture and manufacturing. The size of the cotton ginning factories and the large textile industry help explain the relative size of manufacturing. El Hasaheisa's importance as a centre for trade with village bus services linking it to much of the northern part of the scheme is seen in the fact that 14.2 per cent of the labour force in 1973 worked in wholesale and retail plus transport and storage. The low proportion working in electricity and water reflects the fact that the irrigation headquarters for the Northern Gezira are in Abu Ushar, not El Hasaheisa. El Mustafa in a 1978 survey of 2,850 workers found that around two-thirds were employed in the public sector, although no figures exist to divide these between administration, productive activities and social services.

Fourteen other urban centres were identified as containing significant concentrations of retail stores and social, administrative and commercial services, but with much lower concentrations than El Hasaheisa and El Managil.

These 14 centres included all the urban centres listed in Table 3.8 apart from Wad Medani, El Hasaheisa and El Managil (which have been discussed already) and Mieleg, El Cremet and Wad Ellebieh which had too low a concentration of such stores and services to be included. It also included four other settlements not listed in this table: El Ribie, Wad Raiya, Wad Rabie and Abu Guta, but unfortunately, population statistics are not available for these since they were not regarded as urban centres in the censuses up to 1983.

Retail activities in these 14 centres were almost exclusively for lower order goods; drapers, fruit and vegetable stores, butchers, tailors and general stores were the most common examples. They also serve as markets for produce such as vegetables, grain, goats and sheep for local consumption. Most of these centres had a higher secondary school or a small hospital with between 25 and 82 beds. Abu Ushar has the region's second largest hospital with 242 beds; it is also the only centre among them with a chemist. The spatial distribution of the centres shows remarkable regularity. The mean distance between each centre and its nearest neighbour (or Wad Medani, El Hasaheisa or El Managil) is 35.2 km with a standard deviation of only 2.64 km. In terms of administrative role, three (24 El Qurrashi, El Kamlin and El Hosh) are area council headquarters while all are headquarters for rural councils, which means they are the administrative head-quarters for a number of villages (usually between 30 and 45).

The origins of many of these 14 centres arose from strategic location on transport routes. Three of the largest (El Kamlin, Abu Ushar and El Masudiya) are on or close to the railway and highway linking Khartoum and Wad Medani. We noted on page 91 how one of them, El Messellamiya, lost importance, relative to other urban centres in the region, when it was bypassed by the railway.

Fieldwork in 1982 in these 14 centres found a high proportion of closed shops. For instance, in El Mehereiba, out of 127 shops in the market area, 91 were closed. In Abu Guta, 82 out of 153 shops, were closed. In Abu Ushar, 61 of its 70 shops were closed, while in El Huda, 68 of the 132 shops were closed. Three factors help explain this. Perhaps the most important is the increasing mobility of the consumer which has allowed many purchases formerly made in these centres to be made in intermediate urban centres such as Wad Medani and El Managil. At least up to the Seventies, the absence of all-weather roads and road vehicles had compelled most farmers to u. ' markets which could be reached on foot or by animal. More recently, better roads and more automobiles and lorries have allowed them to go direct to larger centres which have cheaper prices and a wider range of goods and services. The effect of improved transport links is clearly seen in the case of Abu Ushar, which in 1982 had only nine shops in operation compared to a total of 70 shops operating in the early Sixties. Abu Ushar owed its initial development to its location on the railway and then to the construction there of the region's second largest hospital (with 242 beds) in the early Forties. When the Khartoum-Wad Medani road was built in 1969, it lost many of its customers to El Hasaheisa. One village which had been within its zone of influence, El Talbab, was moved some 32 km so that it was sited just by the new road. Today, this village's inhabitants rarely visit Abu Ushar's market.

A second factor in shop closures in the smaller urban centres has been changes in income and consumption expenditure. The 1969 household survey showed that disposable income and consumer expenditure had increased, especially expenditure on durable household goods. Increasing demand for, for instance, clothes, radios, and furniture brought more benefits to enterprises in urban centres such as Wad Medani since it was here that stores selling these goods were based. The continuance of periodic markets is a third factor which helps to weaken the economic base of small urban centres. Owners of permanent retail stores in such centres have to compete with itinerant traders who travel from periodic market to periodic market in villages; better transport systems have tended to help these itinerant traders more than permanent retail outlets in small urban centres.

Below these three categories of central places, settlements generally fall into two other broad categories: large villages with between 500 and 1,000 inhabitants and small villages with 100-500 inhabitants. There are some 700 small villages dispersed over the irrigated areas. Not surprisingly, in a region almost fully irrigated and intensively cultivated with a carefully ordered hierarchy of canals, these villages are regularly distributed with a mean distance between each village and its neighbouring settlement of 3.04 km and a standard deviation of only 0.62 km. Most small villages are located at intervals along the canals or the Gezira light railway or the main railway line. Most do not even have a shop and the only common service found there are primary schools. These villages grew and developed to provide tenants with easy access to their lands.

The small villages usually have a satellite relationship with the 200 or more larger villages whose spatial distribution is more irregular. Large villages often owe their larger size to the location of some publicly-funded service there such as a lower secondary school or a dispensary or to the fact that the Gezira Board has inspection offices there. The mean distance between a larger village and its nearest neighbour is 10.48 km with a standard deviation of 3.04 km. In the south and central parts of the region, these larger villages tend to be closer together while in the north, where rainfall is more scarce and larger patches of uncultivable soil occur, they tend to be further away from each other. In addition to large and small villages, there are the labour camps largely inhabited by share-croppers and resident labourers. Different sources give widely differing estimates as to their numbers, depending on the extent to which they are counted with the villages to which they are linked. The estimate given earlier of some 710 such camps in 1980 is thought to be the most accurate.

Factors underpinning the growth of small and intermediate urban centres

Since the beginning of the Scheme (or indeed before the Scheme began) until today, most of the study region's population derived most or all of its income from agriculture and livestock. Thus, the scale of disposable income generated by these and its distribution among those deriving an income from them are factors of great importance to the level of demand for enterprises selling goods or services, including urban-based enterprises. The other sources of income for the study region's population are: employment in the management of the Gezira Scheme, employment in local government (administration, municipal services such as garbage collection and social services such as health and education); employment in industrial enterprises (some private, some public) providing goods for sale outside the region and employment in enterprises providing goods and services to those deriving incomes from previously mentioned sources. In the last 20 years or so, remittances sent to households in the study region by those working outside have also become important sources of income for many households. Apart from these, there do not seem to be other important sources of income for the study region's population.

Based on the data presented already, it is possible to make some comments about the scale of 'disposable income' available to the study region's population since 1925 and its distribution. Then some comments can be made as to the extent to which this income is spent on goods or services provided by enterprises within the region and the extent to which these are located in different urban centres.

To take first the period 1925-1955, clearly the vast majority of the population derived a living from agriculture and livestock. As the figures in Table 3.2 demonstrate, at least up to 1948, the average profit per tenancy was very low. In some years, tenants made no profit at all. Cotton yields per hectare were usually much lower than had been anticipated when the Scheme was started. So too were prices paid for the cotton on the world market. Although the whole scheme operated with profits to the management company (the Sudan Plantations Syndicate) and considerable benefits to the national (colonial) government, the tenants 'seemed to be little more than labourers on their own land, cogs in the cotton production machine' (Gaitskell, 1959). Thus, much of the income deriving from the production of crops for sale went outside the region – to the national government and the shareholders in the Sudan Plantations Syndicate. Furthermore, the tenants provided most of their food needs through raising livestock and subsistence crops, so they spent little or no income on food. There is no data on the level of income for agricultural labourers, ie from those with no land of their own to farm (whether permanently resident in the study region or coming into the region only for cotton-picking). But if tenants' incomes were low and if there was a plentiful supply of such labour (which seems to have been the case), the incomes earned by agricultural labourers were probably even lower than that of the tenants. After all, the tenants could be regarded as the elite group working in agriculture since at least they had access to cultivable irrigated farmland with their payment for that farmland based only on their cotton production under the Joint Account System. Thus, the level of income generated for those living in the study region and working in agriculture was generally very low. So there was little demand for the kinds of goods and services commonly sold by enterprises in small urban centres to those earning an income from commercial agriculture. It is hardly surprising that only two urban centres with 5,000 or more inhabitants were recorded in the 1955/56 census.

It was in these two urban centres, Wad Medani and El Hasaheisa, that the forward and backward linkages with agricultural production were concentrated. The supply of inputs to the farmers and the transport of their produce to the ginning factories was organised by the Sudan Plantations Syndicate from their main office in Barakat, near Wad Medani. The supply of seeds, agricultural chemicals and credit, and the storing and transport of goods to and from the farmers were controlled from Barakat on a light railway system which was essentially used only to service farmers, not to provide a region-wide transport system for people and other goods. Most of the staff associated with the management of the Scheme lived at Barakat or Wad Medani or at the headquarters of each block; these headquarters were usually sited away from existing settlements. The cotton ginning factories were the most important forward linkages with agriculture and these were located at El Hasaheisa and at Meringan, close to Wad Medani. This centralised control of the whole production system prevented the development of the kinds of activities which frequently develop in small urban centres to serve commercial farming operations in their surrounding areas. Up to 1955 there were no other major industries apart from the cotton ginning factories. And there was very little support for social services such as education and health (which are often located in urban centres) either from the management company or from the national government. Nor was there any evidence of government support for investment in infrastructure to support urban development such as water supply or provision for the hygienic removal of household and human wastes, or for road construction.

Between 1955 and 1983, the most important change in terms of new sources of support for urban-based employment was public sector support for stronger local government, for improved social services and for administration. But incomes for those working in agriculture do not seem to have increased much (if at all), even though more than three-quarters of the study region's population continued to derive their living direct from farming.[23]

Tenants' income did not increase substantially, except in the occasional exceptional year when world prices for cotton were high and cotton yields were good. The principle of a three-way split in the net proceeds from cotton between management, the national government and the tenants did not change until 1980/81, although the tenants did come to receive a slightly higher share in this division. But the national government continued to take a significant proportion of the 'surplus' generated by cotton production which did not support incomes for people in the study region. National government not only received its share of the net proceeds from cotton export but also revenues from export taxes on cotton and other products and duties on machinery and other imported inputs. A World Bank estimate put the Gezira Scheme's contribution in the early Sixties to the national income from the modern sector (then about half the total national income), to foreign exchange earnings and to public finance at around 30 per cent. Although the exact balance between this 'surplus' exported from the region and funds returning to the region through national government investment or support for public sector activities there is not known, existing data suggests a large net export of money out of the region. Some large factories were set up in the study region between 1955 and 1981, some funded by state corporations, but they did not create many jobs.

With the introduction of new cash crops and a more intensive crop production system in the early Seventies, some tenants' net incomes might have risen a little; there is no data to show the extent to which the production of new cash crops like wheat or groundnuts increased tenants' total incomes, although their contribution to tenants' incomes is known to have increased considerably. The Sudan Gezira Board undertakes an annual survey of crop costs and returns for a sample of tenants but this excludes vegetable gardens and livestock and does not differentiate between crops produced by tenants and those produced by sharecroppers. There is little indication of substantial rises in tenants' real income during the Sixties and early Seventies and some indication of a fall in real incomes in the late Seventies. The figures in Table 3.7 show that tenants' average income between 1976/77 and 1980/81 was roughly half that of an unskilled labourer working for the Sudan Gezira Board in 1981. One also recalls that in 1981/82, only 5 per cent of tenants are reported to have made a profit. Early results since the change from the Joint Account System to Land and Water charges and since the beginning of the Rehabilitation Scheme appear promising. The period 1981/2-1983/4 saw a year by year increase in cotton yields per hectare, reversing the declining trend evident in the late Seventies; average tenant incomes also grew. However, the aggregate picture hides substantial variations within the Scheme and the centralisation of decision-making and of control over land use, and input supply is likely to be inhibiting the development of activities based in small urban centres throughout the Scheme.

No data exists as to trends in incomes for the agricultural labourer between 1955 and 1984—whether working as a paid labourer for a tenant or as a sharecropper or a mixture of the two. But two facts suggest that agricultural labourers' incomes did not rise. The first is the unwillingness of tenants to give up their rights to a tenancy but their preference for hiring labour to undertake most or all of the work on their tenancy; the second is the lack of evidence for a large group of seasonal migrants deciding to stay permanently because an adequate living can be made from working as an agricultural labourer. In recent years, the fact that the study region's population seems to have grown more slowly than the national average and the fact that there has been a decline in the number of seasonal migrants both support the suggestion that permanent agricultural labourers' income are not high.

In this period, there are few signs of a growth in backward linkages associated with agriculture in small urban centres. The Sudan Gezira Board, like its predecessor, the Sudan Plantations Syndicate, remained the sole supplier of fertilisers, of credit and of herbicides and insecticides for cotton and wheat. It remained responsible for the storing, transport and processing of the main cash crop (cotton) from the farms to the final market. As in the period 1925-1955, these were not functions which helped expand and diversify the employment and economic base of small urban centres (or proto-centres) since the organisation and distribution of such goods and services was done through the Board's own management hierarchy and transport system which bore little relation to the emerging urban system.

The increase in the number of staff at the Sudan Gezira Board and at the Ministry of Irrigation to manage the Managil Extension (on which construction began in the late Fifties) certainly provided a substantial proportion of the new jobs which underpinned rapid population growth in the urban centres of El Managil and 24 El Qurrashi. But this was not so important in urban centres within the original Gezira Scheme since this administration and management network was already in place by 1950. Apart from the creation of new jobs in the Sudan Gezira Board and the Ministry of Irrigation (which in theory were paid for by the Board's and the Government's share in net cotton proceeds up to 1981/2 and since then by Land and Water charges levied from tenants), the other main sources of new urban-based jobs in the period 1955-1984 seem to have been: those employed in local government administration; municipal services (such as garbage collection, electricity and water supply); social services (such as health and education); and public sector factories.

It is important to distinguish between the new public sector urban-based jobs which had to be funded from government revenues and those which existed because people paid for their products or services. To take first the new public sector jobs which were funded from local government budgets, there was a substantial increase in educational and health services between 1955 and 1984; pages 102-3 described the growth in the number of schools and medical facilities and the concentration of higher education institutions and hospitals in Wad Medani, El Hasaheisa and El Managil. More than a quarter of Wad Medani's and 15.6 per cent of El Hasaheisa's labour force was reported to be engaged in 'community, social and personal service' in 1973 and much of this was likely to be public sector social and municipal services. In El Hasaheisa, the town council is reported to be the largest employer if one combines teachers and hospital staff with staff involved in administration and municipal services. El Mustafa (1978) in a survey of 2,850 workers in El Hasaheisa found that 65 per cent were public sector employees. Clearly, if the expansion of such public sector employment was such an important factor in expanding urban-based employment between 1955 and 1984, constraints on its further expansion arising from limited local government budgets will be an important factor in future prospects for the expansion of urban-based employment.

Public sector jobs in industry are, in theory, somewhat different in that they do not draw on local government revenues. The period 1955-1984 did see the introduction of several new large public sector industrial enterprises such as textile factories which utilised locally grown cotton to produce goods for a market which stretched beyond the study region. But these did not create more than a few thousand jobs in the study region and most of these large factories were located in or close to Wad Medani or El Hasaheisa. There is also evidence of a notable increase in smaller (mostly private sector) industries producing goods for the study region's market although, again, the total number of jobs these created was relatively small—and these industrial plants are concentrated in Wad Medani, El Hasaheisa and El Managil. There has also been a growth in retail trade and in small-scale workshops (for instance repairing machines or making furniture or horse-drawn carts). But for most of the new shops or workshops or industrial enterprises or professional services which have grown up in Wad Medani, El Hasaheisa and El Managil over the last 10-20 years, it is virtually impossible to separate the demand for these generated by those deriving an income from agriculture, or industry, or working in the Sudan Gezira Board, or working in some public sector job, or from remittances sent back to households from family members working outside the study region. Given the trends in agriculture and the expansion of the public sector, it seems likely that much of this increase in demand has not come from the majority of the population who work in agriculture. We noted earlier the extent of shop closures in small urban centres. This might not only be due to the rural population's improved accessibility to the intermediate urban centres such as Wad Medani but also because of the rise in demand created by the increase in the number of public sector employees based in intermediate urban centres.

Low incomes for the rural and agricultural population will go hand in hand with little or no growth in employment in enterprises selling goods or services to this population. Of course, urban centres' employment base might expand if they attract enterprises which sell goods and services outside the region. But there is little evidence of this, apart from some boost to the growth of El Managil from enterprises based there selling goods and services to people to the south of the irrigated area engaged in rain-fed dura cultivation and the raising of livestock, and some boost to the economy of El Masudiya from industries whose products seem destined for the market in Greater Khartoum.

In terms of the factors underlying the development of specific urban centres, the influence of irrigated agriculture can be seen most clearly in the fact that the four largest settlements in 1955/56 (including the only two with more than 5,000 inhabitants) were within the boundaries of the then developed irrigated area. At this point, the Managil Extension had not been developed. By 1964/65, the fourth and sixth largest urban centres (El Managil and El Huda) were in the new Managil Extension while by 1973 it had the third and sixth largest and by 1983 the second, third and sixth. El Managil and 24 El Qurrashi could only develop as substantial concentrations of population and non-agricultural economic activities after the development of irrigated farmland around them, when the Managil Extension was constructed. The proportion of the study region's population living in the Managil extension also rose rapidly: from an estimated 11.3 per cent in 1964/65 to 22.9 per cent in 1983.

The influence of the administrative hierarchy can be seen in the close correlation between the list of urban centres ranked by population size and the administrative hierarchy. Wad Medani has been the largest urban centre and the highest ranking administrative centre since 1925, even if its administrative role has changed from that of capital of Blue Nile Province to capital of Gezira Province to capital of the Central Region. Wad Medani, El Managil, 24 El Qurrashi, El Hasaheisa, El Kamlin and El Hosh, are the headquarters of area councils and these rank first, second, third, fourth, fifth and tenth respectively in population. But it is difficult to separate cause and effect in that the headquarters of area councils would tend to go to the largest urban centre within their boundaries.

The reason for El Hosh's small population relative to its administrative status was investigated. One reason is its location within the Southern part of the Gezira in a clay area which makes roads almost impassable in the wet season. And it did not become an important centre for administration and for higher order public services until the Seventies. In addition, a relatively large village, El Haj Abdallah is close by. This became the headquarters of a rural council, when previously it had been within the rural council for which El Hosh was the rural headquarters. So in addition to three primary schools, two secondary schools are located there to serve the population in its own rural council area. El Haj Abdallah is also a railway station and on the paved road between Sennar (an intermediate urban centre just outside the southern boundary of the study region) and Wad Medani, so its market is better placed than that of El Hosh on the transport network. El Hosh's proximity to Sennar also suggests that people living in and around it with the income to spend on higher order goods or services would tend to go to Sennar – or Wad Medani. However, one notes the relatively rapid population growth El Hosh experienced between 1973 and 1983 compared to the period 1964/65-1973. One reason for this may be the establishment there of one of the study region's six area councils in the late Seventies.

The influence of the development of transport infrastructure can also be seen in the correlation between the spatial distribution of urban centres and the development first of the railway and then the tarred road from Khartoum to Wad Medani and on to Sennar. In 1955, the three largest of the four settlements recognised as towns by the census were on this railway line and the fourth was close to it. In 1973, the first, second, fourth, fifth and seventh largest urban centres were either on the railway or on the new tarred road or both, while in 1983 this had changed to the first, fourth, fifth, seventh and eighth. It is interesting to note that if one considers only urban centres in the Gezira Scheme (ie excluding those in the Managil Extension), all the largest urban centres in 1925, 1955/56, 1964/65, 1973 and 1983 have all been on this one railway or road transport axis.

Some suggestions can be put forward as to the social, economic and political forces which help explain individual urban centres' movements up or down the list of urban centres ranked by population size over the period 1955-1983. However, the lack of data on, say, crop yields over time in different agricultural blocks or areas, or in changes in public expenditure for administrative personnel, for those working in social services (predominantly health and education), for those working in the Sudan Gezira Board and for those working in publicly-owned productive activities ensure that these are, at best, tentative. If we take the rank of urban centres in the region's urban system at different dates (as shown in Table 3.8) and changes in annual average population growth rates (shown in Table 3.10), the social, economic and political forces underpinning Wad Medani's dominance have already been described in considerable detail. Wad Medani's relatively low annual average growth rate for the period 1973-1983 is not easily explained but, as noted earlier, local informants suggest a considerable under-enumeration for its total population in 1983 or a population count within boundaries which excluded population concentrations which function as part of Wad Medani.

The rise of El Managil and of 24 El Qurrashi up the rank of urban centres and their very rapid annual average growth rates reflect their development as centres for commerce and trade and for administration as the new Managil Extension was developed. As noted earlier, 24 El Qurrashi's development has also been stimulated by the location there of the headquarters for the Ministry of Irrigation for that area. El Hasaheisa's decline from second to fourth largest urban centre within the study region and an actual (although slight) decline in population between 1973 and 1983 is not easily explainable although, as noted earlier, there are reasons to suggest that the 1983 census figure for its population may be too low.

Abu Ushar's very low average annual population growth rate between 1973 and 1983 is best explained by improved transport links undermining its role as a centre of trade and commerce for its surrounding population. Fieldwork in 1982 found that only nine shops were open compared to a total of 70 operating in the early Sixties. We noted earlier how the construction of the Khartoum–Wad Medani all-weather road allowed much of the local population to go direct to El Hasaheisa.

The reasons behind El Hosh's relatively low rank in the urban system but relatively rapid population growth between 1973 and 1983 have been discussed already. El Messellamiya's relative decline must be due, in some part, to its much earlier loss of commercial importance as the slave trade was suppressed early in the twentieth century and nearby El Hasaheisa developed as the main commercial and administrative centre in that area with first the railway and then the tarred Khartoum to Wad Medani road passing through it.

El Kamlin's relatively stable rank in terms of population size within the urban system is linked to its administrative role while that of El Masudiya is linked to the location of some industries there, due mainly to demand in Greater Khartoum, and to people who work in Greater Khartoum but live in (and commute from) El Masudiya.

From Table 3.11, it is evident that urban centres usually have more males than females. By contrast, there are usually more women than men in rural areas. In 1983 preliminary census data for the whole of Gezira Province, there were 99.3 men to 100 women, and sex ratios of between 89 and 98 men to 100 women are common in rural areas. The higher proportion of men to women in urban centres usually arises from a higher net in-migration to urban centres by males compared to females.

This is most clearly seen in El Hasaheisa's sex ratio of 121 for 1964/65, 143 for 1973 and 126 for 1983, which is largely the result of male in-migration in response to employment opportunities in the

Table 3.11   *Sex ratios in small and intermediate urban centres (males per 100 females)*

Urban centre	Sex ratio 1964/65	Sex ratio for people over 17 1964/65	Sex ratio 1973	Sex ratio 1983
Wad Medani	115	114	117	115
El Managil	110	117	107	104
24 El Qurrashi	—	—	129	103
El Hasaheisa	121	142	143	126
El Kamlin	96	84	96	97
El Huda	108	—	108	97
Abu Ushar	—	—	106	91
El Masudiya	—	—	107	106
El Meheiriba	—	—	107	95
El Hosh	104	138	111	100
Tabat	—	—	107	108
El Cremet	—	—	—	104
El Messellamiya	97	77	100	93
El Mielig	—	—	114	117

Source: 1964/65 Housing Surveys and Preliminary Results from the 1973 and 1983 Censuses.

urban centre's cotton ginning factories. The sex ratio for El Hasaheisa was particularly imbalanced for older age groups. In 1964/65, the sex ratio for people over 17 years of age was 143 while in the 1973 census, it was 177 for people over 19. There is a relatively strong correlation between urban centres' annual average population growth rates between 1964/65 and 1973 and the proportion of males to females. However, the notable exception is El Managil's relatively balanced sex ratio of 107 for 1973, despite an annual average population growth rate of 9.5 per cent between 1964/65 and 1973. It would seem that El Managil's rapid population growth in this period was largely due to its growing role as administrative and commercial centre for the Managil Extension, which implies in-migration of households rather than single males as in the case of El Hasaheisa in response to employment opportunities in the ginning factories. However, there was no obvious correlation between the proportion of males to females in each urban centre in 1983 and their annual average population growth rates between 1973 and 1983. Nor was there any obvious correlation between changes in sex ratio and annual average population growth rates.

El Messellamiya and El Kamlin are notable for having relatively balanced sex ratios for 1964/65 and for 1973; in the case of El Kamlin, there were more females than males in both years. Figures for the 1964/65 census show that both these urban centres had substantially more females than males over 17 years in the older age groups. For people over 17 years of age on this date, the sex ratio in El Kamlin was 84 while in El Messellamiya it was 77, unlike Wad Medani, El Hasaheisa, El Managil, El Huda, El Medina Arab and El Hosh (the only other urban centres for which such statistics were available). It is worth noting that El Kamlin and El Messellamiya are the urban centres with the closest and easiest transport links with El Hasaheisa, which suggests that migration of adult males from these urban centres to El Hasaheisa to work in factories is one reason for their low proportion of adult males to females.

Sources

This chapter is based on a longer report 'The Role of Small and Intermediate Centres in the Development of the Gezira, Sudan' directed by Professor Omer M.A. El Agraa (who edited this report) and Professor Ian Haywood of the Sudanese Group for the Assessment of Human Settlements of the Department of Architecture, University of Khartoum, the Sudan. Ali M. El Hassan (Economist), Babiker A.A. Rahman (Geographer), Mohammed O. El Sammani (Geographer), Salih A. El Arifi (Geographer) and Hassan M. Salih (Social Studies) contributed to this report, which is available through the Department of Architecture, University of Khartoum, P.O. Box 321, Khartoum, the Sudan or from IIED, 3 Endsleigh Street, London WC1H ODD.

Since the intention of this chapter is to condense the findings of this longer report, those interested in more detail and in an exhaustive bibliography should go to the report on which this is based.

Figures for 1955/56 and for 1973 are based on major censuses. Figures for 1964/65 are based on relatively reliable population and housing surveys which were undertaken in urban centres in the Gezira Scheme. Figures for 1980 are based on estimates drawn from the *Gezira Village Guide and Directory* which were based on the number of homes and consumption figures for rationed food supplies which were provided by local authorities. Figures for 1983 are preliminary census results.

Notes

1 Under colonial rule, the Sudan was divided into nine provinces with the study region being in Blue Nile Province. Wad Medani, the study region's largest urban centre, was the provincial capital. In 1971, as part of a major reform of local government, the nine provinces were subdivided to make a total of 18 provinces; the study region being in the new Gezira Province with Wad Medani being the provincial capital. In 1979/80 there were further reorganisations of local government. The 1980 Regional Government Act established five regions in the north of the Sudan (in addition to what was then the Southern Region). The study

region was in the new Central Region with Wad Medani as the region's capital. The capital of Gezira Province moved from Wad Medani to Rufa'a, an urban centre to the east of the study region, across the Blue Nile from El Hasaheisa (see Map 3.1).

2 Most of Egypt is uninhabited desert because of very low rainfall. More than 90 per cent of the national population live in the Nile Delta and Valley since here water supply is assured. Thus, in the late nineteenth century, Egypt's economy and the livelihood of most of its population depended on a sufficient supply of water from the Nile and it was this supply that was thought to be threatened by the French initiative. The importance to Egypt of water flow from the Nile can be seen in the need for successive agreements to be made between Egypt and the Sudan as to the amount the Sudan is allowed to withdraw from the Blue and White Niles.

3 Gaitskell (1959) notes that British advisers in Cairo, Egypt retained strict control of irrigation developments in the Sudan. The completion of the Aswan Dam (1902) on Egypt's southern border (which allowed the storing of flood water for release during the lower water period) and the raising of its height (1912) eased the problem of insufficient water flow during the low period. This allowed the approval of more than just experimental perennial irrigation schemes in the Sudan. In 1905, permission was given for pump irrigation, but only for the period 15 July to the end of February. The first proposal for the Gezira was a diversion barrage to irrigate 42,000 hectares from the flood; the fact that the Nile experienced its lowest discharge for 180 years in 1913 together with the increase in area of the planned irrigation scheme in the Gezira meant the change to a planned storage dam at Sennar, with surplus flood water used to fill the reservoir.

4 In a meeting in 1913 between the Prime Minister, Mr Asquith and the British Cotton Growing Association (which had shares in the Sudan Plantation Syndicate which managed the Gezira Scheme between 1925 and 1950). Mr Asquith stated that 'it is a matter of interest not only to Lancashire but to the whole of Great Britain and the whole of the Empire, that we should both multiply our possible sources of raw cotton and enlarge the area from which it is grown. Being as we are so largely interested, not only in the cotton industry here, but in the development of the Sudan, we approach the consideration of such a plan as that which you have laid before us with sympathy and indeed with the utmost possible prepossession in its favour.' (Gaitskell, 1959)

5 Throughout this section, figures for areas are given in feddans, the traditional measure used in the Sudan and in hectares; a feddan is assumed to be equivalent to 1.038 acres and 0.42 hectares. Weights are given in kantars, the traditional Sudanese unit of weight and kilograms. One kantar of cotton is taken as the equivalent of 315 lbs of unginned cotton which in turn is taken as the equivalent of 143 kilograms.

6 The word 'Experimental' had been dropped from its name in 1907.

7 Expenses such as fertilisers, insecticides and the ginning and marketing of cotton were deducted first.

8 The Graduate's Congress was a nationalistic, anti-colonial movement begun by the Sudanese intelligensia during the Thirties.

9 Estimates for the number of tenants vary from 96,000 to 110,000. One reason for the variation is probably that the higher estimates include the tenants in two blocks on the east bank of the Blue Nile.

10 Most Gezira tenancies have now been subdivided to form 8.4 hectare tenancies, making them closer in size to those in the Managil extension. With 97,000 tenants and around 880,000 hectares of irrigated land, the size of the average tenancy is thus around 9 hectares, which supports the idea that most Gezira tenancies are half the size of the original 40 feddan (16.8 hectare) tenancies.

11 In 1970, tenants' share did briefly fall from 48 to 47 per cent with the agreement of the Tenants Union so that the Social Development Fund's allocation could be increased from two to three per cent.

12 Average official rate of exchange in 1979 was 1 LS = 2.35 US$ although the market rate was lower.

13 Up to 1980, only the Egyptian type long staple cotton was grown; the American medium staple variety has now been introduced in the South and Centre which gives a higher yield for a lower use of irrigation water, although the crop is less valuable and thus fetches a lower price.

14 For cotton, assumed yields after the implementation of the Rehabilitation Scheme are 5 kantars per feddan for Extra Long Staple Cotton.

15 This process, whereby the cotton fibres are separated from the seeds, greatly reduces the volume of the cotton before it is transported.

16 At a seminar in 1981, mean values for DDT in cow's milk were 0.23 ppm (World Health Organisation/Food and Agriculture Organisation standards in 1969 set the acceptable limit at 0.05 ppm) while concentrations as high as 1.3 ppm have been recorded. Water from surface wells and canals were found to contain 0.2 and 0.16-1.2 micrograms/litre respectively. Maximum acceptable levels in the USA are as low as 0.001 micrograms per litre.

17 National Health Programme 1977/78-1983/84, Khartoum University Press, 1975.

18 These figures come from the *Gezira Village Guide and Directory*, 1981, which include all settlements in the study region except Wad Medani, El Managil and El Hasaheisa, in 1983, the first, second and fourth most populous urban centres. Thus, it will understate the number of services and facilities. But it is interesting to note that 35 per cent of the television sets were in the North Division, the Division closest to Khartoum, the national capital, although this division only contains 10 per cent of the region's population. This reflects the fact that there are some relatively rich households there who commute to Khartoum – although it is also partially due to the fact that this was the area which first received television transmissions.

19 As noted in Table 3.1, this included all settlements with 5,000 or more inhabitants plus El Medina Arab with 4,081 and Wad Ellebieh with 4,098.

20 The population of Gezira Province was recorded in the 1973 census as 1,865,499 but figures are not available for the sub-provincial administrative units and it is not clear whether this figure is fully comparable with the preliminary 1983 estimate for the province of 2,025,215. If it

was, it would imply an average annual population growth rate for the province of 0.8 per cent which seems unrealistically low in view of no evidence of major net out-migration in this period from the study region.

21 Central Place Scores were calculated by the following method. Each place's score was based on the functional index of centrality (FIC), a relationship of the number of points of outlet of the following functions and services between the place and the study region:

— Retail: grocer, greengrocer, general store, draper, bakery, butcher, carpenter, blacksmith, barber, laundry, restaurant, coffee shop, tailor, joiner, mechanic, animal market, grain market, cinema, fueling station, domestic appliances.

— Commercial Services: bank and insurance companies.

— Social Services: schools, university, hospital, social service centre, water supply, electricity, ministry headquarters.

— Administrative Services: rural council, town council, police station.

$$\text{FIC} = \sum \frac{100n}{N}$$

where

Σ = summation of all functions and services in the place.

n = number of outlets of each function and service in the place

N = total number of outlets of each function and service in the whole system of places.

Places are then clustered into discrete tiers of various grades of centrality. Such a tier is defined such that the greatest difference between the FIC of places within it is less than that between the FIC of any place in the same tier and another higher or lower tier.

22 In 1973, 10.9 per cent of Wad Medani's labour force fell into the category of 'electricity and water' which exceeded the 10.2 per cent for those working in manufacturing. The reason for such a high proportion in this sector must be largely attributable to employees in the national Ministry of Irrigation.

23 There are no figures for the distribution of the region's labour force within different sectors. However, 83 per cent ofthe population lived outside small and intermediate urban centres, based on 1983 census data, and a significant proportion of many urban centres' population are known to work in agriculture. For instance, in 1973, roughly a third of the population of El Hasaheisa, then the second largest urban centre in the region, derived a living from agriculture, hunting or fishing and most would have been in agriculture.

References

Ali, K.E. (1982), *The Politics of Agrarian Relations*, unpublished MSc thesis, The Hague.

El Mustapha, Y.Y. (1983), *Capital Accumulation, Tribalism and Politics in a Sudanese Town (Hasaheisa)*, a case study in the political economy of urbanisation, unpublished PhD thesis, University of Hull.

Gaitskell, Arthur A. (1959), *Gezira, a story of Development in the Sudan*, Faber and Faber Ltd, London.

4

Bangalore, Mandya and Mysore Districts, Karnataka State, South India

B.S. Bhooshan (with the assistance of K. Prabhakaraiah)

Background

The study region covers 24,908 square kilometres and is made up of the three districts of Bangalore, Mandya and Mysore in the south of Karnataka State, India (See Map 4.1). The districts are between 915 and 975 metres above sea level and the land is fairly flat. The area lies in the drainage basin of the Cauvery, an important river in South India which rises to the west of the study region and flows through the districts of Mysore and Mandya into Tamil Nadu State to the east, eventually reaching the Bay of Bengal. Mysore and Mandya Districts also have perennial tributaries of the Cauvery while Bangalore District has no major river. A number of anicuts[1] and channels draw water for irrigation from the Cauvery and its tributaries. In 1980/81, close to a third of Mandya District's net cropped area was irrigated compared to a sixth for those of the other two districts. Rainfall is fairly plentiful although concentrated in the period May to September. Average annual rainfall varies from 1,971 mm in Mysore District to 924 mm in Bangalore District. The region lacks great seasonal variations in temperature; between March to May it rarely rises above 33°C while from September to January it rarely drops below 7°C.

The climate was one of the factors which attracted the British to Bangalore City and their preference for locating a garrison and administrative offices there was an important stimulus to Bangalore City's early growth.

Soils are generally fertile, except in the north-east of Bangalore District. Forests cover much of the south-west; forests rich in valuable timber such as teak and sandalwood cover 27 per cent of Mysore District. Only five per cent of Mandya and ten per cent of Bangalore are covered by forest and much of this is bush forest. To the south

Map 4.1 *Mysore, Mandya and Bangalore Districts and their location within Karnataka State and India*

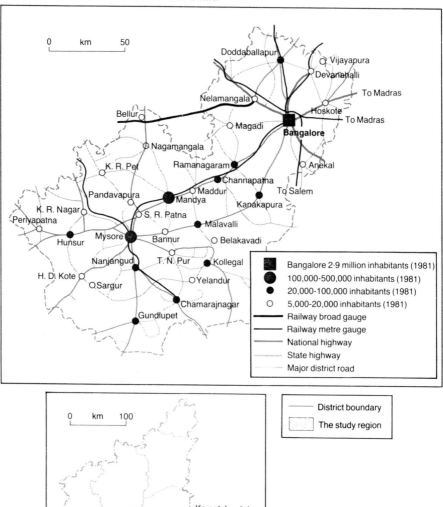

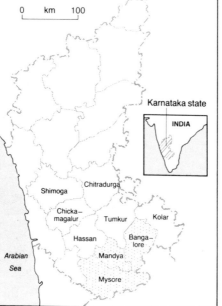

and west are the Sahyadri ranges of mountains and these inhibit communications across the study region's south-western boundaries.

Development up to 1951

The region's development up to 1881

The region has a long history as a densely-settled area. Close to two-thirds of the 35 settlements designated as urban centres in the 1981 census have recorded histories of over 300 years while some (including Nanjangud, Srirangapatna, Magadi, Bannur and Periyapatna) have histories dating back at least to the eleventh century AD. Most existing urban centres owe their origin or early importance to a role as the capital of a local chieftain, petty king, lord or raja, or to being the site of a temple or centre for pilgrims (or both). Only a few are of relatively recent origin.

In the mid-eighteenth century, the region was essentially controlled by local chieftains although they swore allegiance to the Kings (Wodeyars) of Mysore whose court was in Mysore City.[2] In c. 1760, Hyder Ali, the King's Commander in Chief, made himself ruler of Mysore after displacing the Prime Minister and imprisoning the King. It was under his rule and the rule of his son (Tippu Sultan) between 1761 and 1799 that Mysore State was unified. At that time, the study-region made up the southern part of Mysore state. Under Hyder Ali and Tippu Sultan, the capital was moved from Mysore to Srirangapatna. In 1799, the British defeated and killed Tippu Sultan and brought Mysore State under British rule; this marked the beginning of a period of increasing military involvement by the British in India which had been spurred on by the French threat to India with Napoleon's Egyptian expedition of 1798-99 and ambitions further east. There were some links evident with France; Hyder Ali had had some French support and Tippu Sultan had received French Republican envoys and would have made a natural ally for Napoleon. The British also restored the monarchy, installed a loyal king, and appointed a 'Dewan' (Prime Minister) to assist in administration. Mysore City regained its role as the state capital and the state boundaries were to remain unchanged until 1957.

Between 1799 and 1831, various public works were undertaken, including the repair of irrigation tanks and the construction of a bridge across the Cauvery river at Srirangapatna. Though Mysore City remained the official state capital and centre of administration, the Dewan gave increasing importance to Bangalore City. In 1831, Mysore State came under direct British rule, after a revolt against the King's rule in the north-east had to be suppressed. A British

Table 4.1 *Background statistics*

	Area (Km²)	Population (1981) (million inhabitants)
India	3,287,782	685.2
Karnataka State	191,773	37.1
Study region: Bangalore District	8,003	4.9
Mandya District	4,958	1.4
Mysore District	11,947	2.7
Total for study region	24,908	8.9

	1901	1931	1951	1981
Bangalore District[a]				
Population	889	1,221	2,127	4,922
Population in small urban centres (5,000–19,999)	41	60	95	99
No. of small urban centres	6	8	9	6
Population in intermediate urban centres (20,000+ excluding Bangalore City)	0	0	24	172
No. of intermediate urban centres	0	0	1	4
Population in Bangalore City	159	307	16	2,914
Mandya District[a]				
Population	483	581	716	1,414
Population in small urban centres (5,000–19,999)	16	21	46	92
No. of small urban centres	2	3	6	8
Population in intermediate urban centres (20,000+)	0	0	21	125
No. of intermediate urban centres	0	0	1	2
Population in Mandya urban centre	5	6	21	100
Mysore District[a]				
Population	925	1,031	1,424	2,585
Population in small urban centres (5,000–19,999)	38	49	49	73
No. of small urban centres	5	5	7	7
Population in intermediate urban centres (20,000+ excluding Mysore City)	0	0	22	158
No. of intermediate urban centres	0	0	1	5
Population in Mysore City	68	107	244	476

Source: Derived from census data, 1901, 1931, 1951, 1981.

Notes: a—All figures for population in thousands of inhabitants.

All figures include Kollegal taluk which only became part of the district in 1957.

Figures for Mandya District's population are given for 1901 and 1931 even though, up to 1939, its population was officially part of Mysore District.

Map 4.2   *Natural drainage and forests*

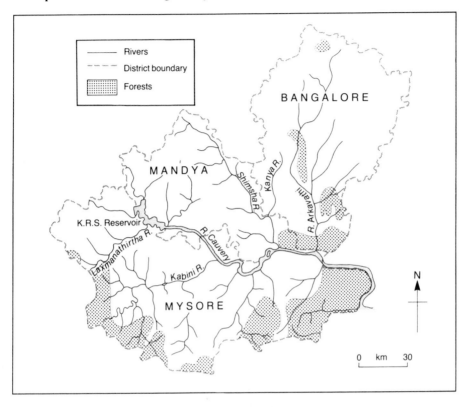

resident commissioner with headquarters in Bangalore headed the administration from 1831 to 1881 when, once again, the state returned to native rule. But the Kings had limited power; the administration was run by the Dewans.

During the period of direct rule by the British, a hierarchy of administrative divisions was established; their administrative headquarters were to have a considerable effect on the later development of the region's urban system for they provided the 'backbone' on which the urban system developed. Bangalore City became the centre for Mysore State's administration although Mysore City remained the capital in name.

At this time, Mysore State was divided into eight districts. The study region covered two of these: Mysore District and Bangalore District. In each district headquarters, there was a government representative responsible for revenue collection and for law and order. Districts were divided into 10-20 'taluks' and each taluk had a headquarters from where an 'Amaldar' presided over the taluk administration. These administrative divisions remain today, almost unchanged[3] and are shown on Map 4.5.

Below the taluk in the administrative hierarchy were 'hoblis' and villages. These did not contain government staff, although hereditary titles were given to certain inhabitants who kept local records. Law courts were established at taluk, district and state capitals. But apart from law and order and revenue collection, the British administration had little interest in local affairs. This administrative hierarchy's influence can still be seen in today's urban system. Out of the 34 urban centres which existed in 1981, 28 were those originally designated in the nineteenth century as taluk or district capitals. The two largest urban centres today, Bangalore and Mysore, were also the district capitals designated by the British at this time. The few urban centres which do not have long histories prior to British rule generally became established urban centres because of their designation as taluk headquarters.

This five-level administrative hierarchy of state, district, taluk, hobli and village remained when native rule was restored in 1881. By this time, Bangalore City's dominance as the largest urban centre had been well established. A permanent Dewanship, instituted by the colonial government, administered the state on behalf of the monarchy and successive Dewans continued to keep their offices in Bangalore City. Most of the main offices of government departments were also at Bangalore City; Mysore City had little role in the state's administration except as the home of the King and, by 1900, as the place where a representative assembly met once a year with representatives from each taluk coming to voice grievances. But this assembly was not to acquire any legislative powers until much later. Most taluk headquarters were not much different from villages in terms of population and economic base. Schools and social clubs for the educated élite were concentrated in some taluk headquarters. And taluk headquarters usually contained a higher proportion of the landed aristocracy, the educated élites and the high caste population.

Thus, by 1881, the cities of Mysore and Bangalore were much the most populous and most important urban centres. The only other urban centres of some importance were a number of taluk headquarters which had developed specialised economic or population bases. For instance, Hunsur was a cattle breeding centre while Ramanagaram was a police camp and a horse breeding centre. A few others were markets or pilgrim centres.

Administrative consolidation 1881-1931

These 50 years of administration under the Dewans brought little significant improvement to the region's economy, although the administrative machinery and the rail and road networks were developed. So too was the idea of government intervention playing a major role in supporting economic development. Public investments in productive activities were to have a major impact after 1931.

Map 4.3   *Transport network around 1920*

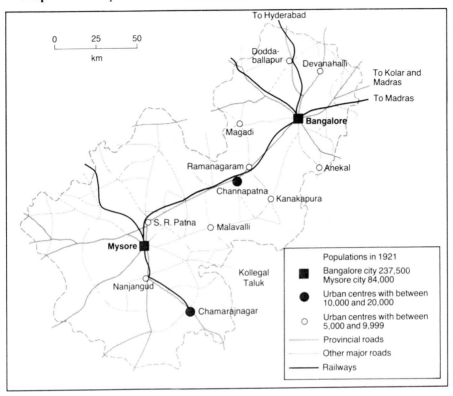

Most of the railway lines shown on Map 4.3 were built between 1870 and 1890. The railway line from Mysore south to Chamarajnagar and from Bangalore north to Hyderabad (outside the study region) through Doddaballapur were built between 1890 and 1910. And by the 1920s, an extensive network of provincial and major roads had been built to link the most important towns and administrative centres.

Even in 1931, the vast majority of the region's population lived in small nucleated villages surrounded by agricultural lands and isolated even from their taluk headquarters. Most villages had less than 500 inhabitants, and the new railways and roads essentially linked state, district and taluk headquarters. They did little to improve village populations' access to their nearest town unless, by chance, their village happened to be close to one of the new provincial roads.

The economic base for most households remained predominantly subsistence farming. The region was plagued by frequent droughts. Where irrigation had been developed, it was based on a few small-scale tanks and wells. The little trading which did take place was in weekly markets (called 'shandies'). There was little external input into agriculture in the form of purchased implements, fertilisers, seeds and labour. There was little industry of any significance outside the cities of Bangalore and Mysore, although some settlements were centres for craftsmen such as weavers, potters and cartmakers. In both Bangalore and Mysore Districts in 1923/24, 89 per cent of the total cropped area was devoted to foodgrains. Between 1881 and 1931, there were no significant changes in average yields per hectare for the major crops. The few small-scale irrigation works which had been developed were not on a scale to have a major impact on district wide crop yields. However, the first signs of the cash crop specialisation which was to develop in later decades, including the growing of tobacco, sugar cane and mulberry (for silk worms), became evident. But by 1923/24, these crops only covered four per cent of total cropped area.

There was very little modern industry in 1901, although two foreign-owned cotton mills had been built in Bangalore City in the 1880s. There were also many small-scale household industries in the cities of Bangalore and Mysore, most of which were related to handlooms or the manufacture of silk fabrics. These and other traditional industries received little government encouragement since the Dewans usually emphasised the need for modern industry based on imported technology.

This is best illustrated in the Dewanship of Visvesvaraya between 1912 and 1918 when ambitious plans were made for iron and steel mills, paper mills, power mills for cloth production, a car factory, and a dam across the Cauvery river. None of these were built during Visvesvaraya's Dewanship although some were built in the late Twenties and Thirties under the Dewanship of Mirza Ismail. Two large textile mills were built, one at Bangalore City (1917) and the other in Mysore City (1920). Alfred Chatterton, head of the Department of Industries and Commerce in Mysore State at that time, stressed the importance of developing industries based on local technologies rather than the import of foreign technology. A sandalwood factory in Mysore City (1916) and the government soap factory in Bangalore City (1918) both used indigenously manufactured technology (the First World War prevented machinery imports from Europe). A Public Works Department Workshop was started in Bangalore to make machines for the soap factory and agricultural implements, sugar cane mills, centrifugal pumps and paddy separators. But the concept of public intervention playing a major role in encouraging economic development became accepted. And Visvesvaraya's ideas of priority to developing modern industry and developments in agriculture concentrating on modern irrigated farming producing cash crops remained influential long after his Dewanship ended. Improving food crop production, raising productivity among existing farm households and support for the development of existing household industries were not regarded as important. In effect, Visvesvaraya's view of the priorities in public intervention prevailed, not Chatterton's.

During the period 1901-1931, the only changes in the region's economy were a few new industrial units in Bangalore City and, to a lesser extent, Mysore City; agricultural production was stagnant. The vast majority of the population remained subsistence farmers and had little or no purchasing power. Education and public health services expanded, with most of the higher education institutions such as medical and engineering schools being located in the cities of Bangalore and Mysore. One of the first universities in Southern India was started in Mysore City in 1916.

The region's population growth was very low for the period 1901-1931, especially for the first two of these decades. Famines and epidemics of malaria and influenza pushed up death rates.[4] The epidemics took a particularly heavy toll on the people living near the forest areas and hilly terrains. The rural population in the 11 taluks which today make up Mysore District actually declined by three per cent between 1911 and 1921. But despite being highly prone to malaria, the region's population growth was well above that for Mysore State as a whole for each of the decades between 1901 and 1941 and above the average for India for the decades between 1911 and 1941. This implies that the study region experienced net in-migration, even for the decades when it had very low population growth, but a lack of supporting data makes it impossible to confirm or to quantify this.

The development of sugar, silk and industrial production 1931-1951.

Perhaps the most far-reaching development in these two decades was the completion of the dam across the Cauvery river in 1931, along with associated canal irrigation developments in that part of Mysore District which became Mandya District in 1939. The region's first modern sugar factory, established in 1933 in the small urban centre of Mandya provided additional encouragement for sugar cane cultivation. At this time, Mandya was 'a sleepy country town' (Hettne, 1977, p. 210); with only 6,000 inhabitants in 1931, it was of little significance either to the region's economy or to its slowly developing urban system. The total cropped area under sugar cane in Mandya and Mysore Districts more than doubled between 1933/34 and 1947/48 to reach 3,260 hectares.[5] The area under rice cultivation grew from 24,830 to 34,020 hectares in this same period while the area under tobacco grew from 1,500 to 2,700. However, total cropped area in the two districts covered 235,220 hectares in 1947/48.

Ragi, the traditional subsistence crop which can be grown without irrigation and is similar to rye, still remained the most widely grown crop although the area under ragi fell from 79,630 to 64,470 hectares between 1933/34 and 1947/48. Rice emerged as an important crop, largely because of rising demand from richer and higher caste farmers and from educated urban dwellers. Originally, the government had planned for a system of crop rotation with rice, ragi (the traditional staple food) and sugar but this was abandoned as agricultural production became more oriented to produce crops for sale. Average yields for both rice and sugar cane increased during these years although there were large annual fluctuations. Yields for ragi and jowar[6] did not show a comparable increase.

Bangalore District experienced no comparable changes in cropping patterns; some vegetables and fruit cultivation developed around the city and mulberry cultivation increased a little. In the southern and south-western parts of Mysore District, there was also some increase in tobacco and mulberry cultivation supported by the government. Although sugar cane in Mandya and tobacco in Mysore Districts only occupied 3.2 per cent and 1.8 per cent of their total cropped area respectively in 1947/48, these districts were the major producers of these crops for the whole of the state. Mandya and Mysore districts together accounted for around 30 per cent of the state's rice production while Mysore District came to play the major role in mulberry cultivation.

These developments in agriculture did not benefit the majority of the rural population, most of whom were agricultural labourers with no land or small, largely subsistence-oriented farmers. Although figures for average land-holding sizes do not exist by district, for the state, around 21 per cent of farmers had less than 0.4 hectares while around 70 per cent had less than two. Around 10 per cent of the rural population had no land. A high proportion of the rural population – perhaps as much as half – had to rely solely or partly on wage labour. Agricultural prosperity was largely confined to those with relatively large farms within the irrigated paddy-sugar cane belt. The movement of population to this belt can be seen in the increasing population density evident in Map 4.4.

Mandya District's growing economic importance is mirrored by the rapid population growth of its new headquarters, Mandya urban centre as it grew from 6,000 inhabitants in 1931 to 21,200 inhabitants in 1951. Mandya's new sugar factory grew to employ 1,200 people and supported increasing sugar cane production through the establishment of demonstration sugar cane farms, credit provision and, on occasion, cane transport to the factory.

Mandya was not the only urban centre to receive a large new publicly-funded factory. A spun silk and filature unit was set up in Channapatna in 1936 (employing up to 3,000 people)[7] and Kanakapura in 1943 (about 600 employees)[8] while a silk filature unit was built near T.N.Pur (around 2,700 employees) and silk weaving and filature units built in Mysore city (which together had around 900

Map 4.4   *How rural population density changed over time*

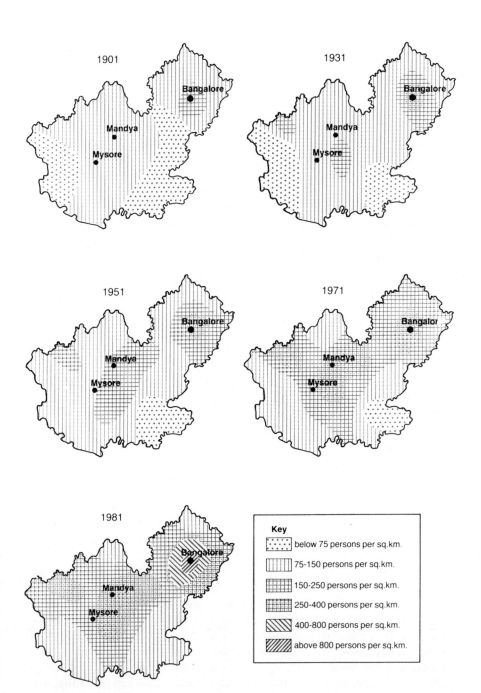

Key

- below 75 persons per sq.km.
- 75-150 persons per sq.km.
- 150-250 persons per sq.km.
- 250-400 persons per sq.km.
- 400-800 persons per sq.km.
- above 800 persons per sq.km.

employees). These helped stimulate demand for raw silk and thus for mulberry cultivation. Many silk weaving units (mostly handlooms) were concentrated around Bangalore City with some also around Doddaballapur. Towns like Chamarajnagar, Ramanagaram, Channapatna, T.N.Pur and Kanakapura had a concentration of reelers, but small-scale and household reeling units were spread in many villages. The Mysore Tobacco Company Ltd had flue curing plants at Channapatna, Ramanagaram, Anekal, Hoskote, Periyapatna and Hunsur (and also in some villages) but these did not provide many jobs and most of the employment created was seasonal. Agro-industrial plants built by private capital were also evident, although these tended to be much smaller.

Apart from such agro-industries, most other new industries were either cotton, textile or engineering and these were heavily concentrated in Bangalore City with just a few in Mysore City. All the large factories were started by the government. The most important engineering industry was the Hindustan Aircraft Factory funded by central (colonial) government. This was located in Bangalore City because it was well away from the coast and the northern borders and thus less vulnerable to foreign attack. This factory later became one of the city's largest employers; it then employed around 3,500 people. By 1947, Bangalore City was the major industrial centre not only for the study region but also for the whole state. Virtually all the 39,613 people employed in industrial establishments with nine or more employees in Bangalore District were in Bangalore city; 54 per cent were in textiles with 21 per cent in engineering. In Mysore District, there were 17,026 people working in industrial establishments of nine or more employees with 55 per cent in textiles and 31 per cent in food, drink and tobacco industries. Most of these people worked in Mysore City.

The making of beedis (small, cheap, hand-rolled cigars) was also an important source of employment, although this was done at home; people were contracted by companies to make the beedis and were supplied with materials. There were several beedi companies in the cities of Bangalore and Mysore and in Gundlupet. Factories making incense sticks had also developed in the cities of Bangalore and Mysore by the late 1940s.

Thus, by 1950, Bangalore City and, to a lesser extent, Mysore City had some engineering, textile and other industries of regional or even national importance. Meanwhile, a few large agro-industrial units had been built in some small urban centres, most of which were on the major provincial roads or on the railway system (or both). The fact that the livelihood of most of the population was largely subsistence farming made rural areas largely independent, economically, of urban centres. Railways continued to dominate inter-urban transport, although motorised road traffic was increasing in importance, especially for the growing number of areas producing commercial crops. Yet in 1946, for the entire study region, there were still only 2,641 cars, 392 buses and 631 lorries. By 1948, only 442 kilometres of road was concreted or asphalted. Public transport existed but connections to most villages were still poor.[9]

The only major change in the administrative system was the creation of Mandya District in 1939 with Mandya urban centre as the district headquarters. For the region, there was a considerable expansion of public services at district and taluk headquarters, although higher order public services remained heavily concentrated in the cities of Bangalore and Mysore.[10]

Changes in population and its distribution, 1901-1951

Population in the study region grew from 2.29 million to 4.27 million between 1901 and 1951. Population growth for rural, urban and total population for each of the three districts tended to increase, decade by decade from 1911-1951; growth rates for urban and rural populations in each district in 1941-1951 were unprecedented. This was attributed to improved medical facilities which helped lessen death tolls from malaria and influenza, whose toll on human life had been particularly heavy prior to this decade, and to rapid net in-migration, into Bangalore district, whose population growth was 27.5 per cent above that of the State average for this decade.

When comparing population growth between the three districts, that of Bangalore district consistently grew faster than the other two for each of the decades between 1901 and 1951. So too did its urban population except for the decades 1921-1931 and 1931-1941 when Mysore District's urban population growth achieved similar rates. In 1901, Mysore District's total population had been larger than that of Bangalore District; by 1951, Bangalore District's population was almost that of Mysore and Mandya district combined.

In 1901, Bangalore City and, to a lesser extent, Mysore City concentrated most of the study-region's urban population. Bangalore City had 41 per cent of the study region's urban population while Mysore City had 18 per cent.[11] No other urban centre had reached 20,000 inhabitants while only two (Channapatna and Kollegal) had more than 10,000.

By 1951, the concentration of the study region's urban population in Bangalore City had increased considerably; between 1901 and 1951 it had grown from 41 per cent to 58 per cent. Mysore City's share of the study region's urban population remained virtually unchanged at around 18 per cent. So by 1951, these two cities contained three-quarters of the study region's urban population.

The figures in Table 4.3 show Bangalore City to be unique in that population growth rates for each of the decades between 1901 and

Table 4.2 *Population growth in the study region's three districts between 1901 and 1951*

	Population (thousand inhabitants)		% of total population		Annual average growth rates	
	1901	1951	1901	1951	1901–1931	1931–1951
Bangalore District						
Rural	659	1,214	29	28	0.8	1.9
Urban	225	913	10	21	1.8	4.4
Total	889	2,127	38	50	—	2.8
Mandya District						
Rural	449	638	20	15	0.6	0.8
Urban	34	78	1	2	0.5	3.4
Total	483	716	21	17	0.6	1.1
Mysore District						
Rural	799	1,017	35	25	0.2	1.1
Urban	126	352	5	8	1.0	3.6
Total	925	1,424	40	33	0.4	1.6
Study Region						
Rural	1,907	2,924	83	69	0.5	1.3
Urban	384	1,344	17	31	1.5	4.1
Total	2,291	4,268	100	100	0.7	2.1

Source: Derived from census data, 1901, 1931 and 1951.

1951 were well above rates of natural increase.[12] Population growth also accelerated steadily, decade by decade. For the other urban centres in Table 4.3, growth rates varied considerably – and, for the decades between 1901 and 1931, were often below natural increase and indeed, in many instances, negative, indicating a decline in population. Population growth rates were generally more rapid between 1931 and 1941 and in all but four of the urban centres listed in Table 4.3, the highest population growth rates for the period 1901-1951 were in the decade 1941-51.

Rapid population growth rates in Bangalore City and the fact that by 1951 it contained nearly half of its District's population and nearly a fifth of the study region's population suggests rapid net in-migration, especially in the decade 1941-1951. Mandya District's rural population growth rate was well below that of the other two Districts between 1931 and 1951 and also below that of the State average. This suggests a substantial migration flow from Mandya District to Bangalore District, especially to Bangalore City. But the magnitude of the increase in population in Bangalore District and City also suggests substantial in-migration from outside the study region.

Table 4.3 *Population growth in urban centres whose population had exceeded 10,000 inhabitants by 1951, 1901-1951*

Urban centres	Population (thousand inhabitants)		Annual average population growth				
	1901	1951	1901–11	1911–21	1921–31	1931–41	1941–51
Bangalore (B)	159.0	799.0	1.8	2.2	2.6	2.9	6.7
Mysore (My)	68.1	244.3	0.5	1.7	2.5	3.5	5.0
Channapatna (B)	10.4	24.0	−3.1	4.5	1.7	1.7	3.8
Chamarajnagar (My)	6.0	22.4	1.0	5.8	2.2	0.7	3.8
Mandya (Ma)	4.5	21.2	0.5	1.3	2.0	6.6	6.4
Kollegal (My)	13.8	19.0	−0.9	0.5	0.4	0.8	2.3
Doddaballapur (B)	7.1	18.1	0.3	0.4	1.6	2.9	4.3
Nanjangud (My)	6.0	16.7	1.8	0.4	0.8	2.7	4.6
Ramanagaran (B)	6.1	16.0	−5.4	4.8	1.7	3.0	6.0
Hunsur (My)	6.7	12.6	−3.3	−0.6	4.2	1.5	4.8
Kanakapura (B)	5.6	12.4	−1.3	1.7	2.2	−1.3	7.0
Malavalli (Ma)	7.3	12.1	−2.8	3.0	1.2	0.9	2.9
Srirangapatna (Ma)	8.6	10.4	−1.2	−0.5	−1.3	2.0	3.1

NB A full list of urban centres' population for 1901, 1951 and 1981 is given on page 176, here the interest is in which urban centres grew to importance up to 1951.

Ma = Mandya District; My = Mysore District; B = Bangalore District.

Source: Census data, 1901, 1911, 1921, 1931, 1941 and 1951.

Unfortunately there is no data on migration flows in this period or of other indicators which might confirm or clarify this.

The links between the emerging urban system and social, economic and political change, 1901-1951

Four factors seem to have played an important role in shaping the study region's emerging urban system between 1901 and 1951: public sector investments in major industries of national importance; public support for cash crop production and processing; the administrative system inherited from the time when the study region was under direct British rule and changes made within this system; and public investment in an inter-urban road network.

Between 1901 and 1951, the increasing concentration of the study region's urban population within Bangalore City reflects the concentration of public sector factories there, as well as the concentration of administrative and military personnel and public services too, and its central location on the main rail and later road networks linking the study region to the wider regional and national markets. The decision taken by the colonial government to locate Hindustan Aircraft Factory there provided an important boost to its industrial development; so too did setting up a workshop to make agro-processing and agricultural implement machines for its development as a centre for engineering industries. Public sector investments in a large textile factory also helped stimulate its role as centre for textile industries. Bangalore City's rapid development from what was essentially a major administrative centre with little industry in 1901 to an important industrial centre by 1951 owes far more to decisions taken by the national (colonial) government and to Mysore State government to promote industries there to meet national and state objectives than it does to forward and backward linkages with the study region's production.

Indeed, in 1951, Bangalore District was the least developed of the three study region districts in terms of commercial crop production. But Bangalore City's central location on the main transport route linking the study region to wider regional and national markets, superior infrastructure (electricity had been provided by the beginning of the twentieth century) and its concentration of public sector employees (whether in public sector factories, state or district administration or military personnel) also meant it became the preferred location for most private sector investment in industries and services. One example of this is the large number of silk units attracted there, even though most of the raw silk was produced in Mysore District. Public sector investments in industries and the city's role as the unofficial state capital up to 1950 (when it became the official state capital), plus the concentration of public services and facilities there explained why its population grew so rapidly. The concentration there of many of the study region's higher income population also helps explain why Bangalore City had two of the study region's three private hospitals in 1948.

Population growth in Mysore City – although slower than in Bangalore City – reflects the fact that after Bangalore City, it was the urban centre most favoured with public investments in industries, infrastructure and public services. It was also the official State capital up to 1950 and the only district headquarters other than Bangalore up to 1939. It too had electricity supplies by the beginning of the twentieth century, although supplies did not match demand. Private investment in a textile factory in 1920 and in silk weaving and filature units allied to government support for silk production within its District helped develop the textile industry; by 1947, this had become its most important industrial activity. Mysore City also received a high proportion of the study region's new colleges and public hospitals, although substantially less than Bangalore City; we noted earlier how one of the first Universities in South India was set up in Mysore in 1916.

Mandya, the urban centre which between 1931 and 1951 rapidly grew to become the study region's fifth largest urban centre (and later to become the third largest), did so largely as a result of public investments. First, public investment in the dam across the Cauvery river in 1931 and associated canal irrigation allowed the rapid growth in cash crop production in and around Mandya. The State government wanted to encourage sugar production so a large new sugar factory was set up there, along with other measures to encourage the growing of sugar cane described earlier. In 1939 it became the study region's third district headquarters; the new district being created by subdividing Mysore District. Seven of the Mysore District's eastern taluks became Mandya District. This meant an increase in public sector employees in the new District headquarters, such as those employed in district courts, administrative offices, police headquarters, schools and health services. This explains why the population growth rate for Mandya urban centre rose from two per cent a year for the decade 1921-1931 to more than six per cent for the decades 1931-1941 and 1941-1951.

Public investments in agro-industries in certain other urban centres also helped strengthen and diversify their economic bases; one recalls the spun silk and filature units set up in Channapatna in 1936 and in Kanakapura in 1943. This, allied to some public investment in social services helps explain the sudden increase in these centres' population growth rates during the Forties. Kanakapura, along with Doddaballapur and Chamaranagar had also developed as centres for the small scale (often household) production of silk and cotton fabrics, beedis and domestic utensils.

Thus, by 1951, Bangalore City had emerged as one of South India's most important industrial and commercial centres for an area wider than the study region. Mysore City remained important within the study region but unlike Bangalore City, it lacked wider markets. Mandya has been transformed from a sleepy market town into one of the study region's most populous urban centres, based largely on its role as a district headquarters and as a market and agro-processing town serving the newly developed commercial agriculture close by. Various taluk headquarters were also beginning to develop more diversified economic bases.

The choice by the national (colonial) and state governments as to which urban centre should receive public sector industries and services, and should be part of the new inter-urban transport system, was much influenced by the administrative hierarchy which had already become consolidated by 1901. By that date, the populations of the study region's urban centres reflected their role in the administrative hierarchy. At this point, there was little economic interaction between most towns. Only 13 towns had 5,000 or more inhabitants and thus qualify, by our criterion, as urban centres. The fact that Bangalore City was much the largest reflects its role as the unofficial State capital; it had functioned as the capital since the period 1831-1881, when the area came under direct British rule. Most of the main offices of government departments were set up in Bangalore. When the region returned to native rule in 1881, the Dewans' offices remained in Bangalore City. Thus, the city was the unofficial administrative headquarters not only for the study region but for the whole of Mysore State, some three times the size of the study region.

In 1901, Mysore City was the only other district headquarter and the only other urban centre with more than 20,000 inhabitants. But Mysore City's population size also reflects the fact that it had been the most important political and administrative centre before colonial rule. It was also an important centre for educational institutions as well as the home of the official (but since 1799, not very powerful) head of the state government, the King.

Of the other 11 centres with 5,000 or more inhabitants in 1901, all but one (Bannur) were taluk headquarters. The taluk headquarters, whose population had exceeded 5,000 inhabitants in 1901, were those which had some specialised functions: for instance, Hunsur was a cattle breeding centre and Ramanagarama a horse breeding centre, also containing a police camp. Others were market or pilgrim centres. The smaller taluk headquarters were essentially villages; the only thing distinguishing them from villages was their administrative status and offices.

By 1951, the urban system still reflected the administrative hierarchy. Bangalore City's dominance had increased; in 1950 it was officially designated the State capital which merely legitimised its existing role. The second, and what was to develop to become the third largest urban centre, were the two other district headquarters. Of the 25 taluk headquarters which were not also district or state capitals (as in the case of Bangalore, Mysore and Mandya), only three had less than 5,000 inhabitants. All urban centres with more than 10,000 inhabitants were taluk headquarters. As in 1901, the most important urban centres after the state and district headquarters were those taluk headquarters in which some specialised economic activities had developed.

The extent to which urban centres were connected to roads or railways depended, largely, on their administrative status. Improvements in the transport network during the period 1901-1951 largely followed the administrative hierarchy. Bangalore City, was the main railway station which linked the study region to other regions. The two other district capitals were also on the railway line, as were most of the study region's urban centres in 1901. Public investments in a road network were essentially confined to improving roads between the cities of Bangalore and Mysore and the taluk headquarters. It is difficult to determine whether a settlement's original designation as a taluk headquarter in the nineteenth century had been because of an already existing importance as the largest, most populous or best-located settlement within its taluk or whether designation as a taluk headquarter established this importance.[13] But the fact that a settlement had been established as a taluk headquarter during the period of direct British rule between 1831 and 1881 largely meant it was the first settlement within its taluk to be connected to to other taluks and to Bangalore and Mysore cities by road.

Since the road network which developed in this period was, like the administrative system, hierarchic (roads connected taluk headquarters to district headquarters and district headquarters, to state headquarters), it meant that the flow of goods and information to and from a taluk essentially had to pass through its taluk headquarters.

In the predominantly agrarian society which existed in most taluks with a relatively low level of demand for goods and services supplied by urban-based enterprises, the few urban-based enterprises which develop within a taluk would tend to go to the taluk headquarters since this is one of the only (or perhaps the only) settlement linked by a good road to other urban centres. The taluk headquarters also had the only significant concentrations of public employees and services which also helped strengthen their dominance as the major central place within their taluk. But even by 1951, the flow of goods and people between most taluk headquarters and the few other urban centres was still very limited. The smaller taluk headquarters had little or no economic activities associated with producing goods or services for more than their surrounding populations.

Urban centres' population sizes in 1951 bear a strong correlation with favourable location on the transport system which had been developed by the 1920s (shown on Map 4.3). Of the 13 largest urban centres in the region (which are listed in Table 4.3), nine (including the five largest) were railway stations and on the highest category of road (provincial road). Of the four others, one (Hunsur) was also on a provincial road while the two others were on a major road. All other urban centres with 5,000 or more inhabitants in 1951 were either on provincial or on major roads.

In terms of urban centres' movements up or down a list based on population size, it was generally taluk headquarters on the main transport routes and within the areas where cash crop production was developing which increased their importance:[14] Chamarajnagar; Nanjangud, K.R. Nagar, K.R. Pet, T.N. Pur and, of course, Mandya which had also become a district headquarters.[15]

There was no strong concentration of urban centres which moved up or down this list in any of the three districts. However, in Bangalore District, most of the urban centres which moved up were headquarters of taluks which adjoined Mandya district including Kanakapura, Ramanagaram,[16] and Channapatna. Most of the urban centres in Bangalore District which had the slowest growing urban populations and moved down the list were in the poorer agricultural areas to Bangalore's north and east; examples include Vijayapura, Devanahalli and Nelamangala.

In conclusion, the factors which best explain the growth and development of urban centres within the study region during the period 1901-1951 were administrative status, concentration of public sector industries and public services there (which was influenced by administrative status), location on transport network (also influenced by administrative status); and extent to which a particular urban centre was able to develop a role in serving the collection, marketing, processing and transport of the small but growing volume of commercial crops (also influenced by public sector investments in irrigation and in agro-industries).

Developments 1951-1981

Agriculture

Existing data suggests a considerable increase in the total value of agricultural production in these three decades. Between 1960/61 and 1975, total income in the district of Bangalore and Mysore more than doubled and increased by 67 per cent in Mandya. Table 4.4 shows how agriculture's contribution to total district income grew considerably in Mandya and Mysore in this period; by 1974/75, agriculture accounted for around four-fifths of the income in both Mysore and Mandya district; In Bangalore district, it accounted for only one-third.

The proportion of districts' labour force working in agriculture also changed little in Mysore and Mandya Districts over this 30-year period; in 1981 some 70 per cent of Mysore District's labour force and some 80 per cent of Mandya District's labour force worked in agriculture. In contrast, the proportion in Bangalore District declined steadily to 34 per cent by 1981.

Between 1951 and 1981, there was a considerable growth in cultivated area, net sown area, irrigated area and total cropped area. As Table 4.5, shows, the proportion of cultivated land devoted to commercial crops such as mulberry and sugar increased while the proportion under food grains decreased. Yields per hectare increased substantially in most instances, as shown in Table 4.6, with the notable exception of sugar cane. Figures for the average for India are included in this Table to show how yields in the study region are much higher than the all India average.

In examining the mix of crops grown within the 28 taluks which make up the study region which are shown in Map 4.5, and how these changed over time, the period 1951-1981 saw the development and consolidation of what can be termed two core areas for commercial crops: one for sericulture and commercial crops apart from sugar cane; the other for sugar cane and rice. The former group are largely dry crops; the latter wet. Table 4.7 and Map 4.5 show the taluks where commercial crop production came to dominate farming.

During the early Fifties, the core area for rice production was the centre of Mandya District and two adjoining taluks in Mysore District. It was here that irrigation had been developed most; the five taluks listed in Table 4.7 with the highest proportion of their cropped area devoted to rice in the Fifties were the five with the highest proportion of irrigated farmland. Sugar cane had not yet come to play a major role in any taluk apart from Mandya, although the taluks where sugar cane was beginning to be grown in higher quantities were also in the centre of Mandya District or in adjoining taluks in Mysore District.

Figures are not available to separate mulberry cultivation from commercial crop cultivation in the early Fifties – but taluks such as Hunsur, Gundlupet and K.R. Nagar in Mysore District, Pandavapura and Malavalli in Mandya District and the two southern most taluks in Bangalore District, Channapatna and Kanakapura, had 11 or more per cent of their total cropped area devoted to these crops. At this time, the six taluks in north and central Bangalore District had the lowest proportion of their cropped area devoted to commercial crops.

The taluks which had specialised in rice in the early Fifties had retained this specialisation in 1981. The taluks of K.R. Nagar and

Table 4.4 *Sectoral composition of district income 1960/61 and 1974/75*

| | Percentage of total district income | | | | | |
| | Bangalore | | Mandya | | Mysore | |
	1960/61	1974/75	1960/61	1974/75	1960/61	1974/75
Agriculture	31.2	32.5	68.5	81.6	58.8	77.1
Manufacturing and Construction	25.6	28.8	7.4	5.1	14.1	5.9
Trade and Services	43.2	38.8	24.1	13.3	27.1	17.0

Agriculture includes animal husbandry, forestry and fisheries. Forestry and fisheries contribute less than one per cent of district income in Bangalore and Mandya in 1974/75. Forestry contributed 1.4 per cent of Mysore district's income in 1974/75 while fisheries contributed only 0.1 per cent.

Manufacturing and construction includes mining which contributed 0.1 per cent or less to each district's income; it also includes small-scale establishments.

Trade and services includes communications, railways, commerce and government administration.

Source: Derived from statistics in Taluk Plan Statistics, Bangalore, Mandya and Mysore Districts, Planning Department, Karnataka Government, Statistical Abstract of Karnataka 1976–77.

Table 4.5 Changes in land utilisation and cropping pattern, 1947/48—1980—81[a]

| | Net sown area (hectares) | Irrigation (hectares) | Total cropped area[c] (hectares) | Proportion devoted to different crops (% of total cropped area) | | | | |
				ragi	rice	sugar cane	food grains[b]	mulberry
Bangalore District								
1947/48	321,107	34,858	325,496	59.3	7.4	0.7	88.2	n.a.
1980/81	474,820	77,510	434,115	51.7	8.0	1.1	79.6	3.0
Mandya District								
1947/48	212,541	53,776	221,972	33.4	20.0	3.2	84.4	n.a.
1980/81	271,306	97,115	327,851	30.7	20.6	7.3	77.0	2.9
Mysore District								
1947/48	317,534	40,037	376,996	23.8	11.1	0.3	85.5	n.a.
1980/81	492,994	85,585	604,409	19.1	11.8	1.1	72.7	10.1

Notes: a—The figures for the proportion of total cropped area devoted to different crops shown here for 1980/81 are in fact averages for the years 1975–78 inclusive, since data was not available for later years.
b—Includes rice and ragi.
c—Total cropped area is higher than net sown area because of some double-cropping.

Source: Statistical Abstract of Mysore, 1947–48 and annual season and crop reports, Karnataka State, 1975–78.

Table 4.6   *Yields for selected crops*

		Bangalore	*Districts* Mandya	Mysore	*India*
Rice	1963/64	1,540	1,640	2,464	—
Kg/ha	1977/78	2,452	3,106	2,525	1,060
Jowar	1970/71	851	956	836	460
Kg/ha	1977/78	2,121	1,936	1,357	640
Ragi	1963/64	945	1,080	1,058	—
Kg/ha	1977/78	1,789	1,721	1,450	800
Sugar	1963/64	86	118	103	—
cane	1970/71	109	88	93	48
Tonnes/ha	1977/78	70	100	88	54

Source: Annual season and crop report of Mysore State, 1963–64, Statistical Abstract of Mysore State, 1970/71 and Statistical Abstract of Karnataka State, 1976/77.

T.N. Pur on Mysore District's border with Mandya District and all taluks in Mandya District with the exception of Nagamangala to the north were the ones with the highest proportion of their cropped area devoted to rice.

Five adjoining taluks at the geographic centre of the study region, four in Mandya District and one in Mysore District, were the ones with the highest proportion of cropped area devoted to sugar cane. Five adjoining taluks in the south-east of Mysore District were the main areas for sericulture. And again it was taluks in the centre and north of Bangalore District which had the lowest proportion of their cropped area devoted to sugar cane, mulberry, tobacco and oil-seeds.

When a comparison is made of the value of agricultural production per person working in agriculture (including both cultivators and agricultural labourers) between the 28 taluks,[17] the taluks with the highest values corresponded to those in the core areas for rice, sugar cane and mulberry[18] except in the case of K.R. Nagar. All taluks in Bangalore District, Nagamangala to the north of Mandya District and taluks outside the sericulture core in Mysore state had the lowest scores.

Growing agricultural production, improved yields per hectare and an increasing proportion of the land devoted to cash crops seems to be accompanied by an increasing proportion of rural population whose living is derived from agricultural labouring and a decreasing proportion of cultivators. The proportion of the rural labour force working as agricultural labourers grew substantially in each of the 28 taluks between 1951 and 1981. Whereas in 1951 it was rare for this proportion to exceed 10 per cent in any taluk, by 1981, in all

Map 4.5   *Administrative divisions, 1981, and core areas for agriculture*

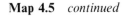

Map 4.5 *continued*

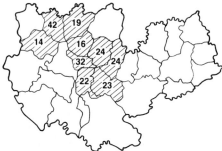

RICE
Taluks with highest proportion of total cropped area
devoted to rice in 1981
(figures give percentages devoted to rice)

SUGAR
Taluks with highest proportion of total cropped area
devoted to sugar in 1981
(figures give percentages devoted to sugar)

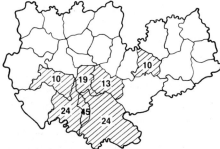

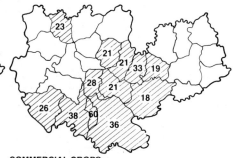

MULBERRY
Taluks with highest proportion of total cropped area
devoted to mulberry in 1981
(figures give percentages devoted to mulberry)

COMMERCIAL CROPS
Taluks with highest proportion of total cropped area
devoted to sugar, mulberry, tobacco and oil seeds
combined
(figures give percentages devoted to commercial crops)

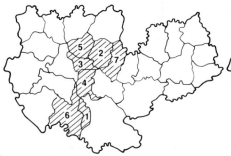

**AGRICULTURAL PRODUCTION
VALUE PER PERSON**
Taluks with the highest production value per person
working in agriculture for 1975-1978
(ranked according to production value)

AGRICULTURAL LABOURERS
Taluks with the highest proportion of the rural labour
force working as agricultural labourers, 1981

Table 4.7 *Changes in patterns of crop specialisation in the taluks, 1950s–1981*

Taluks and % of total cropped area devoted to specified crop

	1950s	1981
Taluks with highest % to rice	S.R. Patna (Ma) 43% K.R. Nagar (My) 35% Mandya (Ma) 33% T.N. Pur (My) 22% Maddur (Ma) 21% K.R. Pet (Ma) 20% Pandavapura (Ma) 17% Malavalli (Ma) 15% Anekal (B) 11%	K.R. Nagar (My) 42% S.R. Patna (Ma) 32% Mandya (Ma) 24% Maddur (Ma) 24% Malavalli (Ma) 23% T.N. Pur (My) 22% K.R. Pet (Ma) 19% Pandavapura (Ma) 16% Hunsur (My) 14%
Taluks with highest % to sugar	Mandya (Ma) 11% Maddur (Ma) 4% Pandavapura (Ma) 2% T.N. Pur (My) 2%	Mandya (Ma) 18% Maddur (Ma) 10% Pandavapura (Ma) 9% S.R. Patna (Ma) 9% T.N. Pur (My) 5%
Taluks with highest % to mulberry	Figures not available	Yelandur (My) 45% Kollegal (My) 24% Chamarajnagar (My) 24% T.N. Pur (My) 19% Malavalli (Ma) 13% Nanjangud (My) 10% Channapatna (B) 10%
Taluks with highest % to commercial crops (sugar, mulberry, tobacco and oil-seeds)	Hunsur (My) 23% Gundlupet (My) 20% Mandya (Ma) 15%	Yelandur (My) 60% Chamarajnagar (My) 38% Kollegal (My) 36% Mandya (Ma) 21% Ramanagaram (B) 19% Kanakapura (B) 18%

Table 4.7 *continued*

	Kanakapura (B) 14%	Channapatna (B) 33%
	K.R. Nagar (My) 14%	T.N. Pur (My) 28%
	Chamarajnagar (My) 12%	Gundlupet (My) 26%
	Pandavapura (Ma) 11%	K. R. Nagar (My) 23%
	Malavalli (Ma) 11%	Malavalli (Ma) 21%
	Channapatna (B) 11%	Maddur (Ma) 21%
Taluks with lowest % to commercial crops	Devanahalli (B) 2%	Bangalore (B) 3.7%
	Bangalore (B) 2%	Anekal (B) 6%
	Hoskote (B) 3%	Doddaballapur (B) 7%
	Anekal (B) 3%	Nelamangala (B) 8%
	Doddaballapur (B) 3%	Hoskote (B) 10%
	Magadi (B) 3%	K.R. Nagar (My) 10%
		Periyapatna (My) 10%

NB   For Mysore and Bangalore Districts, data is for 1953/54 while for Mandya District is for 1956/57.

B—Bangalore District
My—Mysore District
Ma—Mandya District

Source: Derived from statistics in Annual Season and Crop Report, 1953–54, 1956–57 (Mandya) 1981, Bureau of Economics and Statistics.

but two taluks it had exceeded 10 per cent while in 18 it had exceeded 20 per cent and in seven it had exceeded 30 per cent. The taluks with the highest proportions were generally those within the 'sericulture' and 'rice-sugar cane' core areas.[19]

Although a relatively rapid growth in agricultural production and in the value of agricultural produce is evident during the Sixties and early Seventies, existing data suggests that most of the growth in income accrued to a small proportion of the rural population; essentially farmers who had the land and the resources to successfully specialise in commercial crop production. There has been a very rapid growth in the number of electric or oil pumps for irrigation since 1945 and a rapid growth in the number of tractors and power tillers (at least up to 1966, the latest date for which statistics are available). But the growth appears rapid because the numbers of such machines were very low in the late Forties and early Fifties. And while the number of oil or electrical irrigation pumps may have risen from 277 in 1945 to over 52,000 in 1972, for all three districts, this should be compared with a total of 728,400 agricultural holdings in 1970/71.

The average size of holdings has been decreasing. The proportion of holdings with under two hectares rose to 73 per cent in Mysore, 74 per cent in Bangalore and 82 per cent in Mandya districts by 1976/77. It is difficult to judge, merely from land-holding sizes, how many farming households have inadequate incomes. First, some people own more than one holding. Secondly, the net income per hectare depends so much on the crop, on access to water and on the quality of the soil; while a hectare of irrigated land with a good crop of sugar cane or a hectare of mulberry might well provide sufficient income to support a family, two hectares of irrigated land with other crops or substantially larger holdings with no irrigation often produce a totally inadequate living.

However, various indicators suggest that a very high proportion of cultivators have very low and usually inadequate livings. First, around three-quarters of all holdings are below two hectares and most are known to be the sole piece of land owned by that cultivator. Secondly, the area under crops such as mulberry and sugar cane which produce a good return per hectare is not high; in 1980/81 the proportion of total cropped area devoted to these two crops was 10 per cent in Mandya, 11.2 per cent in Mysore and 4.1 per cent in Bangalore District. Thirdly, only 21 per cent of the net sown area in 1980/81 was irrigated. Finally, successful mulberry or sugar cane cultivation both require high initial investment and have overhead costs which inhibits their cultivation by poorer farmers. A land reform act passed in 1961 set a ceiling on land-holdings which varied between four and 22 hectares depending on the quality of the soil and water resources. But it has remained little implemented. And one of its effects has been for those with larger holdings to subdivide them among family members, so expropriation of the land area above the ceiling set by the government can be avoided.

Information on incomes for the increasing proportion of the rural population working as landless labourers is less ambiguous. Consumer prices increased more than threefold between 1960/61 and 1976/77 while wages for the different categories of agricultural labour rarely increased more than twofold. Thus, while it is impossible to state the proportion of the exact agricultural population who lack the land or income to adequately support themselves, the proportion could be judged to be very high; probably over 60 per cent of the rural population in most taluks.

One final point worth considering is the impact on agriculture of Bangalore conurbation's rapid growth, and this impact initially appears less than one might expect. Bangalore draws supplies of fruit and vegetables from well outside the study region; for instance plantains from Salem (to the south of Bangalore in Tamil Nadu state), oranges from Coorg (to the west of the study region in Karnataka state) and Nagpur (Maharashtra State to the north), apples from Simla (one of India's northern most states) and Coorg, and onions from various places in Andra Pradesh, to the north-east of Bangalore. Transport costs in India are not high, especially by rail. Nonetheless, Bangalore is not surprisingly the largest market in the study region for rice grown there. The only area within the study region where between five and ten per cent of the cultivated area is devoted to fruit and vegetables is to the south of Bangalore conurbation, covering parts of Bangalore and Ramanagaram taluks. In addition, between two and five per cent of cultivated area in much of Devanahalli, Hoskote, Anekal and Channapatna (around Bangalore conurbation) and Nanjangud (just to the south of Mysore City) is devoted to fruit and vegetables, while these cover less than two per cent of cultivated area for the rest of the study region.

Urban-based activities directly related to agriculture

Certain urban centres act as the main markets for crops and are important locations for agro-industries and for concentrations of people engaged in agriculture. Urban centres where such activities are important will be briefly described in this subsection.

Agricultural marketing is organised at two levels, regulated markets and weekly shandies. Regulated markets have a defined hinterland from which notified commodities have to be bought and sold only at this market while shandies are smaller, usually take place in villages, draw customers from smaller areas, and tend to be used more by retailers and smaller peasants than wholesalers. At present there are three regulated markets in Bangalore District (Bangalore City, Doddaballapur and Channapatna), one in Mandya District (Mandya urban centre) and six in Mysore District (Mysore City, Chamarajnagar, Kollegal, K.R. Nagar, Nanjangud and Hunsur). Markets in four of these urban centres – Chamarajnagar, Kollegal, Mandya and Channapatna – have submarket yards in other urban centres or villages nearby.

For paddy, Mysore, Mandya (and its seven submarkets which included Maddur, Malavalli, Pandavapura and K.R. Pet and three villages) and Kollegal (with its three submarkets including those at T.N. Pur and Bannur) were the major markets in 1980/81 with both Kollegal and Mandya rapidly increasing the quantity of market arrivals compared to 1971/72. K.R. Nagar had fallen from one of the largest paddy markets to one of little significance in this same period.

For rice, in 1980/81, Bangalore's market arrivals were understandably much the largest followed by Mysore, Mandya and Kollegal. For oil-seeds, Mysore was the largest market followed by Chamarajnagar and Channapatna, while for jaggery, Bangalore and Mandya were the largest markets followed by Kollegal, Mysore and Chamarajnagar.

For silk cocoons, there are eight major markets in the study region. In 1979/80, Ramanagaram was the largest market, followed by Kanakapura, Kollegal, Vijayapura, Channapatna, Chamarajnagar, Santhemarahally[20] and T.N. Pur. Many of these, including the two largest, Ramanagaram and Kanakapura, are outside the core sericulture cultivation area. But the location of government-funded filature units and the availability of traditional reelers provides a stronger influence on cocoon market location than proximity to sericulture areas. One also notes that Kanakapura and Ramanagaram are on the major transport routes linking the sericulture core area to Bangalore.

The links between agriculture and industry can be seen in the agro-processing industries which have developed in certain urban centres. Most of the major centres for agro-processing are also the main agricultural markets. The study region's staple food crop, ragi, requires no processing before being sold, apart from its collection and sales so this implies little support for urban-based enterprises. Rice demands some processing but this can be done using a relatively simple technology with little skilled labour. Most urban centres in Mandya and Mysore Districts have some employment derived from rice mills but in 1975, only in Mandya (with 127 persons employed in rice mills) and in K.R. Nagar (with 119 persons) did total employment in rice mills exceed 100 persons. Many rice mills are located in the villages, as are flour mills. The fact that electricity is available in most villages has helped support the location of such small processing units there. For the processing of sugar cane, traditionally small labour-intensive units in villages made 'jaggery'[21] but their importance is declining in the face of large, more capital-intensive sugar cane mills. In 1975, the urban centre of Mandya had the largest sugar mill in the study region with 2,517 employees; the only other large sugar cane factories were in Pandavapura (732 employees in 1975) and Kollegal (500 employees in 1975) and Kalamudda Doddy village (in Maddur taluk, 400 employees in 1975).

The production and processing of silk has more forward and backward linkages than for sugar. Both traditional and modern techniques are used so both household and factory production are important. One estimate suggests that for every two families engaged in mulberry cultivation, about three are supported by non-farm employment related to silk production or sale. Sericulture has created employment in certain urban centres within the mulberry/sericulture core of Mysore State; Chamarajnagar had 985 people employed in registered factories involved in silk reeling, spinning and weaving in 1975 while Mysore City had 556, T.N. Pur 500, Kollegal 252 and Yelandur 231. But many forward linkages have supported industries outside the sericulture core; the lightness in weight and bulk of the cocoons and the reeled silk or yarns have helped silk industries, especially weaving industries, develop away from the areas where the silk is produced. Proximity to consumer markets or major transport routes and availability of traditional skilled labour has supported the development of silk reeling, spinning and weaving factories in Bangalore District, especially in Bangalore City (1,612 people employed in these in 1975), Doddaballapur (296), Kanakapura (385) and Anekal (with 248).

Figures are not available for the spatial distribution of those employed in household production and small unregistered factories related to silk production and weaving. But there are known to be important concentrations in Bangalore City, Doddaballapur, Anekal, Magadi, Nelamangala and Chamarajnagar. These were the urban centres with the highest proportion of their labour force working in household industries in 1981. The proportion was highest in Anekal with 40 per cent while the others had between 10 and 17 per cent. Anekal, Magadi and Nelamangala have concentrations of silk-based household production while Chamarajnagar, Channapatna, Kanakapura and Doddaballapur have both household production and factory production related to silk weaving, twisting and reeling.

Many of the urban centres in the study region still have a high proportion of their labour force engaged in agriculture. In 1951, this proportion exceeded 40 per cent in Vijayapura, Hoskote, K.R. Pet, Malavalli, Sargur and exceeded 50 per cent in Belakawadi, Bellur, H.D. Kote, Periyapatna and Yelandur. The spatial distribution of these urban centres corresponds neither to the richer or poorer agricultural areas nor to the core areas for commercial crops – but most of them were at a considerable distance from (or poorly located with regard to) main roads and railway lines. The urban centres with the lowest proportion of their labour force working in agriculture – Bangalore, Mysore, Mandya, Channapatna, Doddaballapur, Nanjangud and Chamarajnagar – are all on the railway and major roads; they were also the seven most populous urban centres in 1951,[22] while those mentioned above with a high proportion of their workforce in agriculture were generally among those urban centres with the smallest populations.[23]

By 1981, the proportion of urban centres' labour force in agriculture exceeded 40 per cent in K.R. Pet, Bellur, S.R. Patna, H.D. Kote, Periyapatna and 50 per cent in Devanahalli, Belakawadi and Bannur, while it was below two per cent in Bangalore, five per cent in Doddaballapur and between 10 and 20 per cent in Anekal, Channapatna, Kanakapura, Magadi, Nelamangala, Ramanagaram, Mandya, Nagamangala, Mysore, Nanjangud and T.N. Pur. Again, those with the highest proportion working in agriculture tend to be those at some distance from the main transport axes and are among the less populous urban centres; none of the urban centres listed with 40 per cent or more of its labour force working in agriculture had 20,000 inhabitants in 1981. Those with the lowest proportion included the study region's six most populous urban centres but also small urban centres such as Nagamalgala, Nelamangala and Maddur. But one noticeable change between 1951 and 1981 was the contrast between districts. In 1951, there was no obvious concentration of high and low scoring urban centres in terms of the proportion of their labour force working in agriculture. By 1981 this had changed with Bangalore District containing only one of the urban centres with a high score (compared to four in Mandya and three in Mysore District) and most of the urban centres with a low score (eight compared to two in Mandya and three in Mysore).

Developments in industry and other urban-based employment

By 1974/75, manufacturing and construction were responsible for generating 29 per cent of Bangalore District's income compared to five per cent for Mandya and six per cent for Mysore, as shown in Table 4.4. Between 1951 and 1981, Bangalore City developed to become one of India's most populous and important metropolitan centres, and consolidated its position as the dominant centre for industry within the study region. As in the period 1931-1951, large public sector enterprises provided a substantial stimulus. The Hindustan Aircraft Factory greatly expanded its output; recent estimates suggest a total labour force of around 35,000.[24] Minerva Mills, now under central government control, expanded to employ over 30,000 people. Indian Telephone Industries (18,000 employees in 1975), Hindustan Machine Tools (2,000 employees in 1975) and Bharath Heavy Electricals who recently took over an existing factory were among the other major industries located in Bangalore City by the Central (Federal) Government. All but Minerva Mills are part of larger multi-plant operations. Karnataka State government has also set up public sector industries in Bangalore; its New Government Electrical Factory had 4,000 employees in 1975. Many private sector industries have also set up since 1951 although none are as large as the major government enterprises. They include Nippon Electronics (421 employees in 1975), Alembic Glass Industries (750) and Amco Batteries (900). In 1975, Bangalore District had a total of 168,506 people employed in registered industrial establishments, around four times the total it had had in 1947. Some two-fifths of this total were employed in large public sector industries. Textiles remained the most important in terms of employment followed by mechanical engineering, electronics, and electrical and chemicals. In 1975, Bangalore District had 92.6 per cent of the study region's industrial investment with Mandya district having 3.6 per cent and Mysore District, 3.8 per cent.

In 1975, just 19,060 persons were employed in registered industries in Mysore District, and most of these were in Mysore City. At least up to 1975, Mysore City's industrial base showed little growth from 1951. This city had only received one large new industry between 1951 and 1975; the Ideal Jawa Motor Cycle factory, a private concern, with 2,000 employees in 1975. Perfumed/incense stick production developed from production based in households to that based in factories and Parimala Works was one of the largest factories with 351 employees in 1975.[25] Nanjangud, just to the south of Mysore City, also received some large private sector industries: the South India Paper Mills (400 employees in 1971) and Sujatha Textile Mill (2,800 employees in 1975) located there taking advantage of good transport links with Mysore and Bangalore (it is on the provincial road network and a railway station), relatively cheap land and good perennial water supply (Nanjangud is on the Kabini River). The production of beedis which had been important, especially in Gundlupet, declined due to competition from large-scale manufacturers elsewhere and the penetration of the beedi market by cigarettes.

In Mandya District, a total of 4,679 people were employed in registered industrial establishments in 1975. Among the major new factories were a sugar factory at Pandavapura (732 employees in 1975), an acetate factory (611 employees in 1975) and an agricultural implements factory in Mandya urban centre. The only major public sector enterprise directed into Mandya District was a motor scooter factory set up by the State government near Maddur in 1975.

However, 1975 figures miss a recent trend whereby Mysore City has begun to attract industries and this is a trend being encouraged by the State and the National government. Bangalore's rapid industrial and commercial development has brought with it rapid population growth and urban sprawl. The urban agglomeration has rapidly acquired certain characteristics commonly associated with the rapid development of a Third World metropolitan area—rapid but uncontrolled development of new industries on its periphery,[26] the development of residential areas around the new industries, over-loaded infrastructure and congestion and rapid growth in the number of people living in slums and shanty towns. The State government began to restrict the number of new industries allowed to set up in Bangalore. Meanwhile, the Federal Government declared Bangalore District to be 'industrially advanced' and Mysore District to be 'industrially backward'; this meant tax holidays, cheap electricity and low interest loans for plants setting up in Mysore District. A large area in Mysore City was demarcated as an industrial zone and many new industrial enterprises set up there, including a public sector tyre factory with over 2,000 employees. In all, more than 5,000 new industrial jobs are estimated to have been created in Mysore City since 1975.

In 1971, only 10 of the 35 urban centres, other than Bangalore, Mysore and Mandya, had more than 200 people employed in registered industries.[27] Only in Channapatna, Pandavapura, Nanjangud T.N. Pur and Yelandur did the number of people employed in such industries exceed 10 per cent of their labour force. But census data on occupational structure for 1971 in these urban centres reveals a much lower proportion of the labour force working in manufacturing in Nanjangud, Yelandur and Pandavapura than that expected because of the registered industrial units there. This suggest that a considerable proportion of those working in these industrial units commute to work daily. Many are known to commute from Mysore City, taking advantage of cheap, concessional railway fares. There are also commuting flows from rural settlements, nearby, mainly taking up unskilled, low wage work.

Many goods traditionally produced by artisans in villages and small towns such as earthern pots, handloom fabrics, beedis and wooden ploughs have had to compete with mass-produced goods made elsewhere – such as plastic and aluminium utensils, power tillers and tractors, factory-produced fabrics (including synthetic fabrics) and cigarettes. This is known to have caused a decline in household-industry production in the villages, although this decline has not been quantified. Certain urban centres registered a drop in the proportion of their labour force employed in production between 1951 and 1971 and a drop in the proportion in household industry between 1971 and 1981 (such as Devanahalli, Belakawadi, Malavalli and Bannur), and the declining importance of local artisan production for local consumption was probably a factor in this. The rapid decline in the proportion of Gundlupet's labour force engaged in household production from 21.3 per cent in 1971 to 5.4 per cent in 1981 is known to be related to the decline of the beedi production there as factory produced beedis and cigarettes manufactured elsewhere have widened their market.

As the figures in Table 4.4 show, the contribution of trade and services to the income of each district declined between 1960/61 and 1974/75. While in Mandya and Mysore, this was primarily due to an expansion in agriculture's contribution, in Bangalore, it was related more to an expansion in the contribution of manufacturing and construction.

Data on the occupational structure of urban centres' labour force for 1971[28] shows the enormous variations in the proportion of the labour force working in trade and services: from 63 per cent in Mysore City to 19 per cent for Belakawadi. There is no strong correlation between urban centres' populations and the proportion of their labour force working in trade and services except that the highest proportions are found in the three most populous urban centres, no doubt associated with their roles as centres for higher levels of administration (district headquarters and, for Bangalore, State headquarters) and as major transport nodes. These three centres also had the highest proportion of their labour force employed in transport services of any urban centre: 16 per cent for Mysore and 12 per cent for Mandya and Bangalore. The eight other urban centres with 7.5 per cent or more of their labour force in transport services included most of the study region's other more populous urban centres. Channapatna, Ramanagaram and K.R. Nagar each had between 9 and 11 per cent in transport services while Kanakapura, S.R. Patna, Chamarajnagar, Hunsur and Nanjangud had between 7.5 and 9 per cent. Three of these (as well as Mandya) are on the road and railway linking Bangalore and Mysore while Nanjangud and Chamarajnagar are the major urban centres within the sericulture core and the railway stations and nodes on the main roads linking this area with Mysore and Bangalore.

However, there is very little data on the spatial distribution of private sector services enterprises among the study region's urban centres although, not surprisingly, most of the higher order services are known to be within Bangalore City (or Metropolitan Area) with Mysore City having the second largest concentration. For instance, Bangalore had 609 non-agricultural cooperative societies in 1981 compared to 241 in Mysore, 63 in Mandya, and 10-22 in most of the larger urban centres. Bangalore and Mysore had much the largest concentration of banks although in terms of banks per capita, various small urban centres such as H.D. Kote, Bellur and Yelandur were among the best served in the study region (with twice the score of Bangalore or Mysore) since the location of two banks in such urban centres with small populations gave them a high per capita score.

Map 4.6 *Road transport linkages in the study region*

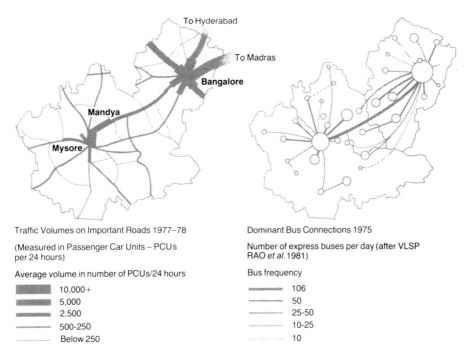

Traffic Volumes on Important Roads 1977–78

(Measured in Passenger Car Units – PCUs per 24 hours)

Average volume in number of PCUs/24 hours

	10,000+
	5,000
	2,500
	500-250
	Below 250

Source: Public Works Department, Government of Karnataka

Dominant Bus Connections 1975

Number of express buses per day (after VLSP RAO *et al.* 1981)

Bus frequency

	106
	50
	25-50
	10-25
	10

Existing data on public services points to a considerable concentration in Bangalore and Mysore, and, to a lesser extent, Mandya. In 1951, of the study region's 11 colleges, five were in Bangalore, five in Mysore and one in Mandya. The period 1951-1981 saw a great expansion in the number of colleges to 75, but their spatial distribution did not change much; Bangalore had 45 while Mysore had 12, Mandya five, Kanakapura two and 11 other urban centres one each; the actual location of recently built professional colleges is influenced, to a considerable extent, by the political strength of local inhabitants and of caste and religious groups. Similarly, in 1981, Bangalore, Mysore and Mandya had much the largest concentrations of hospitals, as well as very high per capita scores. In terms of number of beds per 1000 inhabitants, Mysore had five, Bangalore 3.3, K.R. Nagar 2.8 and Mandya 2.2; most other urban centres had less than one. Bangalore has also emerged as a centre for scientific research. The Indian Institute of Science and the Raman Research Institute there are among the foremost research and training institutes of their kind in India. India's space research programme also has its administrative headquarters and some research facilities in Bangalore, largely due to the existence there of the Indian Institute of Science and research facilities attached to the aircraft factory and the airforce. The Agricultural University of the State and Bangalore University have also been set up since Independence.

Since censuses and state surveys do not provide much information on the kinds of retail establishments, services and industries which exist in urban centres other than Bangalore and Mysore and of their links with enterprises and markets elsewhere, a survey of retail and service enterprises and interviews with a sample of commercial and industrial enterprises was undertaken in three intermediate centres (Mandya, Channapatna and Kanakapura) and two small urban centres (H.D. Kote and Belakawadi). These confirmed the dominant role played by enterprises in Bangalore and, to a lesser extent, Mysore, in supplying goods to other urban centres' commercial enterprises and inputs to their industries, other than agro-industries. It also showed how Bangalore and Mysore were the places to which most finished industrial products were sent and how the region's population relied on enterprises in Bangalore, and to a lesser extent, Mysore for higher order services.

In Mandya, there was little evidence of a range of retail, service or industrial activities to match its place within the urban system or its administrative role as district headquarters, apart from public services. Mandya has a hospital with over 100 beds, a telephone exchange, piped water supply, an undergraduate arts and science college, an engineering college and a polytechnic. But the range of retail and private sector service establishments did not differ much from other less populous and less administratively important centres like Channapatna and Kanakapura apart from a higher concentration of enterprises selling petrol, automobile and tractor spares, and fertiliser and seeds. It was also the only urban centre among the five surveyed which has automobile and tractor repair and service establishments. In Mandya, as in Channapatna, Kanakapura and H.D. Kote, more than half of all retail, trade and service establishments were either selling goods for daily needs – such as food and fuel – or what are termed 'bunk' shops selling such items as cigarettes, beedis, sweets and drinks. When a sample of visitors to Mandya were questioned as to where they had come from, 66 per cent had travelled less than 20 kilometres. A study of traffic volumes within the region in 1977-78 and of the major public express bus connections in 1975 showed that Mandya was not the centre of traffic flows radiating out to other urban centres within its district. This suggests that, at least by the mid or late Seventies, Mandya had not developed as an important central place for its district in terms of a retail, trade or private sector service centre. The only important enterprises it contained relating to more than a local retail and service centre were publicly-funded services, agro-processing activities, support for local commercial crop cultivation and some services like gasoline stations, boarding houses and cafes to serve road traffic passing through it.

The range of trade, retail and service activities in Channapatna and Kanakapur was comparable to that in Mandya, except for a somewhat smaller concentration of enterprises associated with road traffic and commercial agriculture.[29] From interviews with visitors, 72 per cent in Kanakapura and 85 per cent in Channapatna came from within 20 kilometres. Although these urban centres are among the largest within the study region after Bangalore, Mysore and Mandya, their role as central places for retail and service enterprises seems largely confined to serving the population in their taluk.

The range of trade, retail and service activities in H.D. Kote and Belakavadi was, not surprisingly, more restricted than those of the three intermediate urban centres. For instance, they had neither petrol stations nor boarding houses. H.D. Kote with only 6,200 inhabitants in 1981 is the smallest taluk headquarters in the study region. Its taluk is heavily forested and only around a fifth of the land is cultivated. The small range of retail and service establishments and the lack of any industry suggest that it plays little role in the wider regional economy; its existence as an urban centre is largely the result of its administrative status. One fifth of its workforce are administrative personnel while 47 per cent worked in agriculture in 1981. From a sample of visitors, 87 per cent came from within 15 kilometres.

Belakavadi with a comparable range of trade, retail and service establishments to that of H.D. Kote arose originally as a post on the border between Mysore State (later Karnataka State) and Madras State (later Tamil Nadu State); it lost this role when Kollegal taluk became part of Mysore State in 1956. Despite being within 60 kilometres of Mysore city, there was no public transport service there in 1982. It had 72 per cent of its labour force working in agriculture in 1981 and there are no industries of any importance. A public health centre, government veterinary clinic and police station have helped strengthen its role as a central place but its role as a centre for services and retailing covers little more than the surrounding villages.

To complement the surveys of service and retail establishments and interviews with visitors, interviews were also undertaken with samples of commercial and industrial enterprises to find the urban centres with which they had most of their interactions. Links with Bangalore-based enterprises were the most significant. More than half the commercial establishments in Mandya and Channapatna receive their supplies from enterprises inBangalore. Most of those in H.D. Kote receive theirs from enterprises in Mysore which is hardly surprising, given its location and the small size of its commercial base. For those in Belakavadi, links with enterprises in Bangalore, Mysore, Kollegal and Malavalli (its taluk headquarters) are of roughly equal importance while for Kanakapura's enterprises, links with local enterprises and those in Bangalore are the most important.

For the three intermediate urban centres' industries (there is virtually no industry in the two smaller urban centres) Bangalore-based enterprises play an important role supplying raw materials to industries in Mandya and Channapatna while Bangalore is the main market for industrial products coming from Kanakapura and Channapatna. For Mandya, apart from agro-industries based on local products, most of the raw material supplies to industries are shared by Bangalore and Mysore based enterprises while Bangalore and Mysore are the destination for virtually all its industrial products.

Although the network of inter-urban roads and railway lines did not change much between 1951 and 1981, there were substantial improvements in quality.[30] In addition, more villages were connected to the all weather road network; by 1976, there were over 4,000 km of all-weather roads compared to 482 kms in 1949. By 1977, only 26 per cent of the villages in Mysore District and 18 per cent in Mysore District remained unconnected to motorable roads. In 1976/77, there were some 28,000 cars, jeeps and taxis, 1,000 buses, 8,000 goods vehicles, 72,000 motorcycles and 8,000 'other' registered vehicles. But motorised transport is mainly moving goods and people between urban centres; rural-rural and rural-urban transport, especially for agricultural commodities, is still largely by bullock cart (there were 111,000 such carts in 1972).

The telephone network also developed considerably; in 1948, only Bangalore and Mysore Cities had telephone exchanges. By 1983, there were over 100 telephone exchanges which interconnect all the urban

centres and many larger villages. In 1977, electricity had been provided in 83 per cent of villages in Bangalore District, 70 per cent in
Mandya District and 73 per cent in Mysore District.

Statistics on traffic volumes of important roads within the study
region for 1977-78 confirm Bangalore Metropolitan Area's dominance both as the most important node on the road network linking
the study region to other regions and as the centre for the main road
traffic flows within the region (see Map 4.6). The largest traffic flows
– 10,000 or more PCUs per 24 hours – were only evident on the
road linking Bangalore to Madras (outside the study region) and
linking the core of Bangalore Metropolitan Area to its periphery.
Scores of 5,000-10,000 were evident between Mysore, S.R. Patna and
Mandya and on roads linking Bangalore with other urban centres
outside the region – to the north-west through Nelamangala, to the
north-east through Devanahalli and to the south-east to Anekal.
Thus, the most important traffic volumes within the study region,
apart from those linking Mysore, S.R. Patna and Mandya, were all
linking Bangalore to other regions and did not even cross any of
Mandya and Mysore Districts. In terms of inter-urban traffic flows
within the study region apart from the Mysore-S.R. Patna-Mandya
link, only the Mandya-Bangalore link and the Mysore-Nanjangud
link were above 2,500 PCUs/24 hours; all others were below 500,
and most of the more important ones were those which joined small
or intermediate urban centres to Bangalore and Mysore and not
lateral roads linking small and intermediate centres together. Similarly, a study of 1975 of the public express bus connections showed
the Mysore-Bangalore link to be much the most frequent while most
of the other more frequent connections were again linking small and
intermediate urban centres direct to Mysore or Bangalore.

Changes in population and its distribution

The study region's population grew from 4.27 million to 8.92 million
between 1951 and 1981. Total population growth for the region
increased for each decade between 1951 and 1981,[31] although the rate
of population growth during the decade 1941-1951 was higher than
that for the following two decades; the population growth rate for
the decade 1971-1981 was the highest the study region had experienced between 1901 and 1981 and probably the highest for its entire
history. Rural population growth rates in Mysore and Mandya districts were substantially higher for each of the decades between 1951
and 1981 compared to those between 1901 and 1951. Those for
Bangalore District varied considerably; between 1951 and 1961, rural
population recorded a decline while for 1961-1971 the population
growth rate was more rapid than for any of the preceding six decades;
then the rate was much less rapid for 1971-1981. It seems likely that

Table 4.8 Population growth in the study region's three districts between 1951 and 1981

		Population (1000s)		% of total population		Annual average growth rate	
		1951	1981	1951	1981	1951–71	1971–81
Bangalore District	Rural	1,214	1,737	28	19	............1.1	1.5
	Urban	913	3,185	21	36	3.6	5.5
	Total	2,127	4,922	50	55	2.3	3.9
Mandya District	Rural	638	1,194	15	13	2.2	1.8
	Urban	78	220	2	2	3.6	3.3
	Total	716	1,414	17	16ᵃ	2.4	2.1
Mysore District	Rural	1,072	1,877	25	21	1.9	1.9
	Urban	352	708	8	8	2.1	3.0
	Total	1,424	2,585	33	29	1.9	2.2
Study Region	Rural	2,924	4,808	69	54	1.6	1.7
	Urban	1,344	4,113	31	46	3.3	4.9
	Total	4,268	8,921	100ᵃ	100	2.2	3.1

Source: Derived from census data, 1951, 1971 and 1981.

Note: a—Totals differ from sum of components because figures have been rounded.

Figures for Mysore District include Kollegal taluk, even though this did not officially become part of Mysore District until 1956.

these variations were due to increases in the area designated as part of Bangalore urban agglomeration between 1961 and 1971.

With regard to population distribution within the study region, the trend evident between 1901 and 1951 of an increasing concentration of the study region's population coming to live in Bangalore District's urban centres continued between 1951 and 1981. Bangalore District's urban centres contained 38 per cent of the study region's total population in 1901, 50 per cent in 1951 and 58 per cent in 1981. The major reason for this was Bangalore conurbation's population growth. In 1951, this one conurbation contained 85 per cent of the entire District's urban population while in 1981, it contained 91 per cent. In 1901, Bangalore city contained 7 per cent of the study region's population; by 1981, the much expanded conurbation contained 33 per cent.

Looking at trends in the distribution of rural population among different sizes of villages[32] as shown in Table 4.9, clearly there has been little change in the number of villages over the period 1901-1971 (the dates for which data was available). There has been a noticeable reduction in the number of villages with less than 500 inhabitants, a considerable increase in the number with between 500 and 2,500 in this period, and some increase in the number with between 2,501 and 5,000. The general trend suggested by this table and supported by fieldwork and other data sources is that very few new villages have been created in the period 1901-1971 and the increase in the number of villages in the size classes of 501-1000, 1001-2,500 and 2,501-5,000 inhabitants simply reflects population growth in the villages which existed in 1901. Very few villages have 5,000 or more inhabitants. And the increase in the number of villages in the 5,000 or more inhabitant category in Mysore district between 1931 and 1971 was merely due to the declassification of urban centres (and thus to their reversion to being villages) in censuses in 1961 and 1971. The reduction in the number of villages in Bangalore District over these 70 years almost certainly reflects the incorporation of villages into Bangalore conurbation as its demographic growth was accompanied by outward physical expansion. The growth in the number of villages in Mysore District is largely due to the subdivision of villages as their total population and physical area expanded. Most of the population growth in rural areas appears to have been absorbed in villages with between 500 and 2,500 inhabitants and there is no evidence of a significant number of 'large villages' developing to become 'small urban centres'. Of the 34 urban centres whose population exceeded 5,000 inhabitants in 1981, all but seven had had more than 5,000 inhabitants in 1951 and more than half had had populations of 5,000 or more inhabitants in 1931. Thus, despite the fact the study region's rural population more than doubled between 1931 and 1981, there is little evidence of this either creating many

Table 4.9 *Changes in village size classifications, 1901—1971*[a]

District	Year	Size class of inhabited villages					Total
		Up to 500	501—1000	1001—2500	2501—5000	5000+	
Bangalore	1901	2,141	240	59	9	6	2,455
	1931	2,007	362	95	12	7	2,483
	1971	1,347	666	286	37	5	2,341
Mandya	1901	1,104	204	52	6	3	1,369
	1931	986	260	86	11	3	1,346
	1971	686	357	248	44	5	1,340
Mysore[b]	1901	921	321	157	18	5	1,422
	1931	809	357	175	24	4	1,369
	1971	602	432	386	83	9	1,512

Notes: a—1981 figures were not available when this went to press.
b—Mysore District figures do not include Kollegal Taluk.

Source: Census data, 1901, 1931, 1971.

new villages or concentrating in larger villages which over time develop into small or intermediate urban centres.

Looking at how rural population densities change over time, as is shown in Map 4.4, the rural population has become increasingly concentrated along what can be termed the Bangalore-Mysore axis and around Bangalore City. As noted earlier, the first corresponds to a belt of intensively cultivated, irrigated agricultural land producing paddy and sugar cane while the latter is attributable to spill-over activities from Bangalore City.

When looking at the study region as a whole, there is a strong and constant urbanisation trend, with the growth in the population within Bangalore city or metropolitan area being the major factor within this trend. An increasing proportion of the study region's urban population has become concentrated in this one conurbation during each of the periods 1901-1931, 1931-1951, 1951-1971 and 1971-1981.[33] The proportion of the study region's population living in Mysore City increased up to the 1951 census and then declined while the proportion in what we term small and intermediate urban centres grew slowly but steadily from 4.1 per cent in 1901 to 8.1 per cent in 1981.

When looking at urban trends within the three districts, in Bangalore District, the proportion of the population living in small and intermediate urban centres increased very slowly for the period 1901-1981 while the proportion in Bangalore urban agglomeration grew rapidly from 18 to 59 per cent. In Mandya and Mysore Districts, the proportion in small and intermediate urban centres grew more rapidly.

Links between the development of the urban system and social, economic and political change

Between 1951 and 1981, there was relatively little change in terms of where economic and urban development took place from the trends which had already become apparent in preceding decades, even though there were major developments in the scale and mix of economic activities. As in the period 1901-1951, public sector investments in industries of national importance, public investments in roads, and changes in the administrative system played a major role in consolidating the urban system that had developed by 1951 and in supporting the increasing flow of goods, services, people and information between the region's urban centres.

By 1981, Bangalore had become a metropolitan area with its own Development Authority and remained in a category of its own within the study region in terms of population, administrative status and scale and diversity in economic and employment base. In 1950, its unofficial role as state capital was legitimised as India became a federal country and the State of Mysore became one of the federal states.

Table 4.10 Population growth in urban centres, 1951—1981[a]

		Population (thousands of inhabitants)			Annual average population growth		
		1901	1951	1981	1951–61	1961–71	1971–81
Bangalore	(B)	159.0	779.0	2913.5	4.4	3.3	5.8
Mysore	(My)	68.0	244.3	476.4	0.4	3.4	3.0
Mandya	(Ma)	4.5	21.2	100.3	4.6	8.0	3.4
Channapatna	(B)	10.4	24.0	50.7	1.0	2.1	4.5
Doddaballapur	(B)	7.1	18.1	47.2	4.2	2.7	2.9
Ramanagaram	(B)	6.1	16.0	44.0	0.9	6.0	3.4
Chamarajnagar	(My)	6.0	22.4	40.4	0.9	2.5	2.7
Kollegal	(My)	13.8	19.0	35.7	1.8	2.4	2.2
Nanjangud	(My)	6.0	16.7	34.5	0.5	2.5	4.3
Kanakapura	(B)	5.6	12.4	30.2	1.6	3.4	4.1
Hunsur	(My)	6.7	12.6	27.7	1.3	3.3	3.3
Malavalli	(Ma)	7.3	12.1	25.1	1.2	3.4	2.8
Gundlupet	(My)	4.1	8.9	20.0	2.8	2.3	3.1
Anekal	(B)	5.2	9.4	19.2	1.3	1.6	4.3
K.R. Nagar	(My)	2.7	7.9	18.9	2.0	4.8	2.1
S.R. Patna	(Ma)	8.6	10.4	18.1	0.9	2.1	2.5
Magadi	(B)	3.6	8.5	17.6	3.2	1.4	2.8
Hoskote	(B)	3.2	8.4	17.5	0.8	3.0	3.7
Maddur	(Ma)	2.6	5.3	17.4	4.3	4.0	3.8
Vijayapura	(B)	4.0	6.5	17.2	2.4	3.5	4.0
Devanahalli	(B)	6.6	9.5	15.2	0.0	2.4	2.4
Bannur	(My)	5.1	7.6	15.1	1.4	2.9	2.7
Pandavapura	(Ma)	2.0	5.6	14.2	3.0	3.6	2.9
K.R. Pet	(Ma)	2.1	7.0	12.8	1.7	1.5	2.9
Nelamangala	(B)	4.0	5.9	12.6	0.8	3.2	3.7

Nagamangala	(Ma)	3.5	5.5	11.1	1.7	2.8	2.6
Periyapatna	(My)	3.9	4.8	10.0	2.4	2.0	3.1
T.N. Pur	(My)	2.4	5.4	8.9	0.9	1.4	2.7
Sargur	(My)	2.3	3.6	7.5	2.5	2.0	3.0
Yelandur	(My)	3.8	4.0	6.7	1.4	1.0	2.8
Belakavadi	(Ma)	n.a.	4.6	6.4	n.a.	n.a.	1.5
Hongalli	(Ma)	n.a.	n.a.	6.2	n.a.	n.a.	n.a.
H.D. Kote	(My)	1.3	1.9	6.2	4.3	4.3	3.5
Bellur	(Ma)	n.a.	3.1	5.5	n.a.	n.a.	2.5

Note: a—1901 populations are also included for comparison.

Source: Census data, 1901, 1951, 1971, 1981.

B = Bangalore District
Ma = Mandya District
My = Mysore District

The positions of Maharaja (King) and Dewan were abolished. The new Federal State of Mysore obtained a legislative assembly as a lower house and a legislative council as an upper house; the State government's cabinet was responsible to the elected representatives in both of these. Then in 1956, new linguistic states were reorganised and Mysore State (renamed Karnataka State in 1974) was much expanded; the new state had more than double the size of the old state which further increased Bangalore City's administrative role. One reason for Bangalore's rapid population growth between 1951 and 1961 and for Mysore City's annual average population growth rate of only 0.4 per cent a year for this same decade (which implies substantial net out-migration since this is well below the rate of natural increase) was the concentration of new and expanded administrative offices and services in Bangalore City and the relocation of the few such administrative related offices which Mysore had retained in 1950 to Bangalore.

Mysore and Mandya were in a similar category in terms of administrative status for the period 1951-1981, although Mysore had a much larger population and a more diverse economic and employment base. Below these three centres, there are two relatively distinct categories of urban centres within the other 30 urban centres with 5,000 or more inhabitants in 1981: taluk headquarters which have developed more diversified economic and employment bases and have more than 30,000 inhabitants in 1981 (most are also on major highways); and rural-agricultural urban centres where a high proportion of the population still derives a living direct from agriculture and where total population in 1981 was below 20,000 inhabitants. Then there are a few urban centres with between 20,000 and 30,000 inhabitants which have some of the characteristics of urban centres in each of these categories.

Forward and backward linkages with commercial agriculture have been important in helping diversify and develop the economic and employment base of the first category. If Bangalore, Mysore and Mandya are disregarded, the next seven most populous urban centres in 1981 contained most of the study region's agro-industries and agricultural marketing activities.[34]

It is worth noting that many of these urban centres are not within the taluks with the highest proportion of cropped area devoted to commercial crops. Nor are most of them in taluks with the highest value of agricultural produce per person working in agriculture. All are on state highways and five are railway stations. And each had been among the study region's 11 largest urban centres in 1951.

For the urban centres with less than 20,000 inhabitants in 1981 (what we term small urban centres), most had a high proportion of their labour force still working in agriculture. Apart from a few of the largest, virtually all were either taluk headquarters at some distance from the main transport routes or were non-taluk headquarters. Three quarters had more than 25 per cent of their labour force in agriculture in 1981 (nearly half had more than 40 per cent) while six were the study region's only urban centres which were not taluk headquarters. Most had not been on a provincial road by the twenties. and only four (including two of the three largest) had been railway stations by the 1920s. Today six (including the three largest) are railway stations while around half are on state or national highways. Their spatial distribution corresponds neither to the poorest agricultural areas nor to the taluks with the lowest proportion of cropped area devoted to commercial crops; both Yelandur and T.N. Pur are taluk headquarters in core areas of commercial crop production. Yet both had less than 10,000 inhabitants by 1981. However, most of the urban centres in the taluks where commercial agriculture is not particularly important are within this group. Thus, the fact that a high proportion of a taluk's cropped area is devoted to commercial crops is not in itself a sufficient condition to stimulate urban developments within that taluk; in some, forward and backward linkages with commercial crop production did so while in others, these forward and backward linkages supported urban development in urban centres outside that taluk.

When reviewing the whole period 1901 to 1981, the basic structure in terms of what were to be the major urban centres in 1981 was already visible by 1901: the two major urban centres being the two main administrative centres with a tendency for the urban centres located on the road and railway joining them to grow faster. Government intervention since 1901 has played a major role in consolidating and developing this structure through the location of public sector industries and higher order services, through the development of transport infrastructure and through the urban centres which served as state, district and taluk headquarters. No large or rapidly growing urban centre has developed apart from state, district or taluk headquarters.

Vijayapura with 17,200 and Bannur with 15,100 inhabitants in 1981 were the only urban centres which were not taluk headquarters and which might be regarded as having developed beyond what could be termed as large villages in terms of employment and economic base. The other non-taluk urban centres in 1981. Sargur, Belakavadi, Hongalli and Bellur each had a high proportion of their labour force still working in agriculture and between 5,000 and 7,500 inhabitants. It is also noticeable that in the six taluks with two urban centres in 1981, the taluk headquarters were generally small (all but Malavalli had less than 20,000 inhabitants) and most had lost importance in terms of their rank according to population size within the region's urban system. This is particularly noticeable in the cases of Malavalli and Devanahalli which had been the sixth and ninth largest urban centres in the study region in 1901, and were twelfth and twenty-first by 1981.

Changes in population size and economic base within the study region's urban centres between 1901 and 1981 broadly corresponds to the size of their economic role for an area beyond their immediate surrounds. In the case of Bangalore and Mysore, this has been documented in some detail already. Bangalore and to a lesser extent Mysore are the only places where there is a substantial concentration of industries producing for markets outside the study region while these two urban centres also contain most of the higher order services for the study region's population; in the case of Bangalore, its higher order services also serve a market much wider than that in the study region. For the other urban centres, we noted earlier how the eight largest contain most of the agro-processing and agricultural marketing activities related to the study region's commercial crops, apart from those located in Bangalore and Mysore. For other urban centres, most of their productive activities seem to relate largely to demand from population nearby. And it is the lack of a large or growing demand from this population that helps explain their relatively slow population growth and relatively weak economic bases, despite often growing agricultural production nearby. The fact that they were administrative centres and so contained some publicly-funded administrative offices and some publicly-funded health and educational services was a major factor in their development as small urban centres. When the road network linking villages to urban centres improved, their position as the most important urban centre in their immediate area was reinforced since they were favourably located both on this network and on the network linking their area to other urban centres. The level of demand for the kinds of goods and services made or supplied through urban-based enterprises remained low; as noted earlier, a high proportion of the agricultural population did not receive much (if any) rise in real income, even if total agricultural production and total production value was growing.

Much of the demand for goods and services generated by the relatively small group of farmers whose incomes did rise were for goods and services which were not produced or available in small (or indeed in some of the intermediate) urban centres. The demand from richer farmers or public employees for, say, cars or motorcycles, agricultural machinery, better quality clothing and electronic goods had to be satisfied by journeys to the largest urban centres since the level of demand within their taluk was not of a scale which would support their production or supply from the taluk headquarter. Enterprises in Bangalore Metropolitan Area and, to a lesser extent, in Mysore City, are the producers or suppliers of most manufactured goods and higher order services for the entire study region's population. Most of the manufactured goods sold in the study region are

either produced in Bangalore or brought into the region and distributed through Bangalore-based enterprises. Bangalore-based enterprises also seem to play a major role in supplying industrial
establishments in other urban centres with raw materials while many
of the products of industries in small and intermediate urban centres
seem to end up being sold in Bangalore or Mysore.

Bangalore is also where most of the higher order private sector
services such as banks, insurance companies and newspapers are
located. Mysore City has some, but its population still has to rely on,
for instance, architects and travel agencies in Bangalore. Mysore also
lacks its own morning newspaper. Thus, commerce in Bangalore and
Mysore has developed so it can supply many of the consumption
needs, consumer durable and higher level services demanded by richer
farmers and urban dwellers with relatively high incomes. Mandya
has had some development in this too, although the easy accessibility
of Bangalore and Mysore to people living close to Mandya has limited
this. The easy access that most of the richer groups have to Bangalore
and Mysore has also limited commercial developments in their local
urban centres. Thus, much of the commerce in all taluk headquarters
is dominated by small, low capital, low productivity, small cash flow
operations, often run by a single person or a family for the supply
of, say, general goods, or cigarettes. Such small enterprises dominate
commercial activities in virtually all urban centres other than Bangalore and Mysore.

Sources

This chapter is drawn from a doctoral dissertation entitled 'Settlement Structure and Development Pattern; a study of changes in the structure of the
settlement pattern vis à vis spatial pattern of development in Karnataka'
by B.S. Bhooshan at the Institute of Development Studies, Mysore.

Notes

1 small dams built fir irrigation.
2 The urban centres of Bangalore and Mysore are referred to as cities in
  the text since they are distinguished from all other urban centres in the
  study region first by having a substantially larger population and
  secondly by having an administrative status and area of jurisdiction
  wider than the study region (although Mysore City lost this status in
  1950).
3 The taluk boundaries set by the British in the nineteenth century have
  remained unchanged to the present day. Bangalore District's boundaries
  have also remained unchanged from this time. The number of districts
  in the study region was increased from two to three in 1939 when Mandya

District was formed out of seven taluks previously in Mysore District. Then in 1957 Kollegal taluk was reassigned from the neighbouring Madras State to that of Mysore State and Mysore District. In 1974, Mysore state was renamed Karnataka State with its area and population considerably expanded by the addition of additional territory to the north. Madras State was renamed Tamil Nadu State. Bangalore City replaced Mysore City as the official state capital in 1950 although much of the states administration had been there for more than a century before that.

4 Even by 1941, malaria accounted for over 500 deaths per 100,000 population for more than half of Mysore District and three-quarters of Mandya District.

5 The figure for 1933/34 was for old Mysore District which encompassed what became Mysore and Mandya Districts in 1939.

6 Sorghum.

7 The production of silk thread involves the care of domesticated silkworms from the egg state through to the completion of cocoons and the growing of mulberry trees on whose leaves the worms feed. The silkworm builds its cocoon by surrounding itself with a long continuous fibre. A silk filament is obtained by heating the cocoon and unwinding (or reeling) this fibre. Several of these filaments (each with usuable lengths of 500-900 metres) from a single stand which can be combined with others to form a yarn from which silk fabric can be woven. Filature units combine the silk filaments drawn from the cocoons.

8 It appears that a large number of these were casual employees, and figures for later years show a much reduced number of employees in all the filature units.

9 One account of rural transport around 1950 tells of the 'dilapidated war time buses powered by charcoal gas' which 'were so liable to break down that even a village on a bus route presented difficulties. During the period of my study in Rampura, I did not undertake bus journeys which were free from breakdowns' (Srinivas, 1976).

10 In 1948, Bangalore City had 10 of the region's 17 colleges and 37 of the 78 high schools. It also had 14 of the 38 hospitals while Mysore City had 9.

11 The proportion concentrated in Bangalore and Mysore cities would have been higher if the 1981 census definition for what constitutes an urban centre had been used in 1901. Bangalore City would have had around half the study region's urban population in 1901 while Mysore City would have had around 21 per cent.

12 The only figures for rate of natural increase for these decades were for the whole State. Mysore and Nanjangud also had population growth rates exceeding the State's rate of natural increase for each of these five decades but only by a very small proportion for Mysore for 1901-1911 and for Nanjangud for 1911-1921 and 1921-1931. Given that rates of natural increase in the study region might differ significantly from those of the State, only in the case of Bangalore City are population growth rates for each decade between 1901 and 1951 of a magnitude to safely assume that these were well above the rate of natural increase.

13 No comprehensive statistics exist as to the population of urban centres

during the period when the British created the administrative hierarchy. But certainly, taluk headquarters would have been based in existing settlements and they are likely to have been among the largest settlements in the taluks at that time. Most were or had been seats of local chieftains.

14 Population statistics for the study region's 30 most populous urban centres in 1981 exist back to 1901.

15 Yelandur, a taluk headquarters and in a taluk with one of the highest proportions of cropped area devoted to commercial crops was an exception in that its rank within this list dropped within each decade between 1911 and 1951. Yelandur is the smallest of the taluks and as late as 1971 had only 27 inhabited villages.

16 Ramanagaram's movement up the list was only after 1911; between 1901 and 1911 its population is recorded as having declined from 6,100 to 3,500 inhabitants.

17 To calculate these, an average was taken for the years 1975-8 inclusive to smooth out annual fluctuations. For each year, the area under each crop was multiplied by average district yield (no taluk level data was available) and farm harvest price. The value of agricultural production in each taluk was then divided by the number of people working in agriculture. The highest scoring taluks such as Mandya and Yelandur had around twice the value of agricultural produce per agricultural population of the lowest scoring taluks.

18 Ranked in order of value of agricultural production per person working in agriculture, the top seven were Yelandur, Mandya, Srirangapatna, T. N. Pur, Pandavapura, Chamarajnagar and Maddur.

19 The taluks of Mandya, Maddur, Srirangapatna, Gundlupet, Kollegal, T.N. Pur and Yelandur each had more than 30 per cent of their rural labour force working as agricultural labourers in 1981.

20 Santhemarahally is a village 9 km from Chamarajnagar and 6 km from Yelandur; all three of these have reeling and filature units as well as being within the core sericulture area.

21 A kind of lump brown sugar made by boiling and dehydrating sugar cane juice.

22 Not including Kollegal which was the sixth largest urban centre in the study region in 1951; at that time it was in neighbouring Madras (later Tamil Nadu) State and data was not available on its occupational structure.

23 There were some notable exceptions to this. For instance, Malavalli had the twelfth largest population of any urban centre but among the highest proportion of its labour force engaged in agriculture: 49 per cent.

24 This is probably more than the total number of people employed in all registered industries in all of Mandya and Mysore Districts.

25 This figure does not include a very large number of casual workers. This and the Vasu Agarbathi factory (both export oriented with exports to over 80 nations) now employ over 100,000 casual workers on daily wages.

26 In 1975, total industrial investment outside Bangalore Municipal boundaries was more than twice that within the boundaries, although total employment in industries was still higher within rather than outside the municipal boundaries.

27 Channapatna, Kanakapura and Ramanagaram in Bangalore District;

Pandavapura in Mandya District and Chamarajnagar, Hunsur, Kollegal, Nanjangud, T.N. Pur and Yelandur in Mysore District.

28 Data from the 1981 census was not available.

29 Channapatna also had a far smaller number of enterprises selling household articles and consumer durables; this is probably due to its very close proximity to Bangalore Metropolitan Area.

30 This can be seen by comparing Map 4.1 which shows road and rail development in the early 1980s with Map 4.3 which shows road and rail development by the 1920s.

31 Although Table 4.8 does not show population growth rates by decade, the text includes comments about certain decade's annual average population growth rates where these show unusual or notable trends not revealed by more aggregated statistics.

32 Some live outside villages – such as those living scattered in forest – but they represent a very low proportion of total population.

33 This is the case if one uses Indian census definitions for what constitutes an urban centre for the different dates (and this definition changed for different censuses) and if one takes as the 'urban population' the proportion of the population living in settlements of 5,000 or more inhabitants for the different dates.

34 Ramanagaram, Chamarajnagar, Kollegal and Channapatna were the urban centres other than Bangalore, Mysore and Mandya where most of the marketing activities take place within registered markets while Channapatna, Doddaballapur, Chamarajnagar, Kollegal and Kanakapura all had substantial concentrations of agro-industry.

References

Hettne, Bjorn (1978), *The Political Economy of Indirect Rule,* Curzon Press Ltd, London.

Srinivas, M.N. (1976), *Remembered Village,* Oxford University Press.

5

Rae Bareli, Sultanpur and Pratapgarh Districts, Uttar Pradesh State, North India

H. N. Misra

Background

The study region covers 12,800 square kilometres and is made up of the three districts of Rae Bareli, Sultanpur and Pratapgarh in Uttar Pradesh (see Map 5.1). Geologically part of the fertile Ganga plain, the level terrain, fertile soil, good climate and abundance of water have long made this a densely settled area with most of the population relying on agriculture and animal husbandry. By 1981, 5.7 million people lived within the study region which is almost at the centre of the densely populated great north Indian plains; it is among the most economically backward, least urbanised and most densely populated agricultural areas in the country. On this same date, 95 per cent of the population lived in some 6,400 villages and most derived their living from agriculture. Five important urban centres are in districts adjoining the three which make up the study region: Lucknow (Uttar Pradesh's capital) to the north-west; Kanpur to the west, Allahabad to the south, Varanasi to the south-east and Faizabad to the north.

The monsoon climate typically gives a hot dry summer from March to mid-June, a hot and humid rainy season from mid-June to mid-October and a cool, dry winter season from mid-October to February; in May and June, the temperature can reach 48°C. Within the main rainy season, more than 95 per cent of the total annual rainfall of some 1,000 mm falls. January is the coldest month with a mean daily minimum temperature of around 8°C but temperatures can fall as low as 2°C on some occasions.

Relief is characterised by large expanses of featureless alluvial plain formed by sediment deposits from rivers draining from the Himalayas. Elevation varies from 84 to 120 metres above sea level. Virtually all the study region is within the watershed of the Ganga River, the northern part being drained by the Gomti, the middle by the Sai and the south by the Ganga (see Map 5.2). Apart from these rivers, the

Map 5.1   *Rae Bareli, Sultanpur and Pratapgarh districts and their location within India*

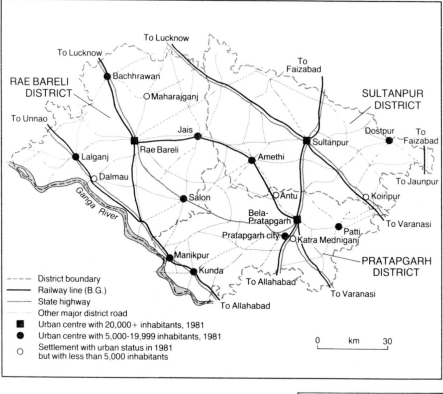

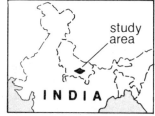

region is also marked by a number of shallow depressions and marshes which fill with water in the rainy season but dry out in the dry season.

These terrain characteristics have influenced the pattern and location of settlements. The poorly drained interfluvial areas tend to have large, compact settlements while in well drained riverine tracts, settlements tend to be smaller and more dispersed. The water courses have provided good sites for many urban centres while the shallow depressions and the many areas with saline and alkaline soils (called 'usar' soils) have proved unattractive to human habitation. Virtually all cultivable land is cultivated and over half the net cropped area

	Area (Km²)	Population (1981) (million inhabitants)[b]	1901	1921	1941	1961	1981
India	3,287,782	685.2					
Uttar Pradesh State	294,413	110.9					
Study region: Rae Bareli District	4,609	1.9					
Sultanpur District	4,436	2.0					
Pratapgarh District	3,717	1.8					
Total for study region	12,800	5.7					
Rae Bareli District[a]							
Population			1,039	941	1,070	1,322	1,888
Population in small urban centres (5,000–19,999)			40	n.a.	15	17	42
Number of small urban centres			4	n.a.	2	2	4
Population in intermediate urban centres (20,000+)			0	0	21	30	90
Number of intermediate urban centres			0	0	1	1	1
Sultanpur District							
Population			1,092	1,021	1,111	1,413	2,038
Population in small urban centres (5,000–19,999)			10	9	13	0	14
Number of small urban centres			1	1	1	0	2
Population in intermediate urban centres (20,000+)			0	0	0	26	40
Number of intermediate urban centres			0	0	0	1	1
Pratagarh District							
Population			908	850	1,036	1,252	1,807
Population in small urban centres (5,000–19,999)			13	n.a.	n.a.	5	33
Number of small urban centres			2	n.a.	n.a.	1	4
Population in intermediate urban centres (20,000+)			0	0	0	21	50
Number of intermediate urban centres			0	0	0	1	1

Notes: a—All population figures in thousands of inhabitants.
b—Provisional.

Source: Censuses of India, district census handbook for Rae Bareli, Sultanpur and Pratapgarh district.

Map 5.2   *Major rivers*

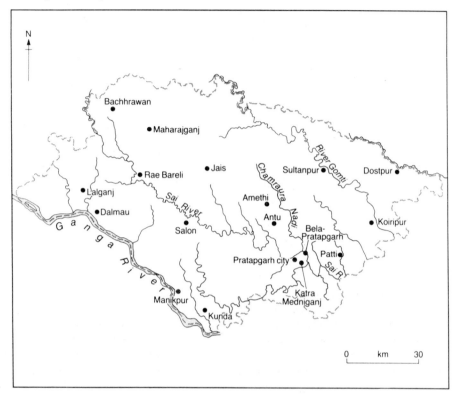

is irrigated; the Gomti-Sai and the Sai-Ganga doabs[1] are highly productive and intensively cultivated.

Developments up to 1951

The region's development up to 1901

Archaeological evidence shows that there have been permanent settlements for at least 2,500 years; the region is known to have been part of the earliest Hindu kingdoms of Kosala[2] and Kausambi in the sixth to fifth centuries BC. With the rise of Buddhism in the sixth century BC, various monasteries developed as nuclei for towns; three were in urban centres in the study region: Sultanpur (then called Kusapura); Manikpur; and Dalmau. As Map 5.2 shows, each of these is on the bank of a major river since until the construction of the railways in the late nineteenth century, rivers were the major transport arteries. The decline of the Hindu kingdoms in the fourth-fifth centuries AD brought an end to a period of peace and the study region came under the influence of tribal chiefs.

For almost ten centuries, the role of the larger settlements within the study region changed to that of defensible seats of political power. The region's inhabitants suffered from frequent disturbances and wars among contending rulers who sought to control what was regarded as a relatively prosperous region. Various settlements became important strongholds. For instance, Manikpur was a headquarter for a local chieftain and later became a centre of control within the study region for the Sharqi dynasty in the late fourteenth and the fifteenth century; this dynasty ruled from Jaunpur, an urban centre just to the east of the study region on the Gomti River. The old town of Kusapura was destroyed by a Muslim army around 1300 AD and a new one built close by, named Sultanpur, after the head of the army, Alauddin Khilji.[3]

The impact of Muslim rule on the study region became more pronounced later, especially under the rule of Akbar (1556-1605) who is often referred to as the greatest of the Mughal emperors of India.[4] Under Akbar, Mughal power was extended throughout northern India and well into southern India and an elaborate administrative system established. His empire was divided into 15 provinces with the study region falling within Allahabad Province with Allahabad City, just to the southeast of the study region, as the provincial headquarters. Provinces were divided into districts and Dalmau, Salon and Manikpur were among the administrative centres which assumed importance during this reign. But after Akbar, there were no major developments within the study region in terms of its economy or an urban system until the period of British domination began in the nineteenth century.

At the beginning of the nineteenth century when British power was consolidating in India, the 'backbone' of what developed as the study region's urban system was put into place. In some instances, the British chose to locate military or administrative functions in existing 'towns', as in the case of the army cantonment set up at Sultanpur. In others, such functions gave rise to new towns; for instance, Bela Pratapgarh, one of the three district headquarters, owes its origin to an army cantonment set up there in 1802 although this was only six kilometres from the already existing Pratapgarh City. It is interesting to note that the three largest urban centres in 1981, Rae Bareli, Sultanpur and Bela Pratapgarh, were the only sites in the study region chosen as army cantonments; they were also chosen as the study region's only three district headquarters in 1858 in the administrative re-organisation which followed the First War of Independence between 1857 and 1859.[5] Allahabad City was also the site of a cantonment, an important administrative and educational centre (the University of Allahabad was founded in 1887) and, from 1875 to

1920, the capital of United Provinces which in 1950 was renamed Uttar Pradesh. It was during this mid-nineteenth century administrative re-organisation that existing district and tahsil[6] administrative headquarters and boundaries were put in place.

New administrative and service functions at these headquarters (such as district courts, post offices, new administrative offices, Christian churches, police stations, hospitals and dispensaries) and improvements to roads and railways linking them to other centres and areas, gave some stimulus to their development. Meanwhile, the towns which existed in 1858 but which were not chosen as district or tahsil headquarters generally lost importance. For instance, before the consolidation of British power, Salon had been a relatively important town within the study region and was designated by the British a district headquarters in 1856. But Rae Bareli was preferred as site of the cantonment and the district headquarters was moved there from Salon in 1858. Rae Bareli's location on the River Sai was one reason for this move.

New markets were built in some of the more important urban centres including MacAndrewganj in Bela Pratapgarh and Perkinsganj and Victoriaganj in Sultanpur; their names giving a reminder of the control exercised by the British Crown. The construction of the railway network meant these replaced the Sai, Ganga and Gomti Rivers as the major transport arteries. By 1901, Rae Bareli, Jais, Sultanpur and Bela Pratapgarh were the largest urban centres within the study region while Dalmau and Salon, important towns prior to British rule, had lost importance. Trade and commerce developed in the 'railway towns' and activities in towns close by often relocated there; for example, Bela Pratapgarh experienced rapid economic and population growth and attracted business formerly undertaken by enterprises in nearby Pratapgarh City and Katra Medniganj. Where railway stations were built in existing towns, they were generally built away from the town centre. Railway colonies which housed the workforce developed nearby and as the urban centres' population and physical area expanded, they became integral parts of these centres. But most of the consolidation and development of the study region's economy and urban system took place after 1901.

Agriculture and rural society, 1901–1951

As noted earlier, the study region has had a relatively dense, predominantly rural population for many centuries; by 1901, 56 per cent of the total land area was under cultivation with 43 per cent of this area under irrigation and 36 per cent cropped more than once a year. In 1901, 85 per cent of the total cropped area was devoted to food staples with rice (paddy), gram (chickpeas), barley and wheat as the four most widely grown crops. By 1951, the proportion of land under

Map 5.3 *Administrative boundaries, 1981*

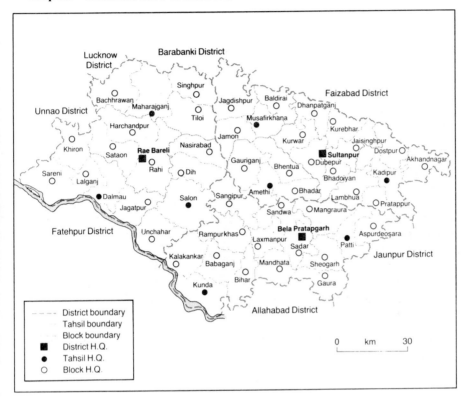

cultivation had grown to 60 per cent although the area under irrigation had hardly grown at all (and the proportion irrigated fell to 41 per cent) while the proportion cropped more than once fell to 30 per cent. The proportion of total cropped area devoted to foodgrains had grown to 94 per cent; paddy, barley, wheat and gram remained the most widely grown crops although the proportion under paddy and barley had grown significantly.

As the figures in Table 5.2 suggest, there were far greater changes in the mix of crops and in the technology and inputs used in farming between 1951 and 1981 than in the preceding 50 years and these will be described later. The increase in the proportion of total cropped area devoted to food grains between 1901 and 1951 was partially due to the reduced importance given to various cash crops first introduced and encouraged by the colonial government – such as indigo, opium and cotton.

Thus, in both 1901 and 1951, most of the study region's population derived a living from largely subsistence-oriented agriculture. Throughout this period, more than 95 per cent of the population lived in rural areas. Most of this rural population lived in some 5,500

Table 5.2   *Cropping pattern in the study region: 1901, 1951 and 1981*

	Percentage of the total cropped area		
Crops	*1901*	*1951*	*1981*
Food grains			
Paddy (rice)	22.7	28.2	31.6
Wheat	11.0	11.3	29.6
Barley	11.8	14.3	6.7
Gram (chickpeas)	14.5	10.2	6.3
Jowar (millet)	5.3	5.5	4.3
Bazra	2.1	2.7	2.9
Peas	—	6.8	2.2
Others	18.0	15.3	4.1
Total food grains	85.4	94.3	87.7
Other crops			
Sugar cane	1.6	1.7	1.4
Potatoes	—	0.8	1.3
Oil seeds	0.3	0.2	1.1
Others	12.7	3.0	8.5

Source: District census handbooks and district annual plans for Rae Bareli, Sultanpur and Pratapgarh, 1980–81.

villages with less than 1,000 inhabitants (66 per cent in 1901 and 61 per cent in 1951). Villages with 2,000 or more inhabitants only contained 10 per cent of the rural population in 1901 and 14 per cent in 1951. It is interesting to note the clear spatial variations in average village size within the study region in 1951: villages with less than 500 inhabitants become more common going from west to east while larger villages with 2,000 or more inhabitants become less common. Two factors help explain this: first, the west of the study region had been more exposed to invasions and security problems in the medieval period which encouraged population to cluster for defence; the second is that a higher proportion of the land in the west is poorly drained, inter-fluvial tracts.

Rural society continued to be dominated by upper caste Hindus as it had been since the decline of the Mughal Empire. Two upper castes, Brahmins (the priest caste) and kshatriyas or Rajputs (traditionally warriors and landlords) maintained control over production through controlling land and labour. In 1901, 14 per cent of the study region's Hindu population were Brahmin while 8 per cent were Rajput. Around 58 per cent were from 'backward' castes such as Murai (who traditionally grow vegetables) or Gadaria (who are traditionally shepherds), while around 16 per cent were from the bottom tier of the caste structure, the 'scheduled' caste, formerly known as the 'untouchables'. Upper castes were the main landowners in both 1901 and 1951 and often did not work the land themselves; Brahmins, as the priest caste, were not meant to work the land themselves. 'Backward' castes often had small landholdings while scheduled castes were usually landless agricultural labourers who worked for very low wages.

The colonial government tried to implement some land reforms to lessen the power of the landlords over their tenants. A first attempt in 1856 had been disrupted by the War in 1857. Acts of 1886 and 1921 sought to give farm tenants more security of tenure and to limit increases in rents charged on the land; meanwhile, land surveys in 1860, 1890 and 1920 classified land according to its productive capacity and rent revenues were fixed according to the average yield in each soil category.

Infrastructure, services and industry, 1901–1951

Map 5.4 shows the development of transport infrastructure over time. Between 1890 and 1901, railways linking Varanasi to Lucknow and Allahabad to Faizabad crossed the study region; both lines met at Bela Pratapgarh while Sultanpur, Rae Bareli, Jais, Amethi, Antu and Bachhrawan were also railway stations.[7] The only paved roads by 1901 were those from Dalmau to Rae Bareli and onto Lucknow and from Allahabad through Bela Pratapgarh and Sultanpur to Faizabad.

Another railway line was built by 1912, part of which ran along the Ganga River's northern bank linking Kunda, Manikpur, Dalmau and Lalganj to Allahabad with a line also connecting this to the Varanasi to Lucknow line at Rae Bareli. Not surprisingly, railway-related activities were important in supporting new developments in certain urban centres; for instance, the relatively rapid population growth in Bela Pratapgarh between 1901 and 1951 was supported by a growth in trade and commerce in response to the location of a railway junction there. One reason for the relative lack of development in nearby Pratapgarh City and Katra Medniganj – both of which had smaller populations in the 1951 census than in the 1901 census – was the fact that trade and commerce formely undertaken in these two towns were attracted to Bela Pratapgarh to get closer to the railway. One reason for Dalmau's relative decline in importance within the study region in these same 50 years was the fact that it was not on one of the early railway lines and it was only at the end point of a paved road in 1901.

The construction of a railway station in certain settlements was an important factor in stimulating some development in what are today small urban centres — Jais, Kunda, Lalganj, Manikpur, Bachhrawan and Amethi. But being a railway station on one of the early railway lines was certainly not a sufficient condition to encourage the development of a small urban centre. For example, Antu, already a railway station in 1901, still had a population of under 5,000 inhab-

Map 5.4 *The development of roads and railways over time*

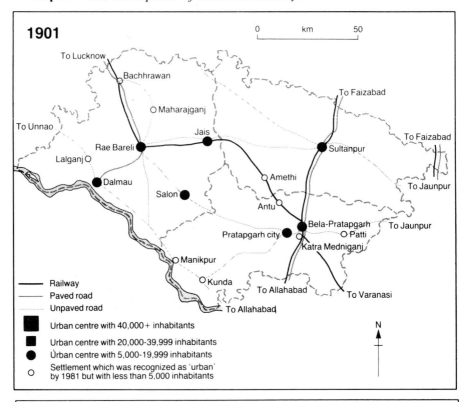

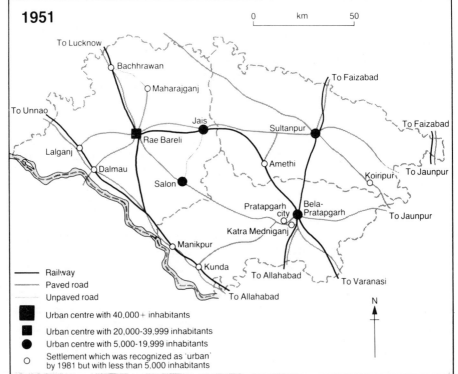

Map 5.4 *Continued*

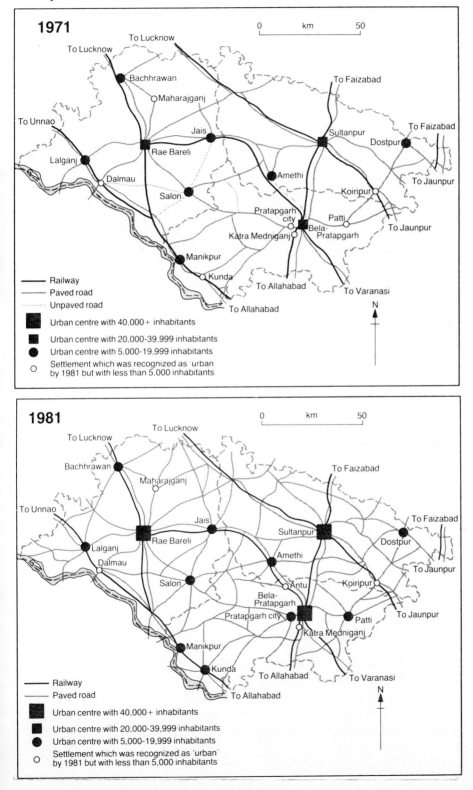

itants in 1981 while Dalmau's population essentially halved between 1901 and 1951, despite the siting of a railway station there early in the twentieth century and the fact that it was one of the first towns in the study region to be reached by a paved road.

The study region once had a flourishing handicrafts industry; the region was well known for spinning and weaving, embroidery and household utensils. But the British policy of promoting textiles produced in Britain and the spread of the railway system which facilitated the import of cheap manufactured goods resulted in a decline in handicrafts and cottage industries. In Rae Bareli District, the 1901 census recorded 11.7 per cent of the labour force working in the secondary sector compared to 5.1 per cent in 1951. The population of Katra Medniganj is reported to have declined from 3,000 inhabitants in 1871 to 2,000 in 1901; the impact of cheap imports on its previously flourishing handloom cotton industry was a major factor in this decline. The migration out of the region of artisans and craftmen during the late nineteenth and early twentieth centuries to industrial centres such as Bombay, Calcutta and Kanpur was also a factor in the very slow (or negative) population growth rates in the early decades of the twentieth century.

Changes in population and its distribution, 1901–1951

By 1901, the study region was already a densely populated area with 3 million inhabitants giving an average population density of 238 persons per square kilometre, compared to a state-wide average of 165 and an all-India average of less than 80. There was also relatively little variation between the 11 tahsils: Pratapgarh tahsil with 270 persons per square kilometre was the most densely populated while Dalmau with 213 was the least densely populated.

Population in the study region grew to 3.6 million between 1901 and 1951. Census data shows a decline in total population for each of the three districts between 1901 and 1911, and 1911 and 1921 although this decline may be overstated since figures in the 1901 census are thought to be over-estimated. But certainly for the first three decades of the twentieth century, cholera, plague and influenza epidemics together with natural calamities,[8] helped keep death rates very high. In addition, in the early decades of this century there was substantial net out-migration from the study region. This shows up in sex ratio statistics since most of this net out-migration is known to have been working-age males. In 1901, there was an average of 1,032 females per 1,000 males in the study region (1,035 in rural areas, 909 in urban centres with only 2 per cent of the population living in urban centres on that date)[9]. Thus, the figures in Table 5.4 show how annual average population growth rates in all three districts were either negative or zero between 1901 and 1931. The population

Table 5.3   *Rural population density: 1901, 1951 and 1981 (inhabitants per square kilometre)*

	1901	1951	1981
Rae Bareli District			
Rae Bareli	222	247	405
Dalmau	213	269	408
Salon	227	248	381
Maharajganj	229	255	354
Sultanpur District			
Musafirkhana	254	297	446
Amethi	229	255	382
Kadipur	233	278	447
Sultanpur	244	297	469
Pratapgarh District			
Pratapgarh	270	327	503
Kunda	234	274	447
Patti	244	280	457

Source: Censuses of India, 1901–1981.

grew by an average of around one per cent per annum between 1931 and 1951; both reduced net out-migration and reduced death rates are known to have contributed to this change although the data does not exist to precisely state the relative contribution of each.

Looking at urban population, it hardly grew at all between 1901 and 1931 which implies net out-migration within the study region, even from urban areas. This is corroborated by examining changes in urban population within tahsils between 1901 and 1951.

Total urban population in four tahsils fell between 1901 and 1931,[10] while five tahsils[11] had no settlements classified as urban either in 1901 or in 1931. The only tahsils with a growth in urban population in these thirty years were Rae Bareli, Sultanpur and Kunda; in each of these, the only town there was the tahsil headquarters of the same name as the tahsil.

Between 1931 and 1951, the tahsils of Sultanpur and Rae Bareli were again among those showing a growth in urban population; they were joined by Dalmau, Maharajganj, Kunda and Pratapgarh. But it was in the three tahsils whose headquarters were also district headquarters that most of the overall growth in urban population took place during these two decades; over 85 per cent of the growth in urban population in the study region in these two decades came from increments in the population of the urban centres of Rae Bareli, Sultanpur and Bela Pratapgarh.

Looking at the population of individual urban centres for 1901 and 1951, as shown on Table 5.5, these same three district headquarters were much the largest urban centres within the study region

Table 5.4 Population growth in the study region's three districts between 1901 and 1981

		Population (1,000 inhabitants)			% of study region's population		
		1901	1951	1981	1901	1951	1981
Rae Bareli District	Rural	999	1,113	1,748	32.9	31.2	30.5
	Urban	40	50	140	1.3	1.4	2.4
	Total	1,039	1,163	1,888	34.2	32.6	32.9
Sultanpur District	Rural	1,082	1,276	1,971	35.6	35.8	34.4
	Urban	10	17	67	0.3	0.5	1.2
	Total	1,092	1,293	2,038	35.9	36.3	35.6
Pratapgarh District	Rural	889	1,081	1,715	29.3	30.4	29.9
	Urban	19	26	92	0.6	0.7	1.6
	Total	908	1,107	1,807	29.9	31.1	31.5
Total for region		3,039	3,563	5,733			

Annual average population growth rates

	1901—31	1931—51	1951—61	1961—71	1971—81
Rae Bareli	−0.2	0.9	1.3	1.3	2.3
Sultanpur	−0.1	1.0	0.9	1.5	2.2
Pratapgarh	0.0	1.0	1.2	1.3	2.4

Source: Derived from statistics drawn from censuses of India, 1901–1981.

Table 5.5 *Population in urban centres: 1901 and 1951*

	1901	1951
Rae Bareli	16,880	24,958
Bela Pratapargh	8,041	15,026
Sultanpur	9,550	17,496
Jais	12,688	8,232
Kunda	n.a.	n.a.
Lalganj	n.a.	3,345
Manikpur	3,673	4,712
Salon	5,170	5,621
Bachhrawan	n.a.	3,447
Amethi	n.a.	n.a.
Dostpur	n.a.	n.a.
Pratapgarh City	5,148	4,576
Patti	n.a.	n.a.
Antu	n.a.	n.a.
Koiripur	n.a.	n.a.
Katra Medniganj	2,123	2,103
Dalmau	5,655	2,766
Maharajganj	n.a.	2,084

NB Settlements listed here include all settlements within the study region
which had urban status in the 1981 census. Antu, Koiripur, Katra
Medniganj, Dalmau and Maharajganj had populations below 5,000 in
1981 – see Table 5.12.

in 1951 whereas in 1901, Jais had been the second largest urban
centre. Of the three centres other than Rae Bareli, Sultanpur, Bela
Pratapgarh and Jais with more than 5,000 inhabitants in 1901, only
Salon registered an increase in population between 1901 and 1951.
And its increase was only some 450 inhabitants compared to the
increment of between 6,000 and 8,000 experienced by the three district
capitals. Meanwhile, Jais's population dropped over 4,000 inhabitants
while Dalmau's population essentially halved.

Developments from 1951 to 1981

Agriculture

As Table 5.6 shows, the proportion of the labour force working in
the primary sector was 85 per cent or more for each district, in 1981;
the proportion increased in both Rae Bareli and Pratapgarh districts
between 1901 and 1951 and between 1951 and 1971. Agricultural

Table 5.6 *Sectoral distribution of the labour force: 1951, 1971 and 1981*

Districts	1951	1971	1981
Rae Bareli			
Primary	79.2	88.2	84.9
Secondary	5.1	4.0	2.4
Tertiary	15.7	7.8	12.7
Sultanpur			
Primary	88.5	88.4	86.7
Secondary	3.5	4.0	3.0
Tertiary	8.0	7.6	10.3
Pratapgarh			
Primary	86.6	87.8	84.4
Secondary	4.7	4.4	2.3
Tertiary	8.7	7.8	13.3

Source: Censuses of India in 1951, 1971 and 1981.

production has grown more rapidly than that of manufacturing; at current prices, the total value of agricultural production grew by 250 per cent between 1960 and 1976 compared to the 97 per cent growth of manufacturing. The slow growth in manufacturing is reflected in its very low (and declining) share in the structure of work participation in these 30 years.

Changes in agriculture between 1951 and 1981 are evident in terms of the net cropped area, the area under irrigation, average yields and the mix of crops grown; Tables 5.2 and 5.7 give some idea of how production, productivity and the crop mix have changed over time.

The area under agricultural production grew substantially between 1951 and 1981 to reach 63 per cent of the region's total area; another 7 per cent is cultivated land left fallow for part of the year. The area under irrigation grew some 40 per cent in this period to encompass 53 per cent of the net cropped area in contrast to the period 1901–1951 when the area under irrigation hardly grew at all. Further increases in net cropped area are unlikely; virtually all cultivable land is now under cultivation. Indeed, net cropped area may fall in the future with an increasing demand for land for such uses as settlements, roads, canals and factories. In 1981, some 10 per cent of the study region's land area was devoted to such non-agricultural uses.

But there remains considerable potential for expanding the area under double cropping, although this is largely dependent on further increases in the area under irrigation. By 1980, 36 per cent of the net cropped area was cropped more than once, compared to 30 per cent in 1951.

Table 5.7 shows the change in the mix of crops grown between 1951 and 1981. Paddy (rice) remained the most widely-grown crop

Table 5.7 *Changes in agriculture during the Sixties and Seventies in the three districts*

	Rae Bareli	Sultan- pur	Pratap- garh
Rice production (1,000 tons) and yields per hectare (tons)			
1961	81 (0.8)	n.a. (0.7)	37 (0.6)
1979	129 (1.1)	117 (0.9)	92 (1.1)
Wheat production (1,000 tons) and yields per hectare (tons)			
1961	51 (1.0)	n.a. (1.0)	23 (0.8)
1979	156 (1.4)	110 (1.4)	107 (1.4)
Sugar cane production (1,000 tons) and yields per hectare (tons)			
1961	n.a. (38)	n.a. (43)	176 (43)
1979	84 (29)	355 (36)	90 (28)
Potato production (1,000 tons) and yields per hectare (tons)			
1961	n.a. (8.7)	n.a. (7.5)	12 (7.0)
1979	56 (15.8)	16.9 (15.3)	110 (15.8)
Area under high yielding variety of rice (1,000 ha)			
1969	5.0	n.a.	5.2
1979	20.0	89.8	66.4
Area under high yielding variety of wheat (1,000 ha)			
1969	22.0	n.a.	14.5
1979	107.0	73.7	59.9

n.a. indicates statistic is not available.

Source: Statistical Bulletin for Uttar Pradesh 1980 and Uttar Pradesh Agricultural Statistics, 1979.

while the proportion of land devoted to wheat grew rapidly. In this 30-year period, the area under paddy grew by only 21 per cent while that under wheat grew by 183 per cent. Barley, gram and peas were the crops which have declined most in importance, due largely to the increasing area under wheat. High-yielding seeds for wheat, the growing use of chemical fertilisers and, perhaps most importantly, improved irrigation facilities have supported this growth in area under wheat. In the kharif monsoon season, rice has become more important for similar reasons at the expense of jowar and bazra (millets). The area under oil seeds (mustard and rape being the two most important) and potatoes also grew rapidly between 1951 and 1980 although neither covered much more than one per cent of the total cropped area in 1981.

Production and yields for sugar cane fell since wheat was found to give a better return. In addition, there were no sugar mills close by and the use of sugar cane for producing jaggery[12] did not give farmers much return compared to other crops. Recently the government has been trying to reverse the decline in sugar production after a sugar mill was set up in Rae Bareli with a capacity of 1,250 tons a year. The Sugar Cane Department installed irrigation in 4,000 hectares of land between 1978 and 1981 and increased the distribution of fertilisers and of high-yielding seeds. In addition, cheap medicines for the farmers and improved provision for transporting the crop to the sugar mill was included in the programme which seeks to raise sugar cane production within a 16 km radius of Rae Bareli. A sugar mill is also being built at Sultanpur; in 1979, 62 per cent of 15,800 hectares devoted to sugar cane within the study region were in Sultanpur District and this and the fact that it has the highest proportion of land area under cultivation help explain why Sultanpur has the highest per capita value of agricultural produce among the three districts.

Crop yields per hectare have risen considerably in the case of rice, wheat and potatoes; average yields per hectare for each grew by more than 40 per cent in each of the three districts whereas average sugar yields fell. The proportion of land devoted to sugar cane also fell. Changes in the mix of crops grown in the study region and the shift in production from that largely oriented to subsistence to an increasing proportion for sale has been very marked in the 1951–1981 period, unlike the previous fifty years. From the mid-Sixties, high-yielding varieties of seeds (especially for wheat), increasing use of chemical fertilisers, improved farm technology and improved irrigation facilities supported the increase in production and yields. Virtually all production remains for local or regional consumption even if more crops are marketed rather than consumed directly by the farming household. Sugar and potatoes are the only crops where a substantial proportion of total production is consumed outside the study region.

The growth in the proportion of net cropped area under irrigation has probably been the single most important factor in changing crop mixes and increasing total production. Water from the Sharda Sahayak Canal and a number of associated lift irrigation schemes provide water for 38 per cent of the net irrigated area. But the study region is at the 'tail-end' of this canal system which means that effective irrigation from the canal hardly covers a quarter of its potential command area. Within the last few decades, several lift

Table 5.8 *Indicators relating to agriculture in the three districts*

	Rae Bareli	Sultanpur	Pratapgarh
Use of fertilisers per hectare (kg) 1979–80	49	39	40
Per capita production of food-crops (kg) 1979–80	271	224	210
Per hectare production value of agricultural products (rupees)	1,950	1,798	1,536
Per head value of agricultural products (rupees) 1979–80	367	403	311
Number of tractors in 1978–79	510	340	385
Area under irrigation (thousand hectares, 1979)	151	137	115
Proportion of holdings under 1 hectare (1977)	75%	79%	82%
Land area under holdings of 2 or more hectares (1000 ha, 1977)	116	119	84
Area under sugar cane (hectares, 1979)	2,871	9,734	3,207
Net cropped area as percentage of total area 1978-79	63%	70%	63%

Source: District Statistical Bulletins 1979 and 1980.

irrigation schemes have been undertaken based on the Sai, Gomti and Ganga rivers. Private tube-wells are the second most important source of irrigation water, accounting for 23 per cent of irrigation water in 1980. While publicly-funded measures to increase the land under irrigation and the efficiency of this irrigation have been slow to come, privately-funded tube-wells with electrically or diesel powered pumps have been installed by richer farmers on their relatively large landholdings; this has helped further widen the income gap between rich and poor farmers. In addition, not all the area recorded as under irrigation receives assured water supplies and this is most common where government schemes are the source of irrigation water. There remains considerable potential for increasing the amount of groundwater used for irrigation; such developments by public authorities to improve irrigation water supply to poorer villages and poorer households are much needed.

However, as in many other areas in India, it is only a relatively small proportion of farmers who have been the main beneficiaries of this rise in production and productivity, since relatively few have access to the land and capital needed to make best use of the new seeds and chemical imputs. While the rise in the number of tractors from 34 in 1951 to 1,235 in 1978 appears dramatic, this still implies little more than one tractor per thousand farming households. The use of chemical fertilisers per hectare for the whole study region also remains low: ranging from an average of 49 kilos per hectare in Rae Bareli to 40 in Pratapgarh and 39 in Sultanpur. Almost 80 per cent of the landholders have less than one hectare with an average holding of only one-third of an hectare; these covered 38 per cent of the net cropped area in 1976. Just 12,000 farmers, one per cent of all the farmers, farmed 11 per cent of the cropped area with an average landholding size of 7.5 hectares. Over time, the trend of increasing proportions of holdings with less than 2 hectares is apparent in all three districts; in 1961, 69 per cent of holdings were less than 2 hectares compared to 92 per cent in 1976.

Government intervention in agricultural production since Independence in 1947 can be divided into four categories: land reform, land consolidation, construction of irrigation facilities and price guarantees for crops. The Uttar Pradesh Zamindar and Land Reforms Act of 1950 allocated land owned by absentee landowners and by landlords whose land was farmed by tenants to those who actually occupied and farmed the land.[13] A large number of farmers acquired land ownership rights and the tenure system was simplified; before this Act, there were a total of 14 types of tenure including categories of tenants with different rights with regard to amount of rent paid and inheritance and transfer rights. After the 1950 Act, most of the farming population acquired a permanent right to till their land and inheritance rights although not all acquired transfer rights. In 1960, the Uttar Pradesh Imposition of Ceiling on Land Holding Act was passed which limited the size of family holdings although the limit was set sufficiently high to mean that this had little effect within the study region.[14]

Two important influences have helped increase the number (and reduce the average size) of holdings. The first is the subdivision of holdings due to inheritance while the second is formerly landless people becoming landowners, usually through purchase of small plots with money acquired through remittances from family members working in major industrial centres like Bombay, Calcutta, Delhi and Kanpur. Another government intervention in the agricultural land market has been land consolidation. Begun in Sultanpur in 1954, a village level programme seeks to rationalise the many small and scattered holdings around a village into holdings whereby each farming household has one plot—rather than plots distributed around the village.

Looking at Table 5.8, Rae Bareli seems the most prosperous of the three districts in terms of agriculture; it has the highest per capita production of food crops, per capita value of agricultural products and per hectare value of agricultural products. In the late Seventies, it also had the largest area under irrigation, the largest number of tractors and the lowest proportion of holdings with under one hectare. The indicators for Pratapgarh suggest that it had the least developed agriculture.

Manufacturing

The slow growth in the value of manufacturing production between 1960 and 1976 was noted earlier; so too was the low proportion of the labour force engaged in manufacturing (3 per cent or less in each of the three districts in 1981). Most of the output and employment in manufacturing is in unregistered units; one estimate suggests that these account for 95 per cent of the value of industrial production. In 1980, there were 1,382 cottage and small registered industrial units with a total employed labour force of around 5,000; 59 per cent were in Rae Bareli with 24 per cent in Sultanpur and the remaining 17 per cent in Pratapgarh. Virtually all were producing consumer goods based on local materials such as flour, oil, bamboo and cane products, leather and leather goods, handloom textiles, soap, pottery and wood products.

Large-scale manufacturing industries only appeared in the study region relatively recently. In all of Pratapgarh, there were just five units employing 72 persons in 1981. However, a tractor factory has been established in Katra Medniganj nearby which should create 600 jobs. Sultanpur has no large-scale industries (apart from a new sugar mill) although a number are being considered. Rae Bareli is the urban centre with much the largest concentration of large-scale industries. The first such unit only came in 1973 and since then 14 others have started, creating a total of 6,000 jobs. These produce a wide range of goods including sugar, cotton textiles, carpets, plastics and chemicals, spun pipes and various engineering products. The most prestigious is Indian Telephone Industries which began production in 1979.

Most of the new industrial units belong to the private sector; Indian Telephone Industries at Rae Bareli and the tractor factory at Katra Medniganj are the exceptions. Jagdishpur is being developed as a centre for industry by the Uttar Pradesh Industrial Development Corporation in collaboration with Bharat Heavy Electricals Ltd, who are building a factory there. Among the other industries proposed for Jagdishpur is another sugar mill. Amethi and nearby Munshiganj also figure in the State government's plans as centres for industrial development; a Hindustan Aeronauticals plant is being built in Amethi. Apart from the stimulus that the State government hopes public sector industries will bring, there are also a range of incentives offered to private sector industries locating within the study region.

Industrial estates with roads, electricity and water supply have been proposed for a number of places and concessional credit is available.

Rae Bareli is seen as an urban centre with considerable potential for developing as an industrial centre with spill-over from Kanpur and Unnao, from outside the region. Apart from the 15 large industrial units, some 51 small-scale industrial units were registered there by 1971, compared to only ten in 1961. Rae Bareli district has been designated as one of the districts to which import licences will be granted for the import of scarce raw materials needed for establishing industrial units. Electricity capacity is also being increased.

Commerce, trade and services

It is agriculture, commerce, trade and services and not manufacturing which dominate the employment base of urban centres and other settlements given urban status in the 1981 census. Antu still had 71 per cent of its labour force working in the primary sector in 1981 while the proportion was 60 per cent or more in Pratapgarh City and Koiripur, and 50 per cent or more in Manikpur and Kunda. Only in the three district headquarters (Rae Bareli, Sultanpur, and Pratapgarh), in Lalganj, Salon and Maharajganj in Rae Bareli District and in Katra Medniganj in Pratapgarh District was the proportion below 25 per cent. The contribution of household industry to total employment was relatively small; it was under ten per cent in all but Katra Medniganj (35 per cent), Manikpur (13 per cent) and Dostpur (12 per cent). In each census between 1951 and 1981, Katra Medniganj has registered the highest proportion of workers in the secondary sector and this relates to its historic role as a centre for producing cloth on handlooms. And although figures from the 1981 census for the distribution of the labour force between non-household industry and services are not available, since 1901 it is very rare for the secondary sector to account for as much as 25 per cent of jobs in any town, and figures of between nine and 20 per cent are much the most common.

To obtain a better idea of the employment base in urban centres, field work was undertaken in Rae Bareli, Sultanpur and Bela Pratapgarh and in Kunda, Manikpur and Katra Medniganj. This revealed a diverse mix of small enterprises in trade, commerce and services, providing the livelihood of most of those not working directly in agriculture. Not surprisingly, the three district capitals had much the most numerous and diverse mix; each had between 1,750 and 2,000 enterprises in 1981. Each had a range of flour mills, carpentry establishments, printing presses and engineering works. Each had more than 250 enterprises selling some mixture of cereals, pulses, dairy produce, vegetables and fruit and over 120 general stores and cloth and hosiery stores. Jewellers, shops selling electrical goods, medical stores and machine tools and auto and cycle stores were generally the next most common with each centre having between 35 and 120 of each of these. Under services, 'hotels, restaurants, tea stalls, sweet shops and betel shops',[15] 'laundry, hairdressing, tailors and other artisans', and 'auto-repair, cycle and rickshaw repair' were three categories which accounted for most private sector service enterprises. What is noticeable – and common to all three centres – is the fact that more than half of the enterprises existing in 1981 only began within the 1971-1981 decade.

In Kunda, Manikpur and Katra Medniganj, not surprisingly, one finds much fewer and much less diverse concentrations of enterprises; Kunda had 360 while Manikpur had 229 and Katra Medniganj 152. Food and general stores and enterprises selling cloth and hosiery account for most of the enterprises in trade and commerce while the three service sector categories mentioned above account for virtually all private sector service enterprises. In Kunda, less than a third and in Manikpur a third of the enterprises recorded in 1981 had begun in the previous ten years; in Katra Medniganj, the comparable figure was close to two-thirds.

The fact that even the three intermediate urban centres of Rae Bareli, Bela Pratapgarh and Sultanpur do not have the concentration of retail, wholesale and service enterprises which one would expect, implies a low level of purchasing power both within their own inhabitants and in the inhabitants of their district. One should also recall that each of these centres is the largest retail and service centre for districts with around two million inhabitants. It seems that a high proportion of the demand for goods and services within each district is met in bi-weekly or weekly markets; in 1981, there was a total of 403 markets. Small bi-weekly markets are held throughout the study region, usually in villages, while weekly markets are usually larger and located in urban centres.

To obtain an idea of the relative importance of both urban and rural centres as concentrations of services, facilities and enterprises, settlements in the study region were assessed according to the number of 'central place functions' they contained, from a list of 28.[16] A total of 58 settlements were found to have central place scores of more than ten; Table 5.9 lists the top 40 and compares their 'central place score' with their rank according to population size and administrative importance. It comes as little surprise to find that the largest three urban centres, which are also the only three district capitals have much the highest scores and thus the highest concentration of services, facilities and enterprises normally associated with urban centres. The next seven largest urban centres with populations ranging from Amethi with 7,132 to Jais with 15,205 in 1981 all have scores of between 48 and 84. Jais's score is relatively low compared to its population size while the scores of Bachhrawan and Amethi are relatively high.

What is also notable is the fact that of the rest of the settlements with urban status in the 1981 census, all but Antu and Katra Medniganj are within the 20 settlements with the highest central place scores. Similarly, relatively large settlements but without urban status such as Nasirabad, Deeh, Sataon, Unchahar, Kurwar, Kheron and Lambhua, all within the most populous 20 settlements in the study region, all have scores which ensure their rank according to population size is substantially higher than their rank according to central place score. In the analysis in the last section of this chapter, the obvious mis-matches between central place scores and settlement sizes will be investigated further.

Changes in population and in distribution

Between 1951 and 1981, the study region's population grew from 3 million to 5.7 million inhabitants. The population growth rate increased for every decade between 1951 to 1981 (as it had done between 1921 and 1951); falling death rates and general improvements in nutrition and health hygiene were important factors behind this. But only in the decade 1971-1981 did the region's population growth rate become comparable to the rate of natural increase. This implies that only during the Seventies did net out-migration not become common.

Table 5.10 shows annual average population growth rates by tahsil for each of the three decades between 1951 and 1981. For each tahsil, population growth was most rapid in the 1971-1981 decade. It is also notable that only in this decade did the population growth rate of most tahsils come to equal or exceed the State average for natural growth. In the previous two decades, population growth rates in most tahsils were well below this average. This also implies sustained net out-migration from most tahsils for the intercensus periods between 1951 and 1971 but net in-migration for many in the period 1971-1981. The next subsection seeks to correlate differentials in tahsils' population growth rates with changes in their economy. But it should be noted that an epidemic of cholera was one reason for the relatively slow population growth rates in the contiguous tahsils of Musafirkhana, Amethi, Sultanpur, Maharajganj and Pratapgarh, during the Fifties.

Sex ratios and the way these change over time give some suggestion of trends in migration flows. For each census since 1901, the study region has recorded a higher sex ratio (ie a higher proportion of women to men) than the average for the state. Over time, the sex ratio has generally declined: from 1,032 females per 1,000 males in 1901 to 999 in 1951 and 970 in 1981. This implies that net out-migration has been slowing down, since migration flows are the principal determinant of change in sex ratios.

Table 5.9 The 40 most populous settlements in the study region with central place scores exceeding 10 – with comparison made between population size, administrative rank and central place score

Rank according to popn.	Name of settlement	Administrative status [a]			Urban status [b]		Population (1981) [c]		Central place Score (1981)	Central place Rank (1981)
		DH	TH	BH	81	51	IUC	SUC		
1	Rae Bareli	x	x	x	x	x	x		267	1
2	Bela Prat.	x	x	x	x	x	x		219	3
3	Sultanpur	x	x	x	x	x	x		231	2
4	Jais				x	x		x	77	6
5	Kunda		x	x	x			x	86	4
6	Lalganj			x	x			x	71	7
7	Manikpur				x	x		x	48	11=
8	Salon		x	x	x	x		x	62	9
9	Bachhrawan			x	x	x		x	78	5
10	Amethi		x	x	x			x	63	8
11	Dostpur			x	x			x	34	15
12	Nasirabad							x	17	48
13	Pratapgarh C.				x	x		x	29	20=
14	Deeh			x				x	18	41
15	Sataon			x				x	15	57
16	Unchahar			x				x	20	28
17	Kurwar		x	x				x	19	33
18	Patti			x	x			x	50	10
19	Kheron			x					19	33
20	Lambhuna			x					20	28

Table 5.9 continued

No.	Name	DH	TH	BH	US-81	US-51	IUC		
21	Antu		×					29	20 =
22	Koiripur		×					34	15 =
23	Musafirkhana			×	×			34	15 =
24	Bhadaiyan				×			18	41
25	Katra Med.					×	×	26	23
26	S. Chandika							18	41 =
27	Rahi				×			48	41 =
28	Dalmau		×		×	×		48	11 =
29	Maharajganj		×		×	×	×	42	13
30	Lakshmanpur				×		×	17	48
31	Bihar				×			19	33
32	Tiloi				×			26	23
33	Jagatpur				×			18	41 =
34	Baldi Rai				×			18	41 =
35	Jagdishpur				×			83	17
36	Pratappur K.				×			22	26
37	Sangipur				×			19	33 =
38	Kadipur		×		×			32	18 =
39	Gauriganj				×			23	25
40	Sareni				×			16	53

Notes: a—DH: District Headquarters
     TH: Tahsil Headquarters
     BH: Block Headquarters

b—US-81: Urban Status in 1981
     US-51: Urban Status in 1951

c—IUC: Intermediate Urban Centres (20,000 plus inhabitants)
     SUC: Small Urban Centres (5,000–19,999 inhabitants)

Table 5.10   *Population growth rates by tahsil: 1951–1981*

Tahsils	1951–1961	1961–1971	1971–1981
Rae Bareli District			
Dalmau	1.4	1.6	1.8
Maharajganj	0.9	1.2	2.0
Rae Bareli	1.5	1.6	2.9
Salon	1.4	1.2	2.3
Sultanpur District			
Amethi	0.9	1.2	2.2
Kadipur	1.0	1.7	2.1
Musafirkhana	0.6	1.5	2.0
Sultanpur	1.0	1.6	2.4
Pratapgarh District			
Kunda	1.5	1.4	2.4
Pratapgarh	1.1	1.2	2.5
Patti	1.1	1.3	2.3
Average for the study region	1.1	1.4	2.3
Natural growth rate for Uttar Pradesh	1.5	2.2	2.1

Source: Derived from censuses of India 1951–1981.

Table 5.13 shows how sex ratios in urban areas are, not surprisingly, much lower than in rural areas – and this has been apparent since 1901. However, census data also shows that over 90 per cent of the study region's population was born in the district of enumeration in both the 1951 and 1961 census and that less than 0.6 per cent were born outside the state of Uttar Pradesh. This implies that, at least up to 1961, changes in population distribution within the region were largely due either to intra-regional migration flows or out-migration flows; flows of in-migration from other areas were not important.

To help get more details about migration flows from rural areas, fieldwork undertaken in December 1983 selected ten sample villages, two from each of the five blocks which make up Musafirkhana tahsil in Sultanpur district. Population growth in Musafirkhana has been relatively slow compared to other tahsils, notably in the decades 1951-1961 and 1971-1981. The fieldwork concentrated on males since female out-migration is known to be relatively small and largely composed on intra-regional migration for the purpose of marriage.

Among the households interviewed in the ten villages, 37 per cent of the males were found to be working elsewhere; the proportion varied from between 32 per cent and 41 per cent of males for the ten villages. Eighty-five per cent of the male migrants were married and 74 per cent were between 15 and 39 years old. Most were literate and generally of a higher educational standard than those remaining in the villages. Seventy-eight per cent were working with 13 per cent as students, five per cent unemployed and four per cent as dependents. Most of those working were unskilled or semi-skilled labourers.

With regards to migrants' destination, most were in metropolitan areas or cities with 100,000 or more inhabitants; 52 per cent were in urban areas within other States but very few were working outside India. Very few were working in small urban centres or rural areas and relatively few were still within Sultanpur District. Two-thirds of the migrants had left after 1970, while a quarter had left between 1980 and December 1983 (when the field work was undertaken). This gives the impression of an area where large-scale out-migration of males of working age has been the norm, at least during the Fifties and Sixties. In the study region, available statistics suggest a comparable flow of out-migration with a change in this only becoming apparent between the 1971 and 1981 censuses when population growth was higher than the average figure for natural growth in Uttar Pradesh State. In addition, seven out of the eleven tahsils had populations growing faster than the State average; in previous decades, no tahsil's population growth rate had exceeded the State average natural growth rate although two (Rae Bareli and Kunda) had equalled it in the 1951-1961 period. Certain tahsils have had populations growing relatively fast compared to other tahsils – notably Rae Bareli and Kunda for the period 1951-1981 and Sultanpur for the period 1961-1981. By comparison, Amethi, Maharajganj and Musafirkhana had relatively slow population growth for the three decades.

The number of rural settlements (villages) has remained remarkably constant over time; the number of villages grew from 6,362 in 1901 to 6,408 in 1971. The growth in the number of villages is largely due to territorial adjustments with adjoining districts or the division of one village into two to provide a more rational administrative grouping.[17] Villages' origins and functions today are predominantly as a home for those working in agriculture; nucleation is far more the result of insecurity in the past and the need to minimise encroachment over good quality agricultural land. Most villages have few (if any) services.

However, some of the larger villages – in 1971 there were 321 with 2,000 or more inhabitants – do have periodic markets and some concentration of services and facilities. In the analysis of central place scores, 11 settlements[18] which were not urban centres had scores of more than 20, while a further 29 had scores of ten or more. However, public services and facilities at designated administrative centres certainly played an important role here; virtually all the settlements with scores of 20 or more which were not urban centres were either tahsil headquarters (Kadipur and Musafirkhana are the only tahsil headquarters not given urban status in 1981) or block headquarters.

Table 5.11   *Urban population: 1951–1981*

District	1951	1961	1971	1981
Rae Bareli	50,453	39,846	51,403	139,833
Sultapur	17,496	26,081	32,330	67,379
Pratapgarh	26,417	21,397	27,909	91,579
Total for study region	94,366	87,324	111,642	298,791

Source: Censuses of India 1951–1981.

Changes in urban population

The study region is one of the least urbanised areas within Uttar Pradesh State which is itself one of the least urbanised states in India. Table 5.11 shows changes in urban population by decade between 1951 and 1981 for each of the three districts, while Table 5.12 gives figures for populations and population growth rates for all settlements recognised by the 1981 census as 'urban'.

While figures in Table 5.11 might be taken to imply rapid population growth in the study region's urban centres between 1971 and 1981 – since total urban population almost tripled in this period – in fact, the inclusion of 14 new settlements in the 1981 census which had not been classified as urban centres in 1971 and the extension of the boundaries of certain urban centres (so that these came to encompass what formerly had been a rural population) contributed more to total growth in urban population than increments to the population of settlements recognised as urban centres in both the 1971 and 1981 censuses.

The study region's urban population grew from 111,642 to 298,791 between 1971 and 1981. The inclusion of the 14 settlements which became recognised as 'urban centres' in the 1981 census was responsible for 50.3 per cent of this total growth; the growth in population of Jais, Sultanpur, Bela Pratapgarh and Rae Bareli (the only settlements recognised as urban centres in 1971 and 1981) accounted for the rest. Population growth in Rae Bareli was the most rapid of the four since its population more than doubled and had an annual average growth rate of 8.8 per cent. Although no figures were available for rate of natural increase in Rae Bareli for this decade, it cannot have been more than around 2.7 per cent per annum, ie accounting for roughly 30 per cent total population growth. The other 70 per cent must be split between net in-migration and the expansion of Rae Bareli's municipal boundaries. However, it is impossible to differentiate between the two although the expansion of municipal boundaries is thought to be of greater importance. The municipal boundaries for the 1981 census figure encompassed some 50 square kilometres compared to the 10 square kilometres used for the 1971 census, and 84 settlements which had been villages outside

Rae Bareli urban centre in 1971, were counted as being within municipal boundaries by 1981. Bela Pratapgarh, which also had rapid population growth between 1971 and 1981, also had its municipal boundaries expanded; while in 1971 they encompassed 8.3 square kilometres, in 1981 they encompassed 11.2. The municipal boundaries of Sultanpur and Jais, remained unchanged in this period.

The drop in urban population for the whole study region between 1951 and 1961, shown in Table 5.11 was due to the exclusion of eight settlements which had been counted as urban centres in the previous census. Each of the four settlements classified as urban centres in both 1951 and 1961 had experienced population growth during this decade – as did most of the settlements declassified as urban centres in the 1961 census.

Since 1961, census definitions for what constitutes an urban area have become more rigorously based on the idea of nucleated settlements with 5,000 or more inhabitants, and the majority of the working population engaged in non-agricultural activities. However, in all censuses since 1901, there have been categories which allow a settlement to be declared an 'urban area' without meeting any minimum population size or concentration of labour force working in non-agricultural activities. Although the ways by which this can happen have varied from census to census (in 1981 a settlement was an urban centre if it was a statutory town),[19] this allowed the classification of such settlements as Maharajganj, Koiripur, Antu and Katra Medinganj as 'urban' in the 1981 census although none had populations which reached 5,000 inhabitants on that date. In addition, in 1981, Koiripur had 61 per cent of its labour force working in the primary sector, while Antu had 71 per cent. Political factors certainly influenced the classification of Antu, Koiripur, Amethi and Dostpur as 'urban'.

Data of sex ratios in urban centres and rural areas as shown in Table 5.13 give some indication as to the scale and direction of migration flows internal to the region. Most out-migration from rural areas is known to be adult males, expecially those of between 15 and 39 years. A correlation between the imbalances in sex ratios within urban centres and population growth rates appears clear. Urban centres with relatively rapid population growth between 1951 and 1981 generally had the most imbalanced sex ratios while those with relatively slow population growth rates had the least imbalanced.[20]

Infrastructure and public services

Considerable emphasis has been placed by Federal and State governments on improving infrastructure and services since 1951. As Map 5.4 shows, an increasing number of the smaller settlements

Table 5.12 Population growth in urban centres: 1951–1981

	1951	1961	1971	1981	Annual average growth rates (%)		
					1951–1961	1961–1971	1971–1981
Rae Bareli	24,958	29,940	38,765	90,442	1.8	2.6	8.8
Bela Pratapgarh	15,026	21,396	27,909	50,188	3.6	2.7	6.0
Sultanpur	17,496	26,081	32,330	48,788	4.1	2.2	4.2
Jais	8,232	9,906	12,638	15,205	1.9	2.5	1.9
Kunda		3,122[a]	4.134	11,776		2.9	11.0
Lalganj	3,345	4,792[a]	6,951[a]	10,596	3.7	3.8	4.3
Manikpur	4,712	5,413[a]	6,666[a]	8,769	1.4	2.1	2.8
Salon	5,621	6,704[a]	7,971[a]	8,113	1.8	1.7	0.2
Bachhrawan	3,447	4,323[a]	5,428[a]	7,682	2.3	2.4	3.4
Amethi		2,551[a]	5,056[a]	7,132		7.1	3.5
Dostpur		3,525[a]	5,393[a]	7,120		4.3	2.8
Pratapgarh City	4,576	4,711[a]	4,714[a]	6,723	0.3	0.0	3.6
Patti		2,546[a]	2,663[a]	5,448		0.5	7.4
Antu		3,724[a]	4,524[a]	4,617		2.0	0.2
Koiripur		2,917[a]	3,610[a]	4,339		2.2	1.9
Katra Medniganj	2,103	1,570[a]	2,026[a]	4,060	−2.9	2.6	7.2
Dalmau	2,766	2,525[a]	3,131[a]	3,891	−0.9	2.2	2.2
Mahrajganj	2,084	2,619[a]	2,880[a]	3,857	2.3	1.0	3.0

Note: a—The settlements were not recognised as a town by this census.

Source: Censuses of India, 1951, 1961, 1971 and 1981.

Table 5.13 *Sex ratios for rural areas in the three districts and for urban centres: 1951—1981*

Urban centres	1951	1961	1971	1981
Rae Bareli	815	838	862	817
Jais	941	964	936	968
Lalgang	798	870	912	866
Salon	932	976	926	966
Bachhrawan	899	942	835	901
Dalmau	854	889	922	902
Mahrajganj	891	921	819	882
Sultanpur	768	790	815	832
Amethi	n.a.	837	847	882
Dostpur	1028	1023	937	934
Koiripur	n.a.	911	910	887
Bela Pratapgarh	811	839	847	818
Kunda	864	977	852	895
Manikpur	1004	966	925	917
Pratapgarh City	880	1016	832	895
Patti	1044	1001	871	865
Antu	916	982	866	912
Katra Medniganj	1062	1065	948	958
Rural population in Rae Bareli District	959	968	946	949
Rural Population in Sultanpur District	1002	1021	973	973
Rural Population in Pratapgarh District	1044	1066	1022	1019

Source: Censuses of India 1951–1981.

became connected to the wider urban system by metalled roads between 1951 and 1981. In each district, the length of such roads more than doubled between 1961 and 1980. The region is served by four major state highways. Railway lines were built after 1951 link Jaunpur and Varanasi (to the south-east of the study region) to Lucknow (to the north-west) via Sultanpur and Dalmau to Rae Bareli. However, many villages still lack easy access to paved roads. Out of the 6,435 villages within the study region, only 28 per cent were within one kilometre of a paved road in 1980 while 42 per cent were not within three km and 22 per cent not within five km. And even villages which are relatively close to a paved road may find their access to this road (and to urban centres) cut off during the rainy season.

While considerable public investment has been made in the region, facilities are still far from adequate for the predominantly village-based population. Literacy reached 24 per cent in 1981 compared to eight per cent in 1951; the change in female literacy in this period was from one per cent to ten per cent. There is now one primary school for every two villages. The number of secondary, higher secondary and degree colleges have grown rapidly. In 1961 there were two higher education colleges; in 1981 there were 17. However, in 1979 there were still some 2,000 villages, (31 per cent of all villages), where children have to walk more than five km to reach the senior basic school. For higher secondary school students, 60 per cent of the boys and a much higher proportion of the girls had to travel more than five km.

There has been a comparable growth in the number of hospitals and dispensaries but again, not commensurate with need. The number of hospitals within the region grew from 54 to 70 between 1961 and 1981, but by 1980 there was still only one hospital bed per 3,500 persons. In 1979, more than two-thirds of the villages were more than five km away from the nearest hospital. Close to three-quarters of all villages had no electricity supply in 1980. It is interesting to note, however, that 55 per cent of the villages in Rae Bareli District had electricity compared to 25 per cent in Pratapgarh and nine per cent in Sultanpur. Rae Bareli also had a higher concentration of agricultural implement repair centres. Rae Bareli urban centre has much the highest concentration of engineering works, while half the villages within the district were within three km of an implements repairing centre. By contrast, 88 per cent of the villages in Pratapgarh and 97 per cent in Sultanpur were more than five km away from such repair centres. Within urban centres, public investment in infrastructure and physical services has been very inadequate. Of the 18 settlements classified as 'urban' by the 1981 census, only five had a protected supply of water and none had a sewage system.

In examining the provision of services and facilities which would support commercial agriculture, the statistics suggest that most farmers still produce for their own consumption with any surplus sold locally. The vast majority of villages are more than five km from the nearest wholesale centre; as we noted earlier, most are also at some distance from a paved road. In 1979, less than four per cent were within five km of a cold storage plant while less than eight per cent were within five km of a food grain store. A third were more than five km from even a small weekly or biweekly market. It is interesting to note that villages in Rae Bareli district are better served than those in the other two districts in terms of access to paved roads, foodgrain stores, cold storage and agricultural implement repair centres.

Links between development in the urban system and social, economic and political change

In the period up to 1901, the location and development of urban centres was much influenced by the location of military and administrative centres. The early development of Manikpur and Sultanpur as military centres through which rulers based outside the study region maintained control in the fourteenth and fifteenth centuries AD and the development of Dalmau, Salon and Manikpur as administrative centres under Akbar's rule in the sixteenth century were noted earlier. Dalmau and Manikpur were sub-provincial administrative centres and Allahabad, a city with over 600,000 inhabitants today, just to the south of the study region, was founded in Akbar's reign as capital of the province which included but extended beyond the present study region. Navigable rivers were the main transport arteries; thus it is no surprise to find Dalmau, Manikpur and Allahabad all on the Ganga River which ensures a direct river link with both Agra (developed as Akbar's capital) and Delhi.

Under British rule, the links between towns and centres of administrative and military control became even stronger; we noted earlier how Rae Bareli, Sultanpur and Bela Pratapgarh (today much the largest urban centres in the study region) were the sites for the only military cantonments, the only district headquarters and the first municipalities. Bela Pratapgarh's origin was as a military cantonment in 1802. In the case of Rae Bareli and Sultanpur, these towns predated their choice by the British as military and administrative centres. But choice as a district headquarters guaranteed Rae Bareli and Sultanpur a stimulus to their development which other towns not chosen as district headquarters did not receive. Settlements chosen as sub-district ('tahsil') headquarters also received some stimulus; the correlation between today's urban centres and district and tahsil headquarters chosen under British rule in the mid-nineteenth century is evident in Table 5.9. And settlements which were important towns before British rule but which were not chosen as administrative centres have generally developed relatively slowly; an earlier section described how Salon was originally chosen as district headquarters in 1856 but the headquarters were moved to Rae Bareli two years later. This move was important both for Rae Bareli's relatively rapid and Salon's relatively slow development ever since. Towns which were known to be important in the early nineteenth century such as Jais, Manikpur and Katra Medniganj lost importance relative to the district headquarters in the late nineteenth and the twentieth centuries. None of these towns was designated either a district or a tahsil headquarters.

The various administrative and service functions associated with district headquarters certainly brought some stimulus to the development of Rae Bareli, Sultanpur and Bela Pratapgarh. So too did the construction of new markets under British rule. To a lesser extent, tahsil headquarters also received some stimulus. But the construction of the railway network was probably more significant, for this freed major inter-urban traffic flows from a dependence on rivers. Obviously, district headquarters were among the first towns to be linked to the railway system which was rapidly expanding over India in the late nineteenth century. In 1901, the four largest urban centres within the study region were the three district headquarters (each on the railway) and Jais, also on the railway. The three district headquarters and Dalmau were also on the only paved roads. Historically important towns such as Manikpur and Salon were neither on the railway nor on the new roads. Between 1901 and 1951, the three district headquarters were the only towns whose population grew significantly; the population of Dalmau, Pratapgarh City, Jais and Dalmau declined in this period while that of Salon hardly grew at all; an earlier section noted how many enterprises in Pratapgarh City and Katra Medniganj relocated to the nearby district headquarters, Bela Pratapgarh.

While as Table 5.9 shows, tahsil headquarters were not necessarily the largest urban centres within their tahsil, by 1981, all 11 tahsil headquarters were among the 18 settlements with the highest central place scores and all but Kadipur and Musafirkhana had urban status. By 1951, all but Kadipur and Musafirkhana either had a railway station or were on a major road. This helps explain why Musafirkhana (with 3,433 inhabitants in 1971) and Kadipur (with less than 3,000 inhabitants in 1971) had not developed as major urban centres.

Nine of the 18 urban centres recognised in the 1981 census are neither district nor tahsil headquarters: Jais, Lalganj, Manikpur, Bachhrawan, Dostpur, Pratapgarh City, Antu, Koiripur and Katra Medniganj. Jais, Manikpur, Antu and Koiripur were among the urban centres with the slowest growing population in each of the decades between 1951 and 1981 while Pratapgarh City was in this category for the first two of these decades. Lalganj was among the most rapidly growing for all three decades while Katra Medniganj was for the last two of these decades. This does not correlate with early access to main roads or railways since Lalganj, Dalmau, Manikpur, Jais and Bachhrawan were each on a major road and were a railway station by 1951.

Thus it seems fair to say that designation as the headquarters of a tahsil in the nineteenth century and the fact that such headquarters were either already on or soon to become linked to a major road and/or a railway station often proved to be a boost for local development there. But it was not a sufficient condition to guarantee local development.

At least up to 1951, there is little sign of much rural-urban interchange in terms of farmers producing sufficient crops for sale to earn income to spend on goods and services supplied from urban-based enterprises. Nor is there much sign of manufacturing in the few urban centres. Indeed, it seems there was a major decline in handicraft production between 1901 and 1951; we noted earlier how the proportion of the labour force working in the secondary sector in Rae Bareli District dropped from 11.7 per cent to 5.1 per cent in this period. The obvious correlation between urban centres ranked by population size and according to rank within the administrative hierarchy reflects the lack of large-scale production for sale either of agricultural goods or of manufactured goods. With most of the region's population deriving a living directly from largely subsistence oriented agriculture, the scale of demand for manufactured goods was insufficient either to stimulate much local manufacturing or to support a strong retail trade. Between 1901 and 1951, the proportion of land devoted to food grains had increased to 94 per cent. In 1951, Katra Medniganj was the only town with more than 25 per cent of its workforce in the secondary sector (which relates to its role as a long established centre for handloom cotton production) while most had a third or more of their labour force working in agriculture.

Between 1951 and 1981, there was obviously a substantial increase in agricultural production and an increase in the amount of crops grown specifically for sale. But this has yet to show much impact on the urban system. Correlations between 24 variables for the 50 blocks in the study region on occupational structure, land and land-use characteristics, infrastructure and services, and distance from urban centres with 500,000 or more inhabitants (outside the study region) were examined. (See Sources, page 224.) Virtually all production remains for local or regional consumption; sugar and potatoes are the only crops where a substantial proportion are consumed outside the study region and in 1981, these two crops combined covered less than 3 per cent of total cropped area. The influence of blocks' distance from the various urban centres of 500,000 or more inhabitants which are close to the study region was slight. And perhaps surprisingly, there is no clear correlation between the areas with the most productive agriculture (or most land devoted to commercial crops) and the areas with growing urban centres or high central place scores. For instance, the block of Akhandhagar, to the extreme east of the study region, has among the highest proportion of land which is cultivated, irrigated and double cropped of any of the 50 blocks. It is also one of the main sugar cane producing blocks. Yet there is no evidence of urban development locally. No settlement within the block has been given urban status; the block headquarters was ranked forty-fourth in terms of population and thirty-third in terms of central place functions among the 58 settlements identified as the main central places within the region. Neither of its two neighbouring blocks (Dostpur and Kadipur) have seen much urban development between 1951 and 1981 although these blocks also have a relatively high proportion of their land cultivated and irrigated and devoted to commercial crops. Indeed, when the spatial distribution of central

Map 5.5   *Spatial distribution, by block, of central place scores, core areas for commercial crops and high agricultural productivity, and number of villages connected by road*

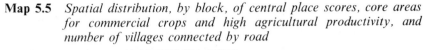

PER CENT CROPPED AREA TO COMMERCIAL CROPS

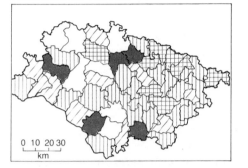

▓	17+
▦	13-16
▥	10-12
▨	6-9
☐	0-5

0 10 20 30 km

NUMBER OF VILLAGES CONNECTED BY ROAD

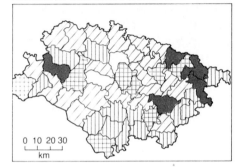

▓	40+
▦	30-39
▥	20-29
▨	10-19
☐	0-9

0 10 20 30 km

CENTRAL PLACE SCORE

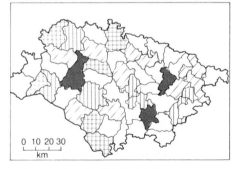

▓	200+
▦	66-200
▥	40-65
▨	20-39
☐	10-19

0 10 20 30 km

AGRICULTURAL PRODUCTION INTENSITY

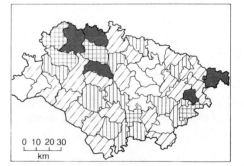

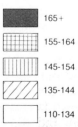

▓	165+
▦	155-164
▥	145-154
▨	135-144
☐	110-134

0 10 20 30 km

Scores for this are the sum of percentage of block which is net cropped area, percentage which is irrigated and percentage which is double cropped; this is a crude indicator of the intensity of agricultural production.

place scores are mapped, the eastern extreme of the study region is one with among the lowest score. It becomes evident from Map 5.5 that there is no clear correlation between blocks with the most productive land and blocks with the highest central place scores. However, it is interesting to note that both total and rural population has tended to become more concentrated in and around the three district headquarters and largest urban centres. Although data on changes in population density between 1951 and 1981 were only available at tahsil rather than block level, clearly it was not only the concentration of urban population within the three headquarters which was responsible for the increasing concentration of population in the tahsils within which the district headquarters are located.

The strongest and clearest positive correlation was between the proportion of land devoted to commercial crops and the number of villages connected by road; this can be seen graphically in Map 5.5. The proportion of land under commercial crops relates negatively to the proportion of land under cereals and there is no significant relationship between proportion of land devoted to commercial crops and central place scores or distances from large urban centres.

When recalling that around four-fifths of the farmers in the study region have less than one hectare holdings with an average holding size of one-third of a hectare, the aggregate level of demand for goods and services is likely to be very low. We noted earlier how a high proportion of existing demand for goods and services from the agricultural population is met in bi-weekly or weekly markets, most of which are not in urban centres. An earlier section also described how most villages have no electricity supply and are at least one km from a paved road, at least three km from an agricultural implement repair centre and at least five km from a wholesale centre, cold storage plant and food grain store.

Manufacturing also provides relatively little stimulus to urban development except in recent years in Rae Bareli urban centre. Less than three per cent of the labour force within the study region is engaged in manufacturing and most of these work in small enterprises producing consumer goods for local sale based on local materials. In 1981, there were just 72 persons employed in 'large-scale manufacturing enterprises' (ie those with nine or more employees) in Pratapgarh district and none at all in Sultanpur. Since 1981, two important factories have been (or are being) built: a tractor factory at Katra Medniganj (with 600 employees) and a sugar factory in Sultanpur.

But Rae Bareli urban centre remains the only major concentration of large-scale industries with some 6,000 people working in such industries in 1981. There has also been a considerable growth in registered small-scale industrial units there. But both past and future development of industry and of the infrastructure to support it has to be understood as much in terms of national and state-level politics as it does in terms of optimum locations for production either to meet demand within or outside the region. The location of the Indian Telephone Industries in Rae Bareli was of considerable importance to the development of a larger and more substantial economic base; its location there was not entirely divorced from the fact that Rae Bareli was the political constituency of the late Mrs Gandhi for nearly two decades. Rae Bareli was also one of the 'Small and Medium Towns' given priority in the Federal Government's Sixth Year Plan. Sultanpur District has benefited from being the political constituency of a Chief Minister (of Uttar Pradesh) and of Rajiv Gandhi. The late Sanjay Gandhi also had his political constituency within Sultanpur District; at that time it was known as Amethi constituency. Recent developments in Amethi including the construction of the Sanjay Memorial Hospital and the Hindustan Aeronautics factory and the fact that Amethi is to be developed as a industrial centre (making use of unproductive 'usar' land nearby) are influenced considerably by the power and position of those representing it in the Federal parliament. The fact that Jagdishpur has been proposed as a settlement well suited to industrial development is also partially due to the fact that it was in Rajiv Gandhi's political constituency.

The selection of other urban centres to be developed as industrial centres has also been based on the political influence exercised by the representative of that particular constituency. The fact that Kunda and Derwa (an important market settlement on the road between Bela-Pratapgarh and Kunda) have been chosen as to be developed as industrial centres, owes much to the political influence of the Muslim M.L.A. which represents the area in the Uttar Pradesh State Assembly and is part of the ruling Congress party. However, in the past, towns having weak representatives did not fare so well; one of the reasons for the relatively slow development of Manikpur and Katra Medniganj in the early twentieth century was the fact that these centres were not favoured with public funds. The establishment of the Auto Tractors Factory in Katra Medniganj is ascribed to the fact that its parliamentary representative was then India's foreign Minister. Finally, as noted earlier, political factors certainly influenced the designation of Antu and Koiripur as urban centres in the 1981 census. Neither had 5,000 inhabitants in 1981. Neither were important central places. And most of the labour force in each still worked in agriculture.

Data taken from censuses on the tertiary sector and from fieldwork in the three district headquarters and in Kunda, Manikpur and Katra Medniganj shows a relatively small tertiary sector and one dominated by small (often one person) enterprises. The three district headquarters had much the highest central place scores. They also had the three highest proportions of total labour force in the tertiary sector of any urban centre in the study region for 1951, 1961 and 1971 (figures for 1981 were not available). The direct and indirect effects of a concentration of district level government offices and public facilities such as schools and hospitals certainly play a significant role in the pre-eminence of these three urban centres as the largest concentrations of tertiary employment.

In looking at the changing fortunes of different urban centres between 1951 and 1981 in terms of population size and population growth rates, the three district headquarters have remained much the largest and were never among the slowest growing for each of the three decades. Each was among the most rapidly growing urban centres between 1971 and 1981. The best explanation is not only related to their administrative status and prime location on roads and railways. It is also that they are the main centres within the study region for meeting the demand for both producer and consumer oriented goods and services coming from the relatively small proportion of farmers with high cash incomes. Neither the concentration of publicly-funded offices and services nor, for Rae Bareli, the recent growth in industries can account for all the recent rapid growth in commerce, trade and services.

Lack of administrative functions certainly correlates with relatively slow population growth. Among the 18 settlements recognised as urban in the 1981 census, six (Jais, Manikpur, Pratapgrarh City, Koiripur, Antu and Katra Medniganj) were neither tahsil nor block headquarters. All had relatively slow population growth rates compared to other urban centres for at least two of the three decades. However, so too did Salon, Dalmau and Maharajganj and each of these was a tahsil headquarters.

Sources

This chapter is based on the report 'Role of Small and Intermediate Towns in the Regional Development process; a Case Study of Rae Bareli, Sultanpur and Bela Pratapgarh, Uttar Pradesh, India' by Dr H.N. Misra from the International Institute for Development Research, 557 Mumfordganj, Allahabad 211 002, India.

The correlation and regression analysis was undertaken with the help and advice of Dr Richard Dunn of the Department of Geography, University of Bristol. The analysis was carried out for the 50 blocks into which the study region is divided using 24 variables:

Occupational structure
1 Per cent labour force in secondary sector, 1971
2 Per cent labour force in tertiary sector, 1971

Land characteristics

3   Per cent total area net cropped area
4   Per cent total area net irrigated area
5   Per cent net cropped area which is double cropped
6   Composite of 3, 4 and 5 to give some indication of blocks with the most productive land
7   Per cent of land area barren, alkaline soil or under non agricultural use

Land use

8   Per cent net cropped area under rice
9   Per cent net cropped area under wheat
10 Per cent net cropped area under barley
11 Per cent net cropped area under pulses
12 Per cent net cropped area under sugar cane
13 Per cent net cropped area under potatoes
14 Per cent net cropped area under commercial crops
15 Per cent net cropped area under non-pulse food crops

Infrastructure and services

16 Central place score
17 Road length (km)
18 Number of villages connected by road
19 Number of telephones
20 Number of seed stores
21 Number of banks
22 Number of post offices

Distance from urban centres

23 Distance from urban centre with 500,000 or more inhabitants
24 Distance from urban centre with 40,000 or more inhabitants

The central place scores are the sum of the number of educational, medical, transport and communication, administrative, agricultural, commercial and industrial services found in any settlement. The following 28 services or functions were counted: primary centre, veterinary hospital, maternity and child welfare centre, private clinic, medical store, post and telegraph office, railway station, bus station, bus stop, municipal board, town area, district headquarters, tahsil headquarters, bank, cooperative society, grain mandi, weekly market, fertiliser store, seed store, auto-repair shop, carpentry/wood product store, printing press.

Notes

1 Area of land between two converging rivers.
2 The capital of this kingdom was close in Ayodhya, to Faizabad, capital of the district just to the north of the study region.

3 In the late twelfth century, Muslim conquests into India led to the establishment of the Delhi sultanate with Delhi falling to the Muslim invaders in 1193 and under Alauddin Khilji, who ruled between 1296 and 1316, the area controlled by the Delhi Sultanate probably reached its zenith.

4 The Mughal dynasty ruled large parts of the present-day India from the early sixteenth to the mid-eighteenth centuries. During this period, many towns were founded in present-day Uttar Pradesh, especially under the rule of Akbar. Allahabad is said to have been founded on the site of an older town (Prayag) during this reign. Akbar also founded Agra, in south-eastern Uttar Pradesh which was the Mughal capital between 1566 and 1569 and between 1601 and 1658. Akbar's reign was notable for the development of trade and commerce, handicrafts, cotton cloth weaving and iron and steel making. The Ganga and Yamuna rivers (which join at Allahabad) were the main arteries for trade; the Yamuna runs past Delhi and Agra.

5 British historians are more inclined to refer to this as the Indian Mutiny which helps reveal their orientation with regard to the event. It was after this event that the transfer of government from the East India Company to the British crown occurred.

6 Tahsils are sub-district administrative units; see Map 5.3.

7 The Jaunpur to Faizabad railway line built by 1874 also crossed the study region – on its eastern end – but with no railway stations located there.

8 In Pratapgarh, the recorded natural calamities between 1901 and 1951 were famine and floods in 1903 and heavy floods in 1935. In Sultanpur, there was a severe flood in 1914, an influenza epidemic in 1916-17, floods in 1923 and an earthquake in 1931. In Rae Bareli, there was a famine in 1901, an attack of locusts in 1903-4, a heavy hailstorm in Rae Bareli tahsil in 1915, influenza outbreak in 1915-16, earthquake in 1932 and outbreak of a Shia-Sunni riot in 1939.

9 See later section on developments in the urban system for more details.

10 Dalmau (with the headquarters Dalmau as the only town) Salon (with Salon and Jais), Pratapgarh (with Pratapgarh City, Katra Medniganj and Bela Pratapgarh).

11 Maharajganj, Amethi, Kadipur, Musafirkhana and Patti.

12 Sugar produced from sugar cane using traditional techniques with no separation of molasses; the loss of sugar in traditional techniques is much higher than in modern sugar cane mills.

13 In Uttar Pradesh, under British rule, a Zamindar had become a land-owner although the term Zamindar had other meanings for different periods in different regions. The origin of the word is Persian and means 'holder or occupier (dar) of land (zamin)' (*Encyclopaedia Britannica*, 1976). In India, Zamindars were originally people who under the Mughals, were given the right to collect revenues on land and to retain a proportion of the collected revenue. For instance, in Bengal, a Zamindar was a hereditary tax collector who could retain 10 per cent of the revenue he collected and in the late eighteenth century, the British government made Zamindars landowners, thus creating a landed aristocracy. In Uttar Pradesh, agrarian reforms under British rule did not try to abolish Zamindars and other intermediaries but to limit the revenue they could

charge and give tenants some security from eviction and clarify (and strengthen) their possibility of inheritance.

14 The limit was 7.3 hectares of irrigated or 11 hectares of un-irrigated land for those with five family members with an additional 2 (irrigated) or 3 (un-irrigated) hectares for each son above this limit for up to three additional sons.

15 Betel nuts (seeds of the areca or betel palm) wrapped in the leaves of the betel pepper plant with other spices, are a popular and cheap item for chewing.

16 These are listed under Sources (page 224).

17 Villages are the smallest areal unit into which the country is divided for the purpose of raising land revenue. Thus, each village has a defined boundary and within this boundary, there may be more than one identifiable population concentration. As a village grows in population and area, it may be divided into two. It is also common for villages close to expanding urban centres to become incorporated within the centre's boundaries.

18 Unchahar, Lambhua, Musafirkhana, Tiloi, Jagdishpur, Pratappur-Kamaicha, Kadipur, Gauriganj, Harchandpur, Kala Kanker, Lalganj (Ajhara).

19 Since 1961, any places with 5,000 or more inhabitants, at least 75 per cent of the working population (1961 census) or male working population (1971 and 1981 censuses) working in non-agricultural activities and a density of population of at least 1000 persons per square mile (1961 and 1971 censuses) or 400 square kilometres (1981 census) is considered an urban centre.

20 Bela Pratapgarh, Rae Bareli, Sultanpur and Lalganj had the first, second, third and fifth most imbalanced sex ratios in 1981 and had had among the higher imbalances for the period 1951 to 1981. By contrast, Jais, Salon, Manikpur and Antu had among the least inbalanced sex ratios for 1951, 1961, 1971 and 1981 and among the slowest population growth rates between 1951 and 1981.

6

South-West Nigeria

David Aradeon, Tade Akin Aina and Joe Umo

Background

The study region is the coastal area stretching some 40 km inland between Lagos metropolitan centre (Sub-Saharan Africa's most populous urban concentration) and Nigeria's border with the Republic of Benin. Covering an area of some 2,200 square km, it had a total population of 344,220 in 1963 (the last date for which reliable census data is available). It is a largely rural region whose development potential has been under-utilised despite its proximity to Lagos – and to Porto Novo and Cotonou, the Republic of Benin's largest urban centres. In this chapter, this region's development is discussed in relation to Lagos to the east. As will be described in detail later, Lagos's physical growth has spread into the study region since the late Fifties and, perhaps not surprisingly, the growth of a metropolitan centre with more than 5 million inhabitants, just to the east has brought significant social and economic impacts.

The region's development is also discussed in relation to developments to its west, in what is today the Republic of Benin. Prior to French colonial rule in Benin (in what was then Dahomey) and British rule in Nigeria, the study region was part of a wider region, known as Yorubaland, which was integrated economically, historically and culturally and which stretched across the present Nigeria-Benin border. The Yorubas are the largest of Nigeria's many ethnic and cultural groups accounting for around one-fifth of Nigeria's total population which is currently estimated to be around 100 million. Four of the main Yoruba sub-groups within the study region – the Egbado, Awori, Ifoyin and Anago – are among seven such sub-groups which can be identified in Western Yorubaland. As Asiwaju (1976) notes, 'Although each of these seven sub-sections is distinguishable by its own dialect and geographical location and was, prior to the establishment of colonial rule, organized into one or more separate kingdoms, they together formed a continuum of the Yoruba culture area characterized generally by the same language, a common tradition of origin, a similar style of socio-political organization, and

Map 6.1   *The study region and its location on the Bight of Benin's coast and within Nigeria*

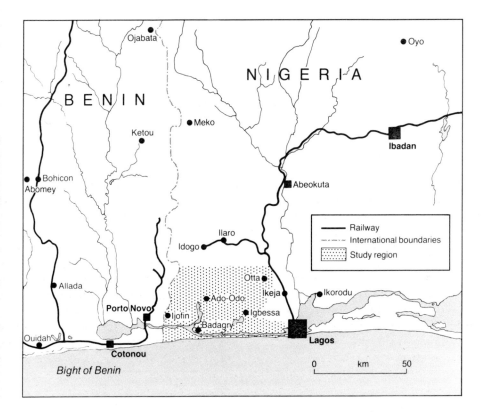

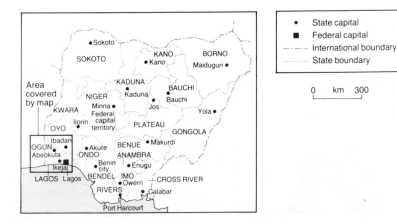

Table 6.1   *Background statistics*

	Area (km²)	Population (1963)	
Nigeria	923,773	55,000,000	
Study Region	2,200	344,220	

	1931	1952	1963
Southern portion of study region			
Population	c. 43,700	65,680	122,159
Population in small urban centres	n.a.	12,158[a]	60,770[a]
Number of small urban centres	n.a.	2[a]	5[a]
Population in intermediate urban centres (20,000+)	0	0	0
Number of intermediate urban centres	0	0	0
Northern Portion of the Study Region			
Population	n.a.	n.a.	22,061
Population in small urban centres (5,000–19,999)	n.a.	38,227	65,242
Number of small urban centres	n.a.	4	6
Population in intermediate urban centres (20,000+)	0	0	0
Number of intermediate urban centres	0	0	0

Sources: 1952 and 1963 censuses; 1931 colonial government estimates.

Note: a—Later sections in this chapter will describe how much of the growth in the population of 'small urban centres' between 1952 and 1963 was the growth of Lagos conurbation into the south-east of the study region; there was only one independent small urban centre in the southern portion of the study region both in 1952 and in 1963.

the same corpus of morals and beliefs' (p. 11). In the north-east of the study region (and beyond its boundaries), are the Egbas, another important Yoruba sub-group. Thus, an understanding of early developments in the formation and development of settlements, in their location and in the early developments of an urban system depends on some knowledge of pre-colonial developments to the study region's west and how the imposition of a boundary separating French Dahomey and British Nigeria affected this.

The study region's boundaries are defined by the coast to the south, the Nigeria-Benin border to the west and administrative boundaries to the north and east. As Map 6.2 illustrates, the southern coastal strip is flat, porous sandy soil interspersed with sea and numerous

Map 6.2 *Physical features*

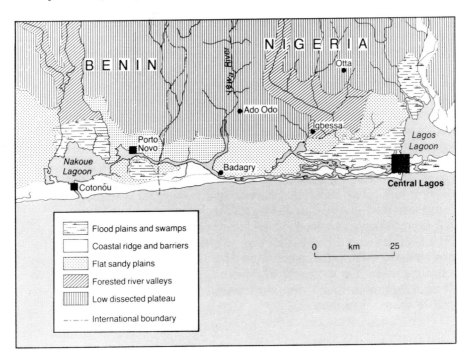

creeks and lagoons with floodplains and swamps to the north. Moving inland, these give way to uplands, often covered by secondary rain forest with a few patches of virgin forest. Much of these uplands have rich agricultural soils. Several rivers and tributaries drain into the coastal creek system. Swampy rich alluvial soil supports mangrove forests and palm tree vegetation beside creeks and lagoons. Intensive use has traditionally been made of these palms for wine, liquor and roofing material. The creeks and lagoons also have a rich aquatic life with considerable potential for fishing. The whole region has a high annual rainfall, much of it concentrated between May and July. Average daily temperatures vary between 20 and 27°C.

The pre-colonial settlement pattern of Yoruba city states is still partially visible today. The settlement pattern in Yorubaland was characterised by relatively large city-states ruled by 'Obas' (Kings) and a council of chiefs, and smaller nucleated settlements over which a 'Bale' (title head) and a council of elders presided, but who owed allegiance to an Oba. Both the towns where the Obas lived and the smaller rural settlements were usually nucleated and surrounded by farmland. In the creek and lagoon area, by the coast, many settlements arose based on fishing; some on patches of firm land by fresh water creeks to exploit fresh water fish; others just by the sea to exploit marine resources.

In discussing social, economic and demographic change, this chapter will often divide the study region into the 'northern' and 'southern' portions because since the imposition of colonial rule in the late nineteenth century these have been part of different administrative divisions for which official statistics exist. In the northern portion, the urban centre of Otta is particularly notable in that it has remained the most important urban centre since pre-colonial times. In the southern portion, Badagry has also remained the most important urban centre since pre-colonial times. But as this chapter will describe, both have lost political and economic importance relative to urban centres such as Lagos to the south-east and Ilaro to the north (see Map 6.1). On this map, note should also be taken of Abeokuta, capital of Ogun State within which the northern portion of the study region is located and Ikeja, capital of Lagos State within which the southern portion is located. The text will also refer to Ibadan, capital of Oyo State. For much of the nineteenth and for the first half of the twentieth century, Ibadan was Nigeria's largest urban centre. But by the late Fifties, the population of Lagos exceeded that of Ibadan and estimates for the early Eighties suggest that the conurbation of Lagos has more than 5 million inhabitants while that of Ibadan has more than 1.5 million.

Developments up to 1963

Pre-colonial developments

The south of the study region close to the coast with its numerous creeks, lagoons, rivers and swamps was not densely populated prior to the twentieth century. This area was on the fringe of Yorubaland. Inland, there was a fairly even spread of farm settlements which were linked both by trade and by allegiance, politically, to larger centres. Such settlements were located within the farmlands their inhabitants worked, and were presided over by a local chief, a 'bale', supported by a council of family heads.

In addition to such farm-settlements, there were settlements which were important political centres, market centres and military centres. The vast and extensive network of markets which stretched across Yorubaland included many settlements within the study region. Most important market and trade centres were inland of the coastal and lagoon strip. The port of Badagry, in the coastal strip, was the exception for Badagry port and market were a key part of the wider regional market system. Badagry was marked on maps dating from the seventeenth century[1] as the major port in what later became south-west Nigeria. It was well located to link the coast and the navigable Yewa river and lagoons to overland transport routes which went up into Northern Nigeria and across the Saharan desert in a period when the main trade routes for inter-regional and international trade were overland or by the river. During the rainy season, the Yewa river is navigable for some 96 km inland; its mouth is close to Badagry and can be reached from Badagry by boat or canoe. Badagry, along with Lagos and Porto Novo (now in Benin) were also important pre-colonial slave ports and the study region was part of what came to be known as the Slave Coast in the seventeenth and eighteenth centuries. Although impossible to quantify, intra- and inter-regional trade and commerce were obviously important for two or more centuries before colonial rule. Otta, today one of the study region's most important urban centres, was an important political centre with an Oba and a council of chiefs. The origin of most of today's urban and larger rural settlements was as population clusters which developed on the main inter-regional roads prior to colonial rule. Thus, the origin of today's settlement pattern was compact, nucleated settlements which were largely self-supporting in food but where craft and some cash crop activities supported inter-settlement trade. One final factor encouraging the development of new settlements was to allow their inhabitants to escape wars or the slave trade; clusters of settlements often developed within the protective covering of forested areas or on islands within the creek and lagoon system.

The most important locally produced goods for trade were foodstuffs, kolanuts and crafts; later, as a transatlantic trade developed, exports from the area included slaves, oil palm and coconuts. Among the imported goods were cattle and leather goods from Hausaland (some 800 km to the north) and European firearms. The settlements from the study region most commonly mentioned with regard to this trade were Badagry, Otta and Ipokia. Of the four main north-south trade routes indentified as running through Yorubaland (Mabogunje, 1969, pp. 86-87), one was the route from Badagry up to Ilaro and on to Northern Nigeria while the other was the route starting in Lagos and passing through Otta and Abeokuta and again up into Northern Nigeria.

In addition to these north-south routes, three other transport corridors passing through the study region are known to have been important: the route linking Ibadan and Abeokuta to Porto Novo (now in Republic of Benin) which passed through Oke Odan; the road network linking Badagry to Ado-Odo and onto Otta, with a branch between Ado-Odo and Otta going down to Igbessa; and the coastal lagoon corridor with movements of goods and people by canoe. Although the historical records are not strong, roads were said to be good and well maintained in this area; tollgates are known to have existed at Badagry, Ipokia and Otta. Two other settlements mentioned in early records with specialised economic functions were

Ajilete as a centre for iron ore mining of some sophistication and Topo as a centre for pottery pots and dishes manufacture.

During the nineteenth century, the growth and development of settlements within the study region (or their decline) has to be understood in terms of a period of rapid and turbulent political change. Successive invasions affected the region, most especially those coming from the Egba (with their headquarters at Abeokuta) to the east and from the Kingdom of Dahomey (with its headquarters at Abomey) to the west. Until the emergence of the French and British colonial systems, ethnic rivalries between the Eguns, Yorubas, Dahomeans and the Otta Awori Yorubas meant a shifting balance of power and shifting allegiances in the wake of the break up of the Oyo Empire. This Empire, a Yoruba state, had dominated much of the present day West Nigeria, Benin and Togo at the height of its powers in the late seventeenth and early eighteenth centuries.

The town of Abeokuta, some 50 km to the north of the region's northern boundary, owes its origin to the foundation of a defence town in 1830 by the Egba-Yorubas who were fleeing from attacks and the break-up of the Oyo Empire. This resulted in Egba incursions into Awori and Egbado territories in the northern part of the study region both for farm-land and through their desire to dominate and protect an open trade route to Lagos. The Awori had developed Otta which was strategically placed on various trade routes, including that between Abeokuta and Lagos and Lagos and Dahomey.[2] They played an important role in the slave trade and in food production to provision the slave caravans heading to Lagos and also to supply Lagos.

Otta suffered repeated attacks[3] and underwent a long period where the threat of attack from Abeokuta was constant and a serious constraint on local agricultural production and on trade. After 1841 and up to the period of colonial rule, being open to attacks from the Egba to the north and from Dahomey to the west and Lagos to the south it was on 'the verge of complete desertion as its population sought shelter in villages south of the town; some even went to settle permanently in Lagos' (Agiri, 1974, p. 471). What is today the urban centre of Oke-Odan owes its foundation between 1832 and 1840 to the Egbado people, fleeing the destruction of their settlements by the Egba. Ilobi, a settlement with 1,362 inhabitants in 1963 just inside the study region's northern boundary, was an important town and capital of an important Kingdom, before its destruction by the Egbas in the 1830s.

Both the town and its surrounding dependent villages were destroyed by the Egba and some of its fleeing population were among those who founded Oke-Odan.

Like Otta, Badagry suffered from the expansionist ambitions of Dahomey and Lagos. Such insecurity obviously acted as a major

Table 6.2 *Population of current urban centres in or close to the study region in pre-colonial and colonial periods*

Urban centres within the study region			Urban centres close to or influencing the study region		
Badagry			Ilaro		
	12,500	(1800)		15,000	(1887)
	5,000–6,000	(1846)		5,000	(1890)
	5,000	(1864)		12,373	(1952)
	4,000	(1890)			
	6,000	(1911)			
	5,917	(1952)			
Otta			Lagos		
	3,000	(1850)		5,000	(1800)
	2,000	(1879)		25,000	(1866)
	8,914	(1952)		74,000	(1911)
				126,100	(1931)
				276,000	(1951)
Ipokia					
	2,000–4,000	(1860)			
	1,500	(1874)			
	4,000	(1860)			
	2,000	(1911)			
Ado-Odo			Ibadan		
	2,000	(1890)		100,000	(1851)
	9,000	(1911)		238,000	(1921)
	16,381	(1952)		459,200	(1952)

Source: Estimates from travellers or by colonial officials and 1952 census.

deterrent to the development of a town whose main economic base was trade (Hodder, 1962, p. 82). The town became a centre for those fleeing wars; for instance, when Oke-Odan was sacked by Dahomey in 1848, only a few years after its foundation, Badagry was one of the recipients of its fleeing population.

Badagry (along with Lagos and Abeokuta) became important points to which repatriated slaves returned from Sierra Leone and Brazil, this immigration beginning with the abolition of slavery in British territories in 1832. Missionaries soon followed and were important because these were among the most vocal agitators for the establishment of British rule in Nigeria. The first mission to be established in Nigeria was in Badagry in 1841. Their involvement in local politics in the mid-nineteenth century had important implications for later colonial and even post-colonial developments. In a major struggle between two rivals for the throne of Lagos, Akitoye and Kosoko, missionaries based in Badagry supported Akitoye; Akitoye sought and obtained refuge in Badagry during this struggle. Then in 1851,

Lagos was bombarded and Akitoye reinstated by the British Navy since he agreed to help suppress the slave trade. Two years later, a British consulate was established in Lagos.

There was some shift in population from Badagry to Lagos as Akitoye and his followers returned to Lagos while both the Church Missionary Society and the Methodists shifted their main centre from Badagry to Lagos. This move is reported to have encouraged a fresh group of immigrants to move to Lagos (Mabogunje, 1968, p. 242). Then considerable pressure was brought to bear on the British Government to tackle the problem of the slave trade and of hinterland obstruction of the trade routes to Lagos. This finally led to the formal annexation of Lagos in 1861 and the first extension of British authority to include Badagry in 1863. Other parts of the study region were added between 1883 and 1895 so by 1895, virtually all the study region was officially part of what was then called Lagos Protectorate.

Political and administrative developments under colonial rule

The Anglo-French agreement in 1889 established the boundary between Nigeria and Dahomey and thus the western boundary of the study region. It was undertaken with no consideration for the inhabitants of the region whose culture, territory and economic organisation it cut across. Certain traditional kingdoms such as Ifoyin and Anago suddenly found the new border dividing their lands. French colonial efforts to establish jurisdiction over the territory they now controlled were said to be more vigorous and coercive than those of the British.

The resentment of certain groups who suddenly found themselves within French Dahomey was illustrated by Asiwaju's documentation of the responses in the Sabe area (well to the north of the study region) where boundary stones were removed and the French authorities brought a charge of treason against the area's traditional ruler in 1902. Although the best documented 'protest emigrations' from French Dahomey into British Nigeria took place to the north of the study region, as in the town of Ifonyintedo which was founded by Ifonyin people who left Dahomey rather than live under the authority of the French-installed chief. Ipokia and Oke-Odan were among the towns to receive people from 'protest-emigrations' from Dahomey. The internal boundaries in Southern Dahomey 'were no less resented by the Yoruba ... the formalized balkanisation of the culture area by the internal boundaries psychologically aroused the people's sense of ethnic unity and infused into them a sustained feeling of irredentism' (Asiwaju, 1976). British policies raised less local resentment since 'British policy was based on the existing indigenous political structures for government. Internal boundary demarcations, particularly at divisional levels, reflected a desire to ensure that lin-

Map 6.3 *The development of overland transport, 1900–1960*

Urban centres and main transport routes around 1950

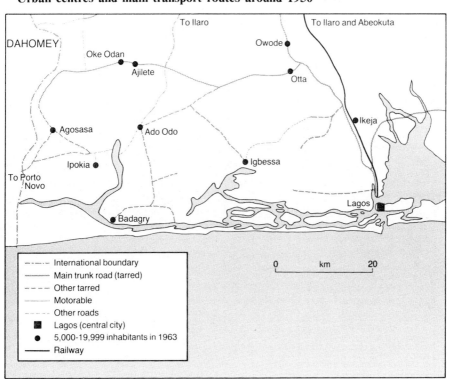

Urban centres and main transport routes around 1960

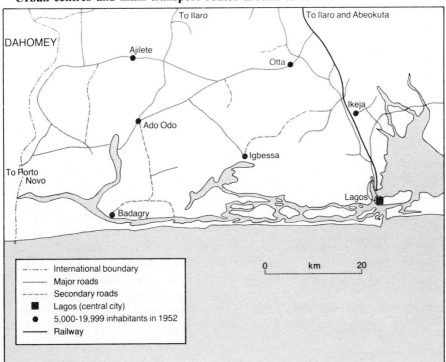

Map 6.3 *continued*
Towns, major villages and transport routes around 1900

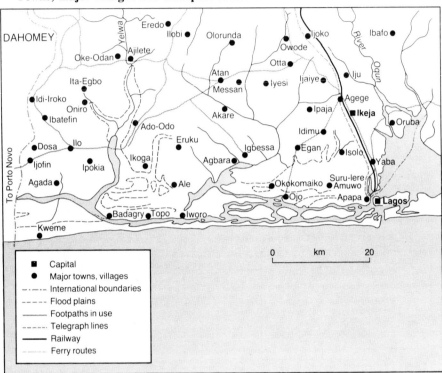

guistic and cultural affinity served as the basis for division'. In terms of administrative grouping, to the south in what was then Badagry District of Lagos Colony, the Eguns were centred around Badagry local government whilst the Aworis and the Egbados had their own local councils. As shown in Map 6.4, Awori and Egun-Awori district councils were later created within what became Badagry Division.

To the north, the divisional boundaries were in place by the late nineteenth or early twentieth century. A divisional boundary divided the areas under Egbado and Egba jurisdiction and Egbado division remained as a single local government unit for the rest of the colonial period. Initially, it was divided into 11 districts of which the districts of Ajilete, Oke-odan, Ipokia, Ado and Igbessa were in the study region; in 1948, the 11 districts were amalgamated into five with the five districts in the study region becoming three: Ado-Igbessa, Ipokia and Egbado-Ifoyin (see Map 6.4). For a few years the town of Badagry was an important administrative centre and served as the seat of the 'British Travelling Commissioners' who administered an area larger than the study region that was initially known as the Western District of Lagos Protectorate. In 1914, what is shown in Map 6.4 as Egbado Division was formed, although at that time it was called Ilaro Division. Ilaro town became the Divisional headquarters in the

Map 6.4   *Regional, provincial, divisional and district boundaries, 1954*

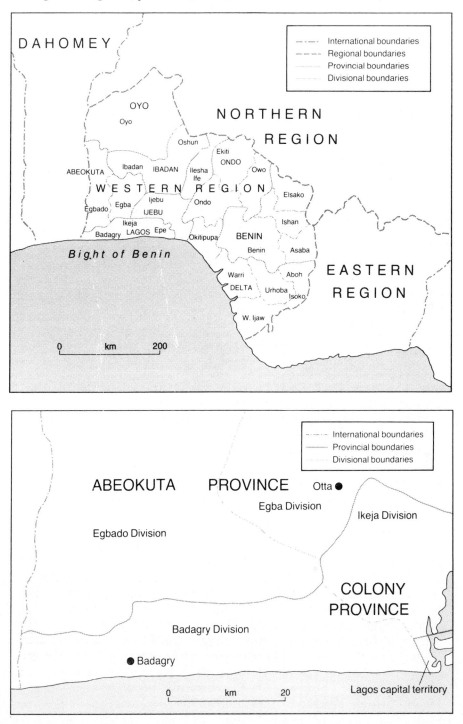

Map 6.4 *continued*

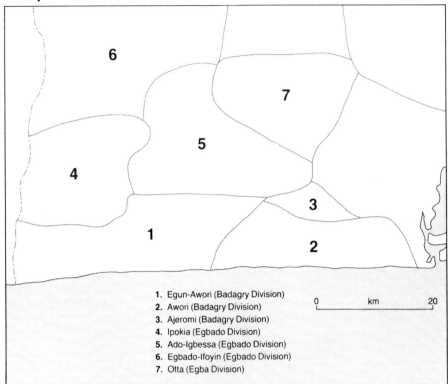

1. Egun-Awori (Badagry Division)
2. Awori (Badagry Division)
3. Ajeromi (Badagry Division)
4. Ipokia (Egbado Division)
5. Ado-Igbessa (Egbado Division)
6. Egbado-Ifoyin (Egbado Division)
7. Otta (Egba Division)

0   km   20

same year. In 1948, Ilaro Division was renamed Egbado Division, although there was no change in divisional headquarters.

In general, each cultural and linguistic group controlled its own affairs. This was in line with the British concept of indirect rule through the traditional power structure, although with most power remaining in the hands of the colonial government. While in Dahomey, the centralised French administration destroyed the institution of 'chieftaincy', the British used it as a tool for government. Indeed, the institution of chieftaincy was preserved and in some instances strengthened. Chiefs of minor kingdoms such as Igbessa, Ado and Ajilete were in effect strengthened both in prestige and in jurisdiction, once they became the centres of new districts created by the British; under pre-colonial rule, they had been subservient to more powerful kingdoms and their chiefs. Meanwhile, the British curtailed the powers and the revenue collection of the Obas of Oyo (heirs to those who ruled the Oyo Empire) and the chiefs of Abeokuta (capital of the Egbas). The British also created a hierarchical administrative structure from the Colonial Administrator through Paramount Chiefs and District Head chiefs to Head chiefs of towns and bales in villages. Asiwaju (1976) commented that 'At their various levels, the chiefs in the British area (of Western Yorubaland) enjoyed the exercise of much larger initiative and greater responsibility, sanctioned by law than their counterparts in the French territory' (p.72).

In 1911, the Native Councils Ordinance prescribed a Central Native Council made up of paramount chiefs to assist the colonial governor based at Lagos. At district level, district councils were set up under the presidency of the chief recognised by the Governor as the principal ruling chief. Where there was no obvious traditional ruler in an area, the British would appoint a 'Warrant Chief' who need not have authority based on lineage or descent from ruling families. A Warrant Chief could also be made a paramount or a minor chief; not surprisingly, the imposition of Warrant Chiefs did not prove to be very successful. Since no Oba (or King) in the study region traditionally commanded the allegiance of all the others, the paramount chief was a warrant chief. One notable example was Seriki Faremi William Abass of Badagry. He was appointed President of Badagry Native Council in 1902 and represented the area on the Central Native Council in Lagos. Then in 1913, he was appointed Paramount Chief for the whole of the Western District. What then had been Western District became Ilaro Division, in 1914. He became senior chief of Ilaro Division until his death in 1919.

Taxation and, in the early years, forced labour, were two important civil conditions imposed by the British on Nigerians. For taxation, initially the British relied on indirect taxes coming from customs and other duties. Direct taxation was introduced to the study region in 1921 with a head tax levied on adult men and women and it was left to local chiefs in their role as heads of native administrations to collect the tax. In addition, tax revenues were raised by licensing certain goods or activities such as lorries, boats, bicycles and imported guns. Until the reorganisation of district boundaries in 1948, native authorities at district level retained around half of locally generated revenues for such tasks as road construction and maintenance, health centres and schools; these were the tasks assigned them by central government. The necessity of paying taxes was probably the most important government intervention in terms of changing the traditional economy and associated social structure. For since taxes had to be paid in British pounds sterling, this hastened the entry of many of the study region's inhabitants into the cash economy. With the French colonial government seeking to establish the exclusive use of the French franc in Dahomey, while the British insisted on sterling as the only legal tender in Nigeria, a further impediment to the traditional west-east trade flows was created. Prior to the colonial rule, a single currency, the cowry shell, had been widely used and accepted in Western Yorubaland.

Forced labour was used for public works although this ceased with the introduction of direct taxation in 1921. Labour recruitment was normally undertaken through local chiefs and those recruited usually worked within these chiefs' areas of jurisdiction. Forced labour was used much more extensively in Dahomey and it only ceased with the post World War II reforms in French West Africa. Forced labour was also used for agricultural projects such as the farms, plantations and seed nurseries set up by the Colonial Department of Agriculture. The French Colonial administration also aided forced labour recruitment for private enterprises. Enlistment often involved force and labour was posted to wherever labour was required, despite the fact that this meant sending labourers far from their home areas. Compulsory conscription into the Army was also practiced in Dahomey; there is no record of compulsory conscription in the study region. The relatively harsh regime imposed by the French in Dahomey was of importance to the study region not only in the comparison it provides for British rule but, more tangibly, in the cross-border emigration it encouraged.

The single entity of Nigeria dates from 1914 when the two British Protectorates of Southern and Northern Nigeria were joined. The area in and around Lagos City had had separate status under a British Governor from 1886 but was amalgamated with the Southern Protectorate in 1906. In 1954, Nigeria became a federation of three regions—Northern, Western and Eastern. Since the major administrative centres for these regions and their sub-divisions were chosen largely for their importance relative to production or commerce, administrative convenience or strategic military location, none needed to be located within the study region. Economically it was of little importance or was connected to Ilaro, the capital of Ilaro Division (renamed Egbado Division in 1948), to the north; militarily, it could be controlled from Lagos.

Lagos became the most important administrative and economic centre for the whole of Nigeria. The entire study region was now within the Western Region whose administrative capital was Ibadan. Lagos was designated a separate federal territory in 1954; in the 1952 census the population of 'Lagos Capital Territory' which covered some 70 square km had reached 267,407 inhabitants. Thus, as Map 6.4 shows, with the whole study region falling into the Western Region, Badagry Division (with the districts of Awori, Egun-Awori and Ajeromi) were in Colony province while the four northern-most districts were all in Abeokuta Province. Three were among the five districts created from the original eleven in Ilaro division and now called Egbado division (Egbado-Ifoyin, Ado-Igbessa and Ipokia) while one (Otta) was within Egba Division. Lagos Capital Territory and Ikeja division into which Lagos city was rapidly over-spilling were by the south-east corner of the study region.

The division of Nigeria into a federation of three major regions was part of the enactment of the MacPherson Constitution which had important implications for Nigeria's economic and urban development and these are discussed briefly on page 246. However it should be noted in passing that no urban centre in the study region benefited much either from the increased pace of industrial development or from the increasing control that Nigerians acquired over the machinery of government. Badagry, the only divisional headquarter in the study region was in no position to benefit from either; its administrative status was below that of regional or provincial capital and it was too small and too isolated to gain any role in the new emphasis given to industrial development.

Economic change under colonial rule

The southern part of the study region's land resources were not judged to be suited either to cash crop production for export or to food production for the rapidly expanding Lagos City; thus it had very poor road or rail connections to Lagos (despite its proximity to Lagos) and to other regions of Nigeria (see Map 6.3). The construction of the western railway began from Lagos in 1895, reached Ibadan by 1900 and then proceeded north. Road construction began somewhat later; an enquiry in 1907 discovered only 92 km of motorable roads in all of Nigeria (Mabogunje, 1968). Major road construction from Lagos also largely bypassed the study region. Some idea of the lack of development of road transport can be seen in the fact that three-fifths of the Nigerian freight traffic was still on the railway in 1953 (Mabogunje, 1968). Despite the fact the Badagry is only some 55 km from Lagos, overland transport between Badagry and Lagos throughout the colonial period (and indeed well into the post colonial period) involved a circuitous route of 125 km on roads which were not completely paved until 1958. Colonial rule with the imposition of a new national boundary between French-controlled Dahomey and British-controlled Nigeria had disrupted what had been a whole series of important east-west trade flows which had helped sustain many producers and trades—and market towns. Paved roads and railways went north from Lagos, essentially bypassing the study region. A road was built to connect Badagry to Ilaro (via Ado-Odo) and on to Abeokuta in the 1920s but given Lagos's dominant role as port and railway terminus, this meant little stimulus to Badagry's economic base. Similarly, in Dahomey, both roads and railways were largely oriented to a north-south direction and production and trade was re-oriented towards French needs with the production and export of cotton and the import of French goods; the east-west movements of population and trade were greatly constrained, although not entirely suppressed.

This combined with the fact that the cost of a road or railway connection running between Lagos and Badagry and on to Porto Novo in Dahomey along a coastal area with numerous rivers, creeks, lagoons and swamps, further guaranteed the insulation of the southern part of the study region from what developed into the largest colonial capital in sub-Saharan Africa just to its east. Largely because overland transport connections between the south of the study region and Lagos were so poor and because little thought was given to developing water-transport (the lagoons had long been the most important transport link between Badagry and Lagos, and Badagry and Porto Novo) the zone of intensive agricultural production which developed in response to demand from Lagos urban consumers, especially after around 1950, was concentrated in a zone running to the north of Lagos, especially on or close to the two major roads out of Lagos; the Lagos-Abeokuta and Lagos-Ikorodu roads. Thus, as Ajaegbu (1970) describes in a paper on food crop farming in the coastal area of south-western Nigeria, the zone of intensive agriculture was to the east of the study region.

Despite the lack of statistics for scale and nature of production and for the sectoral distribution of the labour force until the 1963 census, the economic base for much of the population probably changed little from pre-colonial times up to 1963 except for areas to the north which had become incorporated into cash crop production for export through Ilaro. A census in 1952 revealed that most inhabitants of small urban centres still derived their living from agriculture. Although figures only exist for the whole Western region, in 1953, three-quarters of the population of centres with 10,000–19,999 inhabitants derived their living from agriculture while for those with 5,000–10,000 inhabitants, the proportion was 80 per cent.

Trade was the next most important category of occupation but it only employed 5.4 per cent of the labour force in centres with 10,000–19,999 inhabitants, and 4.3 per cent in centres with 5,000–9,999 inhabitants. Although these figures are for a region with a much larger population and area than that in the study region, at least they give an indication of how agriculture remained the main source of livelihood for those living in small urban centres. One should note that in 1952, the study region had no settlements with 20,000 or more inhabitants and only one (Ado-Odo) with more than 10,000. In addition, there were very few professional and administrative personnel in small urban centres within the Western region. This ties in with the concept of indirect rule and the great weakness of municipal government which was evident in small urban centres, throughout the colonial period.

Thus, in the study region's southern portion, Badagry Division, lack of easy access either to ports for export or to major markets for food crops combined with poor soil and climate for crop production and a preference among many people for fishing led to little agricultural development. Some success was achieved in coconut production; a coconut plantation was established on Topo island, with

support from the Roman Catholic Church, while some coconut production for sale was also undertaken elsewhere. Coconut and associated copra and coconut oil became Badagry Division's main money
crop. Such commonly grown commercial crops as kolanuts and palm
did not do well; yams also did poorly. Badagry town remained an
important market centre for its surrounding area but never returned
to the pre-eminence it had enjoyed in the pre-colonial period. By the
early Sixties, Badagry only handled a tiny proportion of the palm
oil trade in what had been its area of influence prior to colonial rule;
Lagos and ports in Dahomey were far more important. A new market
was founded in Badagry in 1952 with a grant from the Colony
Development Board; by 1969, it had a total of 120 stores or lock-
up stalls and 1425 open stalls. In the 1963 census, the relatively
unimportant role played by agriculture in Badagry Division is clearly
seen in the fact that only 21 per cent of the labour force worked as
farmers, fishermen, hunters or loggers. A substantial proportion of
these would have been largely dependent on fishing.

Agricultural production of both cash crops for export and of food
crops for domestic sale and the road and rail links to support them
were more developed in the northern portion of the study region.
Ilaro, to the north of the study region's northern boundary, became
the main transport and commercial centre for cocoa production and
export out of the region. The exploitation of oil palm, timber and
rubber did affect many areas within the northern portion of the study
region. For instance, a rubber plantation was established in the 1890s
in Oke Odan by the Societe Anglo-Belge. This later became known
as the Ilaro Rubber and Produce Estate Ltd and the management
of the plantation and factory passed to a German firm. But the estate
was confiscated and demolished after the First World War. Up to
1,500 labourers were said to have worked there (Asiwaju, 1976).
When the land was returned to its former owners, the rubber trees
were replaced with cocoa and kolanut cultivation. Cocoa and kolanuts also became popular crops elsewhere. Kolanut production became
an important revenue yielding crop in many areas in the south of
Egbado Division.

In 1941, over 15,000 tons of kolanuts produced in this division
were sold for 585,000 pounds sterling. Much of these were produced
in the northern portion of the study region. The divisional headquarters, Ilaro, also on the railway, received most of the urban stimulus from cocoa production with the enterprises and services growing
up to support its role as centre for transport and trade. As divisional
headquarters, it also had the largest local government budget in the
study region. Corn produced in Ifoyin and Ipokia districts became
important for supplying military garrisons in Lagos and Abeokuta.
Corn production was encouraged by colonial administrators; experimental farms were established in Ipokia and Ado-Odo. Food crops

such as yam, cassava, beans, citrus fruits, pepper and various vegetables were also produced for sale.

The increasing commercialisation of agriculture is known to have had important impacts on land tenure. Traditionally, land was held by tribal groups ('lineage-holdings') with no alienation (ie individual sale) of land. Strangers could be given land grants or the right to use land but this was subject to the sanction of lineage heads. Developments under colonial rule led to the break-up of such traditional tenure systems. First, large areas of land were appropriated by the colonial administration to create State or Crown lands and plots were sold or leased for 99 years to individual and foreign companies. So both freehold and leasehold land became common. In addition, as good quality, well located agricultural land and urban land increasingly acquired a monetary value, so it came to be freely bought and sold. The clash this created with traditional land tenure systems can be seen in the endless litigation in colonial lawcourts about land. (Mabogunje, 1961). Increasing levels of agricultural production for sale also affected the traditional pattern of rural settlements as people bringing new land under cultivation and clearing forests increased the number of settlements.

Thus, it is no surprise to find census data for 1963 showing a much higher proportion of the male labour force working in agriculture, fishing, hunting and forestry in the northern portion of the study region compared to the southern portion. Although statistics are only available for the whole of Egbado Division (of which only half was in the study region), 74 per cent of male labour force worked in agriculture, fishing, hunting and forestry and much the highest proportion of these were in agriculture. There are unlikely to be major differences in the sectoral distribution of the labour force between Egbado South (within the study region) and Egbado North (just to its north). The far higher proportion of the male labour force employed in agriculture in the northern portion of the study region in 1963 ties in with the greater potential and supporting roads there for commercial agricultural production.

For Nigeria as a whole, the period after the Second World War was of particular importance to economic and especially industrial development. With the enactment of the MacPherson Constitution in 1952, political power became more decentralised to regional and provincial level authorities, while more effort was put into promoting industrial development. This certainly affected the larger cities including Lagos but it had little impact on the economy of the study region.

Urban development and population growth under colonial rule

The extension of British colonial rule over Nigeria (including the study region) brought major changes in the relative political and economic importance of the study region (and its main towns and transport corridors) within south-west Nigeria. The most obvious early development affecting it was the development of Lagos just to the east as the colonial capital and main colonial port. From a relatively small and unimportant Yoruba fishing and farming settlement (in the late eighteenth century), it became first the centre of the slave trade and later a centre of agricultural commerce. Once under British rule (commencing in 1861) it developed as a centre for a colonial bureaucracy and then as the port and railway terminus for the railway which opened up the interior of Western Nigeria. Lagos's population grew from around 5,000 inhabitants in 1800 to 25,000 in 1866, 74,000 in 1911, 303,500 in 1952 and 726,6000 in 1963.[4]

Meanwhile, Badagry lost the very foundation of its pre-colonial economic base with the construction and development of Lagos's ports linked to the expanding railway systems. Otta suffered from its exclusion from the railway heading north. Most of the southern part of the study region was completely bypassed by the colonial government's policies to develop a cash-crop export oriented economy in the late nineteenth and early twentieth centuries. Home (1976) noted that the towns which prospered in this period where those in the export-crop areas and favourably placed on the transport network while Asiwaju (1976) noted that towns (in Western Yorubaland) which became administrative headquarters grew more rapidly than others which had been more important in pre-colonial times. Both the period of political instability and warfare in the period prior to colonial rule and the fact that the south and east of the study region were then bypassed by developments under colonial rule can be seen in the lack of development within towns and indeed in the serious decline in population in formerly important urban centres like Badagry and Otta. In the whole study region, only Badagry was recognised as a settlement with urban status in the 1917 Township Ordinance and within this Ordinance, it only received Third Class township status.[5]

In the meantime, Lagos was the only town in Nigeria to receive First Class status. As a Third Class township, Badagry's municipal goverment was essentially left to the native authorities whose knowledge of most basic municipal tasks such as water supply, sanitation and physical planning were very limited. So too were funds. However, its urban status did mean the development of a government reservation area (for whites only) and the construction of some government offices, high class housing for government officials, schools, a hospital, a police station and a prison. But the figures in Table 6.2 suggest a population of between 4,000 and 6,000 for the entire period between 1846 and 1952 in contrast to an estimated population of 12,500 at the beginning of the nineteenth century. Badagry's status as a Third Class township was abolished in 1938.

The town of Ilaro, was also given Third Class township status. Ilaro had received more stimulus from colonial developments than settlements in the study region to its south since it became one of the centres of the cocoa-producing areas developed in the second half of the nineteenth century. As Map 6.1 shows, Ilaro was also on the railway. One sign of Ilaro's role within export agriculture was the offices of various foreign firms which set up there.

Ilaro, like Badagry, acquired the government reservation area with housing and services for its white residents and thus the dualist spatial structure so apparent in most colonial towns in Anglophone Africa. But like Badagry and most Third Class townships elsewhere in Nigeria, it received very little support in terms of funds and profesional help for the provision of basic infrastructure and services. Nor was there any notable public support for education although as headquarters of a Division, it would have had the largest tax base of any settlement within the Division. Various missions were allowed to establish schools and indeed encouraged to compete with Native authorities and private efforts. There were no post-primary educational institutions in all of Egbado Division in 1945.

The already mentioned clash between traditional concepts of tenure and of land freely bought and sold affected urban land. House designs and building materials also began to change. Asiwaju (1976) commented that in Western Yorubaland under European rule, 'the pre-colonial town, as a conglomeration of circular lineage compounds, gradually gave way to a new structure which now consists of individual rectangular buildings with larger doors and windows. Other novel features include planned streets, public conveniences and motor-parks' (p. 210).

A paucity of reliable data on population at district level, apart from that provided by the 1963 census,[6] and the changes in district boundaries makes impossible any detailed discussion of demographic trends under colonial rule. Data from the 1952 census and from various estimates for population size in certain settlements is available, which allows more discussion of the development of the study region's urban system over time.

Table 6.3 gives total and urban population and numbers of urban centres in 1963 for the northern and southern portions of the region and for the districts into which these portions are divided, while Table 6.4 gives population figures for various urban centres for 1952 and 1963. For the southern portion, Hodder (1963) reports that Badagry Division registered a population growth of just over 50 per cent between 1931 and 1952 but with the number of towns and villages increasing over threefold. Most of the increase in population was accounted for by settlements of under 100 persons indicating a dispersion of settlements over the countryside for farming purposes. Part of this growth in population was no doubt the protest emigration from Dahomey mentioned earlier. Total population in Badagry Division is reported to have grown from 65,680 to 122,159 between 1952 and 1963 which implies an annual average population growth rate of 5.8 per cent for these 11 years, more than twice any likely rate of natural increase for that time. This does not imply an area undergoing the very slow economic changes described already. However, most of the growth in population within Badagry Division within these 11 years was the result of the physical expansion of Lagos conurbation into the study region's eastern corner.

By 1963, Ajeromi District which is Badagry Division's easternmost district (see Map 6.4) and one which is just next to Lagos, had four urban centres with 5,000 or more inhabitants including two with close to 20,000; none of these had been recorded as towns in the 1952 census. In the 1952 census, Ajeromi District had some 12,950 inhabitants; by the 1963 census, it had 52,245 and is best classified as 100 per cent urban since it was by then part of Lagos conurbation. Thus, while the population of this relatively small district to the south of the study region (and next to Ikeja Division) essentially quadrupled its population in 11 years, that in the rest of Badagry Division increased by 33 per cent. In addition, population growth in these 11 years in Badagry division was much slower than in the other divisions in Colony State to its east (and to the east of the study region); Ikeja's population grew a phenomenal 366 per cent in these 11 years while that of Lagos Capital Territory grew 149 per cent and that of Epe grew 118 per cent.

Most of this rapid growth in population in Ajeromi District within the study-region and in Ikeja, Epe and Lagos Capital Territory which make up the rest of what was then Colony Province was due to net in-migration flows in response to rapid economic development and rapid growth in the state bureaucracy and associated enterprises in Lagos, the national capital. Apart from Ajeromi District and its very rapid population growth, for the five urban centres within the study region for which statistics for population exist for 1952 and for 1963, Otta and Igbessa registered a considerable increase in population, Badagry registers some increase while Ado-Odo and Ajilete register a decline.

In the northern portion of the study region, there are strong correlations between settlement's administrative rank, urban status and relative population size in 1963. Ilaro, the headquarters of Egbado Division, located to the north of the study region, is larger than any urban centre within the study region while the district headquarters which had existed up to 1948 – Otta, Igbessa, Ipokia Ajilete, Ado-Odo and Oke-Odan were first, second, third, fourth, fifth and seventh[7] largest urban centres. In the southern portion of the study region, the correlation is less obvious with much the two largest urban centres in 1963, Araromi and Ajegunle, both in Ajeromi

Table 6.3 *Population and urban population by district and division for the study region, 1963*

	Total population	Urban centres	Urban population	% total population in urban centres
Southern part of study region[a]				
Awori District	29,778	None	0	0
Egun-Awori District	40,136	Badagry	8,525	21.2
Ajeromi District	52,245	Ajegunle Araromi Aiyetoro Onibaba	52,245	100.0
Total for Southern Region	122,159	Five urban centres	60,770	49.7
Northern part of study region[b]				
Egbado-Ifoyin District	54,232	Ajilete Owode Oke-Odan	16,967	31.3
Ado Igbessa District	61,509	Ado-Odo Igbessa	23,572	38.3
Ipokia District	54,702	Ipokia Agosasa	10,355	18.9
Otta District	51,618	Otta	14,348	27.8
Total for Northern Region	222,061	Eight urban centres	65,242	29.4
Total for study region	344,220	13 urban centres	126,015	36.6

Notes: a—Badagry Division.
b—Egbado-Ifoyin, Ado-Igbessa and Ipokia (in Egbado Division) plus Otta District (in Egba Division).

district. Badagry, both a district and divisional headquarters, had less than half the population of either of these.

But as noted already, the whole of Ajeromi District with its close proximity to the rapidly developing Lagos City/metropolitan area, can by 1963 only be understood in terms of being part of Lagos conurbation. Once Ajeromi's four settlements are excluded, because they are part of Lagos's expanding economic and physical devel-

Table 6.4 *Population growth of urban centres in or close to the study region, 1952 and 1963*

	1952	1963
Northern portion		
Otta	8,914	14,348
Igbessa	6,615	12,179
Ado-Odo	16,381	11,393
Ajilete	6,317	5,795
Oke-Odan		5,607
Owode		5,565
Ipokia	3,607	5,312
Agosasa		5,043
Southern portion		
Araromi	3,877	19,379
Ajegunle	6,241	18,363
Badagry	5,917	8,525
Aiyetoro	2,833	7,427
Onibaba		7,076
Urban centres close to the study region		
Lagos Metro	303,461	1,100,000
Porto Novo (in Benin)		74,500
Ilaro	12,373	20,537

Source: 1952 and 1963 censuses.

opment, Badagry is the only urban centre in the southern portion of the study region and the most important administrative centre.

Developments after independence

Administrative reforms

In the twenty years after gaining Independence in 1960, a series of changes in sub-national and sub-regional boundaries and local government reforms were undertaken. In response to political differences between the north, east and west (and the main cultural groups there), which eventually resulted in Civil War, the number of states was increased from the three administrative regions which existed in 1956[8] to four (in 1963), 12 (in 1967) and 19 (in 1976) (see Map 6.5). In addition, reforms sought to strengthen local government, and in the late Seventies, construction began on a new Federal Capital, Abuja, located almost in the geographic centre of Nigeria. Such changes have important long-term implications for the study region.

Colony Province in Western Region (within which the southern portion of the study region was located) became Lagos State in 1967. This was then subdivided into five local councils in 1968 with the former Badagry Division (and its three district councils) remaining as Badagry Division within the newly named State. Further changes in the subdivision of Lagos State into local government areas occurred in 1971, 1976, 1982 and 1984; for the part of Lagos State within the study region, these simply meant its subdivision into two, then return to one, then back to two and finally, in 1984, back to one again called Badagry Division. For the rest of this chapter, statistics for the whole of Badagry Division will be presented as if it had remained one unit of local government for the period 1968-1984. This also means that statistics for the new Badagry Division are directly comparable to those presented for the Badagry Division which existed under colonial rule and for which statistics are given in previous sections. However, statistics disaggregated below the level of this Division are rarely available, except for some population estimates for 1975 which refer to the three districts used in the 1963 census. These are discussed in the next sub-section.

The northern part of the study region first became part of Western State in 1967 and when this was subdivided into three in 1976, part of Ogun State. Ogun State was divided into ten local government areas and what had been Otta district became part of Ifo/Otta local government area while the three other former districts which had been in Egbado Division became part of Egbado south local government area.

The Local Government Reform in 1976 sought to bring more uniformity to the number of inhabitants under any local government; it also sought to ensure that local government received a direct allocation of state and federal revenues. At least up to the early Eighties, local authorities – like those based in the urban centre of Badagry for Badagry Local Government Area – had received neither the funds nor the revenue-raising powers and resources they would need to play a major role in promoting social and economic development within their area of jurisdiction. While more financial support for local government was envisaged in the 1981-1985 Development Plan, it is too soon to gauge its effects on developments within the study region.

Two other developments are worth noting since these affect the study region: the new state capitals for Ogun and Lagos States and the new Federal Capital.

Ikeja replaced Lagos as Lagos State's capital in 1976 although Ikeja (close to the eastern boundary of the study region) is still part of the wider Lagos conurbation and developed largely as an industrial and residential suburb of Lagos City. And in 1976, with the division of Western State into three, Abeokuta became capital of the new Ogun State. Education, health and agriculture and a substantial amount of infrastructure investment are largely state government responsibilities so it is to state governments located in Abeokuta and

Map 6.5 *Local and state boundaries in the study region, 1976, and state boundaries in Nigeria, 1967 and 1976*

12 States, 1967

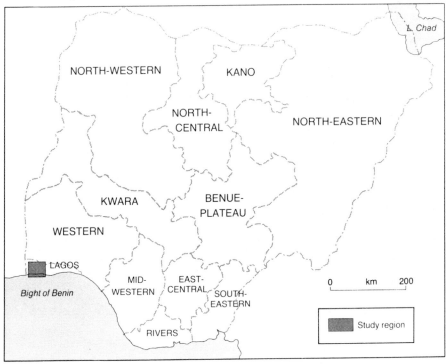

19 States, 1976

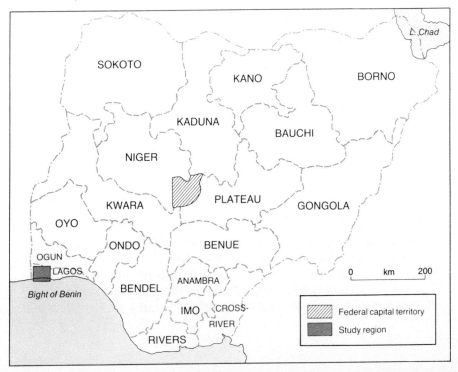

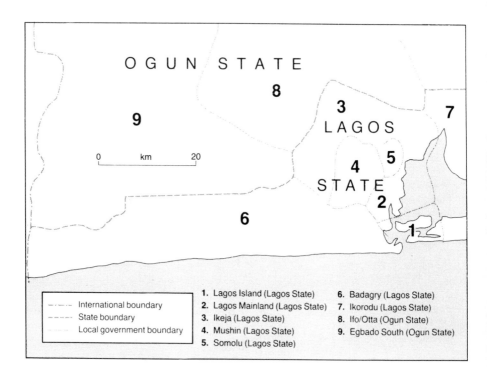

Ikeja that local governments within the study region must look for support in developing the area under their jurisdiction.

Eventually, Abuja,[9] the new Federal Capital now under construction, will take over from Lagos as the Federal Capital with the National Assembly, the Judiciary, the President's residence and the important Ministries. Although the fall in oil revenues (the Federal Government's main source of revenue) and the deteriorating economy have brought cut-backs in the plans for Abuja, in the long term the movement of Federal Government and the many enterprises, services and facilities associated with it will affect Lagos's economic and employment base and perhaps, indirectly, those of the study region too.

Demographic, economic and social change in Badagry Division (the southern portion of the study region), 1963–1982

Total population in Badagry Division grew very rapidly between 1963 and 1975; from 122,159 inhabitants recorded in the 1963 census to an estimated 456,000 in 1975. Population growth in this Division is likely to have continued growing rapidly after 1975. But this is almost entirely due to the increasing growth and spread of Lagos conurbation.

We noted earlier how in 1963, Ajeromi District with 52,245 inhabitants was really part of metropolitan Lagos (see Map 6.4). By 1975, Ajeromi's population was an estimated 388,000 inhabitants. If this 1975 estimate is correct, the population in this relatively small district grew more than sevenfold in just 12 years. This implies an annual population growth rate of over 18 per cent. Meanwhile, in the rest of Badagry Division (which at this date included most of the relatively rural, undeveloped lands west of Lagos) the 1975 estimates suggest that total population actually fell from 69,914 to 68,000. The population in Badagry urban centre only grew from 8,525 in 1963 to an estimated 10,200 in 1975, an annual average population growth rate of 1.5 per cent which suggest net out-migration in this period since this is below any likely rate of natural increase.

The idea of considerable net out-migration flows from the predominantly rural western and central areas of Badagry Division to the highly urbanised eastern area is supported by statistics on age structure which are available for Badagry Division and for Lagos State in 1976. Urban areas in both have a substantially higher proportion of 20-39 year olds than rural areas, while rural areas tend to have a higher proportion of people over 40 years of age. And since the data was for 1976 and the proportion of people in the 20-29 year old age group was noticeably higher in the urban areas compared to rural areas than the 30-39 year old age group, it suggests particularly rapid net rural to urban migration of young adults in the years just preceeding 1976.

Table 6.5 *Percentage of urban and rural population in different age groups for Lagos State and for Badagry Division, 1976*

| | Badagry Division | | Lagos State | |
| | Urban | Rural | Urban | Rural |
Age Group				
0–9	26.3	31.9	28.6	27.1
10–19	19.0	17.6	20.0	20.5
20–29	32.5	15.5	26.3	18.0
30–39	15.1	13.9	13.5	13.6
40–49	5.6	10.1	6.5	10.0
50–59	1.0	5.4	2.7	5.3
60–69	0.4	3.1	1.5	3.1
70–79	0.1	1.5	0.7	1.4
80+	0.0	1.0	0.2	1.0
Total	100.0	100.0	100.0	100.0

Source: Derived from statistics in Lagos State Statistical Survey, 1980.

An examination of changes in infrastructure and industrial development from 1963 to the late Seventies supports the general trends suggested by the 1975 population estimates of rapid economic change in Badagry Division close to Lagos and economic stagnation for much of rest of the Division. Perhaps the most influential development in this period was the construction of an express highway from Lagos to Badagry; this meant that most of Badagry Division was either connected to or relatively close to a four-lane highway giving easy access by car, lorry or bus both to Cotonou (or Porto Novo) in Benin and to Lagos. By 1984, a mixture of illegal and legal housing and shop developments, factories, markets, warehouses, schools, colleges, and other developments lined each side of the road almost continuously for the first 30 kilometres after the expressway begins on the periphery of central Lagos. These include many large Federal or State Government funded developments such as Festac Village (the first large, federally funded public housing project), Satellite Town (a public and private sector development), a large army barracks, the campus for Lagos State University (still under development), a large international trade centre, Lagos State football stadium a large secondary school and a state teacher training college.

Map 6.6   *Growth in the urbanised area between 1963 and 1976 along the beginning of the Lagos-Badagry-Cotonou Expressway*

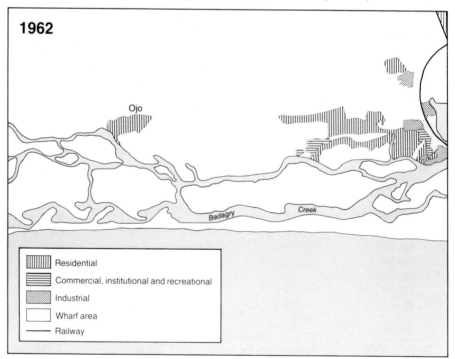

Map 6.6   *Continued*

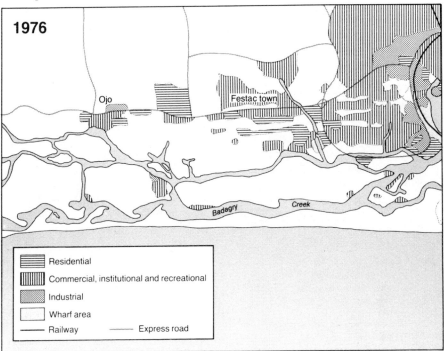

Map 6.6 gives an idea of the speed with which the urbanised area grew on or close to the Lagos-Badagry Expressway between 1963 and 1976; if data was available for 1985, it would almost certainly show an even more spectacular growth in urbanised area over the last ten years. A large Volkswagen automobile assembly plant has been built by the expressway close to Ojo.

Other important new expressways have recently been completed or are now under construction. The first is the 'outer ring road west' which links Apapa Wharf (the port of Lagos's main quay) and Apapa's industrial zone to the Lagos-Badagry Expressway and, further north, intersects the main access route to the Lagos-Ibadan Expressway to the north, through Abeokuta and on to Yelwa in the north-west of Nigeria. Although these expressways pass through the heart of the study region, the Federal Government's funding of the international extension to Porto Novo and the inter-state connection to Yelwa were conceived in terms of the benefits that these would bring to long distance trade and to Lagos rather than to the study region's inhabitants. The expressways should allow goods to move unhindered to and from the port of Apapa, the republic of Benin and the north-west of Nigeria. Perhaps more importantly, large trucks can move

Map 6.7 *Urban centres and major roads*

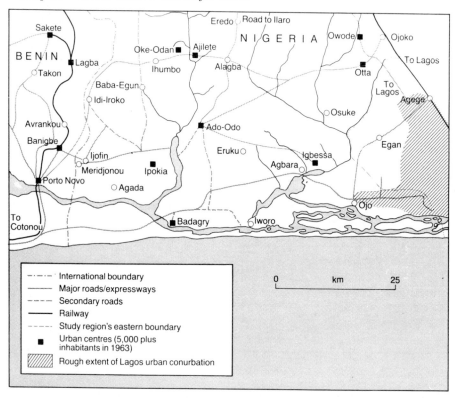

raw materials from the north to Apapa and imports from Apapa to the north without having to pass through heavily congested Lagos.

At Agbara, just north of the Lagos-Ogun State border, close to the Lagos-Badagry Expressway and just next to the new road being constructed to link the expressway to north-west Nigeria, a large greenfield industrial site has been developed originally on the initiative of just one individual who purchased land very cheaply from the village nearby. Several modern enterprises, most of them branches of multinationals, have set up there including Associated Breweries, Glaxo, Metal Box, Reckitt and Colman and Toyo Glass. The estate also includes some residential developments meant for senior or expatriate staff working in the enterprises located there although as of 1984, relatively few were completed and many of the completed units had not been occupied. A discussion of developments at Agbara industrial estate belongs to the next subsection in that it is just inside the northern portion of the study region in Ogun State. But since the discussion here is about the impact of the new Lagos-Badagry Expressway which is in Lagos State, and the Agbara esate is right next to this expressway, it is also relevant to mention its development here.

After the virtually continuous ribbon development along or close to the road up to Agbara, there are relatively few new developments. As of 1984, there was little sign of much new development in Badagry urban centre. Coconut plantations nearby have not been successful and a fibre bag factory has been abandoned. Some new public investments have been made such as a teacher training college and some low income housing, both of which are by the Expressway at some distance from the old town.

A comparison of the sectoral distribution of the labour forces in Badagry Division for 1963 (from census data) and for 1976 (from a survey by the State Government) shows that some significant changes did occur in the intervening 13 years. The figures in Table 6.6 show these changes, although care must be taken in comparing them since the sectoral categories are not the same.

Table 6.6 *Proportion of employed males and females in main occupational groups in Badagry Division, 1963 and 1976*

1963	Male (%)	Female (%)	Total (%)
— Professional, technical and related workers	4.1	1.0	2.9
— Administrative, executive and managerial	0.5	0.1	0.4
— Clerical	9.0	0.6	5.8
— Sales	7.8	26.6	15.0
— Farmers, fishermen, hunters and loggers	32.3	3.2	21.2
— Craftsmen, production-process workers and labourers	31.7	45.9	37.2
— Transport and communications	6.7	0.1	4.2
— Service, sports and recreation	6.0	1.1	4.1
— Others	1.8	21.4	9.3
Total	100.0	100.0	100.0
1976			
— Public administration	26.9	6.5	20.3
— Construction	3.0	0.3	2.1
— Manufacturing	9.3	35.3	17.7
—Agriculture and fishing	12.1	3.4	9.3
— Distributive trades	37.8	53.6	42.8
— Transport	8.1	—	5.5
— Others	2.8	0.9	2.2
Total	100.0	100.0	100.0

Sources: Population Census of Nigeria, 1963, Volume II and Statistical Survey of Lagos State, 1976.

We noted earlier the low proportion of Badagry Division's labour force working in farming, fishing and forestry; in fact, farming and fishing were the main source of livelihood for roughly equal proportions of employed males in Badagry Division in 1963. It is interesting to note the relatively low proportion of women working in this category since women represented around 40 per cent of all 'employed persons' in this census. 'Craftsmen, production process workers and labourers' was the largest category with 37.2 per cent of Badagry Division's employed persons; tailors and other textile workers, millers and mat-makers, were the most important.[10] Crafts were particularly important for women's employment with mat-making accounting for around 90 per cent of all women's employment in the category of 'Craftsmen, production process workers and labourers'. Sales workers, which were 15 per cent of all employed persons, were mostly women street vendors; after mat-making, this was much the most important occupation for women and together they accounted for over two-thirds of all women's employment.

As will be discussed later, this relates to women's roles selling in markets and does not imply a high level of employment in fixed and established retail outlets. However, much of the 'Professional, technical and related workers', the 'Administrative, executive and managerial' and 'Clerical' would be in urban areas; so too would a significant proportion of 'Transport and communications' and 'Service, sports and recreation' workers. Close to half the former category are 'automobile drivers' and 'messengers' while a third of the latter are watchmen. In the absence of employment-related data at district (rather than divisional) level, it is impossible to comment with any accuracy on the spatial implications of these figures. But given the concentration of Badagry Division's urban population in the easternmost district, Ajeromi, and the knowledge that this area had already begun to be engulfed by Lagos's physical and demographic growth by 1963, most of the urban-type employment revealed in the 1963 census is likely to be within Ajeromi District. In 1963, Ajeromi had 43 per cent of Badagry Division's population but 86 per cent of its urban population.

The statistics for 1976 suggest major changes in the previous 13 years. Distributive trades and public administration have become the main sources of livelihood for men, employing close to two-thirds of all employed men. Agriculture and fishing are relatively unimportant while jobs relating to transport have grown more important. For employed women, more than half are in 'distributive trades' while more than a third are in 'manufacturing'; this suggests less rapid change. Although no disaggregation was available comparable to that of the 1963 census, 85.5 per cent of women were 'own account workers', ie self-employed. This suggests the continuing importance of craft-making and street-vending, as in the 1963 census. Thus, most of the women working in 'distributive trades' are likely to be street vendors while most working in ' manufacturing' are likely to be making crafts. Indeed, a higher proportion of employed women were likely to be street vendors or making crafts in 1976 compared to 1963.

By contrast, only 37 per cent of employed males were 'own-account workers' while 61 per cent were employees. The growth in public administration in these 13 years is illustrated by the fact that by 1976, 27 per cent of all employed males were employees in public administration. Most were clerical workers. As in 1963, only a low proportion of women worked in public administration, although the number certainly grew in this period.

But once again, the fact that Badagry Division's eastern-most boundary adjoins Metropolitan Lagos and indeed the increasing overspill of population and economic activities from Lagos into Badagry Division must have played the major role in the changes evident in employment structure between 1963 and 1976. And the rapid population growth for the whole Division caused by this over-spill can give a false impression of what was happening elsewhere. For instance, despite the evident drop in the proportion of employed people in farming and fishing in Badagry Division, there were certainly more farmers and probably more fishermen in 1976 compared to 1963; the drop in the proportion of employed people working in farming and fishing being more than compensated for by the growth in the number of employed persons.[11] Indeed, it seems that the major structural change in employment for males described above was essentially confined to that small portion of Badagry Division into which Lagos over-spilled and little or no structural change took place elsewhere.

In a survey of large and small enterprises in Lagos State for 1980/81, 3,758 people worked in enterprises with ten or more persons in Badagry division (3,359 of these in manufacturing plants) while 1,021 worked in enterprises with between three and nine persons (589 of these being in commerce). 3,000 of these were in the Volkswagen factory, already mentioned. Badagry Divsion's labour force, for that year, must have been well in excess of 200,000 people which implies that only around two per cent of the labour force worked in enterprises with three or more persons covered by the State Government survey. It is also worth noting that Badagry Division with around 12 per cent of Lagos State's population had just two per cent of all employment and three per cent of manufacturing employment of all Lagos State for enterprises with ten or more persons. Neighbouring Ikeja Division, to the east of the study region was the dominant centre for such manufacturing enterprises (45 per cent) while not surprisingly, Lagos Island remained the dominant centre for enterprises with transport, commerce, finance and business services. It also had most of the enterprises with ten or more persons associated with agriculture and fishing; Badagry Division had none.

However, it is interesting to note some signs of industrial development within the study region and some signs of declining industrial investment in Lagos Mainland. The construction of the Lagos-Badagry-Porto Novo Expressway greatly enhances the accessibility of much of the study region to Lagos's ports, central business district and the international airport (at Ikeja). No doubt, this is what helped encourage Volkswagen to set up a plant just by this expressway, close to Ojo. This also underlines the development of Agbara Estate, described earlier, although this just falls within Ogun State, not Lagos State. No doubt, the eastern part of the study region can attract a higher proportion of a new productive investments within Lagos State than it has done in the past.

In the rest of Badagry Division beyond the spread of Lagos urban agglomeration, periodic markets remain both as centres for the purchase of goods and services and for the employment and income they generate for stall-holders, farmers and craft-makers. Such markets continue a role which had been evident throughout the colonial period and is known to have existed for centuries before the colonial rule. Badagry remains the most important market centre to the west, although its importance relative to other urban centres in the larger region has diminished enormously since pre-colonial rule. Within Badagry urban centre, night markets are held every night (in different locations); here locally produced foodstuffs are sold in small quantities. Then there are shops which open every day. Finally, there is the large periodic market. In 1969, it was recorded as having 120 stores or lock-up stalls and 1,425 open stalls (Fadeyi, 1969). Fieldwork in 1982 found 137 lock up stores or stalls and 1,481 open stalls; there were also seven warehouses. Different sections of this market tend to have stalls with similar products; for instance a block of 50 stalls had sellers of used clothing while other blocks specialised in crafts or hair-plaiting, welding, fresh meat, palm oil, dry fish and soup ingredients. Locally produced craftwork included pottery, baskets, brooms and mats. This organisation of the market into blocks specialising in certain commodities was not something planned by the Market authorities but reflects informal arrangements made by women within the Market Authority tenancy agreement. The market is open for three days on a eight-day cycle. The market women have their own association as the umbrella group for various sub-associations such as the fishsellers or cosmetics dealers or foodstuff sellers. These regulate competition and help organise for the welfare of traders. In addition to this main market, there are other markets closeby at Ilogbo, Ikoga and Iworo villages; Ilogbo and Iworo markets are every eight days while that of Ikoga is every four days. Each has

around 80 open stalls and most of the goods there are locally produced – foodstuffs, cloths, mats, baskets, pottery and raffia.

The survival of such periodic markets gives further evidence that
traditional forms of production, consumption and trade had changed
little for much of the population in the western half of Badagry
Division, at least up to the early Eighties. But to test the impact of
the Expressway on a village located near to it, field work was undertaken to Oto village, some 30 km from Central Lagos and right on
the expressway. Oto is a farming and fishing village, traditionally
linked to other settlements in the area by canoe via the lagoons. It
is located right on the Expressway, with most of the settlement and
associated farmlands to the south of the road. Agabara Industrial
Estate is very close by, on the opposite side of the road. During a
survey in 1979, most respondents claimed that they had not been
informed about the construction of the Expressway, even though this
came to cut through their farmlands. However, 44 per cent claimed
to have worked with the road construction company and many built
homes in Oto with their wages. But the construction of the Expressway did not bring much improvement in public services and facilities.

Oto has the traditional Yoruba structure of a central settlement
(with a population estimated at 6,000 in 1979) and a series of subsidiary settlements and farm settlements with another 2,400. Oto
settlement covers some 180 hectares with the old village concentrated
in some 40 hectares; its farmland covers some 16,200 hectares stretching south to the lagoon. The old village includes four churches, three
mosques, a primary school, a dispensary and an open night market
space. The new expressway (including its right of way) took up some
16 hectares within the settlement; in response to this expressway, the
inhabitants had a masterplan prepared with a new site of some 70
hectares developed to include 300 house plots, 30 plots of 0.4 of a
hectare fronting the lagoon, and space for a secondary school, post
office, fire station, petrol station, commercial and community centre,
nursery and primary school, and sewage and waterworks. Coconuts
are much the most important cash crops. Copra emerged as the key
crop on which the village's economy depended, the copra being
shipped on the creek to Apapa, Lagos's main port. But during the
emergence of petroleum as the Nigeria's major foreign exchange
earner in the early Seventies, copra exports declined and eventually
collapsed. In 1979, whole coconuts were locally produced, shipped
to Ojo market and bought by middlemen for sale in Northern Nigeria.

Traditionally, no single individual owns land; the right to admin-
ister its use rests with various family heads and 88 per cent of farmers
questioned aquired their lands through their father or mother. Only
20 per cent of those questioned thought that strangers should be
allowed to acquire land for residential or industrial purposes although

most were happy for strangers to lease land for farming. The accept-able level of rent was put at around 50 naira a hectare per year, or 50 per cent of the crop yield.

However, clearly a major commercial market is developing here for land. In the past, land had been leased to people from the city in return for traditional gifts and a token ground rent. But, land bought in 1979 for some 5,000 naira a hectare in 1979 was being offered at more than six times this price three to four years later. Not surprisingly, 'strangers' wishing to purchase the plots within the new masterplan layout will insist on legal documents as proof of freehold or leasehold; over time this will change the nature of land tenancy and erode the control on land use traditionally exercised by the family heads.

Demographic, economic and social change in the southern portion of Ogun State (the northern portion of the study region), 1963–1982

Data on demographic and on economic trends is even more sketchy in the northern portion of the study region than in Badagry Division. Official population estimates are available for 1976 and for 1977 for each settlement within the study region's districts recorded in the 1963 census. But these estimates simply assume that every settlement, whatever its size, location or economic base, had an annual average population growth rate of 2.5 per cent between 1963 and 1976 or 1977. Thus, this same population growth rate is applied to Otta urban centre where recent industrial developments are likely to have ensured a more rapid population growth rate, and to tiny, relatively isolated villages.

So, there is no data on total or urban population after 1963 from which comments can be made on demographic changes and on asso-ciated economic changes. The only data on economic changes comes from fieldwork on periodic markets (as in Badagry Division), some State Government data on industries and a visit to Otta to gauge the scale of new industrial development there.

Going back to the 1963 Census, there is data on the distribution of employed persons in the (then) Egbado Division. But this is not disaggregated into District level statistics and only three of the five district which made up Egbado Division were in the study region. Furthermore, Otta District, the fourth district in the study region, was in Egba Division.

However, in the absence of any other data, at least the data for Egbado Division might provide some clues as to the scale and nature of production and of urban development. Table 6.7 gives the pro-portion of employed persons by major occupational groupings in 1963.

Table 6.7 *Proportion of employed males and females in major occupational groups in Egbado Division, 1963*

	Male	Female	Total
— Professional, technical and related workers	2.5	0.7	1.8
—Administrative, executive and managerial	0.2	0.0	0.1
— Clerical	0.8	0.1	0.5
— Sales	6.1	80.7	36.5
—Farmers, fishermen, hunters and loggers	75.2	8.9	48.1
— Craftsmen, production-process workers and labourers	10.8	7.6	9.5
— Transport and communication	1.7	0.0	1.0
— Service, sports and recreation	2.6	1.9	2.3
— Others	0.2	0.1	0.1
Total	100.0	100.0	100.0

Source: Derived from figures in Census of Nigeria, 1963, Western Nigeria Volume II.

NB In 1963, there were 18 female administrative, executive and managerial workers and eight transport and communication workers but with 63,132 employed female workers, when percentages are rounded to one decimal point, these show up as 0.0 per cent. The sum of the numbers in the first and third column do not add up to 100.0 due to rounding.

Perhaps the most notable point shown by this Table is the high proportion of employed males working as farmers (over 90 per cent of the 'farmers, fishermen, hunters, loggers and related workers' were farmers) and the high proportion of employed females working as sales workers.

As in Badagry Division, virtually all the women working in sales were street vendors. When compared to the figures for Badagry Division (shown in Table 6.6), Egbado Division's economy is obviously more agricultural and less urban. For males, there are far lower proportions of employed males in clerical work or work associated with transport, communications or manufacturing; there is also a lower proportion of professional, technical and related workers and administrative, executive and professional. For women, there is a much higher proportion working as farmers and much less in manufacturing. Turning to statistics which further disaggregate the occupational groupings, the proportion of employed males in what might be termed typically urban jobs such as typists, clerks, automobile drivers and watchmen was substantially lower than in Badagry Division. For women, 80.5 per cent of all employed females were street vendors while mat-making, so important in Badagry Division, was the occupation of only 5.4 per cent.[12]

This impression of an economy more firmly based on agriculture, and less on crafts and with a lower level of urbanisation than Badagry Division is supported by 1963 census figures. For 29.4 per cent of the northern portion of the study region were in urban centres in 1963 compared to 49.7 per cent in the southern portion.

However, once again, one suspects that if more information were available at district rather than divisional level, the two western-most districts in Badagry Division would have a more subsistence based economy which is far less integrated into the commercial crop production for sale and for export than districts to the north. Once again, it seems the inclusion in Badagry Division of one district which by 1963 was physically and functionally part of Metropolitan Lagos gives a false impression of developments in Badagry Division. It is noticeable that at district level in 1963 the three least urbanised districts in the study region are Egun-Awori and Awori (both in Badagry Division) and Ipokia (the most southern and western district in Egbado Division).

Not surprisingly, in all of Egbado Division, the most urbanised district in 1963 was Ilaro district, just to the north of the study region, with the urban centre of Ilaro both the divisional headquarters and the urban centre on the railway through which agricultural exports from the Division were shipped to Lagos for export; in 1963, 45.6 per cent of the whole district's population was in the district and divisional headquarters. The districts of Egbado-Ifoyin and Ado-Igbessa, both in the study region and both adjoining Ilaro Division, were the next most urbanised. It is worth recalling that roads within Egbado Division capable of taking motor vehicles had been much more developed under colonial rule than in Badagry Division and that, as an earlier sub-section described, cash-crop production and commercial farming had been much more common.

Since 1963, there have been significant developments in the urban and industrial base of parts of the study region within Ogun State, most notably in Otta. The Ogun State Industrial Directory revealed 19 industrial enterprises with ten or more workers in the study region; as Table 6.8 shows, 12 of these were in Otta.

Thus, there were just 675 persons employed in industries with ten or more workers in the urban centres in the northern portion of the study region and nearly three-quarters of these were in just one urban centre, Otta. It is also notable that the only industry which seems to have developed, based on local resources, are wood-based industries. To supplement this information, field visits were made to Otta and to Agbara estate, the new industrial estate mentioned already, which

Table 6.8 *Industrial enterprises in urban centres in or close to the study region in Ogun State, 1980*

Urban centres	Number and type of industries with ten or more employees	Estimated number of employees
Ado-Odo	1 bakery	25
Ipokia	1 bakery	50
Otta	3 food products, 3 wood and wood products, 4 mineral products, 2 fabricated metal or machinery and equipment	475
Owode	4 wood and wood products 1 chemical	125
Ilaro[a]	1 bakery 6 wood and wood products	175

Note: a—Ilaro is just to the north of the study region.

Source: Ogun State Industrial Directory, 1980.

has developed just to the north of the Lagos-Badagry Expressway but just inside Ogun State (rather than Lagos State) boundaries.

A visit to Otta revealed a higher level of industrial development than that implied by Table 6.8 Otta Local Government Area Office have records of 128 industries within the jurisdiction of the local government area. These include several branch plants of large multinational firms such as Honda, Tower Aluminium, Hoechst and Singer. Most are in or close to Otta urban centre, especially on the Lagos-Abeokuta road or on the Lagos-Idi-Iroko road. Around a quarter of them are in Sango-Otta, a settlement with 3,624 inhabitants in 1963 on the main Lagos-Abeokuta road, close to Otta which has undoubtedly developed into a substantial concentration of urban population and urban employment since 1963. An unofficial estimate suggests that the Otta-Sango Otta conurbation probably had over 100,000 inhabitants by the mid-1980s. One of Otta's attractions for industries is that they avoid Lagos State's multi-levy, multi-tax system but retain proximity to Lagos. A visit to Agbara on the southern border of Ogun State in 1982 found 21 industries there; most are quite large and sophisticated operations and involve foreign capital; many are branch plants of firms with their main factory and/or headquarters in Metropolitan Lagos. Although no large population concentration had developed in Agbara (although various residential developments there were seeking to attract middle and upper income groups associated with the enterprises located there), this estate could develop into a substantial population concentration.

One of the reasons for the lack of industrial or infrastructure development in many of the urban centres to the north-west of the study region is probably their location close to the international boundary. As a matter of deliberate policy, both on the Nigerian and on the Beninois side, urban centres close to the boundary have received little or no public investment in infrastructure or services or production. They are neither administrative centres of any importance nor sufficiently well connected to Metropolitan Lagos to serve like Otta as a possible location for new industrial development.

As in much of Badagry Division, traditional markets remain important in much of the study region within Ogun State. Adalemo (1974) investigated 34 periodic markets in the districts of Owode and Otta (within the study region) and Ifo (outside it). Most were small markets acting as important outlets for small-scale farmers to sell produce; over three-quarters had less than 500 people attending market day with the number of people attending varying from around 25 for a very small market to 2,000 for the largest.

In and around the urban centre of Otta, market days are held on a four-day cycle. The market in Otta itself was constructed in the early Fifties by the local government (which replaced an earlier, more informal market) and includes 120 open stalls and 24 closed stalls. Held every four days, there were some 300 people buying and selling when the market was visited in August 1982. Meat, kolanuts and general provisions were the main items on sale although so too was clothing. There were also farm implements, bicycle accessories, books, footwear, medicinal herbs, watch repairers, smith and traditional crafts.

Otta's market serves both local and regional interests; traders from Agege and Mushin (within Metropolitan Lagos) are among those who use this market. There were five smaller periodic markets close to Otta identified in 1974; by 1982, one had ceased operation. None were as large as that in Otta and none had closed stalls.

Badagry Division's share of Lagos State Government funds

Before the final sub-section in this chapter draws on the previous sections to summarise the links between developments in the urban system and social, economic and political change, it is worth looking briefly at how Badagry Division has fared in the allocation of State Government funds in recent years. Unfortunately, data does not exist to allow a similar discussion for Ogun State. Metropolitan Lagos has clearly developed as Nigeria's primate city in terms of the proportion of national non-agricultural activities and of public investment in infrastructure and services. By the late Seventies, Metropolitan Lagos was reported to handle over 70 per cent of all Nigeria's external trade, account for over 68 per cent of total value added in industrial production and contains over 40 per cent of Nigeria's skilled manpower. Yet it contained only some five per cent of the national population.

In the 1970–74 Plan for Lagos State, the headquarters of each of the Divisions which made up Lagos State (including Badagry) received 400,000 naira (at that time around US$500,000) to build industrial estates. But this support for industrial development in Badagry achieved little. It could not hope to compete with other industrial estates in or close to Metropolitan Lagos in terms of (for instance) access to international ports and airports, access to a large pool of skilled and unskilled labour, professionals, services and rich consumers, access to government offices, etc., a mixture of which influences the location of most major enterprises. The 1975–80 Plan brought a different approach to bear on seeking to stimulate economic development outside Metropolitan Lagos; in less developed areas, industrial estates were to be attached to highly subsidised housing estates while in the more congested areas, high rents were to be imposed on industrial estates. But this, too, achieved little with regard to the less developed central and western parts of Badagry Division. Badagry Division received two per cent of the total estimated expenditure in these five years on industrial projects (one should recall that it had around 12 per cent of the State's population). Two industries were sited in Badagry: a coconut processing and a jute factory.

For the 1981-85 Plan, the emphasis was placed on supporting small-scale industries with high potential for employment generation and improvement of infrastructure. Badagry Division was to receive a new burnt bricks factory, a glass and bottle factory, an asbestos products factory and a coconut processing industry. But it is too soon to gauge the impact of this sudden and relatively large share of public investment in industry being allocated to Badagry Division.

However, despite local government reforms, local government below the State level remains weak in most instances and inevitably, this affects the possibilities that any government of a small or intermediate urban centre can have to invest in enterprises or supporting infrastructure and services. Local governments lack the technical and administrative personnel to efficiently promote and support development in their area of jurisdiction. And since so few of the urban centres within the study region have large and easily taxable enterprises, their revenue base is extremely small. In 1980, when Lagos State was divided into eight local government areas (with Badagry being one of these with the same boundaries as the old Badagry Division), Badagry local government received 7.5 per cent of total State revenue, although the proportion of state population it housed was some 12 per cent. Badagry local government also does poorly, compared with other local governments within Lagos State, in terms of public service provision. In 1972, only some ten per cent of secondary school age children were enrolled in secondary school in Badagry – which was much lower than in most other local government areas. In Metropolitan Lagos, the proportion was some 40 per cent.

A comparison of the educational levels of employees in different sectors between Lagos State and Badagry Division in 1976 showed some interesting points. First, in Lagos State, 62.5 per cent of all university graduates were in public administration with manufacturing and distributive trades sharing most of the rest. In Badagry, university graduates were evenly split between public administration and manufacturing. More than 60 per cent of all professional diploma holders in Lagos State and Badagry Division worked in public administration – as did more than half of all secondary school leavers. Distributive trades employed around half of all primary school leavers both in Lagos State and within Badagry Division – and this was the second most important source of employment (after public administration) for secondary school leavers and diploma holders in both. Agriculture and fishing had attracted no university graduates at all although it had around two per cent of professional diploma holders both in Lagos State and in Badagry Division.

Thus, public administration employs more than half of all those who have left secondary school (including those with higher education qualifications). Distributive trades takes around half of those who only finish primary school. It is also interesting (though perhaps not surprising) to note that the local government areas with the lowest proportion of high-level administrative workers, clerks and professionals were those like Badagry with much or all of their territory at some distance from Metropolitan Lagos. In addition, the proportion of the labour force working as employers or employees is lower in more peripheral local government areas like Badagry while the proportion of 'own account' (ie self-employed) workers is higher.

In terms of health services, in 1969, central Lagos had 89 per cent of all Lagos State's hospital beds, 88 per cent of the nursing staff and 94 per cent of the doctors. Badagry had less than one per cent of the doctors and only just over two per cent of the beds and nursing staff. The State plan for 1970-74 allocated five million naira to health but a higher proportion of this was spent in Metropolitan Lagos than in Lagos State's population. Expenditure in the 1975-80 Plan rose to some 54 million naira but those living in Metropolitan Lagos were the principal beneficiaries. The over-emphasis on curative medical care and its ineffectiveness relative to needs even within Metropolitan Lagos where most of the resources were spent, is also notable.

For the 1981-85 Plan, some 74 million naira was allocated for improvements in health services. More emphasis was placed on primary health care and preventive aspects — which also implies a much wider geographic spread of health service establishments. The intention was to make health services available within one km of all inhabitants. In this budget, the urban centre of Badagry was to receive a general hospital.

Links between the development of the urban system and social, economic and political change

The lack of reliable demographic, social and economic data for different dates comparable to those which existed for the regions described in the previous four chapters makes impossible any precise analysis. As noted earlier, the last reliable census was in 1963 and yet some parts of the study region have evidently undergone rapid economic change since then. For example, Otta, and nearby Sango Otta, have certainly experienced rapid population growth since 1963 and may have a total population of more than five times their 1963 population by 1985. Furthermore, since the little official data which does exist is usually for states, divisions, districts or local government areas, the frequent changes in the boundaries of these units hardly help any attempt to describe the links between the development of the study region's urban system and social, economic and political change.

Map 6.7 shows the urban centres which existed in 1963 and the main roads which existed by around 1980. It also gives a rough idea of the area of Lagos conurbation with its main extension northwards and also the considerable extension west along the Lagos-Badagry expressway.

One point of note from the early historial section is the extent to which the urban centres in 1963 had been substantial towns prior to colonial rule. Many large villages also have histories predating colonial rule by decades or even centuries. In the northern portion of the study region (the part which is now in Ogun State), virtually all the urban centres in 1963 had histories as towns going back at least to the eighteenth or early nineteenth centuries. Otta, the largest urban centre in 1963, was politically the most important town in the study region in the early nineteenth century. Although it was not among the most important Yoruba towns in South-West Nigeria of that period, nonetheless it was the seat of an 'Oba' (King). Ado-Odo and Igbessa were the main towns for one of the main Yoruba groups, the Awori, while Ipokia was one of the main towns for the Anago. Oke-Odan was founded in the 1830s. Ilaro, to the north of the study region which under colonial rule became the divisional headquarters for the northern portion of the study region, was established in the late eighteenth century as the capital and main centre of trade for the Egbado, another important Yoruba group.

In the southern portion of the study region, the only urban centre in 1963 was Badagry; the other settlements with 5,000 or more inhabitants listed in Table 6.4 were all part of Lagos conurbation and cannot be regarded as urban centres in their own right. Badagry had been an important port in the eighteenth and nineteenth centuries — and perhaps for a considerable portion of time before that. Until the mid-nineteenth century, it was almost certainly larger and more important economically than Lagos. It was to Badagry, not Lagos, that the first European missions came. Thus, the more important pre-colonial towns were also urban centres in the 1963 census. The only documented exception to this is the town of Ilobi which prior to its destruction by the Egba around 1830, was capital of an important state. Unlike towns such as Oke-Odan and Otta, it was not rapidly rebuilt after its destruction during the period of political instability which characterised much of the nineteenth century, and some of those fleeing from Ilobi helped found Oke-Odan. However, in 1963, a settlement of Ilobi with 1,362 inhabitants was recorded in the census and it was connected to the Ilaro-Odo road by a feeder road by 1950.

The fact that most of the more important pre-colonial towns remained as the most important colonial towns owes much to the fact that these were chosen by the colonial administration as divisional or district headquarters. Ajilete, Oke-Odan, Ipokia, Ado-Odo and Igbessa were the headquarters for the five districts in Ilaro (later Egbado) Division created by the British in the northern portion of the study region. In the southern portion, Badagry initially served as the administrative centre for the entire study region (and beyond), and was the study region's only settlement given urban status in the 1917 Township Ordinance. However, the area under the jurisdiction of the local government at Badagry was cut when new divisional and district boundaries were defined. Ilaro (to the north of the study region) became the headquarters of Ilaro (later Egbado) Division.

But while an urban centre's status as a district or divisional headquarters meant some concentration of public employees, public investment and publicly-funded services for the population in their area of jurisdiction, local government was too weak and too poorly funded for this to have any major effect. Thus, a pre-colonial town's choice as a district headquarters under colonial rule helped ensure its continuance as an urban administrative centre, but by itself, brought no substantial or sustained impetus to economic expansion beyond administrative functions and some retail outlets. If the estimate for Badagry's population of 12,500 at the beginning of the nineteenth century is accurate, then it actually had less population in 1952 and in 1963 than in 1800. Under colonial rule, Lagos the national capital had most of the public employees and public investment and as the railway and road system expanded, completely eclipsed Badagry's role as a port both for receiving imports and for exporting local produce. Badagry might have been the key point of contact between Western Nigeria and Europe for the first half of the nineteenth century but it rapidly lost this role. While Badagry was one of the most important centres of commerce and trade and thus a dominant centre on transport routes in the early nineteenth century, as Map 6.3 shows, it was poorly connected to other urban centres both in 1900 and in 1950.

In Otta too, there is little sign of important urban developments up to 1950. It had been bypassed by the railway line running north from Lagos. For much of the nineteenth and first half of the twentieth century, it too lost political and economic importance relative to other centres close to the study region such as Ilaro and Lagos. The other urban centres in the 1952 census, Igbessa, Ado-Odo and Ajilete, probably received more stimulus from agriculture than Badagry and Otta. As earlier sections described, the northern portion of the study region was far more developed than the south in terms of commercial agriculture and these three urban centres (and Oke-Odan, Ipokia and Agosasa whose population had exceeded 5,000 by the 1963 census) were within or close to important commercial farming areas. It is worth noting that Oke-Odan, Ipokia and Agosasa were each on the study region's main road around 1950 (as shown in Map 6.3) and in or close to the area where there was substantial commercial corn production. However, population growth in Ilaro, just to the north of the study region, was particularly notable between 1952 and 1963; it benefited both from being a divisional headquarters and the railway station through which much of the agricultural produce from the northern portion of the study region was exported out of the region. It was also the main commercial and trade centre within its Division.

In viewing the whole colonial period, no new urban centre grew to challenge the economic and political dominance of towns which had existed since pre-colonial days. But no town in the study region figured prominently in the colonial government's moves to establish control over Nigeria and to exploit its natural resouces. Before the joining of Northern and Southern Nigeria into a single entity, Badagry briefly became an important administrative centre but it soon lost this role.

In large parts of the northern portion of the study region, commercial agriculture and timber production developed, especially over the last 40-50 years of colonial rule. The growth in urban population there between 1952 and 1963 (the only dates for which reliable figures are available) seems best explained by multiplier links from such activities. It is in the urban centres in or close to the commercial farming and timber production areas and centres best located on the main roads which accounted for much of the growth in urban population.

However, most of the forward and backward multiplier effects from such production seem to have chiefly benefited people and enterprises outside the region – such as the enterprises engaged in transport, trade and commerce in Ilaro and Lagos and the colonial government, most of which was located in Lagos. Within the study region, a town's status as a district or divisional headquarters helped it retain sufficient population to remain an urban centre. But as the lack of development in Badagry shows, it did little, by itself, to stimulate growth in the urban economy.

The most rapid urban growth in the study region evident between 1952 and 1963 was in the most south-easterly district. This owes nothing to growing agricultural production for it was due to the physical growth of Lagos conurbation into this district. It hardly relates at all to economic developments within the study region except that its south-eastern corner proved to be a convenient location to accommodate spill-over from rapidly growing Lagos.

The possibilities of identifying links between changes in the urban system and social, economic and political changes since Independence in 1960 cannot be done with any claim of comprehensive coverage since no reliable statistics exist for the population in the various urban centres since 1963. Thus, an analysis after 1963 has to be even more tentative than that relating to colonial rule.

However, it is clear that the largest public investment within the study region made since Independence, the construction of an express-way linking Lagos to Porto Novo and Cotonou in the Republic of Benin (via Badagry), has brought substantial changes, for this accelerated the spread of Lagos conurbation into the study region. An earlier section has already described the rapid development of housing, shops, factories, markets, warehouses, schools, colleges and recreation facilities on each side of this expressway for its initial 30 km. The relatively quick and easy access this expressway gives enterprises along it to downtown Lagos and, perhaps more importantly, to the docks but without going through downtown Lagos, plus the fact that there is still land available for development, has greatly increased the attraction of this part of the study region to both public and private investments. This includes multinational investment; one recalls the Volkswagen plant and the names of various companies which are within Agbara Estate. Indeed, the vast majority of the study region's urban population and urban enterprises are now in this south-eastern corner even if their location here is only understandable in terms of their role as part of the Lagos conurbation.

Similarly, at Otta (and nearby Sango-Otta), rapid industrial development there in recent years is also only understandable in terms of links with Lagos. Being close to Lagos and well-connected to it by road, enterprises (including many branch plants) can locate there and avoid the traffic congestion and high land costs which are associated with much of Metropolitan Lagos. If the rapid growth in industrial production and new investment in industry in the Lagos area continues, no doubt both Otta and sites each side of the Lagos-Badagry Expressway will attract substantial amounts of new industry. A further attraction for Agbara is the residential quarters being developed essentially for professional and managerial staff which are well outside central Lagos with its congestion, high living costs and high crime rates. But obviously, such further developments depend on increasing investments in new enterprises in the wider region. Besides the rapid growth in enterprises in Otta (on the main road from Lagos to Ilaro and Abeokuta) and for the first 30 km of the Lagos-Badagry Expressway, there are no other obvious sign of major economic developments. There is little sign of new developments in Badagry, apart from the few new public developments at some distance from the old town centre by the Expressway.

The survey of markets around Otta and Badagry suggest that these remain important outlets for the sale of local produce by small-scale farmers and fishermen. Both consumers and traders buy such produce. They are also important outlets for selling crafts; one recalls the importance of crafts (especially mat-making) as employment for women in Badagry Division in 1963. Selling goods in such markets, according to the 1963 census, is the most important source of employment for women in both the northern and the southern portions of the study region.

Markets' contribution to total wholesale and retail trade and to service provision within the study region has probably diminished considerably. The relative importance (and spatial distribution) of markets has also changed, influenced considerably by changes in roads and railways. Periodic markets in certain urban centres are now attended virtually on a daily basis, although the official 'market day' is still the most important. Local governments have increasingly taken over the role of organising and supervising the larger markets from the chiefs, guilds and councils of traders. But outside Metropolitan Lagos, clearly they remain important to much of the rural population and many of those in small urban centres. Periodic markets remain an important element within the urban (and rural) settlement system and it seems there is some correlation between urban centres and the larger markets, despite the comment by Hodder (1963) that there was no relationship between hierarchy and functions of settlements, and the existence of periodic markets in Yorubaland.

Certainly, in the west of Badagry Division and in the area around Otta, the main urban centre remains the largest centre for a periodic market, the market with the widest range of goods and services, and with the most extensive hinterland from which people come to the market.

The importance of such periodic markets implies a lack of the kind of prosperous commercial farming and concentration of prosperous farmers which generates sufficient demand for goods and services to support larger and more permanent retail outlets in urban centres. Data on employment in 1976 suggests that in Badagry Division, apart from the highly urbanised eastern end, traditional occupations such as craft-making and street-vending remained the dominant occupation for women, while fishing and farming remain the most important occupation for men. It is worth recalling that the economic boom in Nigeria during much of the Seventies, 'fueled' by rising oil prices and production, also helped strengthen the Nigerian naira against the currencies of those countries to whom Nigerian agricultural exports were traditionally sold. This had the effect of decreasing the incentive to farmers to produce crops for export.

Although one example cannot be representative of a region-wide trend, one should recall that in the village of Oto, whose development was described in some detail, coconut and associated copra production declined and eventually collapsed, no doubt aided both by unfavourable returns because of a strong naira and lack of interest in Federal Government for supporting agricultural development. Although there is disagreement as to the rate at which agricultural production has grown in Nigeria within the last ten to fifteen years, most agree that the average annual growth rate has been well below that of population. Agricultural imports have grown rapidly and agricultural exports have generally fallen rapidly. The priority given to increasing agricultural production nationally, has been very low; even in the 1975-80 Plan which devoted far more than previous plans to agricultural production, agriculture received little over five per cent of all public capital investment (O'Connor, 1984).

Thus, one suspects that urban centres such as Ado-Odo, Ipokia and Oke-Odan whose development under colonial rule was partially linked to commercial crop production, did not develop rapidly during the Sixties and Seventies. They were also too far from (and poorly connected to) Lagos to act as potential sites for industrial branch plants and other enterprises associated with Lagos; one recalls that both Ado-Odo and Ipokia had just one industry with 10 or more employees in the Ogun State Industrial Directory in 1980 (in both cases a bakery) while Igbessa and Oke-Odan had none. Ajilete and Oke-Odan are no longer on the main road linking Lagos and Porto Novo which they had been for decades, before the construction of the expressway in the mid-1970s. And as noted earlier, urban centres close to the boundary with the Republic of Benin have received little or no government investment.

Sources

This chapter is based on a report entitled *The Role of Small and Intermediate Settlements in the Development Process; the Badagry-Porto Novo Region,* edited by David Aradeon and produced by the Human Settlements Research Project team, Faculty of Environmental Design, University of Lagos and the National University of Benin.

Team members from the University of Lagos are David Aradeon (Professor of Architecture and project director), Dr Akin Iade Aina (sociologist), Dr Joe Umo (economist), Mr S. Tomori (economist), Dr A.I. Adelemo (Professor of Geography), Mr Joe Ekpeyong (geographer/cartographer), Mrs F. Obembe (architect/planner) and Mr Joe Igwe (architect).

Team members from the University of Benin are Dr John O. Igwe (geographer) and Mr Kolawole Adams (geographer/cartographer).

Notes

1 A 1631 map shows 'Albufera' on the ocean front opposite the present lagoon-front location of Badagry. According to oral history, 'Gbeferu' (Albufera) was settled in the early sixteenth century and later became a port. Badagry (literally the farmlands of Gbeferu) was settled as a refuge and slave trading community in 1730.

2 The Kingdom of Dahomey was in what is today the Republic of Benin; its capital, Abomey can be seen in Map 6.1. This kingdom developed to become one of the most important inland states during the eighteenth and nineteenth centuries.

3 Otta was conquered by the Egbas, based in Abeokuta, some time after 1832. In 1845 and 1848, Otta was attacked by Dahomey; in 1848, the town was captured and its inhabitants carried off as slaves. But even though it was destroyed, it was resettled and rebuilt by people from that locality.

4 The figures for 1952 and 1963 are for Metropolitan Lagos.

5 There were 74 'townships' which had municipal administrations for colonial urban areas and were not under the jurisdiction of native authorities.

6 Although Nigeria gained Independence in 1960, this section considers changes up to 1963 due to the fact that a census was taken in that year.

7 The readers should recall that only in 1948 were the 11 districts in Egbado Division amalgamated into five.

8 Lagos Federal District was a separate, autonomous unit outside these regions.

9 The new capital is being developed almost at the geographic centre of Nigeria; one of the reasons for its development is the aim of slowing the growth of Lagos.

10 In a further disaggregation of census data, the following professions provided the livelihood of one or more per cent of employed males: crop farming (11.5) fishing (11.4), street vending (7.0), clerks (6.5), automobile drivers (2.4), masons (2.1), watchmen (2.0) teachers (2.0), carpenters (2.0), palm wine tappers (1.6), millers (1.5), market gardeners (1.5), tailors (1.4), textile workers (1.4), mat-makers (1.0) and domestic servants (1.0).
11 Although the proportion of employed persons in the primary sector fell from 21.2 per cent in 1963 to 9.3 per cent in 1976, total population increased more than threefold, and the number of employed persons is likely to have more than tripled as well.
12 The occupations with one or more per cent of employed males were: crop farmers (68.5), street vendors (5.1), market gardeners (2.5), teachers (1.5), fishermen (1.4), tailors (1.4) and carpenters (1.0). For employed females, they were: street vendors (80.5) mat-makers (5.4), crop farmers (2.3) and domestic servants (1.5).

References

Asiwaju, A.I. (1976), *Western Yorubaland under European Rule 1889–1945,* Longmans, London.

Fadeyi, G.A. (1969), 'The growth and decline of Badagry, a geographical analysis', unpublished MA thesis, University of Lagos.

Hodder, B.W. (1962), 'Badagry, I: Slave port and mission centre' in *The Nigeria Geographical Journal,* Volume 5, No 2, pp. 75–86.

Hodder, (1963), 'Badagry, II: One hundred years of Change', in *The Nigeria Geographical Journal,* Volume 6, No 1, pp. 17–30.

Mabogunje, A.L. (1968), *Urbanization in Nigeria,* Africana Publishing Corporation, New York.

O'Connor, A.M. (1984), *Secondary Cities and Food Production in Nigeria,* Report prepared for the European Commision's Directorate General for Development, IIED, London.

7

A Survey of Empirical Material on the Factors Affecting the Development of Small and Intermediate Urban Centres

Jorge E. Hardoy and David Satterthwaite

A comprehensive survey of all published literature of relevance to the subject of small and intermediate urban centres in the Third World would be too ambitious a task for even a small team of researchers. One reason is the enormous range of subjects and papers which are of relevance; any literature which discusses factors that affect urban centres and indeed urban systems as a whole should be included in such a survey. Our original aim was more modest: to review only empirical studies of small and intermediate urban centres. This is a more manageable task since there are relatively few such studies. But this would exclude a large amount of literature dealing with factors shown to be of importance to understanding small and intermediate urban centres' present or potential development in each of the study regions described in Chapters 2 to 6. For example it would exclude literature dealing with the effect on national or regional urban systems of changes in agricultural production or land tenure, or governments' macro-economic and pricing policies, or the structure of government or regional development programmes. It would also miss the growing volume of literature produced by governments and international agencies about present or proposed policies for small and intermediate urban centres and researchers' comments and recommendations with regard to such policies. Thus, both in this chapter, and in Chapter 8 which looks at government policies, we have tried to cover some of these wider issues.

In undertaking a survey, our main concentration has been on papers published in 53 periodicals between 1970 and the most recent issues available at the time of writing; an annotated bibliography based on this survey has been published and the Appendix at the end of this book describes its organisation, and lists the periodicals surveyed. These periodicals were chosen as the focus of the survey since we have found these, rather than books, to be the source of most detailed empirical studies about small or intermediate urban centres. The main exception to these is a collection of papers on small urban centres in Africa (Southall, 1979) and several of the papers quoted in this chapter come from this.

In undertaking the survey, it became clear that most relevant literature could be divided into firstly empirical studies of one or more small or intermediate urban centre and secondly, papers seeking to assess the actual or possible effects of government policies on small and intermediate urban centres. In this chapter, we focus on empirical studies, while in Chapter 8 we go on to discuss government policy effects.

In Chapters 2 to 6, certain issues have emerged as of central importance in understanding the origin of small and intermediate urban centres and changes in their economic and employment base. These are:

1 the extent to which the origins of such centres often correspond to their roles as centres for administration and political and military control;
2 the varying degree of correspondence between administrative rank and size in different nations or regions;
3 the strong and explicit links between agriculture and the development of small and intermediate urban centres and factors constraining the link between agricultural production and local urban development;
4 the often powerful influence of new or improved transport systems on the spatial location of urban development;
5 the diversity of circumstances which explain the growth of industry in any particular small or intermediate urban centre;
6 the importance of trade, commerce and services to total employment;
7 the importance of understanding how international forces impinge on the economy of any urban centre — whether small, intermediate or large; and
8 the diversity of factors and their relative importance in explaining economic and demographic trends for each individual small or intermediate urban centre.

The relevance of each of these issues will be discussed in the light of both material presented in earlier chapters and of literature covered in the survey.

1   The origins of small and intermediate urban centres

Evidence drawn from both the five study regions and the literature survey suggests that most small and intermediate (and indeed large) urban centres owe their initial development and early status as an urban centre to their role as centres of administration or political control; Table 7.1 summarises the findings described in Chapters 2 to 6 on this particular point.

Table 7.1   *Correspondence between the urban centres of the five study regions and their administrative status*

Upper Valley of Rio Negro and Neuquen: The early development in Neuquen, today the region's most populous urban centre, was intimately linked to its role first as capital of the national territory of Neuquen and later, when the national territory became a province, to its role as capital of Neuquen Province. Despite the fact that up to around 1937 the urban centre of Neuquen was relatively isolated from the rapid growth and development of commercial agriculture within the Upper Valley – which was the main factor underpinning economic development and population growth in the area – it was already one of the Upper Valley's largest towns for the period 1910 to 1940 and this owes much to the concentration there of both national and territorial government agencies. Its role as the town with the highest administrative rank within the Upper Valley also encouraged various functions such as banks and foreign consulates which served the whole Upper Valley to locate there. It also became the main location for the wider region's military headquarters. And in the period 1957-1982, as Neuquen urban centre came to dominate the Upper Valley's urban system, its status as capital of a province – a status which no other Upper Valley urban centre has – encouraged a concentration of public investment and enterprises, and private enterprises, to locate there to serve the regional market. National government offices with jurisdiction not only over Neuquen Province but also over Rio Negro Province (within which most of the other Upper Valley urban centres are located) have usually chosen to locate in Neuquen. As Chapter 2 notes, 'it is almost a bureaucratic convention in Argentina to concentrate such national offices in provincial capitals. Even public offices and enterprises which first set up in Cipolletti or General Roca (the Upper Valley's two other intermediate urban centres, besides Neuquen) began to move their headquarters to Neuquen.'

The Gezira Region: Wad Medani, much the largest urban centre within the region, has been the highest ranking administrative centre there since 1925, although its administrative role has changed twice since then. The next four most populous urban centres in the 1983 census were all headquarters of local government units, although at two tiers below that of Wad Medani.

Bangalore, Mysore and Mandya Districts: The 34 urban centres within the study region in 1981, when ranked by population size, correspond closely to the administrative hierarchy set up under British colonial rule in the mid-nineteenth century. The two district capitals established by the British in the nineteenth century were much the largest urban centres in 1981. The only one of these two to have developed beyond an intermediate urban centre into a major city/metropolitan area, Bangalore was the urban centre favoured by the colonial government as the main centre for the administration of the State. The third most populous urban centre in 1981 was the only other district capital, established in 1939 when one of the two existing districts was subdivided. Virtually all other urban centres in the study region in 1981 were sub-district (tahsil) headquarters established by the colonial government in the nineteenth century.

Rae Bareli, Sultanpur and Pratapgarh Districts: Certain contemporary urban centres owe their early development to a role as an administrative centre acquired many centuries ago. For instance, Dalmau, Salon and Manikpur were administrative centres under the rule of Akbar the Great in the sixteenth century. But the link between urban centres and centres of administrative and military control became much stronger under British colonial rule. The study region's only three intermediate urban centres were the site of the only military cantonments, the only district headquarters and the first municipalities under colonial rule in the nineteenth century; in the case of two (Rae Bareli and Sultanpur), a town predated their choice by the British as military and administrative centres while in the case of the third (Bela Pratapgarh), it owes its origin to the siting of a military cantonment there in 1802. Most other urban centres in the 1981 census were also designated by the British as sub-district (tahsil) headquarters in the nineteenth century.

South-West Nigeria: Most of the urban centres recorded in the 1963 census (the last census for which reliable population data is available) were headquarters of kingdoms or sub-kingdoms prior to colonial rule. Otta, the largest urban centre in 1963, was politically the most important town in the early nineteenth century. Most of the other urban centres in the 1963 census have recorded histories as towns going back to the eighteenth or early nineteenth centuries and were capitals for different cultural groups. And most were designated capitals of either districts or divisions early in the twentieth century under colonial rule and have remained the most populous urban centre within their district or division ever since.

The literature survey found relatively few studies which consider the origin and early development of such centres. But the few that do also point to the perhaps surprising similarities between a list of urban centres within a region or nation ranked by current population size and the administrative hierarchy established many decades previously. This is often despite rapid growth in population and considerable change in the economic base of the region or nation; Table 7.2 gives some illustration of this.

Several papers make some reference to the stimulus which a small or intermediate urban centre received due to an administrative role. Miracle and Miracle (1979) note that Grand Bassam in the Ivory Coast (which had an estimated population of 16,500 in 1965) received some stimulus when it was chosen as the first French colonial capital of the Ivory Coast. Lee (1979) describes how Medenine in Tunisia (with 15,826 inhabitants in 1975) became the main urban centre within its region first because it was chosen by the French colonial government as the site for a military base and later because it became the seat of decision-making and local bureaucracy as a regional capital. Hopkins (1979) describes how Kita in Mali (with around 8,000 inhabitants in 1965) owes its origin as an urban centre to a French fort established there in 1881 close to a cluster of villages.

Table 7.2   *Examples of correspondence between regions' or nations' major urban centres and the administrative centres founded many decades or centuries before*

Latin America: Most national and provincial capitals are colonial foundations. The ten largest cities/metropolitan areas today had all been founded by the year 1580 (Mexico City, Sao Paulo, Rio de Janeiro, Buenos Aires, Bogota, Lima, Santiago, Caracas, Guadalajara, Monterrey). In 1930, the four largest cities in Bolivia, Brazil, Colombia, Cuba, Ecuador, Mexico, Peru and Venezuela were colonial foundations; for Argentina, Costa Rica and Chile, three of the four largest in that same year were colonial foundations. All national capitals in the 20 Latin American nations and in Jamaica and Trinidad and Tobago are colonial foundations with the exception of the capital of Brazil. Thirteen were founded in the sixteenth century (although Mexico City had an indigenous precedent), two in the seventeenth century, five in the eighteenth century and one in the twentieth century. With two exceptions (Brasilia and Quito), they are their nations' largest urban centre. All national capitals which were founded during the colonial period played major administrative roles under colonial rule as sites of Viceroyalties (Mexico City, Lima, Buenos Aires and Bogota) in the sixteenth to the eighteenth century and/or sites of regional legal courts (audiencias) and headquarters of universities.

North Africa: The basic outline of current urban patterns was established during the colonial period. The colonial extractive economies, which were well established in the nineteenth century, tended to concentrate urban development in port cities – reviving old ports like Algiers, Tunis and Alexandria and creating new ones like Casablanca, Ismailia and Port Said. The urban centres that developed in the interior were essentially centres for military control or served the mining of a resource or (gradually) expanding European agriculture. Foreign populations were concentrated into ports; meanwhile many rural and nomadic people displaced from the more fertile lands also had little choice but to migrate to the foreign-dominated centres on the coasts (Abu-Lughod, 1976).

East Africa: Virtually every urban centre which had 20,000 or more inhabitants by the mid-Seventies had been an established colonial administrative station by 1910. The size, location and distribution of urban centres in East Africa today is almost entirely the product of British and German decision-making prior to the First World War. Major ports and administrative headquarters were the most important elements in the imposed urban system. Towns built outside these largest urban centres were to serve as trade centres (located to tap accessible resource-producing areas and to help link the interior with international markets) and a network of administrative centres ('probably the most powerful generator of town growth in East Africa', Soja and Weaver, 1976). In Tanzania, 17 of the 18 urban centres with 20,000 or more inhabitants were originally colonial townships; 12 of them were on the railway lines developed under colonial rule to transport cash crops to ports for export.

India: While total urban population increased more than 500 per cent between 1901 and 1981, the number of urban centres increased by only 77 per cent. 'This implies that the majority of settlements now classified as towns have exhibited urban characteristics for a very long time' (Mohan,1983). India's five largest urban centres largely owe their pre-eminence to developments under colonial rule. Trading ports founded by the British East India Trading Company in the seventeenth century provided the initial stimulus for the development of Calcutta, Bombay and Madras as cities. By 1850, they were India's three largest urban centres while by 1981, they were first, second and fourth largest respectively. Delhi had grown to be third largest and it was to Delhi that the British colonial government moved India's capital in 1911 (from Calcutta). Bangalore, India's fifth largest urban centre in 1981, owes much of its early development to the fact that it became the unofficial capital of the State of Mysore under colonial rule.

This attracted African and European merchants with such settlements further encouraged by the arrival of the railway in 1902-4. Hopkins also found that the government was the major wage payer in the town. Saxena (1981) describes how Chandigarh's development as a new state capital for the Punjab in India underlay its rapid growth. Some three-fifths of the labour force in 1971 worked in government service and no doubt their demand for goods and services underlay a substantial proportion of the other jobs there. Kulkarni (1979) describes how most of the cantonment towns established in India under British rule during the eighteenth or nineteenth centuries formed the nuclei for urban growth or stimulated the development of nearby urban centres. Agiri (1979) notes how in Nigeria, the designation of Ikorodu by the British colonial government as administrative headquarters for a new district reinforced its traditional role within its region as the largest and most important urban centre. In 1963, Ikorodu's population was some 20,000.

Although few papers discuss the extent to which an administrative role has helped support urban centres' development, many note that the public sector is important for the employment it creates directly or indirectly. For instance, Hjort (1979) notes how in Isiolo, Kenya (with some 6,000 inhabitants), those employed within the local, district and provincial administration (including labourers, messengers, drivers and typists) and the demand they generate for goods and services (including maids to do housework) is important in Isiolo's whole employment base. Dike (1979) describes how the establishment of a University in Nsukka (which had 26,206 inhabitants in 1963) was a major factor in stimulating its development from a small, isolated farming town. The construction of the university attracted skilled and unskilled construction workers and the demand for goods and services generated by its personnel and its operation became a mainstay of the urban centre's economy. Hermitte and Herran (1970) note the numerous public officials and professionals in Huarco in Argentina, an urban centre with some 6,000 inhabitants in 1969; since it is the main urban centre of its Department, it has representatives of national, provincial and municipal government.

In Kafanchan, Nigeria (with some 15,000 inhabitants in the mid-Seventies), public sector employees of all kinds (including teachers, hospital staff, policemen, personnel in administrative offices, road and rail workers) make up one of the most important sources of employment. However, many of the public employees are working on the railway system since Kafanchan is on the railway and has important technical facilities for the railway belonging to the Nigerian Railway Corporation. Thus, a substantial number of the public employees owe their job more to Kafanchan's role on a main transport route rather than to administration (Hannerz, 1979).

The importance to an urban centre's development in receiving relatively high administrative status is well illustrated in the case of Owerri, the development of which is briefly summarised in Table 7.3. Clearly, its choice as capital of a new Nigerian state in 1976 has given a considerable stimulus to what was previously a poor and stagnant economic base. Similarly, acquiring the status of provincial capital has probably helped slow Hamadan's economic stagnation (See Table 7.4).

Table 7.3 *What were the main factors behind the development of intermediate urban centres — some examples*

Ikorodu (Lagos State, South-West Nigeria): With around 20,000 inhabitants in 1963, it has been the most populous and most commercially important town in its area since the nineteenth century. It achieved this role through its inhabitants' control of trade between its hinterlands and Lagos. Its status was enhanced when it became a district headquarters under British (colonial) rule and the colonial government sought to encourage commercial crop production around it. By 1973, Ikorodu had not developed a strong economic or employment base; there was large net out-migration from the urban centre and from the surrounding areas to Lagos as there had been in the Thirties and Forties (Agiri, 1979).

Ismailia (Egypt): With around 175,000 inhabitants in 1975, it had been established some 100 years earlier as the headquarters for the Suez Canal Authorities when Egypt was under British rule. The Suez Canal Authority remains the largest employer while small-scale ship-building, light manufacturing and service industries also provide employment (Davidson, 1981).

Owerri (Imo State, South-East Nigeria):   With some 9,331 inhabitants in 1953 and 90,000 in the late Seventies, the modern urban centre dates from 1901 when the colonial (British) government established a small military/ administrative headquarters there. Much of its early development related to the location there of public services and facilities – a native court, government station, barracks, prison, school. It became a provincial headquarters in 1914 but was bypassed by the railway; other urban centres nearby developed stronger economic bases. The residency and consulate of the Province moved to Port Harcourt in 1927. But with the creation of Imo State in 1976, many civil servants, professionals and traders came to Owerri since it was chosen as the new state capital. It became the centre for numerous Federal and State Government departments, parastatal organisations and corporations (Nwaka, 1980).

Although we found no empirical studies on urban development in recently settled territories, the government is likely to be a major source of employment in many urban centres in such areas. For instance, in southern Patagonia in Argentina, this is the case in Ushuaia, capital and port of Tierra del Fuego and in Rio Gallegos, port and capital of Santa Cruz. Military garrisons can also provide an important support to employment in small or intermediate urban centres and such garrisons are still sought by local or provincial governments, especially in frontier territories as a way of promoting local business. For example, such garrisons are important for Iquitos, capital of a department in north-eastern Peru and for Punta Arenas, a provincial capital in southern Chile; both centres had more than 100,000 inhabitants in 1985. Military garrisons also contribute to the economic base of Ushuaia and Rio Gallegos.

In any discussion of the development of small and intermediate urban centres, it is relevant to consider why so many owe their origin to roles as centres of administration or political control under colonial rule. In many of today's poorer and less urbanised nations – such as the Sub-Saharan African and Asian nations for which examples are given above – the administrative hierarchy imposed under colonial rule in the nineteenth or first half of the twentieth century was often the first nation-wide set of inter-connected urban centres. The less developed and less diversified the urban economy prior to the imposition of this administrative structure, the more powerful its influence. For example, Soja and Weaver (1976) noted that the size, location and distribution of urban centres in East Africa today is almost entirely the product of British and German decisions, prior to the First World War. In nations or regions where important urban centres predated colonial rule, the choice of colonial centres of administration

was usually greatly influenced by existing urban centres or by concentrations of rural population – or by existing transport routes which
usually linked existing urban centres. The pre-colonial origin of most
of today's urban centres in both the North and the South Indian
study regions in Chapters 4 and 5 and in South-West Nigeria (Chapter
6) are good illustrations of this. The Argentinian and Sudanese
regions described in Chapters 2 and 3 are different because only
relatively recently did they become densely populated; neither had
an established urban tradition prior to the twentieth century.

Most of the examples given of the similarities between the list of
current urban centres, ranked by population size, and the administrative hierarchy created decades or even more than a century before,
relate to former British colonies such as India, Nigeria and the Sudan
– although we have also noted examples from former German and
French colonies. In the poorer and less industrialised former British
colonies, this is hardly surprising given the extent to which the British
used indirect rule through indigenous power structures and centres
of authority. If in South-West Nigeria, the native authorities in the
traditional capitals of the Yoruba city states remained the local focus
for government, although with powers and tasks assigned them tightly
constrained, there would be little or no change in the administrative
centres. But if the colonial government chose to concentrate its administrative offices, troops and related services elsewhere, as in the case
of the South India region, it is hardly surprising to find that their
chosen administrative centre (Bangalore) came to grow and develop
more rapidly than the traditional political centre (Mysore) even
though Mysore remained in name of higher administrative rank – a
state capital rather than a district capital.

Even in Latin America, where most nations gained political Independence more than 150 years ago, as the example given in Table
7.2 illustrates, most of today's national and provincial capitals were
founded in colonial times. All national capitals which were founded
during the colonial period played major administrative roles under
colonial rule as sites of Viceroyalties and/or of regional legal courts
and headquarters of universities. But given the fact that most Latin
American nations have developed larger and more diversified economic bases than most African nations and most regions in Asia,
the match between sub-provincial colonial administrative centres and
current urban centres is unlikely to be as strong as that shown in,
for instance, the North and South Indian study regions.

2 Correspondence between administrative rank and urban scale

The influence of a colonial or post-colonial administrative hierarchy
in forming or stabilising the employment base of urban centres does

not imply that an urban centre's designation as an administrative centre necessarily provided a *long-term* stimulus to its development. By being designated an administrative centre, that particular centre was likely to become the first within its area of jurisdiction to be linked by road or rail to other areas or regions. It was also likely to monopolise most public investments and to contain most of the public employees within its area of jurisdiction. But this, in itself, was rarely sufficient to provide a sustained stimulus to its development.

First, connection to other areas or regions by road or rail might be a necessary condition for growth and diversification in local production – but it could not be a sufficient condition; one recalls that Badagry in Chapter 6 had an essentially stagnant economy after the imposition of colonial rule despite its administrative status. Both Badagry and its surrounding area came to play little role in the new economic orientation introduced by colonial rule. The same is true for Ikorodu (Agiri, 1979). Similarly, many small or intermediate urban centres have experienced rapid economic and population growth which owe little or nothing to any administrative role. In the Upper Valley of the Rio Negro (Chapter 2), rapid growth and diversification of agricultural production and a relatively equitable distribution of agricultural land ownership were far more important in underpinning rapid urban growth in most urban centres than any administrative role. As will be discussed in more detail later, the rapid growth of industry in Otta (Chapter 6), in Rae Bareli (Chapter 5) and in other industrial centres owes little to their administrative status. In the rest of this chapter, other important factors underlying rapid development in small and intermediate urban centres will be discussed.

However, it is clear that the administrative hierarchy of national, regional and sub-regional capitals imposed to consolidate political control within existing national boundaries has had a profound effect on the location of urban development, most especially in relatively unurbanised nations. This seems best explained by the fact that this administrative hierarchy, when imposed over any national or regional territory with little or no urban development, essentially imposes the first (although very undeveloped) urban system. Given that most important administrative centres have a long history as administrative centres, the establishment of much of the current administrative hierarchy usually predated an urban system developed to the point where there were substantial inter-regional and inter-urban centre flows of goods, people, capital and information. For instance, as Scott (1982) noted, even in Mexico, one of the more urbanised and industrialised Third World nations, up to around 100 years ago, the national territory was functionally divided into largely self-contained agrarian systems where towns and cities served the limited commercial needs of their own rural areas and provided the location for political and administrative control. As inter-regional production and trade developed, the administrative centres were usually the main nodes on the transport network which stimulated their development relative to other urban centres nearby. This essentially created the 'backbone' on which the urban system developed because it provided the inter-regional transport and communications infrastructure which allow such a development.

However, it is worth recalling that investments in roads or railways have been powerfully influenced by the need not only to link administrative centres to guarantee political control but also to promote commercial interests. For example, the initial development of railway networks was frequently only to link key ports to major regional centres where commercial agriculture or mining had developed. Thus, neither Otta nor Badagry were connected to the railway network in South-West Nigeria because political control had been secured and their surrounding areas were not judged to have land well suited to commercial agriculture (Chapter 6).

In many nations, it was only the regional or sub-regional capitals in the more productive areas which were linked to the national capital and/or the main port. Wad Medani in the Gezira region (Chapter 3) was linked by railway both to the national capital (Khartoum) and to the main port (Port Sudan) by around 1910 not so much because it was an important administrative centre but because it was the main administrative centre close to an area where export agriculture was to be developed.

Today, the extent to which the original administrative hierarchy closely resembles the urban system depends on the level to which an urban system has developed. If relatively little production and inter-regional trade has developed, administrative centres may remain the main urban centres. If administrative centres remain the best locations for enterprises associated with growing production and trade – because of their pivotal location on inter-regional transport and communications networks – the original administrative hierarchy will continue to resemble the developing urban system. But if the original administrative centres were poorly located to serve a rapidly developing economic base and the (often powerful) regional, national and international economic vested interests, urban centres with little or no administrative importance might well develop rapidly and eclipse nearby administrative centres in terms of population and economic importance.

So, while the list of existing urban centres in many Third World nations seems to bear considerable similarities to the list of administrative centres founded in the past, the relative importance of individual centres within their national or regional economies and within the national urban system has often changed substantially. The changes are most evident in those nations or regions where there has been the largest mismatch between the location-needs of the most important economic activities and the urban system created earlier largely for administrative purposes. The greater the change in scale and in type of economic activities since the original administrative hierarchy was set up, the greater the potential for such a mismatch.

Table 7.4 *Examples of how cities' importance in their national economies declined as the orientation of national or regional economies changed*

North Africa: Many of the great historical cities developed during the Islamic period (ninth to fifteenth centuries) were inland, reflecting the importance of land trading routes – Meknes, Fez, Tlemcen, Constantine, Kairouan, Marrakesh being examples. But these generally played little role in the extractive economic models introduced by the European powers. For instance, such illustrious cities as Tlemcen, Kairouan and Fez found their economic bases of handicraft production and trade systematically undermined by the new commercial firms in the ports which had grown to serve the colonial economy (Abu-Lughod, 1976).

Brazil: Under Portuguese colonial rule, in the late sixteenth and seventeenth centuries, urban centres grew and developed to serve the sugar plantations producing for export in the north-east. By 1600, Salvador/Bahia was the most important and prosperous urban centre and the national (colonial) capital. With Brazil's economy firmly based on the export of sugar, cotton, hides, and fine woods from the north-east, Sao Paulo, today Brazil's largest city, was only a small frontier town. The gradual decline in the European sugar market during the second half of the seventeenth century shifted the economic centre south. Rio de Janeiro grew as the port serving the mines and it became the national capital in 1762. As gold deposits became exhausted, coffee exports became the main commercial activity and the coffee boom helped develop the urban economy in the south-east with the expansion of railroads increasing the importance of certain centres, notably Santos (a major port) and Sao Paulo (Hardoy, 1975).

Hamadan and Qazvin, Iran: Hamadan, with around 150,000 inhabitants in 1978, became famous as one of the cities on the silk route during the eleventh and twelfth centuries, but collapsed when invading armies overran it in the early thirteenth century. Its role as a major commercial centre was restored in the second half of the nineteenth century with the flow of goods to and from Britain and British-controlled India through Baghdad, Hamadan and Tehran. It has long been famous as a centre for leather goods and carpets. But as Iran became consolidated as a nation-state with its economy based on oil extraction and export and industrial development, so Hamadan lost its role as an important transport and manufacturing centre; it was bypassed by the new inter-regional rail and road systems built during the Thirties and Forties. By 1976, its role as a sub-national administrative centre (it became a provincial capital in 1966) and a centre for public services had become more important than its traditional commercial and manufacturing activities (Kano,1978). The city of Qazvin, with around 100,000 inhabitants in 1972, has also declined in importance. The centralisation of government functions in Tehran some 150 km away drew to Tehran most of the nation's international import-export trade in which Qazvin had formerly played a major role and on which much of Qazvin's wealth had been based (Rotblat, 1975).

Potosi, Bolivia: Around 1640, Potosi was the largest city in both North and South America with some 140,000 inhabitants, and its rich silver deposits were a symbol of wealth around the world. During its peak years, silver mining in Potosi stimulated other economic activities in various regions such as mule raising in central Argentina (the mules were crucial for transporting minerals and people and they were sold in the markets of Tucuman and Salta), mercury (quicksilver) production in Huancavelica (Peru), wines from Central Chile and Western Argentina and food from the lower and warmer valleys around Sucre and Cochabamba (Bolivia). Potosi was never an important religious, administrative or educational centre but was an important stop on the old land route connecting Lima-Callao (Peru) with Buenos Aires (Argentina) via Huamanga (Ayacucho), Cusco, Puno, La Paz, Oruro and Potosi and then Jujuy, Salta, Tucuman, Cordoba and Buenos Aires. As silver became increasingly difficult and more costly to mine, Potosi's population declined. So too did the regional economies it had stimulated. It experienced a brief revival in the late eighteenth century due to the import of improved extraction technologies, but then declined to 26,000 inhabitants in 1854 and 21,000 in 1900. Today it has around 45,000 inhabitants and mining is still the main economic base.

In the poorest and most agrarian economies where much of the population derive their living from largely subsistence based agriculture or livestock raising, the relative importance of urban centres within the urban system is usually little different from the original administrative hierarchy. This is certainly the case in the North Indian and for much of the South-West Nigerian study regions. It is also largely the case in the South Indian and Sudanese regions, even though a higher proportion of the agricultural population are producing most of their crops for sale rather than household consumption. If most of a nation's or region's population earn little or no cash income, the demand for consumer goods and services will be too low to sustain much urban development.

In nations or regions with larger and more diversified economic activities, and a higher proportion of the labour force receiving sufficient income to generate demand for goods and services, it is generally the old colonial administrative centres best located to serve the new economic activities which have grown, although new urban centres with no major administrative role may have also developed. In the following sections, we will look at cases where agriculture and industry have provided this stimulus. Meanwhile, the old administrative centres in less developed regions or those which have not come to serve the new or expanded economic activities have often stagnated, even if their administrative roles help to ensure that they retain their urban status. The profound influences that changes in nations' economic orientations have had on urban centres' relative positions within national or regional urban systems can be seen in the fact that cities such as Fez in Morocco, Salvador (Bahia) in Brazil, and Potosi in Bolivia were once their nation's most important cities. Indeed, Potosi was once the largest city in all North and South America. Table 7.4 gives some brief explanations as to their history. Other examples include Mombasa in Kenya and Ibadan in Nigeria which where their nation's largest and most important urban centres during the first half of this century.

But before considering how growth in agricultural or industrial production affects small and intermediate urban centres, note should be taken of a few empirical studies which point to the lack of power and resources available to local governments in small and intermediate urban centres. Although this is a subject to be discussed in more detail in Chapter 8, it is worth noting these since they describe how local governments have little possibility of helping develop local resources, improve local infrastructure and services, and generally help strengthen the local economy.

At the level of small urban centres, Hermitte and Herran (1970) note how the local government in Huarco, the administrative centre of a department and also the nearby intermediate urban centre of Catamarca which is a provincial capital have very weak fiscal bases and are strongly dependent on funds from national government. The same is true in two Tunisian urban centres, Testour (Hopkins, 1979) and Medenine (Lee, 1979). Despite the fact that Medenine is a regional capital, regional plans lack any long-term development strategy based on local needs and resources.

Various empirical studies of intermediate urban centres with much larger economic bases also point to the weakness of local government. For instance, in Ismailia and Suez (Egypt), the gouvernorat level governments have increasingly inherited powers devolved from central government but still have limited revenue raising capability and limited trained personnel to undertake the tasks now assigned to them. They also remain dependent on central government for funds and for approval of investment plans (Davidson, 1981, Steward, 1981, Blunt, 1982). In the Philippines, local governments in Iloilo and Bacolod have their expenditures heavily influenced by the restrictions imposed by central government on their revenue raising powers. Central government defines local revenue powers including rates, levels and categories of taxation and 'these powers have been extended only grudgingly and slowly to Philippine city governments over the last 25 years' (Leichter, 1975, p. 91).

While papers noted above provide no basis for generalisations, papers reviewed in the section on local government in Chapter 8 suggest that in most Third World nations, local governments in both small and intermediate urban centres do have very limited powers and resources and have little possibility of stimulating and supporting local development.

3 The links with agriculture

A substantial proportion of the population in each of the five study regions derive their living directly or indirectly from agricultural production. But it is worth considering small and intermediate urban centres separately to see if there are important qualitative differences in the scale and type of linkages both for the study regions and for small or intermediate urban centres described in other studies.

The clear and explicit linkages between small urban centres and agriculture (or incomes earned from agriculture) in the five study regions are summarised in Table 7.5.

Table 7.5 *Linkages between agriculture and small urban centres*

North Indian Region: Between 84 and 87 per cent of the labour force in each of the three districts worked in the primary sector in 1981 and virtually all of these worked in agriculture. And in 1971, the last date for which data on the occupational structure in urban centres was available, 13 of the 15 small urban centres registered in the 1981 census had more than a quarter of their labour force in the primary sector while six had more than half. Apart from those working in the public sector, a very high proportion of those working in the secondary and tertiary sector largely depended on selling goods and services to farmers or to households whose main income was derived from farming.

South Indian Region: Of the 21 small urban centres in the 1981 census, 15 had more than a quarter of their labour force in the primary sector (which is predominantly agriculture) while ten had more than two-fifths and four had more than a half. Much of the employment in the secondary sector relates either to those employed in agro-processing industries or silk production and weaving, utilising locally produced silk-cocoons. And apart from those working in administration, much of the employment in the tertiary sector relates to those selling goods and services to farmers or households whose main income is derived from farming. And most of the forward and backward linkages with commercial agriculture are in intermediate or large urban centres.

Upper Valley, Argentina: While a much lower proportion of the labour force in the five small urban centres noted in the 1980 census work directly in agriculture, compared to the two Indian regions, much of the small urban centres' economic and employment base derives either from forward and backward linkages with agriculture (for instance cold storage and packaging plants for local produce, a factory producing biocides and fertiliser for which farmers in the Upper Valley form an important part of its total market) or from demand generated by those deriving a living directly or indirectly from agriculture.

Gezira Region, The Sudan: For the 12 small urban centres noted in the 1983 census, there is no data on occupational structure, although a substantial proportion of the labour force is known to work directly in agriculture. Their employment structures are dominated by trade and commerce producing a relatively limited range of goods and services to meet local demand – most of which derives from agricultural production or income derived from such production. The relatively slow population growth and lack of diversified employment bases in these small urban centres is best understood in terms of a regional labour force largely working in agriculture (more than three-quarters of the labour force work in agriculture) and the relatively low incomes that those working in agriculture have received. Most forward and backward linkages with agricultural production are concentrated in intermediate urban centres.

South-West Nigeria: Of the 13 small urban centres which existed in the 1963 census, four developed because of the growth of Lagos conurbation into the study region; their development owes little or nothing to agricultural production. The development and diversification (or lack of this) in the other nine is best explained by the extent to which they came to serve and support commercial agriculture in their surrounding areas. Periodic markets where local produce and crafts are sold remain important to the economic and employment base of many of them. However, the recent growth and development of one of them (Otta) is more related to its development as an industrial satellite of Lagos than to local agricultural production.

Among published empirical studies of small urban centres, 12 contained sufficient information to be able to judge the importance of agriculture to their development and in most, their development was as intimately linked to commercial agriculture as in most small urban centres in the five study regions. In Chinchero, Peru, a town which has existed since the Inca Empire, the economic base largely derives from a market where the produce of the highlands and the warmer, lower valleys are exchanged (Esteva Fabregat, 1970). The lack of development in Chinchero was noted and linked to poor soils. The economic and employment base for Castro, Chile, is essentially a market for local farmers and fishermen; it boomed when prices for the most important local product (potatoes) rose but slumped when these prices fell (Morawetz, 1978). Grand Bassam in the Ivory Coast grew and developed as a market for the exchange of agricultural produce from different ecological areas (Miracle and Miracle, 1979). The development of Akropong, Ghana, was linked both to its political role as a seat of a king and to the fact that oil palm and then cocoa production generated sufficient income locally to support it. During the boom in cocoa production, Akropong and several nearby settlements flourished; now their economies have declined (Middleton, 1979). Testour in Tunisia is the main market in a rich agricultural area while Kita in Mali has developed as the market and organisation centre for local peanut production (Hopkins, 1979).

Among the two exceptions where agriculture was not the most important underpinning to a small urban centre's economy, were Medenine in Tunisia, which developed as an administrative centre and the point through which the area under its jurisdiction was linked to other regions and not as a market, and Isiolo, Kenya, which developed more as an administrative centre and as a market for animal trophies sold to those passing through it to reach game parks to the north (Hjort, 1979).

When we turn to intermediate urban centres (ie those with 20,000 or more inhabitants), perhaps a less explicit link with agriculture and associated commercial operations would be expected. Certainly, as Table 7.6 shows, lower proportions of the labour force work in agriculture in the North and South Indian study regions – and almost certainly in the other regions, although data was not available to confirm this. But as summarised in Table 7.6, the incomes generated by those engaged in agriculture and forward and backward linkages with agricultural production and sale were of considerable importance to the economic and employment base of many intermediate urban centres in the South India and Gezira regions and in the Upper Valley (Argentina).

Table 7.6   *Links between agriculture and intermediate urban centres*

South Indian Region: Of the 12 intermediate urban centres in the 1981 census, five had more than a fifth of their labour force working in agriculture while one (Malavalli) had 39.4 per cent. The more populous intermediate urban centres usually had the lowest proportions. However, a high proportion of the forward and backward linkages with agricultural production were in intermediate urban centres – or the one large urban centre, Bangalore. Most of the large, government regulated markets for agricultural produce are in intermediate urban centres or Bangalore. For instance, in 1979/80, of the eight largest markets for silk cocoons (an important local product), the first, second, third, fifth and sixth largest were in intermediate urban centres – and few of these urban centres were in or close to the main silk-cocoon producing areas. Similarly, silk reeling, spinning and weaving factories were often in intermediate urban centres at some distance from the area of production; proximity to consumer markets or major transport routes and the availability of traditional skilled labour were more important than proximity to area of production.

Gezira Region, The Sudan: Although data on the occupational structure of intermediate urban centres was very limited, the fact that 33 per cent of the labour force of El Hasaheisa was in the primary sector in 1973 suggests that employment in agriculture could still be important. Most of the forward and backward linkages with agricultural production were in intermediate urban centres. Most were in Wad Medani, the capital of Central Region (within which the study region is located). Because the Sudan's largest (and earliest large) irrigation development is close by, Wad Medani contains the

National Ministry of Irrigation. The headquarters for the 900,000 hectare irrigation scheme is in a settlement just on the periphery of Wad Medani; so too is the agricultural research station and cotton ginning industries. Wad Medani is also an important livestock market for the region; many animals are brought from the west, fattened on plots on the outskirts and then sold. Textile mills utilising local cotton are also located here. The other intermediate urban centres serve as agricultural markets for their surrounding areas and contain most other agro-processing industries.

Upper Valley, Argentina: Most of the industries which have grown up based on forward and backward linkages with local agricultural produce are in two of the three intermediate urban centres, General Roca and Cipolletti. These include wine and cider production, fruit juices and conserves, the manufacture of packaging for fruit and fruit products and cold storage plants. A high proportion of the demand which supports service enterprises in all three of the intermediate urban centres comes from incomes earned from fruit or vegetable production or activities which depend on such productions.

South-West Nigeria: The fact that there are no reliable statistics on urban centres' populations after 1963 makes it impossible to know which urban centres have grown beyond 20,000 inhabitants, apart from Otta, Araromi and Ajegunle. Certainly Otta has grown beyond 20,000 and has the largest periodic market in its area which includes agricultural produce. But agricultural production in its surroundings area has been far less important than a growth in industry in stimulating and supporting the growth of its economic and employment base. The growth in population of Araromi and Ajegunle beyond 20,000 inhabitants owes even less to local agricultural production than in Otta; population growth here has been the result of their incorporation into Lagos conurbation's physical growth and economic structure. Developments in intermediate urban centres owe less to links with agriculture than in the other four study regions; perhaps the most important reason is that export-agriculture became increasingly unprofitable during the Seventies.

North India: Enterprises in the three intermediate urban centres meet most of the demand for both producer and consumer oriented goods and services which arises from the small proportion of farmers with relatively high cash incomes. But region-wide, there is a very low demand for such goods and services, given the fact that over five million people depend on farming in an area of only 12,800 square kilometres. The fact that some four-fifths of the farmers have holdings of less than one hectare and the average holding size is one-third of a hectare ensures that most farmers have little or no cash income.

Among other empirical studies on intermediate urban centres, many point to the intimate link between their development and to agricultural production (or incomes earned by surrounding inhabitants from agriculture). In a description of the development of Ikorodu in Nigeria, Agiri (1979) notes how the colonial government sought to encourage cash crop production for export there with Ikorodu becoming a centre for bulking crops from nearby villages and small towns for transport to Lagos (the main port). In describing the development of Owerri, Nwaka (1981) points to its original development based on local agricultural produce which was marketed there – although the location of a University there and various public functions have also been important. Sidon in Lebanon, up to 1970 at least, had had much of its development underpinned by production from surrounding olive and citrus groves although its role as a terminal on the Trans-Arabian oil pipeline had also been important(Abu-Laban, 1970). Iloilo and Bacolod both grew and developed as centres for the processing and shipping of locally grown sugar cane (Leichter, 1975). Onyemelukwe (1974) describes how Onitsha in Nigeria grew very rapidly as the centre from which oil palm production and export was organised and, later, as the main agricultural market within a large region.

We found seven empirical studies of intermediate urban centres whose development owed little to local agriculture. Three were the main urban centres on the Suez Canal in Egypt and their development will be described briefly in the next section which discusses transport. So too will the development of two others, Hamadan and Qazvin in Iran. The final two, Chandigarh in India and Owerri in Nigeria, essentially owe their origin and development to their administrative role, as described in a previous section.

Although the five study regions and the urban centres whose development has been described in other empirical studies is a very limited sample from which to draw conclusions, at least some tentative generalisations emerge. The first is that rising agricultural production can sustain the rapid growth and development of a relatively urbanised and diversified economic base, as illustrated by developments within the Upper Valley (Chapter 2). Within a 700 square kilometre area – a fertile river valley – total population has grown from around 5,000 inhabitants in 1900 to over 300,000 in 1981 with around 80 per cent of the population now living in small and intermediate urban centres. One of the most important factors in this has clearly been the increasingly intensive farming which has developed in response to demand originating from outside the region. But another critical factor has been the division of most of the best land into relatively small but prosperous farms cultivated by their owners.

Increasing purchasing power for farmers' households and forward and backward linkages with commercial agriculture, have underpinned the rapid urbanisation there between around 1920 and 1980; one recalls the measures implemented by the government when the Upper Valley was first developed for commercial farming to restrict absentee landownership and to attract farmers to the area with the capital to invest in developing intensive cultivation. One should also recall the government's investment in flood control and gravity irrigation, and to ensure the provision of a railway without which local produce could not have reached extra-regional markets. Although – as in all other areas – there are many factors accounting for the Upper Valley's development which are unique only to this area, the example is particularly interesting in that it shows how a relatively equitable pattern of land-ownership combined with good soil, government support for intensive cultivation and farmers with the resources to invest in farms can produce a very strong stimulus to local urban development and diversification.

In contrast to this, various studies, including the chapters on the South India and the Gezira regions, show how growth in agricultural production is not necessarily accompanied by development in the local urban economy. Another example is a study in the Muda River Valley project in Malaysia which found that although there was a substantial rise in output and in local farm incomes, the inter-industry links within the region were very limited and many of the goods purchased by households had to be imported into the region; as Renaud (1981) notes: 'the local urban centres could not provide the appropriate goods' (page 126). Furthermore, 'only 45 per cent of regional private savings found its way into regional investment' and 'estimates of government flows show a net tax burden for the region even though the area is poorer than the average'.

The ways in which the returns generated by agriculture are steered away from local small or intermediate urban centres are very varied. But all imply that a substantial proportion of the value created by agricultural production and by those who actually undertake the production is appropriated and spent (or invested) outside the area or spent on goods produced outside the area. Among factors which can exacerbate this are the structure of land ownership, the structure of marketing operations, poor or unpredictable crop prices, and government taxation. Examples of each are given here but in reality a combination of these and other factors is likely to be present.

The existence of inequitable land-owning structures is perhaps the best documented of the four. If within any agricultural area, only a relatively small group of people earn high incomes with the majority engaged in largely subsistence farming or low paid wage labour, this small group may find that their demand for goods and services, both for production and consumption, cannot be met by enterprises in the nearest small urban centre. With only relatively few farmers in the area around a small urban centre having sufficient income to generate this demand, the demand for many of the items or services they need could not support an enterprise in that local urban centre. So the forward and backward linkages that rising commercial crop production usually generates, and the 'demand' it creates by providing income, benefit enterprises in other, more distant, urban centres. For these urban centres have sufficient size and hinterland populations to support enterprises making or supplying the range of goods and services that richer farmers want. These might be intermediate urban centres or even the primate city. For instance, Collin Delavaud (1974) describes how large cattle ranches in Uruguay have tended to deal directly with enterprises such as banks, export houses and industrial and transport enterprises in the national capital, Montevideo. The range of goods and services that the richer farmers wanted were not available in small and even intermediate urban centres locally. Cattle raising also illustrates the different influences that various kinds of agricultural production imply for urban development. Farming activities which generate the highest income per person working in farming and per unit area can be expected to provide the most concentrated demand for goods and services both for consumption and production inputs. Cattle raising on grasslands can generate enormous wealth (although the rising value of the land itself can be more important than the produce from the land). But at best, it generates relatively few jobs and produces among the lowest income per unit area of any farming activity. This has particular relevance to the discussion by Jacobs (1984) as to why Uruguay failed to develop beyond a 'supply region' in the world market. For she considers neither the structure of land ownership not the nature of the agricultural produce as relevant factors in determining the kind of urban base that expert-agriculture can help generate.

Chapter 4 on South India also suggests that inequitable land owning structure is one of the main reasons why rapid growth in agricultural production has not stimulated development in many small urban centres. A relatively small group of farmers with the land and capital to invest in commercial farming have been responsible for most of the growth in production. As in the Uruguayan cattle ranches, the demand for both production and consumption oriented goods and services bypassed local urban centres. So too did much of the marketing and agro-processing which, as noted in Table 7.5, tends to be in intermediate urban centres, including some well outside the main crop producing areas. Saint and Goldsmith (1980) describe how the Brazilian Government's promotion of citrus production in Cruz das Almas helped increase land ownership concentration and had the net effect of stimulating increased out-migration. The example is particularly interesting in that one of the purposes of government support to growing citrus production was apparently to slow out-migration from the area. Citrus production requires extensive land holdings, high capital investment and less labour compared to the small farmer's usual mix of cassava (the main subsistence food), tobacco (for sale) and other food crops. Tobacco is intensively cultivated on small plots and needs high labour input; citrus is cultivated extensively and requires barely a third of the labour input per hectare of cassava and tobacco. Cattle raising requires even less labour input per hectare than citrus.

With favourable market prices and government support, citrus cultivation has expanded, absorbing small farms and lowering demand for labour. Between 1960 and 1975, the area under permanent crops (including citrus) nearly tripled; the area under pasture also increased while that under annual crops such as tobacco and cassava nearly halved. There was also a rapid drop in the number of tenants and sharecroppers, which suggests that these people are being forced out as land ownership and cultivation become more concentrated in larger units. The paper also describes how as families grow too large for the land on their farm to support them, individuals migrate and the cropping pattern on the farm changes to reflect the fact that there is less labour available to work the land. This paper illustrates how the mix of crops and market forces which change the profitability of different crops over time have profound effects not only on the value of production but also on the level of labour absorption in agriculture and on land-ownership concentration. All three have important implications as to the stimulus (or lack of it) produced for local urban centres.

Herbert (1970) in a description of Santa Maria, a small urban centre in Guatemala, also mentions that the inequitable land-owning structure in the surrounding area is a major constraint on its development. But perhaps the best documented examples of how inequitable land-owning structures inhibit local urban development are from descriptions of settlements which do not have as many as 5,000 inhabitants.

Although 5,000 inhabitants was chosen as the minimum population figure for the discussion of small and intermediate urban centres, it is worth noting studies of smaller centres since these give detailed descriptions of how land-owning structures greatly inhibit the kind of growth in demand from farming households which can stimulate the development of small urban centres. The first is Smith (1979) in a historical description of Huasicancha in Peru, a 'town' with about 1,750 inhabitants in 1970. This paper documents how a hacienda (large ranch) close to Huasicancha monopolised most of the best land and increased its boundaries. This meant that herders from Huasicancha were forced to go further in search of pastureland and inhabitants were driven off hacienda land which they had invaded in desperation. At the height of its power, the hacienda had 28,000 hectares while the people from Huasicancha had less than 120. The second is a paper on Barro in Brazil (Soiffer and Howe, 1982), a settlement with around 2,000 inhabitants in 1974. This study describes the changes over 80 years in the relations between the élite and the rural masses in Barro which grows to be a small farming town. The third is a narration by an inhabitant of how life had changed in the town of Santiago de Cao on Peru's northern coast; the town had around 2,000 inhabitants in 1974 (Sabogal Wiesse, 1974). Within the municipality, just two landowners possessed 67 per cent of the land, leaving the other 194 with just 33 per cent. In recent decades, there has been rapid out-migration from the town as land ownership became increasingly concentrated.

The fourth is the historical reconstruction of developments in a Chinese settlement with 2,465 inhabitants in 1980 (Thaxton, 1981). This looks at the problems faced by peasants in obtaining a livelihood between 1911 and 1943. As in Santiago de Cao, increasing concentration of land ownership forced out-migration. But in this case, it was generally the men who migrated, leaving their wives to work the tiny plots (whether owned or rented) and undertake other sideline activities such as the raising of livestock to survive.

Each of these papers gives some picture of the very specific and particular circumstances relating to land tenure which help define the level of production, the distribution of the returns from the sale of that production and the pressures on lower income groups to move elsewhere. It may well be that given a more equitable distribution of land ownership in the agricultural lands around these settlements, they would have developed to become small urban centres.

If the suggestion that the structure of land ownership can be a crucial determinant of whether or not agricultural production supports local urban development is true, it is worth looking at agrarian reforms to see if these changed urban trends locally. Although we found no detailed studies of the impact of agrarian reforms on urbanisation in South Korea and in Taiwan (China), we suspect that the 'land to the tiller' programmes implemented there in the Fifties initially provided a substantial boost to many small (and perhaps intermediate) urban centres' development. For these agrarian reforms increased the number of farmers with sufficient income to represent the kind and scale of demand for goods and services which supports local urban development. Considerable stimuli to small urban centres' development has been documented for Mexico during the 1920s and 1930s and in Bolivia during the Fifties after agrarian reforms. But in neither was the stimulus sustained. It seems that the redistribution of land-holdings – which was very considerable in both nations – was not accompanied by management of land-subdivision to ensure plots could produce adequate incomes. Neither was there support for the beneficiaries to develop their land and market their produce, nor improvements in basic services.

Many studies of the local impact of the Green Revolution in Asia and of the development of commercial farming in several Latin American nations have also shown that increasing agricultural production and productivity can also mean impoverishment for many rural dwellers in the area (usually through a combination of increasing land concentration in larger commercial units and the decrease in the demand for labour on the commercial farms as the capital:labour ratio changes). The result is often forced out-migration from the area. Thus, increasing crop production has been shown to be supportive of rapid growth in small urban centres. But in other circumstances, it can provide little or no support and create impoverishment and rapid out-migration. The mix of crops and the pattern of land-ownership seem the most crucial variables determining what actually happens between these two extremes when there is a rapid growth in crop production.

But there are other ways in which the potential stimulus to small urban centres from rising agricultural production can be steered elsewhere. One is through much of the profit from rising production simply being appropriated by people outside the area, for example, absentee landowners or foreign owners of cash crop plantations. The Gezira Scheme described in Chapter 2 provides an interesting illustration of how the stimulus from rising crop production need not benefit local urban centres, even when the land is farmed by a dense agricultural population with relatively equitable and commercially viable holdings. The Scheme was developed by the Anglo-Egyptian Condominium Government to produce long staple cotton for British textile mills and to generate an income for the Sudan Government. Between 1925 and 1950 it succeeded in these objectives. The management of the whole operation was undertaken by a private company which also made a profit. But the way in which the Scheme was managed and the share of the profits taken by the government and the management company limited farmers' incomes. Low incomes for those involved in production (except in the occasional boom year when high yields combined with high world market prices), a lack of publicly-funded services, weak or non-existent local government and a management and internal transport system[1] which tended to consciously avoid strengthening and supporting any developing 'urban system' meant very little support for the development of small urban centres.

The Gezira Scheme also illustrates the vulnerability of many small (and indeed intermediate) urban centres to world market forces. If these urban centres grow to serve the production, processing and transport of cash crops for export, then declining world prices mean a direct effect on these urban centres' economic bases and their potential for further development. It is difficult to determine the relative contribution of different factors to the lack of growth and development in small urban centres. But the often low, frequently unstable and sometimes declining real prices that agricultural export crops have realised in the last 20-30 years must be one important factor in the lack of development in urban centres associated with the production and export. We noted earlier how many urban centres' early development was linked to a role in commercial crop or mineral exports. The development potential of many small and intermediate urban centres throughout the Third World is dependent on the surrounding farmers having the land, access to extra regional markets, good fortune to choose to grow a crop for which prices will remain high (or at least stable in real terms), and the capital to afford intensive production. First and Second World nations have shown little interest in arrangements to provide Third World farmers with improved access to markets and more stable prices.

Another common (but little documented) way in which potential stimulus to small urban centres from rising crop production is steered elsewhere is through vertically integrated marketing operations. One example is the state or parastatal marketing board whose operations bypass local small urban centres. It is quite common for parastatal marketing organisations to have their own hierarchical organisation in terms of storing, processing and transporting crops or in supplying inputs to farmers which take these functions away from enterprises located in small urban centres. Indeed, according to some critics, their inefficient operation is one of the factors in the poor agricultural performance of many Sub-Saharan African nations. *Accelerated Development in Sub-Saharan Africa* (World Bank, 1981) points to the extent to which governments in the region have made public sector agencies responsible for supplying inputs and for marketing and exporting many (or most) commercial crops. It suggests that centralising control over such activities within one or two agencies makes it very difficult for such agencies to efficiently provide inputs or services to match the differing needs of farmers within each locality. This in turn will inhibit growth in production which would hinder small urban centres' development. And the hierarchical organisation of such agencies and the fact that their monopoly powers inhibit the development of alternative suppliers of inputs and services would also inhibit local small urban centres' development. Another example is an organisation like the kibbutz in Israel, as Soen and Kipnis (1972) show. They attribute the lack of development in three small new urban centres in Israel partly to the fact that so many of the economic links that the kibbutzim have are not with local urban centres but within the hierarchical kibbutzim regional and national organisation and with large but more distant urban centres.

4 Transport

Not surprisingly, virtually all the urban centres in Chapters 2 to 6 which have grown rapidly have been relatively well located on transport corridors. The first urban centres within any region to be connected to the railway or improved roads were usually those with the highest administrative rank – although this does not necessarily imply a simple cause and effect relationship, as will be discussed later.

In the five study regions, urban centres which received some initial stimulus to their development through their location on the railway line in the late nineteenth or early twentieth century are generally those which have retained their economic importance today. Where road systems have developed to diminish the dominance of railways as the main movers of people and goods, the urban centres which developed most as centres of the railway system generally became those best served by the road system; Table 7.7 gives some examples of this.

Table 7.7   *Transport systems and the development of urban centres*

Upper Valley, Argentina: Each railway station gave rise to an urban centre or at least a small service centre; stations are on average only some 7 kilometres apart. Only with the arrival of the railway line in 1899 was it feasible for intensive agricultural production to develop – for the railway provided the possibility of reaching extra-regional markets. All the small and intermediate urban centres have railway stations, although road transport has become of increasing importance both for intra-regional and inter-regional traffic.

South Indian Region: The six most populous urban centres in 1981 were all railway stations and on major roads by 1920; the seventh was on a major road by that date and soon to become a railway station.

Gezira Region, the Sudan: Five of the six most populous urban centres developed on or close to the study region's main transport corridor – which contains both a railway and a main road connecting the regional capital (Wad Medani) to the national capital (Khartoum).

North Indian Region: The construction of the railways in the late nineteenth century changed the relative importance of urban centres since it freed the major inter-urban traffic flows from a dependence on rivers. The seven most populous urban centres in the 1981 census were all stations on the railways built in the nineteenth century and all are on main highways today.

South-West Nigeria: Since the mid-nineteenth century, two fundamental changes in the main transport corridors have brought about important changes in the form and spatial distribution of urban development. Until the mid-nineteenth century, a port within the study region (Badagry) was the main port in South-West Nigeria; in 1800 it was both larger and more important economically than Lagos (which today has more than 100 times Badagry's population). Colonial rule disrupted Badagry's role as a major regional market and port in two ways. First, the imposition of a boundary to divide French controlled Dahomey (later Republic of Benin) and British-controlled Nigeria put a boundary in the middle of what had previously been a culturally and economically integrated region and essentially cut Badagry's economic hinterland. Secondly, Lagos, some 55 km to the east of Badagry, became the major port, railway terminus and point from which all major roads radiated – as well as the colonial capital. Inter-urban trade within and beyond what had been Western Yorubaland was replaced by a concentration on developing agricultural crops for export. The railways, built both to consolidate political control and to facilitate the movement of export crops, bypassed the study region. And since at least up to the 1950s, railways remained the main mode of inter-urban and inter-regional transport both for people and for goods, this led to a considerable decline in the economic and political importance of the main urban centres in the study region. However, the two most significant recent urban developments have been greatly influenced by improved roads. The first is the increasing volume of industrial investment going to Otta which is developing as an industrial satellite (and location for branch plants) for Lagos. The second is a very rapid growth in population and in urban enterprises as Lagos conurbation has increasingly spread into the study region along a new Express highway built in the mid-Seventies east-west across the southern portion of the study region.

The economic effects of linking some settlement (whether a village or small or intermediate or large urban centre) to a railway system or improved road system can be divided into two categories. The first relates to economic activities which develop in direct relationship to the new road or railway facilities – for instance, the offices needed to run the railway system and railway related facilities located there such as workshops, petrol stations and garages to serve road traffic, public works offices set up to maintain the road system and hotels, cafes, foodstalls and food-hawkers which develop to serve the traveller. The second is the change in the economy of that settlement and the surrounding area brought about by lowering the cost of transporting people, goods and information to and from it.

In each of the five study regions, there are obvious examples of the first category – for instance the concentration of hotels, travel agents and many other services in Neuquen within the Upper Valley as air-transport grew and its airport served the whole Upper Valley. The way that the gasoline stations, boarding houses and cafés have developed in Mandya in the South India region to serve road traffic passing through it, or the way that railway colonies sprang up in two of the intermediate urban centres in the North India region and bus and train stations attracted tea-stalls and hotels are also examples. Other case studies present such examples as the importance of the railway workshops and associated facilities for providing employment in the small urban centre of Kafanchan in Nigeria (Hannerz, 1979).

But it is the second category which generally brings more important and more fundamental changes to the economic base (and economic prospects) of urban centres. In each of Chapters 2 to 6, there are numerous examples of settlements developing into urban centres or rapid growth in existing urban centres as they came to serve as the centre for the sale of goods brought in from other regions or as the centre through which local products were assembled, stored, sold and perhaps processed before being transported to other regions. As Chapter 2 describes in considerable detail, rapid growth and diversification of agricultural production for sale outside the Upper Valley was the main factor behind rapid population growth and urbanisation and this was only made possible when the railway arrived there in 1899. In South-West Nigeria, as noted in Table 7.7, the rapid growth in productive investment in Otta and in the south-east of the study region was largely made possible by improved transport links with Lagos. In the South India region, the urban centres which contain most of the agricultural markets and large agro-processing industries are not those within the main crop producing areas but generally the intermediate urban centres best located on the highway system and with good access to the main consumer markets. The same is true in the Sudanese region.

But it is worth differentiating between regions where the improvements in their connections to other regions supported a rapid growth in local production for sale outside that region and where this was not the source of new developments. In the Argentinian, South Indian and Sudanese cases, improved transport links to other regions allowed rapid growth in production there for sale outside. This also happened to some extent in the northern part of South-West Nigeria, at least up to the early Sixties. But this has not been the case in much of the North Indian region and the south and east of the South-West Nigeria region. In North India, most of agricultural produce is either for direct consumption by the farmer or for sale locally; this is not a region with substantial crop exports (or any other form of exports based on local products) to other regions. In South-West Nigeria, improved transport connections encouraged rapid urban developments in Otta and in the south-east as these increasingly came to function as part of Lagos conurbation; the growth in new industries and other developments in both these places cannot be explained by any growth in production based on local crops, local produce or locally generated capital.

Empirical studies of individual urban centres covered in our literature survey also contained many examples of centres whose development was a result of the growth and diversification of local production to meet extra-regional demands when road or railway connections allowed cheaper transport of the goods to other markets. Miracle and Miracle note how Grand Bassam (Ivory Coast) developed as a centre for commerce and finance and as a centre for bulking, breaking-bulk, trans-shipping, storing and processing commodities by being the hub of a well-developed transport network. Medenine in Tunisia (15,826 inhabitants in 1975) also developed as an important centre for distribution but in this instance, it was not as a centre for the collection and transport of regionally produced goods but as a centre through which goods brought into the region were distributed to smaller settlements (Lee, 1979). Onyemelukwe (1974) notes how new, paved roads and the occasional steamer call from Europe helped increase the sphere of influence of Onitsha's agricultural market, and even the largest periodic markets nearby were quickly dwarfed and their areal influence engulfed. The population of Onitsha grew to over 160,000 before the Civil War (1967-70) largely based on its role as a trade centre for local produce transported out of the region.

There are also many examples of urban centres which lost importance relative to other places as improved road or rail connections allowed goods to be brought from other regions and to destroy or damage local production or inhibit further development. For instance, two ports in the Comahue region, Argentina (the wider region within which the Upper Valley is located) declined as the railways helped steer goods formerly using these ports (Carmen de Patagones and San Antonio) to Buenos Aires. Until roads replaced the railway as the main mode for transporting goods in the late 1940s and 1950s, the port of Bahia Blanca also lost out to Buenos Aires for produce exported from the Upper Valley, despite the fact that it too was on the railway and closer to the Upper Valley; the reason for this lies more in the structure of transport charges made by the railway company for it suited them to use their facilities in Buenos Aires rather than Bahia Blanca. When the transport of produce from the Upper Valley transferred from rail to road, Bahia Blanca rapidly supplanted Buenos Aires as the main export port for produce from the Upper Valley and has developed into a port of national importance and an industrial centre.

In each of the study regions, the construction of a railway station or linkage to a major road has often meant little or no stimulus to that particular urban centre because no new economic activities developed there as a result. There are also examples of local handicraft or artisanal industries in both villages and small urban centres which declined or even disappeared when mass-produced goods made elsewhere penetrated their market formerly protected by its relative isolation. In the North Indian region (Chapter 4), the decline in the proportion of certain small urban centres' labour force working in industry between 1951 and 1981 is linked to this.

This is illustrated by the case of Gundlupet where the proportion of the labour force engaged in household production fell from 21 per cent in 1971 to five per cent in 1981 and this is known to be related to the decline in the production of beedis (small, cheap, hand-rolled cigars) due to competition from factory-produced beedis and cigarettes. The lack of enterprises providing higher order goods and services in Mandya urban centre in this same region, despite rapid population growth since 1941, is best explained by the cheap and rapid road or rail services to Mysore and Bangalore, two much more populous urban centres. A similar reason helps explain why many higher order services utilised by people in Mysore are located in Bangalore. In the North Indian region, the colonial government's policy of promoting textiles produced in Britain and the spread of the railway system facilitating the import of cheap manufactured goods led to a decline in handicrafts and cottage industries in the late nineteenth and early twentieth centuries and help explain the rapid out-migration of craftsmen and the decline in population of certain urban centres.

Empirical studies of two Iranian intermediate urban centres, Qazvin (Rotblat, 1975) and Hamadan (Kano, 1978) also show how two places with long histories as important centres on trade routes lost out to other urban centres (especially Tehran, the capital) as new roads and railways and the centralisation of government functions in Tehran drew much of the international import-export trade away from them. Hamadan had been famous in the Middle Ages as one of the cities on the silk route and regained a role as an important transport node in the early nineteenth century with the inflow of goods from Britain and British India sent to Tehran via Baghdad. Its traditional carpet and leather industries were also well-known. But with the trans-Iranian railway completed and central highways built, the main trade routes came to bypass Hamadan.

By way of contrast, three papers include some documentation of the development of the three intermediate urban centres on the Suez Canal in Egypt, whose growth was essentially the result of the construction and running of this canal. Ismailia owes its origin to the establishment there in 1875 of the headquarters of the Suez Canal authority (Davidson, 1981). The urban centre of Suez had a long history as a settlement – dating back to pre- Roman times as a caravan watering point, then as a Roman settlement and later as Egypt's Red Sea port closest to Cairo. But its development was greatly stimulated by the construction of the Canal and the growth of associated industries and port activities (Stewart, 1981). Port Said owes its origin to being the Mediterranean supply base for the Suez Canal's construction and for nearly 100 years after its foundation in 1860, it was isolated from the rest of Egypt and grew and developed almost entirely due to its role on the Suez Canal (Welbank and Edwards, 1981).

5 Industry

Many references have been made in previous sections of this chapter to the kind of industry developing in certain small or intermediate urban centres – for instance, the links between agricultural production, agro-processing industries, and industries relating to forward and backward linkages with agricultural production and their location within the study regions. Under the section on transport, note was taken of the growth in industrial investment in Otta and in the south-eastern portion of the South-West Nigeria study region, made possible by improved roads. So too was the decline in traditional household industries in the two Indian study regions made possible by the expanding railway system.

There is a considerable amount of documentation on how agro-processing or agriculture-related industries develop in small and inter-mediate urban centres in or close to areas with an intensive production of certain crops. Clearly, some crops can be processed locally, gen-erating considerable employment and added value in the process, as the description of industrial development in the Upper Valley in Chapter 2 and the description of silk and silk product fabrication in the South Indian region in Chapter 4 illustrate. Other crops such as wheat produced in the North Indian region and corn formerly pro-duced in the north of South-West Nigeria do not.

A few empirical studies on industrial production in particular nations note the link between agriculture and industry. Liedholm and Chuta (1979) in a study of industrial establishments in Sierra Leone with less than 50 employees note the importance of forward and backward linkages with agriculture. For instance, one dollar of output in blacksmithing (primarily in the form of knives, machetes, hoes and axes) was demanded for every 100 dollars worth of agricultural out-put. Child and Kaneda (1975) in a study of small-scale agriculturally related industry in the Punjab in Pakistan note that there was a rapid growth in small-scale engineering industries supplying tube-wells (including diesel engines and pumps) and farm implements during the Sixties; this accompanied rapid growth in agricultural output. Most of the larger, more diversified firms producing such equipment were in Lahore, the largest urban centre in the Punjab and Pakistan's second largest city (with 2.17 million inhabitants in 1972). However, an equally large number of somewhat smaller firms were located in Daska, an urban centre whose population is not given but which does not appear in the 1972 census list of urban centres with 50,000 or more inhabitants. Daska had acquired a region-wide reputation as a centre of excellence in the production of tube-wells.

It is also interesting to note that in the Upper Valley, the prosperity underpinned by growth in agricultural production has helped to stim-ulate the development of a more diverse industrial and commercial base to serve local demands in addition to enterprises which grew to process and sell local produce elsewhere. But most of this diversifi-cation has taken place in an urban centre whose initial development owes less to prosperous commercial agricultural production around it than to the two other intermediate urban centres. As noted ear-lier, Neuquen's rapidly growing economic and employment base owes more to its role as a provincial capital than to links with agriculture. The fact that it has the highest administrative rank within the Upper

Valley, and associated public investments, has allowed it to attract many of the enterprises providing goods or services to the whole Upper Valley and the region beyond this Valley. The main factor attracting such enterprises has been the existence of a relatively prosperous consumer market of over 300,000 people within a 700 square kilometre area – and much of the income generated for this market comes directly or indirectly from agricultural production.

The North Indian region provides an interesting contrast since there is little sign either of the prosperous intensive agriculture that produces crops which can be processed locally or of the level of consumer demand which might support local consumer industries. In 1981, some three per cent of the labour force was in the secondary sector and a considerable proportion of these worked in small, low productivity cottage and small-scale industries producing for local consumption. Although Chapter 5 documented how in recent years, some large-scale industry has come to the study region, this is based neither on regional demand for the goods produced, nor on utilising local products. Indeed, the main reason for this as Chapter 5 describes, seems to be political patronage.

In the South India region, most of the large and high productivity industries are in Bangalore metropolitan area. Of the 1,300 industries with more than nine workers in the whole region in 1975, 1,005 were in Bangalore City with 115 in Mysore. Most small urban centres had, at best, just one or two industries with more than nine workers, while 11 had none at all. And for those industries which do exist in small or intermediate urban centres, it is often Bangalore-based enterprises which supply the raw materials and Bangalore consumers who finally consume the products. However, one trend which the 1975 figures did not reveal was a considerable flow of new industrial enterprises to Mysore City, many of them linked to enterprises based in Bangalore.

Among the articles surveyed about industrial development in small and intermediate urban centres, most pointed either to how limited it was or to how – as in Otta and Mysore – it had developed as that urban centre had come to function as part of a large urbanised region. Industrial developments in Neuquen were rather exceptional in that they were for the regional market and not a byproduct of local agricultural production.

However, many intermediate urban centres in South Korea and in Taiwan (China) seem to be exceptions. According to Rondinelli (1982), urban centres in South Korea with between 60,000 and 99,999 inhabitants had 19 per cent of their labour force in manufacturing, while those with between 100,000 and 249,999 had 22 per cent in 1974. Ho (1979) states that in Taiwan (China), the industrial and commercial census in 1971 reports that manufacturing establishments located outside the 16 largest urban centres accounted for half of all manufacturing employment and produced 48 per cent of the manufacturing value added. Comparable contributions of manufacturing to total employment in intermediate urban centres in some of the more industrialised Latin American and Asian nations (or sub-national regions) is also likely. Despite the high concentration of industrial employment in Mexico in or close to Mexico City, many of Mexico's intermediate urban centres had 25 or more per cent of their workforce in manufacturing in 1970 (Scott, 1982). Agro-related industries were important in certain centres in or close to major agricultural regions. But it is interesting to note that it was mostly consumer goods industries which were distributed roughly according to urban size. This suggests that they developed there because there was sufficient local or regional demand to encourage their location there – rather than this demand being supplied from units based in large urban centres such as Mexico City, Guadalajara and Monterrey.

Scott (1982) also notes how different urban centres in Mexico developed different specialisations for industrial production. When examining the economic base of the 37 most populous urban centres, which ranged from Pachuca with 92,000 inhabitants to Mexico City with 8.6 million in 1970, many had specific industries which dominated that centre's industrial sector. For instance, in many urban centres, food industries accounted for a third or more of all industrial employment; in two they accounted for more than half. Other centres had a third or more of all industrial employment in metallic-mineral mining, footwear, textiles, beverages, chemicals, vehicles or electrical goods.

Similarly, a study of 126 urban centres in south/south-east Brazil which had 20,000 or more inhabitants in 1970, found a comparable pattern of industrial specialisation. Apart from eight large multinucleated metropolitan areas which produced a whole range of products, most others had more specialised economic bases. Around half specialised in the production of locally exported manufactured goods. Many specialised in textiles or food processing while some specialised in iron and steel or non-metallic minerals, and one or two specialised in leather, pulp and paper, transport equipment, chemicals, beverages or non-electrical machinery. Then over 30 of the 126 centres could be classified as agricultural service centres, with their employment tending to be in warehousing, transport, wholesaling and some food processing. Finally, more than 10 had high concentrations of state or federal government employees, including those working in defence (Hamer, 1984). Given the diversity both in the extent to which industry contributes to the economic base of any particular intermediate urban centre and in the kind of industries located there, once again it becomes difficult to find any valid generalisations as to the potential for industry to contribute to the development of intermediate urban centres.

One implication is that industrial development within any inter-mediate (or small) urban centre will essentially depend either on demand for goods that it can sell competitively in external markets or sufficient growth in the number of prosperous consumers within its area to encourage the development of consumer goods industries there to meet this demand.

6 Commerce and services

In looking at commerce and services, the main focus will be on enterprises meeting effective demand, and their contribution to employment in small and intermediate urban centres. But before this, note must be taken of the importance of employment in administration and publicly-funded services such as hospitals, schools and colleges to total non-agricultural employment in many small and intermediate urban centres. In each of the study regions (Chapters 2 to 6), examples were given of the dependence of certain centres on such publicly-funded employment – for instance, the high proportion of public employees in Wad Medani, El Managil and El Hasaheisa in the Gezira region, the high concentration of public services and administrative offices in Bangalore and, although to a lesser extent, Mysore in the South India region, and the importance of a concentration of administrative and military personnel in Neuquen in sustaining its growth to increasingly dominate the urban system in the Upper Valley (Chapter 2). In addition, in many small urban centres, public sector employees in administration or services were the largest category of non-agricultural jobs. To give only one example, one recalls H.D. Kote with only 6,200 inhabitants in 1981 and one-fifth of its work force as administrative personnel and 47 per cent working in agriculture. Section 1 of this chapter also gave many examples of the extent to which public employees in administration or services made major contributions to total employment in certain small or intermediate urban centres.

But while such public sector employees may help provide a most useful and stable proportion of jobs and level of demand for goods and services, their concentration is rarely sufficient by itself to provide a major stimulus to any particular urban centre's long term development. It did so in national capitals in many countries soon after they achieved independence; this is especially the case in nations which only gained independence in the last 30-40 years and had to build or greatly strengthen a national government. But this was only a temporary stimulus to urban development and the generally high degree of centralisation of power and resources meant that most of the stimulus was in or around the national capital. There are also examples of the construction of new national or regional capitals where a similar effect can be detected; such is the case in Brasilia and Chandigarh. Saxena (1981) describes how Chandigarh and its concentration of demand (largely from public employees), higher education colleges and infrastructure stimulated agricultural growth in its surrounding region and attracted industry. However, these are exceptional and isolated cases, when viewing the whole Third World, and while Chapter 8 will discuss the need to strengthen the power and resources of local governments and the need to consider improved public service provision in small and intermediate urban centres, the increase in the number of public employees which results from such changes will not in itself be an important factor in supporting local urban development.

Perhaps the two most notable points with regard to commerce and services in the study regions of North and South India, the Sudan and Nigeria, are first, the small size of their total value relative to population and secondly, their importance in terms of providing most non-agricultural jobs. In addition, in all five study regions, it is demand from within the region which is the dominant factor in influencing the kinds of commercial and service enterprises and the scale of their total value. And for small and intermediate urban centres in all but the Argentinian region, most of the demand for such enterprises comes from incomes earned either in agriculture or in enterprises which grew up because of forward or backward linkages with agriculture. This is also the case in the small and intermediate urban centres in General Roca County, within the Upper Valley in Argentina. Thus, the diversity of trade and service enterprises within most urban centres in the study regions, and their total value, depend on the value of total agricultural production and the distribution of income generated among those involved in its production. This also holds true for many of the urban centres described in other empirical studies.

In urban centres in the North India region, if those working in agriculture are disregarded, most of the economically active population work in commerce or services. Most enterprises are small, often operated by one person or household with small cash flows, little capital equipment and often low returns. Examples include shops or stalls selling goods for daily needs such as cereals, pulses, fruit or vegetables or sweets and snacks. The scale and range of retail and service enterprises in the whole region is very low when one recalls that it had 5.7 million inhabitants in 1981. There is also no evidence of the region's inhabitants making much use of urban centres outside the study region. This reflects the low level of purchasing power among most inhabitants. And a high proportion of the limited demand for goods and services is met in bi-weekly or weekly markets; in 1981, there were 403 such markets and most were held in villages rather than urban centres.

In the South India region, surveys in three intermediate urban centres (including Mandya with over 100,000 inhabitants) showed that more than half of all commercial and service establishments were shops or stalls selling goods for daily needs or cigarettes, sweets and drinks. Most people not living in these centres but using them come from within 20 km. Of the 34 urban centres within the region, only two have a large and diverse mix of commercial and service enterprises other than small scale operations catering largely for local demand. The first is Metropolitan Bangalore with 2.9 million inhabitants in 1981; this has developed into a service centre of national importance and provides higher order services and a large range of goods for a region stretching far beyond the boundaries of the South India study region. The second is Mysore with 476,400 inhabitants in 1981, but even in an urban centre of this size, many of the higher order services used by its inhabitants are supplied by Bangalore-based enterprises.

In the Gezira region, just one intermediate urban centre (Wad Medani) is the centre for professional services, specialist medical services and wholesale trade. People from the region also use Khartoum, to the north of the region's boundaries (Khartoum is the national capital and largest urban centre in the Sudan) and Sennar to the south. Only two other urban centres in the whole study region have some concentration of service enterprises and a diversity of goods available. Temporary markets remain important channels through which those deriving a living from agriculture gain access to goods and services and to markets for their crops. Many such markets are held in villages, not urban centres.

In South-West Nigeria, apart from the areas where Lagos conurbation's growth has spilled over into the region, periodic markets remain important for the purchase of goods and services both for urban and for rural inhabitants. They also remain the main outlet for selling locally produced goods. Fieldwork in two areas found periodic markets working on an eight-day cycle with the largest market in that particular area's only urban centre. Despite the fundamental changes brought to the region's population, economic structure and level of urbanisation by the growth of Lagos conurbation, this impact has been largely concentrated in the east. What aggregate statistics for the whole region cannot show is how most of the people to the west continue to rely on traditional forms of production, consumption and trade.

The Upper Valley in the Comahue, Argentina, provides a contrast to the other four regions in that the total value of commerce and service enterprises is much higher per capita, their distribution within the urban system is much less concentrated in the most populous urban centre, there is a much greater diversity in the goods and services sold, and the enterprises themselves are larger. With a rapid growth in the value of agricultural production and with a relatively large group of people gaining good incomes from this, various small and intermediate urban centres grew up as retail and service centres for those living nearby. At least up to 1970, one particularly interesting characteristic of rapid urbanisation was the fact that no single urban centre emerged as the dominant centre for commerce and services – or indeed for manufacturing. Enterprises providing higher order services and drawing customers from a much wider area than the surrounds of their particular urban centre developed in several urban centres. And by 1980, the Upper Valley, with its three intermediate and five small urban centres within 700 square kilometres, contained a range of higher order services and retail outlets which are commonly associated with a regional metropolitan centre, even if these were not concentrated within one core city.

In concluding this rather cursory review of commerce and services in the study regions, it should be noted that in all but the Argentinian region, most enterprises are of a size (in terms of numbers of people employed and value of output) to be termed 'informal sector' operations or 'petty commodity producers'. In addition, periodic markets remain important and many take place outside urban centres. Both of these features point to the low purchasing power of most inhabitants within all but the Argentinian region. Periodic markets also suggest that only by traders having 'mobile' retail enterprises, which can move from temporary market to temporary market, can they gain sufficient returns to survive. Only rarely is there sufficient concentration of demand for any service or range of goods to support a permanent shop and those that do exist are usually in the intermediate urban centres which are best located on road networks.

Among other empirical studies, there are relatively few which concentrate on the economic or employment base of small or intermediate urban centres. But many state that a lack of effective demand from those living within the centre or closeby accounts for the lack of retail or service enterprises which have grown beyond one person or one household enterprises and which provide stable, remunerative employment.

In many small urban centres, periodic markets remain important. In Chinchero (Peru), when fieldwork was undertaken in the late Sixties, weekly or fortnightly markets were the most important outlets for goods and services. At that time, barter was still widespread and Chinchero provided the place where products from the warm valleys such as maize, cocoa, fruit and vegetables could be exchanged for products from the highlands such as potatoes and quinoa (Esteva Fabregut, 1970). In Kafanchan (Nigeria), demand locally had reached a scale where it could support a daily market; commerce was centred around this market although some permanent retail stores and service enterprises such as bars and lodging houses had also developed (Hannerz, 1979). In Testour (Tunisia), the market was part of a five market cycle involving other settlements nearby (Hopkins, 1979). In Akropong (Ghana), a large market was held twice a week with many smaller daily markets. There were around a dozen shops of various sizes and many stalls which set up outside individual houses, selling foodstuffs and everyday goods; there were also several bars, hair-dressers, seamstresses and cloth-sellers. In describing this centre, Middleton (1979) notes how a substantial proportion of local demand for goods and services derived from remittances or gifts to local residents from kin living elsewhere. In Castro (Chile), the waterfront market remains the economic core (Morawetz, 1978). Trager (1979) describes how she found 28 marketplaces in Ijeshaland (Nigeria); Ilesha which had 165,000 inhabitants in the 1963 census, had the only daily market. Other markets operated on a two, four or eight day cycle. It is interesting to note that many of the larger markets in terms of number of commodities and establishments were not in small urban centres but in settlements with 700-3,000 inhabitants. In Grand Bassam (Ivory Coast), fieldwork undertaken in 1965 revealed at least 112 different commodities and a great number of services in the market. One interesting characteristic of the market was not only the diversity of goods or services but the distance from which many goods had come. Furthermore, many goods were sold for consumption in areas at some considerable distance from the market, including nearby nations (Miracle and Miracle, 1979).

The importance of periodic markets is less evident in empirical studies of intermediate urban centres. However, most studies note that small-scale 'informal sector' enterprises dominate commerce and service provision. Dannhauser (1980) looked at the role of the so called 'sari-sari' (neighbourhood) store in Dagupan, the main urban centre and commercial node in the north-central end of Luzon Island's central plain in the Philippines. In 1969, 70 per cent of all retail establishments, nationally, were 'sari-sari' stores, small to medium size retail stores typically run within or attached to a house. They are in effect general stores which stock items that nearby households might need at short notice and in small quantities. In Dagupan, most such stores do not provide a high income but are usually operated by women to supplement the income of the main income earner. The paper notes that perhaps such neighbourhood stores become important at an intermediate stage in development 'in which cash resources among a consuming population are slowly developing and into which distributive channels that are linked to a manufacturing-import sector begin to penetrate...This is especially the case if the labour market is characterised by chronic under-employment. It is no accident that most accounts of this retail type are derived from societies that are currently moving slowly on the road towards de-peasantisation and development' (p. 174).

At an earlier stage, rotating markets will probably remain the main retail operation. If demand grows, then larger enterprises will find it profitable to tap this demand. But at the level of demand reached in Dagupan, sari-sari stores are the retail outlets through which large, wholesale or manufacturing enterprises can reach consumers.

The process by which periodic markets are increasingly replaced by permanent markets and with permanent, larger-scale retail and service enterprises seems quite common in the limited number of empirical studies of intermediate urban centres which touched on this point. Rotblat (1975) notes that in Qazvin, an Iranian urban centre which had around 100,000 inhabitants in 1972, the importance of the bazaar to the commercial base has been declining as retail stores have become dispersed either along major thoroughfares or in small clusters in residential areas. Similar changes are beginning to appear in smaller provincial urban centres, although in these centres, the bazaar generally remains the main centre for wholesale and retail trade, finance and production. Kano (1978) notes that in Hamadan, another Iranian urban centre with around 150,000 inhabitants in 1978, the bazaar has lost importance but Hamadan had not grown sufficiently to have a fully developed 'western style' commercial area.

One interesting case study of an intermediate urban centre's development almost entirely based on commerce is Onyemelukwe (1974) which describes the growth of Onitsha to over 160,000 inhabitants, before the Civil War in Nigeria (1967-70). Onitsha's origin was a village in the seventeenth century and it was chosen as a centre for trade in 1857 because of its well-drained riverain site close to oil-palm rich Iboland in east Nigeria. With rising demand for oil-palm in Europe, Onitsha became the centre for the export of oil-palm out of Iboland and the centre through which goods were imported in exchange. Onitsha developed first as a periodic market within a four-day cycle of markets in its area but by 1917, when it became the headquarters of Onitsha Province, it had a daily market. By 1953, nearly 70 per cent of the adult population were involved in trade. Onitsha's main economic function was thus the collection, sale, bulking and transport of local produce to major urban centres throughout Nigeria. It is interesting to note the strong correlation between the size of the volume of trade from Onitsha to urban centres outside Iboland and the number of Ibo who had migrated to live in these urban centres. There is also a significant (but less strong) correlation between trade flows and freight rates. The Civil War devastated Onitsha's economy; apart from other factors, it caused the withdrawal of the market's main economic agents elsewhere – the Ibo merchants in other regions. The example of Onitsha, like the example of Grand Bassam for small urban centres, suggests the need for a certain caution in making judgments as to either the range of goods traded in markets in small or intermediate urban centres or the size of the 'hinterland' whose population the market serves. Pre-civil war Onitsha's prosperity depended on demand from markets far beyond its immediate region. Grand Bassam's market depended to a considerable extent on demand and on produce from distant markets for its prosperity, including demand and produce from other nations.

Various other papers note in passing how street vendors, peddlers, periodic markets or small neighbourhood stores in small and intermediate urban centres often sell imported goods or goods produced many hundreds of kilometres away from the area in which they operate. Indeed, as Dannhaeuser (1980) notes when discussing the neighbourhood stores in an intermediate urban centre in the Philippines, it is through the willingness of such operations to cater for numerous minute transactions and to have very small turnovers that they provide a means through which large industries or importers or wholesale-retailers are able to reach a widely dispersed and poor consumer population. While this point was made only in relation to neighbourhood stores in one particular urban centre, it is also true for many other small retail operations in many Third World small and intermediate urban centres.

One final empirical study whose findings have relevance to this section on commerce and services, is a study of street food trade in four intermediate urban centres which is summarised in Cohen (1984). In looking at street food trade in Iloilo in the Philippines and Bogor in Indonesia (both with around 250,000 inhabitants in 1980) and in Ziguinchor in Senegal (86,925 inhabitants in 1980) and Manikganj in Bangladesh (38,000 inhabitants in 1981), the study revealed the importance of such trade in terms of employment and income (especially for women in the case of Iloilo and Ziguinchor) and in terms of providing cheap and often nutritious food. In Bogor, there is one street food establishment for every 14 inhabitants; in the others, it varied between 49 and 69 persons to every establishment.

In summary, there seem to be few generalisations which can be made as to the size or form of the commercial and service sector in small and intermediate urban centres – just as generalisations about their links with agriculture or industry were avoided in previous sections. Certainly, a high proportion of the economically active population in many such centres derive a living from retail or service operations which are one person or one household enterprises with small cash flows and little capital equipment. Although often described as a major part of the 'informal sector' in such centres, the futility of seeking to understand the dynamics of the 'informal sector' without understanding its complex linkages and dependent relationships with 'formal sector' enterprises has been demonstrated (see, for instance, Moser, 1978). And as Moser (1984) notes, the 'identification of the extent to which the economic function of the city, rather than its size per se, determines the occupational composition of both the formal and the informal sector, requires an understanding of the manner in which the urban economy is linked to systems of production both in the surrounding areas, and in other urban areas, as well as to the wider regional, national and international economy' (p. 13).

7 Small and intermediate urban centres and the international market

The international market has an important influence on the type, quantity and spatial distribution of economic activities and thus on the urban system in virtually all Third World nations, especially in those with the more export-oriented economies. The possibilities for governments to moderate these effects are often slight. Since, in many regions, the growth and development of small and intermediate urban centres is related to international prices for crops, perhaps the most important factor impinging on the economic prosperity of some urban centres is the size of the soya or the orange crop in the United States, or the sugar beet harvest in the EEC, or Brazil's frost-damaged coffee crop, or the extent to which the Indian Government is going to permit the export of certain kinds of tea. Such factors can be of vital importance to millions of farmers and, through them, to the economies of the urban centres with which their incomes and economic activities interact.

Certain case studies have pointed to a 'boom or bust' cycle; Gaitskell (1959) reports a boom in consumer expenditure, in people taking out trade licences, in funds donated to build mosques and schools, in competition for flour mill sites and in house building activities in the Gezira scheme in the Sudan after two years in which cotton prices were very high on the world market and good yields were achieved. But as Chapter 2 describes, this was in stark contrast to the returns achieved by the cotton farmers in most previous or subsequent years.

In considering the relationship between small and intermediate urban centres and the international market, it is also relevant to examine the problem of protectionist barriers surrounding the richest consumer markets, such as those around the United States and the European Economic Community. While certain Third World nations are allowed to export most primary products duty free to such markets (as is the case of the so-called ACP States to the European Economic Community), their full utilisation of such markets is often inhibited both by protectionist barriers on processed or semi-processed goods and by the fact that farmers operating in the United States and the EEC are among the most highly subsidised economic enterprises in the world. This may seem a little removed from the question of Third World small and intermediate urban centres. But the kind of industry which frequently helps to diversify and develop the economic base of such a centre is agricultural processing. If the structure of the world's major consumer markets prevents or inhibits the import of, say, fruit juice, cotton, silk cloth or meat from Third World nations, the development of certain small and intermediate urban centres in these nations is likely to be inhibited.

8 Do small and intermediate urban centres share common characteristics?

Drawing on the data presented for the five study regions and from the survey of other empirical works on small and intermediate centres, it is possible to consider the usefulness of talking about these two categories of urban centre.

Many small urban centres (ie those with between 5,000 and 20,000 inhabitants) seem to share four common features:

(i) a substantial proportion of their labour force engaged in non-agricultural activities;

(ii) a relatively minor administrative role and usually some concentration of lower order public services such as a health centre or school;

(iii) a relatively minor role in regional and national production but an important role as a centre through which people in their surroundings have access to the goods and services their enterprises provide and access to wider regional and national transport networks;

(iv) linked to (ii) and (iii) above, the category of urban centre with which most of the rural and agricultural population have most of their links.

Examples which run contrary to each of these could be found — for instance, small urban centres with no administrative role or with virtually all the labour force working in agriculture. In addition, the choice of a population threshold of 5,000 inhabitants above which a settlement becomes 'an urban centre' is known to be arbitrary – but as was discussed in Chapter 1, there is often little or no other data available on which a more rigorous division could be made. In many nations or regions, settlements with fewer than 5,000 inhabitants will have important concentrations of the kind of retail, service and perhaps manufacturing enterprises which are normally associated with urban centres – especially in richer, more industrialised nations or regions.

Within the Upper Valley in Argentina, for example, many settlements with fewer than 5,000 inhabitants contain a range and scale of retail and service enterprises substantially larger than those contained in many small urban centres within the other four study regions. Some relatively important administrative centres will not have 5,000 inhabitants; for example, in Bolivia, the capital of Pando Department, Cobija, had only 2,700 inhabitants in 1970. For both researchers seeking to understand how urban systems grow and develop and, within this, the role of smaller urban centres, and for government agencies seeking to design special programmes for small urban centres, the criteria used to define urban centres of different sizes and scales should be developed to be of relevance to the particular nation or region under consideration.

The chosen definition for intermediate urban centres was nucleated settlements which have 20,000 or more inhabitants but which cannot be regarded as making major contributions to national production and trade and regional service provision (see Chapter 1 for a discussion of how this definition was reached). Most intermediate urban centres whose development has been described already have four characteristics which distinguish them from small urban centres within or close to their own region. These are:

(i) a lower proportion of the labour force working in agriculture;
(ii) a higher administrative rank, generally a higher concentration of public services and facilities and some mix of urban services or facilities which are not so evident in small urban centres. For instance, many intermediate urban centres will have some intra-urban bus services, a more diverse range of professionals and of services such as banks and higher education institutions;
(iii) a larger, more widely distributed group of people living in surrounding areas which use businesses there to acquire goods and services;
(iv) better location on regional and national transport and communications systems, and often the settlement through which small urban centres are connected to major inter-regional transport systems.

It sould be noted that these are the characteristics that most intermediate urban centres have relative to small urban centres within or close to their region; these should not be taken as the basis for inter-regional or international comparisons. A cursory read of the five case studies in Chapters 2 to 6 will show the lack of validity in such comparisons.

It is also possible to point to numerous exceptions to these characteristics, such as intermediate urban centres with higher proportions of their labour force working in agriculture than certain small urban centres in the North and South India region. There are also many urban centres whose population size within their national urban system might at first sight make them appear as 'intermediate urban centres' but whose concentration of productive activities is of national significance; examples of this would include San Nicolas and Villa Constitucion (Argentina), Volta Redonda (Brazil), San Vicente (Chile) and Paz de Rio (Colombia) with large steel mills.

Earlier sections in this chapter have discussed, at some length, features and characteristics of small or intermediate urban centres and their development which imply that there are valid inter-regional or international comparisons – for instance, the fact that many owe their origin or initial development to a role as an administrative centre, or the extent to which prosperous intensive agriculture and a relatively equitable land owning structure can provide strong stimuli to the development of their economic and employment base.

The question as to whether such centres do have common characteristics is of considerable relevance in that implicit in many government policies for small and intermediate urban centres (which will be discussed in Chapter 8) is the idea that they do have common characteristics on which a national policy can be based. This idea is given further credence by similar assertions by many researchers – notably Bairoch (1982), Johnson (1970), Knesl (1982), Mathur (1982), Meissner (1981), Rondinelli (1982), Rondinelli, Lombardo and Yeh (1979), and Rondinelli and Ruddle (1978).

But the characteristics which small or intermediate urban centres seem to share, including those outlined above, seem to relate little (if at all) to their development potential. Indeed, perhaps the most notable aspect of intermediate urban centres' development is the phenomenal diversity in the factors which were largely responsible. Some, such as Owerri (Nwaka, 1981) largely developed because of an administrative and public service role; others such as Ismailia because of their service role on a major transport axis; others, like Mandya in Chapter 4 or General Roca in Chapter 2 because of multiplier links with growing agricultural production (and, for Mandya, a growing administrative role). Others, such as Puerto Stroessner in Paraguay have their origins and early developments linked to their role as headquarters for large public works – in this instance, the construction of the Itiapu dam. Social unrest in rural areas can help swell the population of an urban centre to over 20,000 and thus into our category of 'intermediate urban centre.'

Some intermediate urban centres develop a role almost totally unrelated to local, regional or even national demand. Harris (1983) cites the example of Novo Hamburgo in Brazil whose growth prospects (and indeed pattern of land use) is intimately linked to the demand for shoes in the United States of America since this is the point of origin for many of Brazil's shoe exports. International tourism has provided sufficient employment to help in the development of many intermediate (and indeed small) urban centres. To give only a few examples, Montego Bay and Ocho Rios in Jamaica, Punta del Este in Uruguay, Bariloche in Argentina, Malindi and Lamu in Kenya – the list could be multiplied many times for each region of the Third World. The growth of various intermediate urban centres on the Mexican-United States border can only be understood in terms of the products and services they provide for United States citizens and the cheap labour they include for foreign enterprises. Political factors may be of considerable importance – as illustrated by the rapid growth in industrial investment in Rae Bareli in Chapter 5 which was greatly helped by by the fact that it was the political constituency of India's late Prime Minister, Mrs Gandhi. Chapter 5 also documented how the fortunes of certain urban centres changed with the extent to which the interests of their region were represented in state government. Similarly, Hannerz (1979) noted how Kafanchan's development was constrained because the main ethnic group in its population was different from that controlling the government of the state in which it was located.

Thus, the one characteristic which is so evident in the empirical studies of small and intermediate urban centres is the phemomenally rich and diverse set of circumstances which led to the growth and development (or stagnation) of each. In Chapters 2 to 6, the diversities in terms of local resources, local histories, cultural traditions, links with surrounding areas regions and urban centres should have become apparent.

There may be some basis for comparing historical experiences (for instance among Sub-Saharan African nations which were former British colonies), or comparable administrative roles, or comparable roles with regard to local agricultural production, or comparable market forces affecting them. But the relative importance of such factors and their mix and interaction with a whole range of factors particular to each region or urban centre are as varied as the number of such centres. As Chapter 8 will develop, in a discussion of the relevance of special government policies for such centres, it does not seem appropriate to consider policies based on any judgment as to their common characteristics related to potential for development. It is far more appropriate to change the sectoral, structural and macro-economic biases which provide the context within which such urban centres operate in their national or regional economies and about developing plans which are based on the needs, skills and resources specific to each urban centre and its environs.

Perhaps the enormous lack of data about small and intermediate urban centres on, say, occupational structure or type of manufacturing activity and the technology used, or on what '30 per cent of the economically active population in service provision' means in reality has been partly to blame for an assumption by researchers and governments that populations of comparable sizes in urban centres imply common characteristics. For instance, researchers have on occasion made generalisations for a continent or even for the Third World about the proportion of intermediate urban centres' labour force working in different sectors. Governments have made similar generalisations for their nations. But such comparisons even within one nation may have little validity.

The remarkable diversity in the distribution of the labour force between different sectors in Tanzania's urban centres with 20,000 or more inhabitants as shown by the 1978 census (Bryceson, 1984) and in the 37 urban centres in Mexico which had more than 90,000 inhabitants by 1970 (Scott, 1982) or in 34 urban centres in three districts in Karnataka, India (Chapter 4) – among others – implies that a certain caution is needed in making such generalisations. Furthermore, the highly aggregated sectors commonly used to describe occupational structure hardly allow precise judgements to be made; for instance, a high proportion of a workforce employed in 'manufacturing' could be due to a concentration of high productivity factories producing for export, or to the survival of many artisans making goods for local markets, protected from competition from manufactured goods by the area's inaccessibility and its population's low incomes.

The examples already given on the different ways in which the economy of a small or intermediate urban centre might develop are illustrations of the difficulties in identifying common characteristics. Because of the lack of data, there is a tendency to try and generalise about, in particular, population growth rates (see Rondinelli, 1982, Mathur, 1982). This is commonly done using statistics which show that the populations of smaller urban centres in some population size category (or the population in smaller urban centres of some population size category[2]) are growing more slowly than the population in primate cities or large cities. The (admittedly limited) empirical base we examined to test this[3] suggests that such generalisations are of very limited validity, and that population size at the beginning of a census period is little guide to the population growth rate of any small or intermediate or large urban centre up to the next census. The examples given in Table 7.8 and the few detailed analyses of the factors underpinning urbanisation and its spatial distribution within Third World nations or regions suggest that only one generalisation is valid about population growth rates for the largest city (or cities) against those of small and intermediate urban centres. This is the truism that for some considerable period of time, the largest city or cities sustained population growth rates well above the average for all urban centres – or above average for small and intermediate urban centres.

Even if two small or intermediate urban centres do have comparable population growth rates, we cannot deduce that the forces underlying these growth rates are comparable. For instance, the relative contribution of natural increase and net in-migration to population growth may be different. Or indeed, one urban centre may have a rapidly expanding population as a result of an inflow of refugees or surrounding rural peoples because of a drought – while another urban centre's population may be expanding at exactly the same rate because of rapid growth in production in surrounding agricultural areas which then stimulated rapid growth in services and retail trade. The contribution of wars, droughts or floods to sudden rapid increases in population might be considered a special case; the migration flows might be assumed to be temporary. But in making this assumption, it should not be forgotten that the impact of natural disasters has so frequently been enormously exacerbated by human action or inaction and that the influence of such disasters on population movements seems to be growing. It also underestimates the extent to which such migration flows are permanent or at least of considerable duration. For instance, the more accessible intermediate urban centres in the east of the Sudan have had their populations swelled by those fleeing war and drought for several years; a substantial proportion of these migrants are likely to be permanent or at least relatively long-term residents. Many of the migrants who moved to the intermediate urban centre of Potosi in Bolivia after the droughts during 1981-1983 have stayed.

Table 7.8 *Comparison between population growth rates of intermediate and large urban centres*

Tanzania: Taking the two intercensal periods 1952-67 and 1967-78, the largest city in 1978 (Dar es Salaam) did not have the most rapidly growing population in either of these periods. Taking the 18 urban centres whose population had exceeded 20,000 inhabitants in the 1978 census, three (Arusha, Singida and Iringa) had population growth rates higher than Dar es Salaam for the period 1952-1967 while Mbeya, Shinyanga, Mwanza, Tabora and Singida had higher population growth rates than Dar es Salaam in the 1967-1978 period. In neither period was there a strong correlation between population size at the beginning of the period and population growth rate. Broadly speaking, the break up of the East African Community and its common transport and communications services constrained urban development in the north (especially in Arusha, the headquarters of many East African community services) while many of the more rapidly growing urban centres were those in areas where cash crop production had been successful. One important component of migration to the urban centres in the Fifties and early Sixties was women coming to join their men to make up a family unit; until then, the colonial (British) government had sought to keep wives and children in the countryside so they could support themselves so only bachelor wages had to be paid (Bryceson, 1984).

The Sudan: If the population growth rates of the capital and the largest city, Greater Khartoum, are compared with those of the 19 other urban centres which had more than 20,000 inhabitants in 1973, seven had higher population growth rates than greater Khartoum for the period 1955-1965, while five had for the period 1964/65-1973 (Simpson, 1984).

Peru: Taking the periods 1940-61, 1961-72, and 1972-81, annual average population growth rates for Lima-Callao, much the largest urban centre, were neither among the highest nor among the lowest for any of these periods. Population growth rates for 23 urban centres with 50,000 or more inhabitants in 1981 showed no obvious correlation with population size in any of these three periods (Richardson, 1984).

Mexico: For each of the decades between 1940 and 1970, there were always some intermediate urban centre population growth rates which were well above of those of Mexico City and the two other largest cities (Guadalajara and Monterrey). Among the 37 urban centres which had 100,000 or more inhabitants in 1970, Scott (1982) commented that for the three decades before 1970, 'there was no general relation between relative population size and subsequent growth in 1940 and there were great variations in growth rates between cities as well as for individual cities in different periods'. Indeed, some intermediate urban centres which were among the most rapidly growing in one or two of the decades were among the slowest growing in the third. And many of the slowest growing populations in urban centres for two or three of the decades (such as in Pachuca, Aguascalientes, Queretaro and Merida) were in urban centres which were among the largest in Mexico in 1940 apart from Mexico City, Monterrey and Guadalajara. The only way in which the relative performances of the different urban centres can be understood is through an analysis of developments within their region or the concentration of activities within that urban centre relating to their role in regional, national or international production. The growth of Tijuana and Ciudad Juarez, two of the most rapidly growing urban centres, relates to their role linked to the economy of the United States. Relatively rapid population growth for this period in Hermosillo relates to the development of prosperous commercial agriculture in the wider region. Acapulco's relatively rapid population growth relates to its role as a tourist city, while that of Puebla, Cuernavaca and certain others close to Mexico City relate to their role within the city region of Mexico City.

Perhaps the most useful set of indicators is not to do with urban centres' population growth rates but the scale and direction of migration flows within a region or nation, and how these affect the relative population growth rates in different urban centres. A study of migration patterns can reveal and clarify trends which population growth rates alone obscure. For example, a primate city or major regional metropolitan centre might have a slower population growth rate than several small or intermediate urban centres, but still be the dominant centre for receiving net migration-flows. In Mexico, many intermediate urban centres had more rapid population growth rates than Mexico City between 1940 and 1950, and 1950 and 1960, but Mexico City still attracted many times the number of migrants of any other urban centre for both periods. It is interesting to note that Mexico City attracted 49 per cent of all migrants between 1940 and 1950 and had nine times the number of migrants of the next city (Guadalajara). Between 1950 and 1960, Mexico City's share in attracting migrants for the nation was down to 42 per cent and the number of migrants it attracted was only three times that of Guadalajara (Scott, 1982).

Table 7.9 gives the proportion of net rural to urban migration received by different urban centres in Colombia, classified by population size for two different time periods; this shows the substantial increase in Bogota's attraction for such migration flows between the

Table 7.9 *Proportion of net rural to urban Migration by Different Urban Centres in Colombia Classified by Population Size: 1951–1964 and 1964–73*

	1951–1964	1964–1973
Bogota (National capital)	28.6	46.4
Medellin, Cali and Barranquilla (next three largest urban centres with between 500,000 and 1.5 million inhabitants in 1973)	29.6	31.8
Seven urban centres with between 150,000 and 499,999 inhabitants in 1973	14.5	1.3
Six urban centres with between 90,000 and 149,000 inhabitants in 1973	6.2	3.2
Thirteen urban centres with between 30,000 and 89,999 inhabitants in 1973	8.4	3.2
Other urban centres (number not available)	12.7	14.0

Source: Derived from tables in Linn (1978) quoted in Renaud (1981).

first and the second period. The decreasing attraction for the 26 urban centres with between 30,000 and 499,999 inhabitants in 1973 is also notable. Analyses of migration flows can also identify areas or regions with constant out-migration flows which in turn allows careful analyses of the causes of such flows and judgements as to whether social and economic development goals are best met by encouraging such out-migration (perhaps to lessen over-exploitation of soils there) or addressing the factors causing the out-migration.

But since data on migration is generally scarce and since in certain nations, data on urban centres' populations is so weak, governments and researchers may draw conclusions from the distribution of urban population between different sized urban centres and how this distribution is changing or about degree of 'primacy', which seem to us of limited validity. For instance, drawing on United Nations statistical sources, Rondinelli (1982) suggested that Nigeria has one of the least primate city-dominated urban hierarchies of any nation in the Third World. But in terms of concentration of a nation's industry, services and trade, Lagos is certainly a primate city. Similarly, reseachers and governments frequently compare different nations' urbanisation levels or rates of urbanisation or rate of urban population growth despite the fact that these are not comparable because of the enormous differences in the measures or criteria used by different national governments to define what constitutes an urban centre and thus set the parameters for the measurement of urban population. For instance, if India was to adopt Colombia's or Kenya's urban definition, it would become one of Asia's more urbanised nations, while if Mexico chose to use the criteria at present used to estimate urban population in Nigeria, it would become one of the least urbanised nations in Latin America.

But in conclusion, perhaps there are two characteristics which are shared by many small and intermediate urban centres in most Third World nations. The first is the vulnerability of their economic and employment base since these are so often largely dependent on just one good or service. The second is the lack of power and resources in the hands of the local government based there to play much role in encouraging a larger and more diverse economic base.[4]

We have noted how many urban centres only experienced population growth because enterprises there came to play some role in meeting demands originating outside their area or outside their wider regions. In nations and regions with low per capita incomes, the scale and distribution of incomes within the immediate area of such centres is rarely sufficient to be a major influence on the centre's growth and development. Since such centre's growth is often underpinned by the demand for one good (for instance one cash crop) or one service (for instance, international tourism), if demand for this one good or service falters, so too does the economy of the centre. The depletion of mineral or timber resources or a decline in demand for them frequently produces serious declines in the economic and employment base of urban centres which grew to serve their extraction. This may well be the fate for Catriel in the Comahue, Argentina, as described in Chapter 2. This seems to be happening in Poza Rica, an intermediate urban centre in Mexico which grew to over 200,000 inhabitants in 1980, with its economic base derived from oil activities. But it is no longer a major centre for the Mexican oil industry and has very high unemployment and under-employment (Sanchez, 1983). There are some instances where public companies are kept alive, despite producing large losses, because their production underlies the employment base for entire urban centres. This is the case in, for instance, several mining towns in Bolivia and in Rio Turbio in Santa Cruz, Argentina.

Changes in the political orientation of governments can frighten off foreign tourists as has happened for tourist centres in the Caribbean. So too can internal unrest (and guerrilla movements) which inevitably discourage tourism and thus the urban centres which grew to serve such tourism, as has happened in recent years in parts of Sri Lanka and Peru.

The fickleness of prices for primary commodities in the international market has already been noted; but the national market may be as fickle. For instance, Morawetz (1978) writes of the stimulus a small Chilean urban centre received when potato prices were particularly high in the early Seventies – and of the slump in economic activities once the prices fell. But govermnents can help to stabilise national markets for foodstuffs more easily than international markets for cash crops – and there seems to be a considerable need for more attention in many nations to food crops for national consumption rather than a long-standing concentration only on government support for export crops. Then, of course, there is the weather – and many hundreds of small and intermediate urban centres contain enterprises whose viability and profitability vary as much as those of the farmers with the timing and quantity of rain. Governments can moderate such influences. Certainly the rapid expansion of irrigation in India and in China has lessened the perennial dependence for survival of so many of their inhabitants on unpredictable rainfall patterns. However, neither investments to lessen farmers' dependence on rainfall nor measures to change the balance between agriculture production for export and for the domestic market is easily implementable in many instances. First, there is the lack of investment capital for flood control and irrigation development (or rehabilitation). Secondly, agricultural crops are often the main source of foreign earnings and there is a widening balance of payments deficit and increasing foreign debt.[5] Food crops often give farmers a lower return than cash crops for export and the transfer from export crops to basic food crops can imply the write-off of large investments as the land is converted from perennial crops to annual food crops. Problems facing governments in seeking to strengthen and diversify the economic and employment bases of small and intermediate urban centres can only mirror the wider problem of how to strengthen and diversify the economic and employment base of the whole nation.

Notes

1 The internal transport system was a narrow gauge railway which was essentially used to distribute inputs into agriculture and transport cotton from the farms to ginning mills for processing before being exported. This railway did not facilitate the movement of other goods or people and served district and sub-district management centres which were often consciously located away from existing towns or 'proto-towns'.

2 The distinction between population growth in some size class of urban centres and population growth in urban centres of some size class is important. In the former, population growth between two points in time will exclude the entire population of urban centres which grew out of that particular size class during this time and include the entire population of urban centres which grew into the size class; it may thus have little or no relation to population growth for urban centres within that size class.

3 Two intercensal periods in Mexico (Scott, 1982) three intercensal periods in Peru (Richardson, 1984), two intercensal periods in Tanzania (Bryceson, 1984), two intercensal periods in Sudan, between six and eight intercensal periods in two regions in India and one in Argentina (Chapters 2, 3, 4 and 5).
4 A discussion of the link between stronger, more effective local government and a special government programme for small and intermediate centres is in Chapter 8 and is not discussed here.
5 In many instances, the potential conflict between agricultural crops for export and food crops for local or national consumption is perhaps overstated; shortage of cultivable land is often not the major constraint although the capital investment and supporting infrastructure needed to bring it into commercial production may be.

References

Abu-Laban, B. (1970), 'Social change and local politics in Sidon, Lebanon', *The Journal of Developing Areas,* 5, October, pp. 27-42.

Abu-Lughod, Janet (1976), chapter on 'Urbanization in North Africa' in Berry, B.L.J. (editor), *Patterns of Urbanization and Counter-Urbanization,* Sage Publications, Beverly Hills.

Agiri, Babatunde (1979), 'The changing socio-economic relationship between Ikorodu and its neighbouring villages, 1950-1977', in Southall Aidan (editor), *Small Urban Centers in Rural Development in Africa,* African Studies Programme, University of Wisconsin, Madison.

Bairoch, Paul (1982), 'Employment and large cities: problems and outlook', in *International Labour Review,* Volume 121, Number 5, September-October.

Blunt, Alistair (1982), 'Ismailia sites-and-services and upgrading projects – a preliminary evaluation', in *Habitat International,* Volume 6, Number 5/6, pp. 587-97.

Bryceson, Deborah (1984), *Urbanization and Agrarian Development in Tanzania with Special Reference to Secondary Cities,* IIED, London.

Child, Frank C. and Kaneda, Hiromitsu (1975), 'A study of small-scale, agriculturally related industry in the Pakistan Punjab', in *Economic Development and Cultural Change,* Volume 23, January.

Cochrane, Glynn (1983), *Policies for strengthening local government in developing countries,* World Bank Staff Working Papers, Number 582.

Cohen, Monique (1984), *The Urban Street Food Trade, Equity Policy Centre,* Washington, D.C.

Collin Delavaud, Anne (1976), *Uruguay: medium and small cities,* Institut des Hautes Etudes de l'Amerique Latine, Laboratoire Associe du Centre National de la Recherche Scientifique, Paris.

Dannhaeuser, Norbert (1980), 'The role of the neighbourhood store in developing economies: the case of Dagupan City, Philippines', in *The Journal of Developing Areas,* 14, January, pp. 157-74.

Davidson, Forbes (1981), 'Ismailia: from master plan to implementation', in *Third World Planning Review,* Volume 3, Number 2, May.

Dike, Azuka A., 'Growth and development patterns of Awka and Nsukka, Nigeria', in Southall, Aidan (editor), *Small Urban Centres in Rural Development in Africa,* African Studies Program, University of Wisconsin, Madison, pp. 213-25.

Esteva Fabregat, C. (1970), 'A market in Chinchero, Cuzco', Actas del XXXIX Congreso Internacional de Americanistas (Peru, 1970), Special Issue of *Anuario Indigenista,* published by El Instituto Indigenista Americano, Volume XXX, Mexico, December, pp. 213-54.

Gaitskell, A. (1959), *Gezira: A Story of Development in the Sudan,* Faber and Faber, London.

Hamer, Andrew (1984), *Decentralized Urban Development and Industrial Location Behavior in Sao Paulo, Brazil: a synthesis of research issues and conclusions,* World Bank Report No. UDD-29.

Hannerz, Ulf (1979), 'Town and country in southern Zaria: a view from Kafanchan', in Southall Aidan (editor), *Small Urban Centers in Rural Development in Africa,* African Studies Programme, University of Wisconsin, Madison.

Hardoy, Jorge E. (1975), 'Two thousand years of Latin American urbanization', in Hardoy (editor), *Urbanization in Latin America: Approaches and Issues,* Anchor Books, New York.

Harris, Nigel (1983), 'Spatial planning and economic development', in *Habitat International,* Volume 7, Number 5/6.

Herbert, Jean Loup (1970), 'A community facing the capitalism of a social structure', in *Revista Mexicana de Sociologia,* Volume XXXII, Number 1, pp. 119-45.

Hermitte, Esther and Herran, Carlos (1977), 'Productive system, intersititial institutions and ways of social articulation in an Argentine North-western community', in Hermitte and Bartolome (editors) *Procesos de Articulacion Social,* Amorrortu-CLACSO, pp. 238-56.

Hjort, A. (1979), 'Sedentary pastoralists and peasants: the inhabitants of a small town', in Southall, Aidan (editor), *Small Urban Centres in Rural Development in Africa,* African Studies Program, University of Wisconsin, Madison, 1979, pp. 45-55.

Ho, Samuel P.S (1979), 'Decentralised industrialisation and rural development: evidence from Taiwan', in *Economic Development and Cultural Change,* Volume 28, Number 1, October.

Hopkins, Nicholas S. (1979), 'A comparison of the role of the small urban center in rural development: Kita (Mali) and Testour (Tunisia)', in Southall, Aidan (editor), *Small Urban Centers in Rural Development in Africa,* African Studies Programme, University of Wisconsin, Madison.

Jacobs, J. (1984), *Cities and the Wealth of Nations,* Random House, New York.

Johnson, E.A.J. (1970), *The Organization of Space in Developing Countries,* Harvard University Press, Cambridge, Mass.

Kano, Hiromasa (1978) 'City development and occupational change in Iran: a case study of Hamadan', in *The Developing Economies,* Volume XVI, Number 3, September.

Knesl, John (1982), 'Town & Country in development from below: the emerging paradigm for the decade', in *Ekistics,* 292, January-February.

Kulkarni, K.M. (1979), 'Cantonment Towns of India', in *Ekistics,* 277, July-August, pp. 214-20.

Lee, Concepcion E. (1979), 'Medenine: regional capital and small urban center in the Tunisian South', in Southall, Aidan (editor), *Small Urban Centers in Rural Development in Africa,* African Studies Programme, University of Wisconsin, Madison.

Leichter, Howard M., (1975), 'Political change and policy change: the case of two Philippine cities', in *The Journal of Developing Areas,* 10, October.

Liedholm, Carl and Chuta, Enyinna (1979-80), 'The role of rural and urban small-scale industry in development: empirical evidence from Sierra Leone', in *Rural Africana,* Number 6, Winter.

Mathur, Om Prakash (1982), 'The role of small cities in national development', in *Small cities and national development,* United Nations Centre for Regional Development, Nagoya, Japan.

Meissner, Frank (1981), 'Growth without migration: towards a model for integrated regional/rural development planning', in *Ekistics,* 291, November-December.

Middleton John (1985), 'Home Town: a study of an Urban Centre in Southern Ghana' in Southall, Aidan (editor), *Small Urban Centres in Rural Development in Africa,* University of Wisconsin, Madison.

Miracle, M.P. and Miracle, D.S. (1979), 'Commercial links between Grand Bassam, Ivory Coast, and rural populations in West Africa', in Southall, Aidan (editor), *Small Urban Centres in Rural Development in Africa,* African Studies Program, University of Wisconsin, Madison, pp. 175-98.

Mohan, Rakesh (1983), 'India: coming to terms with urbanization', in *Cities,* August.

Morawetz, David (1978), 'Castro market: slice of economic life in a poor Chilean fishing town', in *World Development,* Volume 6, Number 6, June.

Moser, Caroline O.N. (1978), 'Informal sector or petty commodity production: dualism or dependence in urban development?', in *World Development* Volume 6, Numbers 9/10, September/October.

Moser, Caroline O.N. (1984), 'The role of the informal sector in small and intermediate sized cities', in *UN Centre for Regional Development,* Nagoya, Japan, September.

Nwaka, Geoffrey I. (1980), 'Owerri: Development of a Nigerian State Capital', in *Third World Planning Review,* Volume 2, Number 2.

Onyemelukwe, J. (1974), 'Some factors in the growth of West African market towns; the example of pre-civil war Onitsha, Nigeria', in *Urban studies,* Volume II, Number 1, February.

Renaud, Bertrand (1981), *National urbanization policy in developing countries,* World Bank, Oxford University Press.

Richardson, Harry W. (1984), 'Planning strategies and policies for metropolitan Lima', in *Third World Planning Review,* Volume 6, Number 2, May.

Rondinelli, Dennis A., Lombardo, Joseph F. and Yeh, Gar-on Anthony (1979), 'Dispersed urbanization and population planning in Asia', in *Ekistics,* 277, July-August.

Rondinelli, Dennis A. and Ruddle, Kenneth (1978), *Urbanization and Rural Development; A Spatial Policy for Equitable Growth,* Praeger.

Rondinelli, Dennis A. (1982), 'Intermediate Cities in Developing Countries', in *Third World Planning Review,* Volume 4, Number 4, November.

Rotblat, Howard (1975), 'Social organisation and development in an Iranian provincial bazaar', in *Economic Development and Cultural Changes,* Volume 23, Number 2, January.

Sabogal Wiesse, Jose (1974), 'The town of Santiago de Cao, yesterday: Don Enrique's narration', in *Anuario Indigenista,* Volume XXXIV, December, pp. 91-151.

Saint, William S. and Goldsmith, William D. (1980), 'Cropping systems structural change and rural-urban migration in Brazil', in *World Development,* Volume 8, (English version) and CEBRAP Number 25 (Spanish version).

Saxena, K.K. (1981), 'Chandigarh City – its influence on regional growth', in *Habitat International,* Volume 5, Number 5/6, pp. 637-51.

Scott, Ian (1982), *Urban and spatial development in Mexico,* World Bank, The Johns Hopkins University Press, Baltimore and London.

Simpson, I.G. (1984), *Secondary cities and food security – the Sudan,* IIED, London, February.

Smith, G.A. (1979), 'Socio-economic differentiation and relations of production among rural-based petty producers in Central Peru 1880-1970', in *The Journal of Peasant Studies,* Number 6/3, April, pp. 286-310.

Soen, Dan and Kipnis, Baruch (1972), 'The functioning of a cluster of towns in Israel: an analysis of real and expected zones of influence', in *Ekistics* 205, December.

Soiffer, Stephen M, and Howe, Gary N. (1982), 'Patrons, clients, and the articulation of modes of production: an examination of the penetration of capitalism into peripheral agriculture in north-eastern Brazil', in *The Journal of Peasant Studies,* Number 9/2, January.

Soja and Weaver (1976), Chapter on East Africa in Berry, B.L.J. (editor), *Patterns of Urbanization and Counter-Urbanization,* Sage Publications, Beverley Hills.

Southall, Aidan (editor) (1979), *Small Urban Centers, in Rural Development in Africa,* African Studies Program, University of Wisconsin, Madison.

Stewart, R. (1981), 'The development of the city of Suez', in *Third World Planning Review,* Volume 3, Number 2, May, pp. 179-200.

Thaxton, R. (1981), 'The peasants of Yaocun: memories of exploitation, injustice and liberation in a Chinese village', in *Journal of Peasant Studies,* Number 9/1, October, pp. 3-46.

Trager, Lillian (1979), 'Market centers as small urban places in Western Nigeria', in Southall, Aidan (editor), *Small Urban Centres in Rural Development in Africa,* African Studies Program, University of Wisconsin, Madison.

Welbank, M. and Edwards, A. (1981), 'Port Said: planning for reconstruction and development', in *Third World Planning Review,* Volume 3, Number 2, May, pp. 143-60.

World Bank (1981), *Accelerated Development in Sub-Saharan Africa.*

8

Government Policies and Small and Intermediate Urban Centres

Jorge E. Hardoy and David Satterthwaite

Introduction

In surveying published literature on government policies or government actions which affect small and intermediate urban centres, it is difficult to know what to exclude. Virtually every government policy, action or item of expenditure has some effect on the spatial distribution of development – and the form this development takes. Directly or indirectly, each affects the fortunes of some people living in some small or intermediate urban centre. Concentrating only on policies explicitly directed to such centres would miss the fact that many of the most powerful influences affecting these and other urban centres originate from governments' macro-economic or pricing policies, or from sectoral priorities which may have no explicit urban or spatial goals.

Map 8.1 seeks to illustrate the range of forces which can impinge on and influence a region and the urban centres within it. Similarly, as described in previous chapters, the structure of government – the distribution of power and resources between national, regional and local level government and agencies – also has an important direct and indirect impact on small and intermediate urban centres. So a discussion on the influences of government policies, actions and expenditures must look not only at the small and intermediate urban centres themselves but also at their context: the national or regional structure of production and urban system of which they are a part.

A survey of the literature describing or analysing explicit government policies on small and intermediate urban centres shows that such policies usually have more than one aim; this is illustrated by the range of explicit aims given in the summaries of recent or current government policies in Table 8.1. When goals are expressed in terms of spatial or socio-economic development within national plans or

Map 8.1   *Examples of external forces influencing and interacting with a region and its urban system*

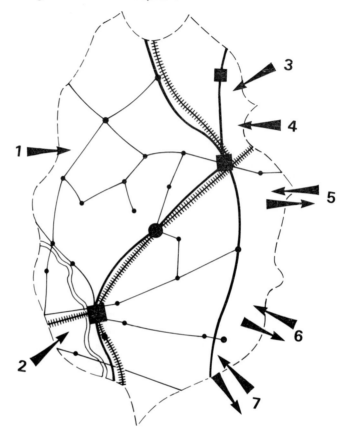

Key

1 *National Public Policy*

(i) Non-Spatial

** Import controls (taxes, licences, quotas, etc.) and import-substitution. Which industries/activities benefit and in which settlements are these located?

** Exchange rate controls/policies. Do these promote exports or imports? Which sectors/settlements/regions benefit and which lose out?

** Taxation system at national and regional level; from what activities/ sectors are revenues raised; what spatial implications does this have — for example, are taxes drawing heavily on certain agricultural regions producing export crops?

** Agricultural crop prices — public control/influence; are these in effect taxing or subsidising crop producers?

** Transport and energy tariffs — which settlements or regions are favoured and which lose out?

** Special incentives to encourage specific sectors or activities such as cheap loans for purchasing equipment, etc. Which sectors/activities/settlements benefit?

** Attitudes to foreign investments; if positive, which sectors benefit, where are foreign investments encouraged to invest; size of subsidy (e.g. tax holiday, infrastructure provision); spatial biases inherent in policy?

** Government intervention in ownership of productive assets or their use; for instance, agrarian reforms — and implications for, for instance, income distribution within society and spatially.

2 (ii) Spatial

** Transport system — its development and the effects this has on the regional and national distribution of production, trade and services.

** Land colonisation programmes.

** Special regional or metropolitan area or city or rural area development programmes and/or authorities.

** Special incentives to attract productive investment to specific settlements/regions — for instance, financial incentives (cheap loans, tax holidays) or infrastructure provision.

** National or sub-national government aid to local government to encourage development there — for example, training programmes or institution building to improve local government competence and involvement in development programmes.

** Controls or dis-incentives on new enterprises in certain cities/regions and other measures to lessen attraction of larger urban centres to productive investment.

3 *National government public spending (Where is it spent?)*

** Public investments in industry and other enterprises.

** National infrastructure (roads/railways/bridges/ports, airports, electricity, etc. to meet national priorities).

** Regional infrastructure (for regional goals/priorities).

** Social and physical services (water supply, removal of household and human wastes, education, health care, etc.).

** Agriculture (including new irrigation development, support for land colonisation and extension services).

** Financial support to sub-national (state/province/region) sub-regional and urban governments — grants/loans, tax sharing, etc.

** Housing programmes.

4 *Sub-national government public spending*

As above but for state/regional/provincial government.

5 *Structure of government*

** Distribution of power, resources and personnel for formulating and implementing development plans between national, sub-national, sub-regional and urban governments; extent of commitment to building up and supporting local government in being major actor in development plans and in acquiring strong and stable revenue base.

6 *Private sector/individual action*
In-flows and out-flows of
** Capital investment
** Goods
** Services and information
** Profits, savings, tax payments and remittances leakage of savings, profits and forward and backward linkages with production within region of particular concern; also extent of such linkages within region and origin of new capital investment within region).
** Local leadership within the region and its capacity to negotiate with central and state governments.

7 *International policy of government, blocs and aid agencies*
** Protectionist barriers (tariffs/quotas, etc.) inhibiting or preventing export of any good/service from region to market overseas.
** Special privileges given to any good/service from region in export to market overseas.
** Aid flow into region — which sectors/activities/settlements benefit?

---

as part of political platforms, small and intermediate urban centres (or comparable settlement categories such as secondary cities, growth centres, medium size cities, etc.) are often given special roles. For instance, governments might seek to enhance the role of such centres as 'interceptors' of migration flows heading for the primate city (or other large cities) or as 'dynamisers' of rural and regional development or as locations for new or relocated industries or as the urban centres around which a strategy seeking to reduce regional differences in per capita income or per capita GDP is constructed. On occasion, these centres are also assigned more specialised roles such as consolidating population in a border area or serving a land colonisation programme.

There are also many instances where one or more urban centres are created or developed for a specific task – for example, to serve the extraction of some timber or mineral resource or to serve as the centre for the construction and, later, management of a hydro-electric dam or to develop a port. The multiplicity of social, economic and political objectives explicit or inherent in different government policies for small and intermediate urban centres makes any concise general discussion difficult. But if we limit the discussion only to regional or national policies for small and intermediate urban centres, these policies can be divided into five broad categories. The first is the development of such centres in more 'backward' (and generally more rural) regions. The second is policies for such centres specifically aimed at stimulating and supporting rural and agricultural development. The third is to develop such centres in more urbanised (and usually more industrialised) regions as part of what is essentially a 'growth management' strategy to lessen the concentration of population and productive investment in larger cities or metropolitan areas within that same region. The fourth is to slow migration flows to large urban centres – or to address what is usually a major cause of such migration flows, the concentration of new productive investment in such large centres. Finally, the fifth is to strengthen local or regional government (including improving public service provision there). These will be discussed in the first five sections of this chapter.

Our literature review suggested two other categories of government policies of relevance to small and intermediate urban centres: sectoral priorities and their spatial implications; and macro-economic and pricing policies. These will be discussed as the last two sections in this chapter.

Table 8.1 *Examples of special government programmes related to small and intermediate urban centres in Africa, Asia and Latin America*

Kenya: Seven small or intermediate urban centres selected as growth centres in the 1970-74 Plan, a further two added in the 1974-78 Plan and a further nine added in the 1979-83 Plan. Kisumu, Kenya's third largest urban centre, is to receive priority. The 18 growth centres are to receive priority in social and economic infrastructure investment. Differing roles have been assigned to them. For instance, Machakos and Thika, both close to Nairobi, are to receive industrial investment while Garissa, Isiolo, Kapenguria and Narok are to be developed as 'gateway towns' linking arid and semi-arid areas to more developed regions and their markets. The 1974-78 and 1979-83 Plans also outlined a National Service Centre Hierarchy through which the government aims to reach 90 per cent of the population with 86 urban centres (not including the 11 major urban centres), 420 market centres, 1,015 local centres and 150 rural centres; each category aims at a different mix of services and infrastructure for the surrounding area (Richardson, 1980; Kenya, Republic of, 1975 and 1979). However, it seems that a concentration on the 18 growth centres outlined in the 1979-83 Plan is being replaced by a new Secondary Towns programme, supported by the World Bank and the US Agency for International Development. The projects being implemented in the first phase of the programme are oriented towards the servicing of urban land and provision of construction loans for residential and small enterprise development, construction of local authority revenue generating projects such as bus parks, markets and workshops, and financial project management and maintenance support to the local authorities. But what distinguishes this programme from most other government programmes is a concentration on the specific needs of each urban centre and on building up and supporting the capacity of each centre's government to become more effective in supporting that centre's development.

Tanzania: As a complement to the villagisation programme, national development plans have sought to stimulate the development of nine regional 'growth centres' (each of which were already substantial urban centres and regional headquarters); these nine growth centres were first identified in the 1969-74 Plan and they include Dodoma which is being developed as the national capital. Various measures have sought to stimulate their development including improved infrastructure and fiscal incentives to attract public and private enterprises. The Small Industries Development Organisation has been developing industrial estates in these nine growth centres – and other regional capitals. The 1976-1981 Plan sought to support the development of basic consumer goods' industries and to promote and develop small and medium industries in regional and sub-regional (district) headquarters. Two-fifths of the budget and the civil service have been decentralised to the regional level (Tanzania, Republic of, 1976 and 1975).

Tunisia: Various measures, apparent in successive development plans, have sought to stimulate development in small and intermediate urban centres. Efforts have been made to strengthen municipal government. Investment and land development programmes have been undertaken by national or regional government bodies in smaller urban centres and various initiatives have sought to promote tourism, and housing developments there (Rivkin, 1982).

Asia

Philippines: As part of a long-term national settlements policy, a total of 346 settlements have been identified as potential growth centres; these should serve as focal points on intra-regional and inter-regional transport and communications linkages and help encourage urban development away from Manila (the primate city and national capital). For the first 5-10 years of this plan (first outlined in the early Seventies), 30 centres were to be given top priority including two metropolitan centres (Cebu and Davao), eight regional centres, 15 sub-regional centres (including four in Manila Bay Metropolitan Region) and five growth centres also within this metropolitan region. New industrial developments within a 50 kilometre radius of the centre of Manila City centre are to be restricted (Task Force on Human Settlements, 1975; ESCAP, 1984).

Nepal: During the Seventies, the nation was divided into four regions, each with its own centre for implementing development plans – and within each of these, one or two major north-south growth axes linking each region's urban centres were identified. The aim is to stimulate their development – and links between them (Nepal, His Majesty's Government of, 1974).

India: Various Federal Government initiatives have sought to encourage development of relatively small urban centres since the advent of national planning. An explicit scheme for such centres was introduced for the Sixth Five Year Plan (1980-85) as a Federal Government sponsored scheme for 'Integrated Development of Small and Medium Towns', which arose out of recommendations from a Task Force set up in 1975. The scheme provides for central loan assistance on a matching basis with State and local government (40:40:20) to support land acquisition and development, traffic and transport, industrial estates and certain services for rural hinterland. The State level government has to fund slum improvement, and water supply, sanitation and preventive health care facilities. The scheme was restricted to urban centres with less than 100,000 inhabitants in the 1971 census with preference given to certain types of urban centre such as district headquarters. By 1 April, 1983, projects for 230 towns had been approved (India, Government of, 1984).

Thailand: The fifth Plan (1982-86) designated five regional cities in the three poorest regions which will receive investments in infrastructure (roads, drainage, flood protection, solid waste disposal site), revenue-earning facilities, such as markets, fishing ports and industrial estates, slum improvement and institutional development. Efforts are also being made to develop 'sub-regional' cities and their peripheral rural communities (ESCAP, 1984).

Indonesia: During the 1979-83 Plan, 10 major cities, 40 smaller cities (with 50,000-100,000 inhabitants) and 150 towns were chosen for kampung improvement programmes with improved water supply, sewage, drainage and solid waste removal/treatment. The public housing and serviced site programmes were to be decentralised, the national housing agency (PER-UMNAS) having projects underway in some 30 urban centres (Rivkin, 1982).

Latin America

Ecuador: The National Development Plan 1980-1984 emphasises the need to support the growth of 16 'Intermediate cities' (with between 40,000 and 200,000 inhabitants in 1981) to strengthen their role as centres or urban sub-systems and alternatives for internal migration and neutralising population flows towards the two largest cities (Guayaquil and Quito). There are also plans for smaller 'minor' cities (with between 10,000 and 40,000 inhabitants in 1981) to promote rural services and agro-industries and for rural centres (3,000-10,000 inhabitants). Government plans include improved coordination between central planning and municipal action; industrial location policy; programme of urban infrastructure; a cadastral and planning programme aiming at rationalising municipal affairs and improving small and intermediate urban centres' tax base (Ecuador, Government of, 1980).

Chile: A paper in 1983 prepared by the Urban Development Division of the Ministry of Housing and Urbanism stated that the recent process of political and administrative regionalisation, based on 13 regions, has provided a boost to the regional capitals since it concentrates on improving administration and services (Chile, Government of, 1983).

Nicaragua: The Housing and Human Settlements Ministry (MINVAH) set up in 1979 has defined a national urban system with a national centre, nine regional centres (20,000-100,000 inhabitants), 19 secondary centres (10,000-20,000 inhabitants) and below these service centres and base villages. The distribution of investments in urban infrastructure and services will be made through this system; measures will also seek to decentralise investment away from the Pacific Coast and from Managua and decentralise industry, especially towards centres with limited agricultural potential, control Managua's growth and strengthen border centres for defence purposes. The government also aims to strengthen regional and local government and to promote people's participation in, for instance, municipal affairs (Mayors were replaced by Municipal Councils) (MINVAH, 1983).

Panama: A Programme for the Development of Integrated Urban Systems was prepared in 1976, its aim being to strengthen urban centres in inner areas of the country so that migration to the capital would be decreased. This has 14 sub-programmes which have included promoting small industries, agro-industries and industrial parks in small and intermediate urban centres, and preparing master-plans (Panama, Government of, undated).

Peru: The government is seeking to decentralise administrative decisions, putting the emphasis on each departmental government and on municipal governments. Self-government at the municipal level is considered as the main instrument for economic and institutional development. Autonomous municipal governments are considered as the guarantee of an effective decentralisation. Through the creation of a Multisectoral Committee for the Co-ordination of the Decentralisation of Metropolitan Lima, new economic activities should be incorporated into two development corridors; one in the north between Huacho and Pativilca, the second in the south between Canete and Pisco. In addition, the development of certain intermediate urban centres around Lima will be promoted (Peru, Government of, 1981; Richardson, 1984).

Source: Derived from UNCHS (1985b).

Small and intermediate urban centres and 'backward' regions

There have been many attempts by governments to stimulate urban and industrial development in small and intermediate urban centres in regions labelled as 'backward' or 'lagging' or 'peripheral' – although these attempts have often gone under the name of 'growth centre' policy.[1] It has been common for governments to designate certain intermediate urban centres as 'growth centres' and, through concentrating public investment there in infrastructure and services and sometimes in public sector enterprises, to hope that these centres will achieve some level of self-sustaining development. Such policies usually relate to a desire to lessen regional imbalances in per capita income or per capita production and to steer productive investment away from the larger city (or cities). One notes, for instance, the designation of intermediate (and in some instances, small) urban centres as 'growth centres' in national plans in Kenya, Tanzania, Philippines and Nicaragua, in Table 8.1.

Until the last ten years or so, most 'growth centre' policies concentrated on stimulating industrial development in the designated centres. This probably relates to the original use and development of growth centres in Europe after the Second World War. This helps explain the lack of attention to agricultural or rural issues, since growth centre policies were first applied in nations in which only a small proportion of the labour force was working in agriculture and where there was rapid growth and change in the industrial sector – and indeed in the whole economic and employment base of urban centres. Friedmann (1981) notes the failure of some of the most important and influential books on regional policy and regional development economics to give much attention to rural development. But the concept of the growth centre as a device to encourage urban and industrial development away from larger cities became widespread in the Third World, despite the major differences that usually existed in the scale and structure of production and the sectoral division of production and employment compared to First World nations. The poor results achieved by 'growth centres' based on industrialisation to stimulate development in their surrounding regions have been described in many case studies and criticised in theoretical papers published in the last ten years.

Stohr and Todtling (1979) have summarised the failings as follows. First, the growth centre may have proved to be a much smaller stimulus to surrounding regions than was first expected, and the stimulus was often counteracted by negative effects. Secondly, increases in rural incomes or in incomes in smaller urban centres create strong multiplier links in larger urban centres – but it is not necessarily the case that comparable multiplier effects flow from larger to smaller urban centres. The hope that the benefits of growth would 'trickle down' from larger to smaller centres was not fulfilled.

One reason for the lack of success of 'growth centres' in meeting social goals such as stimulating development in poorer, more 'backward' regions was the confusion between 'social' and 'spatial' equity. While government intervention might increase the relative role of a region or urban centre in national production, this need not mean that there were important social and economic benefits for most of the population living there. As Stuckey (1975) comments, regional theory and the notion of growth poles or growth centres 'were derived from the observation of growth and development in North America and Europe' but 'in a Rostowian manner, they were marched off into the world of underdevelopment in the Fifties and Sixties and asked to solve the problems of poverty' (p. 90). While few macroeconomists and development theorists subscribe to the Rostowian theory of a historically linear development process, Stuckey notes that this theory retains a pervasive influence on spatial development theories. Indeed, explicit or implicit in the writings of many urban specialists today is the idea that all Third World nations will undergo comparable transformations to those experienced in the richer First World nations in terms of levels of urbanisation and the spatial distribution of urban population.

Another possible explanation for the uneven results of policies on 'growth centres' as planning tools to redistribute urban and industrial development, lies in the fact that the term 'growth centre' has been used to cover so many different kinds of policy intervention. Gilbert and Gugler (1983) note that the term 'growth centres' includes:

everything from villages of 5,000 people to the world's largest metropolis. Industrial areas, administrative centres, university cities and sleepy market towns have all been labelled growth centres. As a result, the growth centre has been used as the intellectual rationale for every spatial strategy from Dodoma to the continued growth of Mexico City. It has been used in one form or another in Tanzania, Brazil, Poland, Chile, China and India. Its blandness has allowed it to be the handmaiden of whatever regime found it useful. It is not the regional approach that is the villain but the development model which limits and dictates the manner of use. (p. 175)

A report on 'Middle Rank Human Settlements in Territorial Organisation Strategies in Latin America and the Caribbean' (ECLA/UNCHS, 1984) lists a series of failings in policies to stimulate intermediate urban centres including: imprecise diagnosis of existing circumstances in such centres and their region of influence; simplistic and obviously piecemeal understanding of the factors behind its development; a lack of integration of proposed policies with macro-development policies and sectoral priorities; inadequate recognition of factors and aspects specific to each centre; and unrealistic and imprecise projections of needed investments to implement proposed policies. A survey of national spatial policies in 17 Third World nations during the Seventies suggests that despite the ambitious social and spatial aims stated in development plans, rarely did such plans contain policies which had any hope of meeting such aims and they all too frequently ended up enriching already privileged social groups, regions and large conurbations (Hardoy and Satterthwaite, 1981).

In the literature surveyed, the nations whose national policies have been described and analysed in most detail are Kenya, Thailand, Cuba, China, Israel, Brazil and India. The discussion of these papers is perhaps made more coherent by dividing the nations according to whether the public or the private sector is the main source of productive investment. If it is the public sector, government bodies have a much greater influence on the kinds of productive investment, the technology used and the location. When viewed as a single entity, the 'public sector' has far more power to determine the form and the spatial distribution of urban development if it is the main source of productive investment. In a largely market oriented economy, government has less direct influence on the nature and spatial distribution of productive investment – although the location of infrastructure, services and government offices has an important influence, and a variety of direct and indirect subsidies or penalties are also often used to promote spatial aims. Many nations do not fall easily into one of the two categories; for instance in India, national and state governments are important sources of productive investment. In Israel, explicit government policies to influence the spatial distribution of urban development bears comparison to some of the so-called 'Centrally Planned Economies'. Let us first discuss the examples of Kenya, Brazil, India, Thailand and Israel before looking at the examples of Cuba and China which are usually categorised as 'Centrally Planned Economies'.

Richardson (1980) critically evaluates Kenya's urban development strategy as first outlined in the 1970-74 national development plan and further developed in successive Plans (see Table 8.1). He criticises the idea, then current within the Kenyan government, that Nairobi is becoming too big and suggests that it would be incorrect to base a growth centre strategy on this belief. Nairobi has important agglomeration economies which make it attractive to both industry and people while diseconomies such as pollution, congestion and crime are less serious than in most other large cities. Richardson suggests that given effective planning, even a Nairobi with more than four million inhabitants by the year 2000 would be quite acceptable. However, he does point out that there is a stronger case for a growth centre (or small and intermediate urban centre) strategy if it were based on Kenya's comparative advantage in agriculture and resource-based industries and on its policy objectives emphasising rural development. The paper then outlines how the government should concentrate on developing one intermediate urban centre, Kisumu, which is already Kenya's third largest urban centre. The national government does not have the resources to develop all 18 small or intermediate urban centres designated as growth centres in the 1979-83 Plan, and several of these growth centres are too far away from Nairobi to benefit from its agglomeration economies but perhaps too close to escape its competitive influence.

Two papers on north-east Thailand, Fuller (1981) and Hafner (1980), touch on the national government's decentralised urban strategy which seeks to upgrade several urban centres into 'regional urban growth centres' with between 100,000 and 300,000 inhabitants. The strategy follows on from earlier government policies which identified regional growth poles, although the commitment to encouraging decentralised urban development is more explicit and more integrated into national planning in the 1977-81 national plan. This designates nine provincial capitals as regional urban growth centres, four of which are in the north-east. Neither papers' main concentration is on assessing this strategy, although both authors quote criticisms of it by others. Hafner also notes that initiatives to try and attract industrial investment to the north-east's intermediate urban centres must be accompanied by a transformation of the rural agrarian sector. 'If raw material outputs falter and regional per capita incomes do not grow, the regional markets essential to an expanding manufacturing sector will not provide the economic environment necessary for protracted industrial investment ... the success of these programmes depends as much on rural investment as it does on urban investment' (Hafner, 1980, pp. 499-500).

One of the best documented attempts by a government to stimulate and support urban development in a backward region has been the Brazilian government's efforts in the north-east, a region with more than 30 million inhabitants. Dickenson (1980) describes the various initiatives tried by the Federal government over the last century to reduce poverty and stimulate development there. Among the special incentives during the Sixties and early Seventies was the so-called '34/18' legislation which allowed Brazilian industries to reduce their tax liabilities if the money saved was used for approved investments in the north-east. Several hundred new factories were built and many existing factories modernised. Most new or expanded industries were not consumer goods industries, presumably because there was a lack of demand for such goods from the region's inhabitants as most have very low incomes. Most of the new jobs created by the new or expanded industries went to the north-east's larger urban centres in the richest states. Dickenson suggests that the main beneficiaries of 100 years of Federal Government attempts to stimulate development there, including this programme to stimulate industry, have been groups outside the region and small groups within the region who were neither the poor nor those in need of government help. Gilbert and Goodman (1976) suggest that increasing inequality in the north-east 'severely qualifies any claims that the 1960s witnessed a period of development, irrespective of progress towards regional income equalisation' (p. 131). Hamer (1984) in a study of urban development and industrial location in Sao Paulo State (the richest and most industrialised state in Brazil) found that for rapidly growing intermediate urban centres there, the expansion of existing enterprises and the establishment of new enterprises were more important than enterprises from Greater Sao Paulo relocating there – or establishing branch plants. This implies that government policies to encourage industrial growth in any particular urban centre may have to concentrate more on improving local conditions and supporting local firms than incentives to attract branch plants or to encourage plants to move there. Hamer also notes the very high cost to the government in the tax credits given to industries which located in the north-east; the average federal tax credit subsidisation was the equivalent of US$15,000 per job. Hamer suggests that this is best described as 'monument building' and 'as with most monuments, it is difficult to replicate without bankrupting the public treasury' (p. 88).

In reviewing the evolution of an urban growth policy for India, Jain (1976) notes the increasing interest being given by national plans to spatial questions. The first two five-year plans (1951-60) gave little attention to spatial aspects. The Third Plan called for new industries to be established away from major cities and for rural and urban components to be combined in community development projects. The Fourth (1969-74) had a similar approach and called for the development of urban centres other than Metropolitan Bombay and Calcutta. By the Fifth Plan (1974-79), among the objectives were the development of smaller urban centres, the strengthening of local authorities in implementing urban development schemes and the formulation of an urban land policy. But the author takes issue with the approach in this plan because urban development programmes were seen as social welfare schemes, outside the mainstream of national development. In addition, physical plans lacked economic, social and political content; the preparation of masterplans for small and intermediate urban centres appeared random and devoid of both economic analysis and development orientation.

The author went on to compare two ways in which urban development has been stimulated by public sector intervention. The first was through investments in capital intensive industries with their location determined by resource efficiency criteria; some new steel plants built in the Second Plan have served as centres for rapid growth in intermediate urban centres. By contrast, efforts to improve 'regional balance' with subsidies and investments in basic infrastructure have failed; infrastructure provision in backward regions is not sufficient to induce industrial growth. Mohan (1985) reports on the result of offering incentives to industries to locate in 'backward areas'. Districts so designated cover around 60 per cent of India's entire population and 70 per cent of its total area. Industry has not invested in some of the least backward areas. Almost 90 per cent of the concessional investment funds went to just 22 districts and most of these were near metropolitan areas. 'Furthermore, at least three of the metropolitan cities (New Delhi, Bangalore and Hyderabad) had 'backward areas' in their backyards in adjacent districts. Not surprisingly, private industry has been quite happy to take advantage of the incentives to locate in these areas' (p. 53). But this hardly provides much stimulus to poorer areas.

In Israel, there are more than 30 'development towns' with a total population of over half a million inhabitants; only five are based on settlements which existed prior to 1948 (Meissner, 1979). Although perhaps this is more a 'new town' programme than a programme to develop existing small and intermediate urban centres, the example is interesting both because its aim was to steer urban and industrial development away from the larger urban centres and because the approach is still, on occasion, recommended to Third World nations as an example from which they could draw lessons (see Meissner, 1981).

The government gave considerable resources to housing and infrastructure investment in these development towns, each of which was planned to accommodate between 15,000 and 60,000 inhabitants. Industrial development was heavily subsidised and there were lower personal and business taxes on incomes originating in these areas. Comay and Kirschenbaum (1973) found that some of the initial hopes for the development towns had not been fulfilled. In a study of migration, they found that between 1965 and 1968, these centres were net exporters of population; among 23 investigated, only three had positive net in-migration. Much of the migration out of these towns was to the larger, established urban centres, ie the very areas from which they were meant to draw population. In a study of 18 of these centres, the level of unemployment was found to be the most potent explanatory variable for in or out migration.

Soen and Kipnis (1972) look in more detail at three urban centres and suggest why two failed to grow in population and develop economically in the manner planned. The three had been planned in a cluster, close to an existing Arab urban centre; by 1969, they had populations of 8,500, 13,200 and 16,700 with the Arab urban centre having 32,900. But by this date, there were stronger economic ties between the inhabitants in these urban centres and Haifa, a city with over 300,000 inhabitants some 30-40 km away, than between the different urban centres within the cluster. One reason was that many of the residents in the old Arab centre worked in Haifa. A second was because Jews preferred to shop in Haifa than in the local Arab centre. A third was due to the form that agricultural production took. Production and consumption in nearby kibbutzim (large collective farms) largely bypassed enterprises in their local centres within the cluster; the kibbutz, by its nature, tends to have most economic ties through its parent organisation and with enterprises in larger urban centres. So kibbutzim generally make their purchases in Haifa, or even in more distant Tel Aviv.

But there are broader issues to consider if the relevance of Israel's experience with 'development towns' is to be assessed for other Third World nations. These should include the recognition that Israel has a per capita GNP of over US$5,000 and probably receives more aid per capita than any other nation in the world. Furthermore, in linking the idea of 'development towns' to agriculture, note should be taken that Israel is one of the world's most urbanised nations and in 1980 had just seven per cent of its labour force working in agriculture.

In considering government policies in market or mixed economies which seek to encourage industrial development in small and intermediate urban centres, there is a danger that all the lessons learnt from 30 years of 'regional development' and 'growth centre' policies will be forgotten. As Renaud (1981) points out, prematurely forcing the relocation of major manufacturing activities to urban centres such as the capital of a poor, low income province can prove costly to the national economy and fatal or near-fatal to the company. This has special relevance to the poorer Third World nations with small and less diversified industrial bases. It may be that only the primate city has the factors which allow many industries, whether in public or private hands, to operate efficiently and produce the goods cheaply. In the Sudan, for example, many factories placed by government in intermediate urban centres are working far below capacity. One reason is their dependence on imported goods, especially machinery, so that difficulties in transporting inputs to intermediate urban centres in backward regions, allied to foreign exchange shortages and associated controls on imports inhibit efficient industrial operations there. So also do power cuts, poor infrastructure and lack of skilled personnel (Simpson, 1984).

In addition, in a stagnant economy, where the volume of manufacturing investment is low, there are unlikely to be many opportunities for the spontaneous decentralisation of productive investments because most firms are operating below capacity and much of the investment in manufacturing will be to replace equipment or expand existing facilities (Townroe, 1979; Renaud, 1981). Furthermore, the study on 'Decentralised Urban Development and Industrial Location Behaviour in Sao Paulo, Brazil' (Hamer, 1984) quoted earlier suggests that the potential for branch plants or relocation of productive activities from large urban centres to small or intermediate urban centres may have been over-estimated. Once again, this strengthens the argument that government policies for small and intermediate urban centres must be based on careful assessment of the local needs, local resources and local potentials which are particular to each urban centre.

Perhaps there are possibilities in some Third World nations for supporting the development of certain basic consumer goods industries in intermediate urban centres in particular, backward regions. For example, in relatively large African nations with poor inter-regional transport links, regionally based consumer goods industries meeting regional demand for the most common and widely used items might improve the supply and reduce their cost. Improving the intra-regional rather than inter-regional transport infrastucture to facilitate this should be cheaper too. But caution is also needed here in that if such industries in backward regions need critical inputs from the national capital or from abroad, the advantage in having a regional market protected by poor transport links with richer core areas becomes outweighed by the disadvantages that these same poor transport links imply for the industries in obtaining the inputs vital for their efficient operation. In addition, if there is little or no growth in production in the poorer region, there will not be a growth in demand for such industries' products.

In regional or national economies less influenced by market forces, national government initiatives to support the development of small and intermediate urban centres are less constrained by such factors. Perhaps it is for this reason that the surveyed literature gave considerable attention to Cuba and China. Acosta and Hardoy (1973) note that agrarian reform laws in Cuba, implemented shortly after the revolution in 1959, removed the main cause for rural to urban migration. Investments in transport and communications reduced the isolation of small and intermediate urban centres. A number of intermediate urban centres were selected for concentrated investment in industries and housing and their population growth rates were roughly twice the national average in the mid-Sixties. New small and intermediate urban centres (and rural settlements) were developed. As the authors note in the Preface, 'perhaps the most important lesson to be derived from it is the recognition that the basis for the solution of urban problems is not of a technical nature but essentially political and socio-economic. The solution cannot be found by concentrating efforts solely in urban areas, but only by means of a territorial plan of national goals that spatially and socially reflects the orientations of the economy.'

Gugler (1980) in his paper on Cuba notes the importance of the improvements of living standards among the rural population and of involving urban dwellers in rural activities in order to slow urban population growth. The ending of wage differentials between rural and urban areas were erased and the rationing system and expansion of free social services were also important. The goal of urbanising the countryside led to a large programme for the construction of small urban centres and rural service centres. The paper ends with the comment that despite the paucity of data, the existing evidence suggests achievements in the policies to reduce the dominance of Havana, to slow down urban growth and to urbanise the countryside, although these achievements were as yet quite limited by 1970.

Two aspects which distinguish the policies undertaken by Cuba from most of those described for market or mixed economies are first the structural changes which underpin them (for instance the agrarian reform) and secondly, the fact that the national government can direct the sectoral and spatial distribution of productive investment. The experience of China in seeking to promote the growth and development of small and intermediate urban centres is also interesting in this light. Kwok (1982) in talking of urban centres with under 100,000 inhabitants points out that urban development after 1949 has responded more directly and positively to specific national strategies for agricultural or industrial development, administrative reform and technological adaptation than to the perhaps better known and more frequently cited principles promoted by the government, such as eliminating rural-urban disparities, developing interior regions and decentralising administration.

The period 1949-1980 reveals many major policy changes relating to economic development or administration which affect small and intermediate urban centres' development. The period 1947-1957 was not conducive to such centres' development since government's priority was on developing heavy industry, and planning and administration were strongly centralised. Then in the Great Leap Forward, 1958-61, small-scale industries were promoted in smaller urban centres and rural areas. But after three years of failure in industry and agriculture, this was quickly terminated before it produced any significant results. The period 1961-65 saw power again decentralised, small-scale industries no longer encouraged and slower development of small and intermediate urban centres. The decades after 1966 produced stronger development for these centres as administration was decentralised and small-scale industries producing for local needs were emphasised again.

The costs and benefits of Cuba's and China's policies are not discussed in any great detail. But their relevance in this survey of government policies is their example of the powerful influence on development prospects in small and intermediate urban centres of governments' chosen socio-economic orientation in terms of sectoral and social priorities and of government structure.

In concluding the discussion on the possibilities of encouraging industrial development in small or intermediate urban centres in backward regions, note should be taken of the problems facing the poorer and less industrialised Third World nations in developing a large and diversified manufacturing base. Most Third World nations lack an internal market for manufactured goods of sufficient size to provide the demand needed to support successful and sustained industrial development. One alternative is to develop the industrial sector by producing goods for export. But export markets are intensely competitive. While the export of manufactured goods has allowed several Third World nations (notably the so-called Newly Industrialising Nations) to build diversified industrial sectors, the possibilities for many nations of finding a range of manufactured goods they can export for a good return is very small. Yet the potential for industries to develop in small and intermediate urban centres is much influenced by the size and structure of the industrial sector.

It is worth considering the factors listed in Table 8.2, since an appropriate mix of these can encourage industries and service enterprises to invest in intermediate urban centres in backward regions. Many of the listed factors have been instrumental in regions in the First World in encouraging new productive investment in small and intermediate urban centres and on greenfield sites. A Third World government which wants to encourage industrial investment in backward regions might run through this list and consider how many apply to the regions in question. Few (if any) of these factors seem to be present in more than a small proportion of Third World regions. First, backward regions' attraction for productive investment is usually much smaller than in backward First World regions; low incomes there mean lower demand for the goods or services that new enterprises might provide; the infrastructure, services and facilities in the intermediate centres there and their connections with the primate city or with large cities, are often very poor; labour is no cheaper (the large pool of un- or under-employed labour in the larger cities keeps labour costs down); local government is often very weak; and the labour force there does not have high levels of education and literacy.

Secondly, few nations' economic bases are sufficiently large and diversified to have supported the development of the kinds of enterprises which can more easily invest in peripheral regions – branch plants of large commercial or manufacturing concerns. Thirdly, the 'pull' of primate cities is very powerful; perhaps only here are there the needed contacts with government agencies, transport connections to national and international markets, and a substantial pool of professionals, managers, sub-contractors and service industries.

If the factors listed in Table 8.2 become apparent within the national economy, it might be possible for governments to encourage industrial development in certain small and intermediate urban centres. Premature attempts to steer industry away from primate cities or large cities are likely either to be very expensive for what they achieve, or very expensive for national production because the industries pushed to small or intermediate urban centres produce high cost goods and/or work far below capacity. Intermediate urban centres in the Third World are littered with industrial parks (built at considerable expense) with very few industrial operations. In addition, many factories are working at only a small fraction of their capacity or indeed lying abandoned because their location proved incompatible with their efficient functioning, or because industrial policies changed and they did not receive the expected support.

Table 8.2   *Factors which can encourage industries and service enterprises to invest in intermediate urban centres in backward regions*

(a)   A sufficient level of demand for goods and services from the population of the backward region which is most profitably met by enterprises based there. This implies a relatively high per capita income and relatively equitable income distribution.

(b)   Good inter-regional transport and communication systems (e.g. telephone systems, telex systems, radio, television services) of comparable quality to those in largest cities, access to national newspapers, all weather roads, bus services.

(c)   Industrial and retail/wholesale/services sector within a nation with size, diversity and concentration of many units within one enterprise to allow the decentralisation of branch units outside large cities to lower production costs or better tap markets there.

(d)   Cheaper labour (partially due to lower living costs) and cheap and plentiful land in peripheral regions.

(e)   Good infrastructure and service provision within the backward region including important business support services like banking, development credit agencies, technical assistance facilities, etc. for encouraging the 'birth' and development of local firms and good cultural/entertainment/recreational facilities for managers, executives, professionals ... including even a preference among many people for life in an intermediate urban centre.[b]

(f) High level of literacy and education in population in backward regions and active regional/local business community.

(g) Large national market (production for export in peripheral intermediate urban centres less likely).

(h) Efficient intermediate urban centre level government and strong data base about local climate, water availability and resources.

(i) Strong tourist sector related to natural sites (beaches, parks, lakes, rivers).

(j) No need for long negotiations with bureaucrats, government agencies located in primate city.

(k) Powerful and influential labour movements developing in existing main industrially developed areas which can be avoided by investing in peripheral regions.

(l) Advanced systems of management and control linked to sophisticated communications systems allowing spatial dispersion of large enterprises' plants (each seeking location best suited to its operation) with no loss of management/control of whole enterprise from head office.

Notes: a—Many of these are factors which have contributed to a decline in population in large cities or metropolitan areas in the First World, as enterprises which formerly thrived there closed down or relocated, and new investment sought sites in smaller urban centres or in greenfield locations.

b—Various surveys in different First World nations have shown that a substantial proportion of the urban population would prefer to live in relatively small urban centres.

This is not to imply an 'anti-industrial' or 'anti-small and intermediate urban centres' bias. But in current circumstances, most Third World governments lack resources, lack capital and lack a stable and growing economic base. Inappropriate public expenditure aiming to decentralise industry and to distribute it in too many intermediate centres (by whatever means) can only impose a hardly needed additional burden on what are often already fragile economies and create unfulfilled expectations and higher operational costs.

Small and intermediate urban centres and rural development

The concept of the growth centre applied to small or intermediate urban centres in the rural and agricultural context may have a much wider relevance to most Third World nations than when applied to changing the spatial distribution of industrial development. Although it is not valid to generalise from the findings in Chapters 2 to 6 on other Third World regions, the intimate links between the development of small or intermediate urban centres and the kinds of agricultural development and land tenure structure are worth recalling.

So too are comparable links from other studies summarised in Chapter 7. Since the attempts to encourage industrial development in Brazil's North-east were described earlier in this chapter, it is also worth noting a study on the agricultural economy of this region (Kutcher and Scandizzo, 1981) which emphasises what might be regarded as an alternative approach to stimulating and supporting the development of small and intermediate urban centres there. This policy is based on making better use of the region's two abundant resources – land and labour.

The study shows that there are nearly one million viable farming units and sharecropped plots in the North-east which provide an acceptable standard of living for those who have the land. There are also 'nearly 30 million hectares of underutilised land of similar if not superior quality on the estates' on which 'nearly another million families could achieve comparable living standards' (p. 216). Agricultural production in the north-east could increase the supply of traditional foodstuffs – corn, beans, manioc and rainfed rice – to meet demand in the region and ultimately even to export a surplus to the south. The extent to which this would help slow out-migration from rural areas in the North-east to the region's large urban centres such as Recife, Salvador and Fortaleza or to Sao Paulo or Brasilia can be seen in the fact that the smallest farmers there

> employ 25 times more labour per hectare on their land than do the largest farms and obtain vastly higher productivity levels. The smaller farms (less than 50 hectares) though only 10 per cent of the agricultural land, produce over 25 per cent of the region's sugar, cotton and rice and 40 per cent of the beans, corn and manioc. Yet two million agriculturally dependent families own no land at all while an area of land the size of France is un- or under-utilised (p. 218).

Out-migration from rural areas in the north-east to urban centres both in the North-east and outside the region has been an important factor in the rapid population growth experienced by many of Brazil's larger urban centres. But to slow such out-migration demands the implementation of a land reform; just four per cent of landowners own more than half the land in agricultural properties and only one in four families dependent on agriculture owns the land it works.

Scott (1982) in his analysis of urban and spatial development in Mexico also points to the links between the growth of small and intermediate urban centres and rural and agricultural development. He suggests that in several of the poorer states, urban economic growth could be stimulated by increasing agricultural productivity and raising rural incomes – through 'small-scale irrigation, reforestation, flood control works, rural roads, rural electrification and improved land use practices' (p. 271). He goes on to add that 'an approach to economic growth based exclusively on cities – such as growth centre strategies sometimes imply – might not work as well as one that pays equal attention to the rural population and economy' (p. 271).

It is worth noting the importance of coffee production in the second half of the nineteenth century around the city of Sao Paulo in providing a major stimulus to commercial and industrial activity in the city ånd to generating the incomes which then represented demand for goods and services met by enterprises in the city (Hamer, 1984). Examples in Chapters 2 to 7 have already shown how growth in agricultural production coming from a large group of farming households with sufficient land and labour to obtain adequate incomes from intensively cultivated land is a powerful stimulus to small and intermediate urban centres' development. Many of the forward and backward linkages are often internal to the region. If such policies are shown to have relevance to regions in Brazil and Mexico, two of the most urbanised Third World nations, then their relevance to nations with higher proportions of their labour force working in agriculture and higher proportions of GDP and export earnings dependent of agricultural crops has perhaps been under-estimated. In many regions, appropriate land, agricultural and rural development policies can reduce migration from rural areas to larger urban centres because they provide a better livelihood for potential migrants; the Upper Valley in Chapter 2 was shown to be one of the major magnets for inter-regional migration in Argentina. Such policies can also help meet such national goals as increasing food production for the domestic market and increasing the proportion of the population above the poverty line. But as noted earlier, each region will have problems specific to its own resource base, population characteristics and distribution, income levels, connection to other regions and so on.

Misra (1981) notes that in recent years the concept of the growth centre has come to be applied in the rural context. Perhaps in agriculture, as in industry, the fact that sectoral plans give little consideration to their spatial implications led many researchers to consider the settlement or urban component of rural and agricultural development. This means impinging on small and intermediate urban centres. Many research studies and policy documents including those by Knesl (1982), Brutzkus (1975), Rondinelli, Lombardo and Yeh (1979), Meissner (1981), ESCAP (1979) and Johnson (1970) have given increasing attention to the importance of an adequate hierarchy of small and intermediate urban centres to serve and support rural and agricultural development. This work led to recommendations that one of the most important government actions should be to create or impose a settlement hierarchy of market towns or rural service centres in poorer and more rural areas.Clearly, in terms of public service provision, both rural and urban populations' access to different levels of education and health care is maximised by the location of an apropriate level of services through large, intermediate and small urban centres – and indeed, for some lower order services in rural settlements. It seems that it is this kind of thinking which lay behind governments' declared aims and objectives of creating an articulated hierarchy of urban centres or settlements – which can be seen in the plans of the Ecuadorian, Nicaraguan and Kenyan governments summarised in Table 8.1.

The empirical studies reviewed in the previous chapter, however, suggest that at least in predominantly market or mixed economies, this will not necessarily have the hoped for impact. It is not clear how a government policy to create or strengthen the 'varied hierarchy of central places' which Johnson (1970) regards as a crucial government intervention would necessarily stimulate social and economic development. Empirical studies – including those summarised in Chapters 2 to 6 – suggest that the lack of a varied hierarchy of central places is usually due to such factors as the poverty of most people in the area surrounding potential 'central places'. Government provision of an accessible market centre cannot address the needs of lower income groups if they lack the land or the capital or skills to increase production for sale at that market.

The earlier discussion on Brazil's North-east suggests that providing a varied hierarchy of central places with good intra-regional and inter-regional roads would do little to address the most pressing social and economic problems there. Improving a fertile region's access to external markets has often stimulated major increases in production and productivity. Most Third World nations have small and intermediate urban centres whose initial development coincided with the arrival of a new road or railway which allowed the production and export of some crop out of the region. But as described in Chapter 7, the extent to which such action stimulates local urban development will depend on such factors as the landowning structure and the arrangements by which the crops are marketed, as well as such factors as the price received by the crop producer – and this can be diminished by (among other things) high values of the national currency against currencies in the nations to which the produce is exported, low prices paid by national government to farmers or low world prices for that crop. A new road which suddenly links a formerly isolated micro-region to a wider regional or national economy can actually mean the destruction of or damage to many local inhabitants' livelihoods. Goods brought in for sale from elsewhere can destroy or damage local artisanal or crop production formerly protected by that micro-region's isolation. The agricultural land market can become increasingly commercialised and land ownership more concentrated – including, perhaps, a rise in the number of absentee owners.

The cases of Tanzania and Algeria are notable in that governments in both have long-term village programmes which seek to improve service provision to rural inhabitants and reduce their isolation. They also have other aims like the adoption of communal crop production as the main and eventually the only form of crop production, but a discussion of such aspects is beyond the scope of this chapter. While most of the settlements affected by these programmes have less than 5,000 inhabitants, the programmes are worth considering in that they seek to provide rural inhabitants with the kinds of services and facilities which one would normally associate with small urban centres. As Brebner and Briggs (1982) point out, there are social advantages to these village programmes since economies of scale for social service provision are gained and it becomes economically feasible to provide schools, health facilities and clean water. Providing these to a dispersed rural population would be much more expensive.

Sutton (1982) describes Algeria's '1000 socialist village' programme as the settlement component of an agrarian reform which began in 1971. Land from large and absentee landowners was be be nationalised and redistributed mainly in production cooperatives to landless peasants. The new socialist villages were to provide the technical base for agricultural production and improved housing, and services for their inhabitants and for the population nearby. It was also hoped that they would hold back rural to urban migration; land abandonment by agrarian reform recipients as they moved to urban areas has become common. Initially, three village sizes were planned: primary with 700-1,400 people; secondary with 1,750-2450; and tertiary with 2,800-4,900. The larger the village, the more services and facilities it should provide.

But this programme's implementation has fallen far behind initial targets as the costs for constructing the villages has grown. While housing standards and the quality of services and facilities in the completed villages are impressive, the programme has been criticised not only on the grounds of expense and of slow implementation but also on the fact that there was little or no consultation with the intended beneficiaries as to their needs and preferences, before designing and building the new villages (Sutton, 1982). As Brebner and Briggs (1982) point out, the new socialist villages can be seen as a way through which political control can be exercised over the rural population; most decisions concerning the villages are taken through local, regional and ultimately central ministerial levels.

Although Tanzania's villagisation programme is different both in its form and in the way it was implemented, it too has facilitated the degree of government and Party control over the rural population and over its crop production (ibid). Under this programme, over 8,000 villages were established, most with between 1,250 and 7,500 inhabitants and estimates for 1980 suggest that 82 per cent of Tanzania's population live in 'ujamaa villages and development villages'. Unlike Algeria's village programme, this was implemented much more rapidly and did not include a large house construction component, undertaken by the government. By 1980, 38 per cent of villages had running water and 35 per cent had dispensaries while 92 per cent had primary schools. Ward centres, which are to act as nuclei for rural development serving between five and eight villages, will be developed as market and production centres for rural produce and centres for small scale or craft industries; in effect to develop as small urban centres. The government's Small Industries Development Organisation seeks to promote small-scale industries in villages and low interest loans are available to allow individuals or groups in villages to buy building materials. A model village plan handbook was produced in 1976 and various campaigns have sought to encourage housing and health improvement (Kulaba, 1982).

Various problems have arisen in implementing this ambitious programme. First, some villages were sited on lands susceptible to seasonal floods or lands far from dependable water supplies or where there was poor soil. In some areas, the model village plan handbook was applied too dogmatically. In some villages, it has proved costly and difficult to maintain water pumps (ibid). The speed with which the villagisation programme was implemented between 1974 and 1976 also had a negative effect on agricultural production (Brebner and Briggs, 1982).

Small and intermediate urban centres within urban regions

Many specialists agree that as a large urban centre grows and develops, there are many more opportunities for decentralising urban and industrial development within rather than outside the surrounding region with intermediate – and perhaps small – urban centres playing a role. Clearly, government intervention in encouraging such a process is essentially a 'growth management' policy since it cannot encourage urban and industrial development in backward regions; indeed, it may help increase the concentration of economic activities in core regions.

The attraction of intermediate and, on occasion, small urban centres (or greenfield sites) for many industrial and service activities has become apparent in many First World nations. There is also an increasing number of Third World examples of rapid growth in urban centres outside large metropolitan areas but where activities in these centres are intimately linked to those in the metropolitan area. For instance, Townroe and Keen (1984) have documented the 'polarisation reversal' in the State of Sao Paulo, Brazil as the population growth rates of intermediate urban centres located outside Sao Paulo Metropolitan Area have come to exceed that of the Metropolitan Area during the 1970s.[2] Various intermediate urban centres close to Mexico City Metropolitan Area are also tending to have population growth rates more rapid than that of the Metropolitan Area itself.

In South Korea, many small and intermediate urban centres with good transport connections to Seoul, the national capital and much the largest city, have populations growing more rapidly than that of Seoul (Song, 1982). As Chapter 4 described, Mysore City, at one time one of South India's most important urban centres, seems to have had its relative economic decline halted because of increasing industrial investment as a result of its close location to and strong transport links with Bangalore Metropolitan Area, one of India's most rapidly growing large cities. Similarly, as Chapter 6 described, Otta, an important urban centre in south-west Nigeria (Yorubaland) prior to colonial rule, is also finding that its relative economic decline is being reversed by industrial investment there linked to Lagos Metropolitan centre. But, as Townroe (1982) has pointed out, the phenomenon of 'polarisation reversal' is not simply a function of a city's population size and population growth rate; the question of when (or if) it will occur is also dependent on many city-specific factors such as topography, income level and its distribution, resources in the city-region, government structure, quality of infrastructure, strength of city government in nearby intermediate urban centres and quality of transport and communication links between them and the major city, together with the nature of the organisation and technology of manufacturing.

The prevailing advice of specialists who have examined 'polarisation reversal' and its relevance to better managing the growth of large cities in the Third World could be summed up as a need for careful analysis of whether polarisation reversal is already happening 'spontaneously' and the extent to which this can be supported by strategic government investments in infrastructure and services, changes in the spatial biases of current policies, and programmes to better inform enterprises in the city core of costs and benefits for plants outside the core. Renaud (1981) also points to the fact that the expansion and improvement of transport systems over time will relax constraints on productive investment in locations other than major cities and that certain intermediate urban centres located on major transport corridors close to large cities may well be the first urban centres which attract productive investment away from large cities. The cases of Otta and of Agbara Estate in Chapter 6 illustrate this.

Various papers have described and analysed government attempts to decentralise urban and industrial development within or close to a major metropolitan area. Jenssen, Kunzman and Saad-El Din (1979) describe the enormous expense incurred by the Egyptian government in developing three satellite cities within 30 to 100 km of Cairo to divert commercial and industrial development there. The paper points to these new cities' lack of linkage to an agricultural hinterland (they are largely built on desert land), the lack of benefit they provide for low income groups and – perhaps most crucial in terms of obtaining a viable economic base – the fact that few local or foreign enterprises are likely to move there.

Controlling large urban centres' growth

Discussions on steering urban growth from larger to smaller urban centres usually hinge on steering industrial investment from larger to smaller urban centres, and the rationale for this has been debated for decades. There is general agreement that, for many industrial activities, important economic benefits derive from their concentration in larger urban centres – intra- and inter-industry linkages are facilitated; the large concentration of demand by different industries for labour, goods and services helps to ensure the needed diversity in supply; and access to large consumer markets which allows economies of scale in production, distribution and marketing is guaranteed both through proximity to that city's population and through good location on intra- and inter-regional and international transport networks. Similarly, for city governments, there are economies of scale in providing the infrastructure and services that industries need – including roads, ports, airports, transport terminals, telephone systems, water supply, and waste disposal management. And as Renaud (1981) points out, a certain minimum population size and concentration of income is needed for the profitable operation of specialised business services, shippers and jobbers, financial offices, legal offices, trade associations, repairs, specialised printing, consulting firms, equipment leasing, laboratories and professional schools. For many businesses, these more than cheap labour affect the attractiveness of a city.

Despite what might be termed a minor resurgence in interest in the concept of optimum city size,[3] generalisations about relative 'costs' and 'benefits' for different city-sizes have little or no validity. Any rigorous evaluation of such costs and benefits must be city specific, depending on many factors unique to the city, region and nation such as the type and mix of industrial activities, income levels, income distribution and availability (and cost) of land and water for city expansion. Furthermore, discussions about such costs and benefits sometimes fail to differentiate between the industries, the public authorities charged with providing the infrastructure and services, and the different interest groups within the city's population. Most government actions (or the lack of them) affect the balance of these costs and benefits. For example, governments' neglect of the needs of lower income groups for improved shelter and access to basic services within urban centres often helps to keep national or city taxes low, thus keeping down industrialists' costs. Governments' lack of action to mitigate the forces in rural areas which deprive many households of their livelihood, and governments' discouragement of labour unions, can both act to keep city wages down. Such factors somewhat complicate any careful cost-benefit evaluation in that industries' concentration in large cities may be much influenced by the fact that they pay very little towards the social and environmental costs they generate. Manufacturing and service sector enterprises rarely pay high city taxes to ensure, for instance, that the city government can afford to extend piped water, health care services and provision for the hygienic disposal of household and human wastes to their workforce and the wider labour pool from which they benefit. Manufacturing enterprises rarely have to pay for pollution control equipment or for the safe disposal of toxic liquid and solid wastes; many large cities in the Third World have far higher incidences of air, land and water pollution than First World cities and even where environmental legislation exists to control pollution, it is rarely enforced (Hardoy and Satterthwaite, 1985). Health and safety standards for their workforce often do not exist – or those that do exist are ignored. There may be agglomeration *economies* for many firms (or types of firm) in large cities but agglomeration *costs* are often borne by lower income groups and by national and city governments.

Implicit or explicit in earlier sections has been the suggestion that the best strategy for stimulating development in small and intermediate urban centres is to change those economic, social and political factors which at present inhibit their development and which essentially subsidise capital investment and industrial operations in larger cities. Later sections of this chapter will also describe in more detail how macro-economic priorities and sectoral and pricing policies have directly or indirectly subsidised productive investment in large urban centres. Some governments have sought to limit or to control new industrial investment in certain large cities or to control the movement of labour there; the attempt by the Philippine Government to restrict industrial investment in and around Manila, described in Table 8.1, is one example.

One of the most ambitious plans to control a primate city's growth was the national spatial plan prepared in Egypt in the second half of the Seventies. Cairo was declared 'over-congested' and, with Giza (nearby) and Port Said, was to have its population reduced by the year 2000. Various other areas and urban centres were declared 'saturated' with no more room for population growth. Meanwhile, much of Egypt's projected population growth between 1978 and 2000 was to be accommodated in various satellite cities around Cairo and Alexandria (Egypt's second largest city), the Canal Zone and the so-called 'virgin areas' which included the Red Sea Coast, the New Valley, the area around Mirsa Matruh and the Sinai. These four 'virgin' areas which had relatively little population in 1978 were to have 14 million people by the year 2000. Such a radical attempt to completely reshape population distribution and to halt and then reverse Cairo's population growth seems unimplementable. Cairo's first masterplan, published in 1958, suggested that Cairo's population should be kept to 3.5 million; current estimates suggest that it has around three times this population today.

But what is more relevant to this book is the fact that such a plan calls for enormous public investments in the 'virgin areas' and the new satellite cities. This can only drain resources that could have been used to improve infrastructure and basic services in all the small and intermediate urban centres and rural settlements in the Nile Valley and Delta. Even if private investment is persuaded to go to the three large, new satellite cities in the desert, 50 kilometres or more from Cairo, and indeed to the 'virgin areas', one wonders at what cost to the government in terms of public investment and incentives. A careful examination of current trends within the national economy and of the developmental possibilites in certain existing intermediate urban centres might well point to many cheaper and more effective ways of managing Cairo's physical growth and population growth. Jenssen, Kunzmann and Saad-El Din (1979) suggest a possible deconcentration of population to selected urban settlements within Cairo's metropolitan region. But as in most Third World cities, there are also substantial amounts of undeveloped or poorly utilised land within Greater Cairo (US AID, 1977). Their appropriate development could ease the uncontrolled physical growth of Greater Cairo over valuable and scarce irrigated farmland, which was one of the justifications for the elaborate spatial plan.[4]

Some governments have also tried to slow population growth in primate cities by seeking to prevent in-migration or forcing out-migration. Indeed, several governments have tried to forcibly relocate those inhabitants of large cities which they judge to be 'unemployed' or 'non-functional' to the cities' economy. Such public actions seemed to diminish during the Seventies; governments began to recognise the high social and economic cost of bulldozing squatter settlements and to recognise the importance of the contribution made to the city's economy by the inhabitants of such settlements. But in several nations, government attitudes seem to be returning to forced relocation programmes again; no doubt, economic crises or rapid migration into cities by those fleeing droughts or wars have helped trigger this. However, if migration flows are essentially responses to the location of better economic opportunities or rational choices about how best to survive (which research into migration in the Third World supports), then migration patterns are one effect of the changing spatial distribution of economic opportunities. The assumption by governments that many of the people in a large city are 'unemployed' or not functional to that city's economy and thus should be forced out to other areas has rarely (if ever) been shown to have any economic rationale and usually implies considerable suffering on the part of those forced to move. Rapid in-migration to any urban centre (whether small, intermediate or large) is the migrants' response to changing economic circumstances. Table 8.3 gives some examples of the extent to which certain large cities contain a high proportion of the non-agricultural enterprises within their national economies. Strong net migration flows to such cities as they came to concentrate such a high proportion of investment is hardly surprising. If governments are concerned about the size of such migration flows, then they are best changed by addressing the causes of such flows.

Table 8.3: *Examples of primacy in terms of one city's dominance in national production or trade*

Nairobi (Kenya):   In 1975, it had 57 per cent of all Kenya's manufacturing employment and 67 per cent of its industrial plants in 1974. By 1975, Nairobi and its industrial satellite, Thika, had 61 per cent of all industrial wage employment (Richardson, 1980). In 1979, it contained 5 per cent of the national population.

Abidjan (Ivory Coast):   In 1978, some 70 per cent of the nation's economic and commercial transactions were said to take place in Abidjan (Ivory Coast, government of, 1984). On this same date, it contained around 15 per cent of the national population.

Manila (Philippines):   Metropolitan Manila produces one-third of the nation's GNP, handles 70 per cent of all imports and contains 60 per cent of all manufacturing establishments (Apacible and Yaxley, 1979). In 1981, it contained around 13 per cent of the national population.

Lima (Peru):   The metropolitan area of Lima accounts for 43 per cent of GDP, four fifths of bank credit and consumer goods production and for more than nine-tenths of capital goods production in Peru (Richardson, 1984). In 1981, it contained around 27 per cent of the national population.

Managua (Nicaragua):   A report in 1983 stated that Managua concentrated 25 per cent of the national population and 38 per cent of the GDP (MIN-VAH, 1983).

Lagos (Nigeria):   By 1978 it was reported to handle over 40 per cent of the nation's external trade, account for over 57 per cent of total value added in manufacturing and contain over 40 per cent of Nigeria's highly skilled manpower. It contains only some 5 per cent of the national population (Chapter 6).

Mexico City (Mexico):   In 1970, with 18 per cent of the national population it contained 30 per cent of total employment in manufacturing, 28 per cent of employment in commerce, 38 per cent of employment in services, 69 per

cent of employment in national government, 62 per cent of national investment in higher education and 80 per cent of research activities. In 1965 it
contained 44 per cent of national bank deposits and 61 per cent of national
credits (Scott, 1982).

Sao Paulo (Brazil):   Greater Sao Paulo, with 12.7 million inhabitants in
1980, contained around one-tenth of the national population and contributed one-quarter of the net national product and over 40 per cent of Brazil's
industrial value-added (Hamer, 1984).

Rangoon (Burma):   Located at the centre of the national transport and
communications network, Rangoon is the economic, political and administrative heart of Burma. It is the dominant tertiary service centre and
virtually all the import and export trade passes through its port. More than
half of Burma's manufacturing industry is said to be located there (Leonard,
1985). In 1981, it contained 6 per cent of the national population.

Port Au Prince (Haiti):   Approximately 40 per cent of the national income
is produced within the capital although only 14 per cent of the national
population live there. It virtually monopolises all urban economic activities.
'Its primacy is buttressed by both a highly centralised political and administrative system as well as development policies geared towards the manufacturing sector which have favoured a high level of expenditures within
Port-au-Prince.' (US AID, 1980, p. 22)

Notes: a—The share in national urban population of each of these cities
or metropolitan centres is not given since the different criteria
used by national governments as to what constitutes an urban
centre within national censuses varies so much as to give little
validity to such international comparisons.

Governments which have recently tried to transport some of the
people in their primate city back into the countryside or to other
locations might consider the current spatial distribution of economic
opportunities and the extent to which government expenditure and
policy is in fact responsible for the prevailing migration flows. It is
perhaps worth noting that while colonial governments often achieved
a control of migration movements, the only government within a
'market' or 'mixed' economy with a 'relatively successful' long-term
policy to control migration flows to large cities is South Africa. There,
apartheid with its denial to the majority of the country's population
of their most basic political, economic and social rights also denies
them the right of free movement in response to, for example, the
lack of employment and the poverty in the homelands to which many
of them have been forcibly relocated. The example is relevant only
in that it shows the degree of government repression and control
which is needed for a long-term policy to control migration flows to
major cities. And even though the controls on migration are so severe
with illegal migrants facing jail, forced relocation to their 'homeland'
and even police brutality, there are still strong 'illegal' in-migration
flows to major city regions such as Johannesburg and Cape Town.
Most actions by Third World governments to decentralise urban devel-

opment, however, have been based not on controls on investments or migration flows into large cities but on the initiatives to stimulate urban development outside large urban centres, as discussed already.

As national governments and the governments of larger urban centres are confronted with large and usually growing populations in inner city slums and illegal housing developments in squatter settlements or on illegal subdivisions, the idea of a nation's urban system appearing to be dominated by a single city or being 'unbalanced' because of the size of the largest city relative to other urban centres has often been used to justify special policies for small and intermediate urban centres. But the empirical findings presented earlier suggest that such judgements – usually based on mathematical abstractions on degree of 'primacy' – seem of little value in assessing government's potential role either in slowing large cities' growth or in stimulating smaller urban centres' development. As Richardson (1977) comments, 'attempts to control and influence city sizes to conform to some preconceived theoretical model (e.g. rank size distribution) are usually unsound'. In this volume, the various statistical techniques for determining whether a national or regional urban system is characterised by being a 'primate city dominated' or 'unbalanced' are not discussed; the lack of utility in such discussions has been covered elsewhere.

However, there is one question about small and intermediate urban centres which is of great relevance to governments. This is whether the exisiting concentration of urban based activities in the largest urban centre (or centres) is serving national, social and economic development goals. This is a question which can only be addressed first, by examining the factors particular to each nation or region which are causing or contributing to the largest centres' economic and population growth; secondly by considering the social and economic costs and benefits of current urban trends; thirdly by evaluating the role of government policies and structure in contributing to or causing these trends; and fourthly, and perhaps most importantly in the context of this book, in evaluating the extent to which changes or innovations in government policies to lessen this concentration would further social and economic development.

Such a consideration may also reveal regional concentrations of productive activities which are missed by a focus only on the distribution of urban population among different urban centres. For instance, many of the larger, more populous and more industrialised Latin American nations have what might be termed 'regional' rather than 'city' primacy – for instance the La Plata-Buenos Aires-Campana-Zarate-San Nicolas-Rosario-San Lorenzo region in Argentina; Caracas-La Guaira-Maracay-Valencia in Venezuela; the triangle of Rio de Janeiro, Sao Paulo and Belo Horizonte in Brazil; and Mexico City-Toluca-Cuernavaca-Puebla   in   Mexico.   Comparable concentrations of productive activities within a region seem to be occurring in and around many other Third World cities such as Bombay, Lagos, Manila, Lima and Abidjan.

Strengthening local government

As noted already, power and resources are frequently highly centralised within Third World government structures; usually much more so than in First World nations. And the centralisation of power and resources is known to contribute to the domination of a national urban system by one or a few major cities. Similarly, stronger and more effective 'local' governments are known to be a factor in influencing a less primate city dominated urban system.

It is also increasingly argued that a stronger and more effective 'local' government can make valuable contributions to national and local development goals. This has an important bearing on intermediate urban centres not only from the point of view of their own urban governments but also because they are frequently the location of sub-national and sub-regional levels of government.[5] The lack of power, personnel and resources at these levels of government means that small and intermediate urban centres cannot play such important developmental roles as: the centres through which sub-national and sub-regional populations' needs and priorities are articulated and passed to higher levels of government; the centres from where many sub-national and all sub-regional resources and development potentials are assessed; the centres through which many developmental tasks are planned and implemented, taking the responsibilities off national agencies; the centres through which infrastructure and public services should be provided and maintained for urban centres and for the region or sub-region over which they have administrative jurisdiction; and the centres through which local revenues are raised.

National and sometimes sub-national levels of government are too distant and too far removed from the local realities to be able to undertake many essential developmental tasks. As a newly published review of recent experiences concerning decentralisation in the Third World noted, centralisation can bring some heavy costs:

> A ministry of agriculture that applies crop production quotas to all areas of the country without taking regional variations in soil and climate conditions into account ... hinders production and wastes resources. When central planners design rural development projects in the national capital without thoroughly understanding local, social, economic, physical and organisation conditions, they often generate opposition among local groups or encounter such apathy that the projects are doomed to failure at the outset. Overworked and cautious central finance officers, who typically are responsible for approving even petty expenditures for local devel-

opment projects, often release funds for agricultural projects so late in the fiscal year that optimal planting times are missed ... Central administrators cannot know the complex variety of factors that affect the success of projects in local communities throughout the country. In their attempt to cope with this uncertainty, they create highly centralised and standardised procedures; or through fear of making mistakes, they do nothing about urgent decisions that are essential for implementing local projects and programs'. (Rondinelli, Nellis and Cheema, 1984, pp. 3-4)

Local levels of government should also have the resources and staff to ensure better co-ordination between the various public agencies and ministries working on sectoral projects within or affecting their area.

Although the amount of documentation about government at sub-national, sub-regional and sub-metropolitan area is not very extensive – and there is a tendency to refer to all of these as 'local government' which makes it difficult to distinguish between these different levels – what exists suggests that sub-national, sub-regional and urban levels of government are often very weak. Existing literature suggests that typically they lack the funds and the staff to carry out either those tasks assigned to them or the tasks which are most effectively under-taken by government at their level. In a World Bank paper about strengthening local government, Cochrane (1983) noted that many local governments are 'fragmented, confused about their functions and all too often either invisible or largely ceremonial' (p. 5).

Latin American nations provide a number of examples. There, as in most African and Asian nations, local governments generally have difficulty in covering their operating expenses, training the personnel they need, purchasing equipment, making organisational improve-ments, obtaining technical assistance and expanding the range and quality of public services (Rondinelli, Nellis and Cheema, 1984). Townroe (1982) notes that even in Sao Paulo State, Brazil, one of the richest and most industrialised areas in Latin America, munici-palities' abilities to raise finances either to offer industrial incentives or to prepare infrastructure improvements and factory sites in advance of demand is very circumspect. In Thailand, total munic-ipal expenditure in all urban centres other than Bangkok was less than one per cent of total public sector expenditure in 1980 (ESCAP 1984). In studies of policies for intermediate urban centres in Tunisia, Kenya, Brazil, South Korea and Indonesia, Rivkin (1982) noted that central rather than local government was the principal source of public investment capital in such centres.

One of the problems confronting local governments is their lack of capital for investment within their area of jurisdiction. Cochrane (1983) notes that higher levels of government generally take the most lucrative, elastic and easily collected taxes such as income tax. If these are largely spent on government administration and services (often concentrated in the national capital) and sectoral projects which also favour larger cities, the spatial bias is obvious. Little attempt has been made by national governments to guarantee lower levels of government the power and skilled personnel they need to develop and collect their own revenue base. Bird (1978) notes that in most Third World nations, there is a truly 'formidable list of restraints on the taxing powers of local authorities' (p. 68) and that 'access by urban area governments to the most productive tax sources is commonly denied or severely restricted' (p. 69). Indeed, most small and intermediate urban centres lack an up-to-date cadastral survey which is essential for any planning and important for any revenue collection based on land or property. Lower levels of government frequently lack the personnel to plan and implement improvements in local infrastructure and services; indeed their funding and personnel base is so weak that they often cannot adequately maintain what they already have.

Cochrane (1983) notes that the national goverment may be the most efficient collector of certain taxes, in which case the issue is not so much who collects the taxes but who receives them once they are collected. But the very heavy dependence of lower levels of government on grants from national (or on occasion sub-national) levels of government can mean that these are among the first expenditures to be cut when cutbacks are undertaken. And perhaps more importantly, only lower levels of government are able to collect efficiently many kinds of taxes (such as property taxes) and other revenues such as user charges for public utilities. A failure to ensure that lower levels of government have the power, personnel and resources to collect such revenue – and to keep tax assessment procedures up to date – means a wasted resource for development. A training exercise for local government officials in the Philippines included mapping many local government units; in so doing, it was discovered that just collecting the property tax from only a few of the largest property tax delinquents would be equal to one year's total local government revenue (Cochrane, 1983). A similar exercise in Ghana found that the potential returns from local revenues from a variety of taxes, fees, tolls and licences were usually five times or more the amount collected. In one district, the amount collected in 1980-81 was more than four times that collected in 1978-79 (Warrena and Issachar, 1981, quoted in Cochrane, 1983).

In general, First World nations have government structures far less dominated by national government. For instance, 69 per cent of the government wage bill in Japan is paid to local government officials; in Denmark it is almost 70 per cent and in Netherlands 58 per cent. Although data on local government personnel in the Third World is lacking, its share in total government wage bills is likely to be much smaller than in most Western nations, particularly in the case of Africa. Similarly, the number of local government employees outnumber central government employees in such nations as Japan, the United Kingdom and the United States – by a factor of more than 3:1 in the United States. But in nations such as the Philippines, India and El Salvador the reverse is true – most especially in the Philippines (Cochrane, 1983). In 1972, there were 74 established posts for economists in Lusaka, Zambia's capital but 'not a single economist or planning specialist in the provinces' (Chambers, 1974, p. 117, quoted in Johnston and Clark, 1982). This gives some idea of the relative strengths of national and sub-national levels of government, although there are central government employees in sub-national government administrations as, for instance, representatives of national ministries.

Clearly, the need to strengthen and consolidate national unity after Independence has been one factor in this centralisation. Perhaps another which helps explain differences between First World and Third World nations is that strong local governments developed much earlier in the First World and thus, as national government came to play a larger role in economic development, local governments were already sufficiently powerful, established and organised to ensure that their roles remained important as national governments' roles and tasks increased.

In several Third World nations, governments have recently sought to strengthen sub-national and sub-regional levels of goverment. For instance, in Nigeria, the process by which the national territory was increasingly subdivided into states (from three regions inherited from colonial rule to four, then to 12 states in 1967, 19 in 1976 and the designation of a Federal Capital Territory) has strengthened the urban centres chosen as state capitals; however, most of the state governments' resources come from their allocation of oil revenues from Federal Government and not from their own tax base (O'Connor 1984). A reform of local goverment below the level of the States in 1976 has sought to rationalise this level of government but it also has limited powers to raise revenues. It largely depends on annual statutory grants from federal and state governments (Rondinelli, Nellis and Cheema, 1983). It is not yet clear whether the resources allocated to this level of government will match the responsibilities it has been given. In the Sudan, the sub-division of the national territory into an increasing number of provinces and the recent move to devolve a large portion of government to six regional governments has provided some stimulus to the development of certain of the intermediate urban centres which serve as regional capitals.

A comparable stimulus to certain intermediate urban centres can be seen in Tanzania with the decentralisation of government employees to provincial capitals in the early Seventies and the more recent moves to strengthen this level of government. In China, Kwok (1984) documents how changes in national government policy in terms of centralisation or decentralisation of power or resources affected smaller urban centres with less than 100,000 inhabitants. For those periods during the last 30 years when local authorities were given a greater share in planning and management of production and distribution of services and income, small urban centres' development was stimulated. The stimulus was lessened or disappeared when administrative centralisation was the rule (as, for instance, between 1949 and 1957). In Cuba in 1976, elected local government was established as part of a long-running goal of the government to lessen Havana's dominance (Gugler, 1980).

But the long-term stimulus to a small or intermediate urban centre deriving from decentralisation of power and resources to the administration located there depends on the extent to which this increase in power and resources allows the administration to stimulate increased production in and around the centre. Although it is far beyond the scope of this book to discuss reforms in local government and the decentralisation of power and resources in general, this is clearly a subject of considerable relevance to stimulating the role of small and intermediate urban centres in national and regional development strategies. Indeed, most of the aims and objectives of a special government policy on small and intermediate urban centres can only be achieved if lower levels of government acquire more power, resources and trained personnel. As Linn (1983) notes,

> the quality of management by the urban authorities may have an important effect on whether and how a city grows... Among the elements of urban management at issue here are: the provision of adequate public utilities for industry and commerce; the existence of a well functioning urban transport system for the speedy distribution of goods and services; availability of developed land for new industrial developments; adequate public marketing facilities, both wholesale and retail; a good communications system (telephones and postal); and a public administration that minimises efficiency losses and compliance costs for regulations and taxes (p. 57-57).

Thus for sub-national and sub-regional governments, more successful regional and local development plans almost certainly depend on an increase in their power, resources and trained personnel. 'Central government's attempts to stimulate economic growth are likely to be improved significantly with assistance from local government ... central government cannot afford to ignore the manpower resources available at local level; neither can local government afford to ignore the assistance central government could give towards upgrading performance of local government workforce' (Cochrane, 1983, pp. 49-

50). Similarly, Uphoff and Esman (1974) in their study *Local Organisation for Rural Development in Asia* note that:

'... successful local ... and participatory development depends very much on a high frequency of both top down and from below development impulses: local automony in isolation provides little leverage for development' (quoted in Douglass, 1981).

Macro-economic policies and sectoral biases

One of the most powerful mix of factors influencing where urban development takes place and the form it takes, arises from the social and economic orientation of the national government and the sectoral and development priorities it implements. We have already noted how in a centrally planned economy the form that an urban system and its evolution over time takes is unlikely to be similar to that in an economy where market forces are much more influential in resource allocations. And clearly, as Lentnek and Green (1985) point out, where government plays a significant role in economic planning (which it does in most Third World nations), the choice by government as to which economic sectors to emphasise and the choice of industries within these sectors, has a major influence on the form that developments take in the urban system. Sectoral and industrial choices can also have important influences on income distribution, both socially and spatially, which in turn influences urban change. Lentnek and Green also discuss the different implications for changes in the urban system that a priority given to, say, basic industries has compared to priority to exports or to an agriculture-based settlement strategy. Care must be taken, however, in seeking to fit nations into any one category. For example, the discussion of the changes in developmental orientation in China beteen 1949 up to 1980 presented earlier (Kwok, 1982) warns against categorising China's chosen development path as simply an agriculture based settlement strategy.

Despite Tanzania's villagisation programme, characterising its government's development strategy as an agriculture-based settlement strategy tends to obscure changes in priorities since gaining Independence in 1961. As will be discussed later, the government's agricultural price policy could not be said to favour farmers, during the Seventies.

Thus, to understand how and why a national or regional urban system is changing, it is important to understand how national government's past and present economic and development orientation are influencing it. For instance, Scott (1982) describes how many of the forces listed in Map 8.1 which influence the spatial distribution of urban development helped reinforce the dominance of Mexico

City's Federal district within Mexico. These included public investment in infrastructure (transport, power and water) in which the
Federal District received the largest share of total outlays; education
(in which the Federal District 'again received a disproportionately
large share of the total', p. 111), administration (because of its role
as the seat of the Federal Government), and subsidised prices for
water, corn, electric power, diesel fuel and public transport in the
Federal District. Furthermore, railroad freight rates 'were structured
to favour routes to or from Mexico City' and property in the Federal
District 'was relatively undervalued for tax purposes, and other states
were taxed at relatively high rates' (p. 118).

Mexico City, or the wider city region, also received many of the
new industries encouraged by Mexico's import substitution policy.
Although a growing body of literature has recently begun to point
to the spatial effects of such factors, their importance relative to
others is not yet clear. Nor is there a clear idea of whether what are
judged to be undesirable spatial impacts of non-spatial policies and
sectoral plans can be lessened without altering their aims and purposes. This section will look in turn at the spatial influences of: public
service provision, macro-economic and pricing policies, spatial biases
in public investments, and spatial biases in subsidising or supporting
industrial investment.

Public service provision

Many studies have shown how government expenditure on low cost
housing and on physical and social services (including water supply
and sanitation, health care, education and public transport) are frequently heavily concentrated in the largest city—or in a few large
urban centres.[6] For instance, a study of education and health services
in Colombian urban centres found that 'a strong positive relationship
existed between service provision and size of city among the larger
cities of the country ... among these cities, the quality of health and
education provided in the larger cities was far superior to that in the
smaller cities. There were no exceptions to this rule.' The number of
doctors and of dentists per thousand inhabitants dropped with declining population size and dropped dramatically for urban centres with
less than 100,000 inhabitants (Gilbert, 1974, quoted in Rondinelli,
1982).

Linn (1982) also noted that per capita expenditure in 1971 by the
city of Bogota's government was almost seven times the average per
capita spending by the municipal governments in urban centres with
between 50,000 and 90,000 inhabitants. In Thailand, Bangkok has
many times the number of doctors and hospital beds per 1,000 inhabitants of most other urban centres while a much higher proportion
of Bangkok's residents have access to electricity and piped water than

in other urban centres; and the two regions encompassing and surrounding Metropolitan Manila in the Philippines have consistently
received a much higher proportion of total investment in buildings,
schools and hospitals than their share in national population would
warrant (Rondinelli, 1982). In Indonesia, in 1980, 30 per cent of all
households in Jakarta (the primate city and national capital) received
piped water compared to a figure of 23 per cent for Bandung (Indonesia's third largest urban centre) and a figure of little more than 10
per cent for households in urban centres in the province of West
Java other than those in Jakarta and Bandung (ESCAP, 1984).

In Mexico, the Federal District within Mexico City's Metropolitan
Area is approximately three times better off than the national average
for doctors and hospital beds (Ward, 1985). Many other examples
could be given of the high concentration in primate cities of investments in water supply and sanitation or in housing projects or programmes to improve lower income groups' housing and living
conditions or in services related to health care. This concentration
cannot be explained simply by pointing to the fact that only in larger
urban centres can the more specialised services be efficiently provided;
the concentration of government expenditure in such services in larger
urban centres is usually greater than that implied by the 'optimum'
distribution of different levels of services through the settlement system in terms of impact on health per unit cost.

This concentration has been reinforced by the fact that much of
the multilateral aid given to housing construction or upgrading programmes for lower income groups and to water supply and sanitation,
has also been concentrated in national capitals and large urban
centres. For instance, around three-quarters of the loans given by
the World Bank and the Asian Development Bank for urban development in Asia during the Seventies went either to capital cities or
to urban centres with 500,000 or more inhabitants; a similar proportion of World Bank loans for Africa in this period also went to
capital cities and urban centres with 500,000 or more inhabitants
(Blitzer, Hardoy and Satterthwaite, 1983). However, it is interesting
to note that certain multilateral and bilateral agencies, notably the
World Bank Group, the United Nations Development Programme
and US AID's Office of Housing and Urban Programs, have in recent
years begun to change the concentration of aid for urban projects
in the largest cities to include small and intermediate urban centres,
while others are at least beginning to discuss whether they should do
so.

One final example of the spatial bias in national governments'
investments in social and physical services is investments in public
transport. For example, the construction of the metro in Santiago,
Chile's primate city, essentially starved other sectors and other urban
areas of much needed investment funds in the late Sixties and first

half of the Seventies. Every person in Chile who directly or indirectly contributed to government revenue helped to finance the construction of a system on which some 500,000 people travel daily and which 'almost' covers its operating costs from revenues from fares (Ortuzar, 1983).

Comparable biases in terms of concentrating investments or subsidies in public transport in primate cities could be given for many other nations, including metros in Caracas, Lagos and Mexico City.

But as Linn (1982) points out, the crucial issue is far more the spatial distribution of government subsidies on social and physical services rather than the spatial distribution of government investments. High per capita investments in larger urban centres also reflect higher 'demand' there, ie more people with the ability to pay for social and physical services. However, most of the examples in the previous paragraphs cannot be explained simply by the higher demand that exists in larger urban centres. Indeed, despite higher demand in larger urban centres, large subsidies are frequently given to social and physical services even though a high proportion of the lower income groups – such as those living in shelters built on illegal subdivisions or in squatter settlements – may not have access to these services.

Prices for enterprises and households fortunate enough to be connected to piped water supplies and sewage systems rarely reflect the real cost of providing these services or of increasing the capacity to cope with increased demand. Automobile owners in large cities rarely pay the full cost of city or national government expenditure to ease traffic congestion; indeed such automobile owners may be heavily subsidised by taxpayers from all over the nation who have to pay for the highways, ring roads and other facilities designed to ease traffic congestion in the large cities. As Hamer (1984) notes, firms and workers in larger urban centres contribute to the creation of negative externalities such as pollution and congestion yet these economic agents are rarely taxed to help pay for the costs these impose on city inhabitants and city or national governments. Firms and middle and upper income groups (since these are generally the ones to receive subsidised infrastructure and services and who own automobiles) are thus subsidised from resources raised nationally. Yet these are the groups with the highest ability to pay for the full cost of the pollution, congestion and public service provision which they generate or receive. It has been suggested that governments' failure to structure prices to reflect real costs in larger urban centres has provided a strong stimulus to over-concentration of production and urban population there.

In addition, there seem to be few (if any) cost penalties in improving service provision in small and intermediate urban centres. Linn (1982) and Kalbermatten, Julius and Gunnerson (1980) demonstrate how the per capita costs of providing many basic social and physical services do not necessarily decrease with population size in urban centres. For instance, Linn (1982) states that

> water supply and sewerage systems typically involve technological economies of scale for given technologies, but the potential cost savings from increased size are counteracted by a number of factors: first, human settlements do not grow in discrete jumps but continuously over time. Thus, capacity must be added sequentially, frequently involving units of constant rather than increasing size. Second, as cities grow they tend to expand into areas which are more difficult and costly to service. Third, increased congestion and pollution, and reduced carrying capacity of the environment associated with increased density and city size, result in the need for more treatment at the source of water and more costly technologies of sewage disposal to ensure comparable levels of environmental quality.
>
> Given the complexity of the cost structure of water supply and sewerage systems and the many different factors influencing these costs (many of which are dependent on very specific hydrological, geological and geographic characteristics of a particular settlement), it is not surprising that comparative estimates of unit costs for settlements of different sizes are very difficult to make. Allowance must also be made for differences in quality of service, in capacity utilisation, and many other factors in order to avoid estimation biases. Usually, this is not done and therefore any correlation between unit costs and settlement size may be quite spurious. On the other hand, engineering cost studies, such as the one carried out by the Stanford Research Institute for India, tend to show declining costs because they capture the impact of economies of scale and density but fail to allow for differences in accessibility to water resources, for differential needs for sewerage-treatment and disposal technologies, and for the fact that systems are built sequentially. As a result of these estimation difficulties, very few cost studies emerge with reliable conclusions regarding the impact of settlement size and density on water supply and sewerage costs (pp. 636-637).

The claim that the installation of piped water supplies and systems to dispose of human wastes is too expensive for small and intermediate urban centres is also frequently based on cost estimates for installing systems to First World standards. World Bank research involving field studies in 39 communities in 14 nations found a wide range of household and community systems which would greatly improve the hygienic disposal of human wastes. Within this range were options which could be implemented to match local physical conditions, social preferences and economic resources. Several of these options had a total annual cost per household of between one-tenth and one-twentieth that of conventional sewerage systems both in terms of investment and recurring costs. Most demanded far lower volumes of water to allow for their efficient operation while some demanded no water at all, although household water needs for drinking, cooking and washing were essential. It is also possible to install one of the lower cost technologies initially and over time upgrade it in a series of steps (Kalbermatten, Julius and Gunnerson, 1980). Similarly, improvements in the quality of water supply and its availability may indeed be self financing in many urban centres. Many urban residents at present have high daily expenditures buying water from water vendors when a proper piped water system can often provide a far more economical and accessible supply for similar costs (Briscoe, 1983).

For solid waste disposal, existing empirical evidence suggests that costs 'are largely invariant with city size on a per unit basis' (Linn, 1982, p. 640). For public transport, clearly per capita costs are likely to rise with city size but then so too is demand. But in many intermediate urban centres, appropriately designed public transport systems may well be largely self-financing. Providing basic health care services and schools is likely to be cheaper in small and intermediate urban centres than in larger urban centres (land and labour costs are cheaper there) if facilities are appropriately located within the urban hierarchy to provide maximum accessibility at minimum unit costs. Unit costs for police and for fire fighting probably increase with city size, as more sophisticated equipment and organisation is required (Linn, 1982).

It is interesting to note in this context that in Cuba, it has been the primate city which suffered from a spatial bias in public spending on housing and service provision, at least up to 1970. While there is considerable debate as to the net costs and benefits of the Cuban government's spatial policies, the high quality of social and physical services available in rural areas and in small and intermediate urban centres has helped reduce the primacy of Havana and has contributed to an exceptionally high average life expectancy for a Third World nation and, in recent years, a relatively low rate of infant mortality (Gugler, 1980 and World Bank, 1984).

Thus, it does not seem too optimistic to say that if governments at sub-national, sub-regional and small and intermediate urban centre level have more power, resources and personnel, the wider provision of public services can be achieved outside the larger urban centres without major cost penalties. Indeed, on occasion, per capita costs will be lower and in some instances, largely recoverable from user charges, if the technology and organisation for the provision of each particular service is chosen to match the needs and resources of that particular locality.

Macro-economic and pricing policies

Various recent papers (Richardson, 1984; Renaud, 1981; Ruane 1982 and 1982b; Townroe 1979 and 1982; Douglass 1981; Mohan, 1983; Filani, 1981) have pointed to the powerful spatial impacts of various macro-economic policies such as those which promote import substitution or affect national exchange rates. Similarly the sectors, activities or incomes which governments choose to tax and the sectors or activities in which they choose to invest or to subsidise can also have powerful spatial impacts. In this section, brief comments are made about the spatial influences of various non-spatial policies, although as noted earlier, more often than not it is a combination of these policies which is in force in a country, at any one time.

Import Substitution Government support for the development of particular industries or industrial sectors through providing them with some protection from competition by imports (whether through subjecting imports to tariff barriers, or quotas or through some other protectionist policy) has the effect of subsidising productive investments in the locations which best serve the new or expanding protected industrial activities.[7] In most Third World nations, it is the larger cities (and often only the largest city) which have been the favoured locations for protected industries, although a few governments have also encouraged import substitution and industrial development outside the primate city at the same time. One of the reasons for the increasing domination of national capitals in national production in Latin American nations after the 1930s was the support given by governments to import substitution; most new industries became established in national capitals and/or large cities. Tyler (1983) describes the complex mix of sectoral incentives in Brazil, including those used to restrict imports, and how this mix changed over time, reflecting both changes in government priorities and changes in the world market. Although imports have been restricted or controlled by direct or indirect means for decades, it was in response to balance of payment problems arising from the oil price rise of 1973-74 that the move began to increase import restrictions. Such restrictions include tariffs, *de facto* surcharges on imports, import licences, import quotas and the prohibition of certain products. The paper analyses the sectoral and spatial impacts of these and of sectoral incentives such as fiscal and credit subsidies, export controls and domestic price controls. Overall, sectoral incentive policies provide the greatest protection to sectors located in the higher income south-east while discriminating against the south and the north-east. The states of Sao Paulo and Rio de Janeiro in the south-east are the main beneficiaries. 'Their benefit, however, comes at the expense of the country's poorer states such as Ceara and Pernambuco' (ibid, p. 39), both of which are in the north-east. Within Sao Paulo State, Greater Sao Paulo metropolitan area benefited more than the rest of the state.

Richardson (1984) notes that both the import-substitution policy adopted in Peru and the growth of a central government benefited Lima, the national capital and much the largest city, at the expense of the rest of Peru. Scott (1982) describes how Mexico City or the area around the city, received a high proportion of the investment and employment generated by new manufacturing whose market was protected and/or whose production was subsidised. Jones (1982) notes how manufacturing industries in Caracas and Valencia had been the major beneficiaries of the Venezuelan government's import substitution policies during the Sixties. Thus, in the case of Brazil, Peru, Mexico and Venezuela, at least for substantial periods of time, the economic interests served by import substitution prevailed on governments to implement policies favourable to them; the net spatial effect, in broad terms, seems to have been that of helping concentrate industrial development in the largest urban centres.

In sub-Saharan African nations, the support for import substitution industries since Independence has encouraged most new industries to set up in the largest urban centres. In a report on trade protection and industrial incentives in Nigeria, for example, the Lagos region was found to receive some 90 per cent of the indirect subsidies provided by national trade policies (Renaud, 1981). Daly (1977) noted that import-substitution industries in Nigeria are 'often high cost, tariff-protected and monopolistic enterprises' (p. 2, quoted in Filani, 1981). Filani noted the 'spectacular' spatial implication of Nigeria's import substitution strategy by pointing out that apart from Lagos (which had been the main beneficiary), Port Harcourt (along with Lagos, one of the major ports) and some regional capitals and cities strategically placed on major transport routes had also benefited considerably. Filani also noted that Metropolitan Lagos's dominance of the entire nation in terms of concentration of industry is also mirrored within states by state capitals.

Douglass (1981) notes that in Thailand, by the end of the Sixties, 'full duty exemption on capital goods and raw material imports was given for protected industry, which almost without exception chose to locate in the metropolitan area', that is Bangkok, the primate city. Between 1960 and 1973, '86 per cent of all new, promoted industry' located in Bangkok metropolitan area (p. 194). Mohan (1983) suggests that the strong support for import substitution and trade protection in India may be one of the reasons for the fact that a large proportion of the industrial growth since the mid-Fifties has occurred in inland cities such as Bangalore, Delhi and Hyderabad; meanwhile the great port cities of Calcutta and Madras have languished.

An example from Pakistan shows the very high subsidies which import substitution can receive – which in effect means heavy subsidies to certain manufacturing operations which tend to be in large cities. In 1963-64

the average annual subsidy to large scale manufacturing and the corresponding implicit tax on agriculture represented 6.6 per cent of total domestic expenditures. The conventional contribution of industry was measured at 7.0 per cent; its actual contribution after allowing for protection was estimated to be a dismal 0.4 per cent of domestic value added' (Beier, Churchill, Cohen and Renaud, 1975, page 47).

In addition, lengthy and complex procedures for importing machinery or production inputs will work to the disadvantage of individuals and enterprises outside the major ports and centres of government which are so often also the primate city. It can also take up an inordinate amount of administrative capacity (which in itself may be a scarce resource) and create bottlenecks in production because critical inputs are not available in the right quantity or at the right time (World Bank, 1981).

Trade and exchange rate policies in many sub-Saharan African nations are systematically biased against exports and in favour of import substitution industries producing consumer goods with little local value added (e.g. packaging and assembly type operations) – some of which actually lose foreign exchange rather than save it. Furthermore, such policies may encourage an expansion of manufacturing industries which make little use of local materials and, because they favour packaging and assembly type operations, create relatively little employment (including hoped for multiplier linkages) and mean little support for skill development. In Zambia, for example, the expansion of manufacturing for the domestic market has not been based on developing the considerable agricultural potential (which could, in turn, support smaller urban centres' development) but on textiles, rubber and chemicals, all of which are highly dependent on imported inputs (World Bank, 1981).

Many governments have also restricted imports to conserve foreign exchange. In sub-Saharan Africa, more and more nations have higher tariffs, quotas and bans on what are judged to be 'non-essential' imports which reinforce import substitution industrialisation policies. With increasing balance of payments crises, such restrictions intensified the import substitution bias. To give only one illustration of possible effects, in Burkina Faso (formerly Upper Volta), engines used for irrigation pumps had to pay a 58 per cent tariff (World Bank, 1981). The spatial bias of such policies is evident, even if it is impossible to be precise about their exact effect on small and intermediate urban centres.

National exchange rate policy   If a nation's currency maintains a high exchange rate with the currencies of its main trading partners, this will tend to cheapen imports and reduce returns for exporters. The (not very extensive) documentation on the sectoral and spatial effects of 'over-valued' national currencies suggests that such action can have the effect of subsidising goods for those living in or close to large cities since a high proportion of the households who can afford to purchase imported goods live there.[8] It lowers incomes and inhibits growth in production in certain rural areas in most Third World nations since they still rely heavily on primary commodities for export earnings. One reason for the rapid growth of Lagos City and metropolitan area and other large urban centres in Nigeria has been the fact that during the Seventies, oil exports helped keep the exchange rate of the naira high against other currencies. This led to extremely unattractive prices for export crops and lowered the cost of imports, including imported basic foodstuffs (O'Connor, 1984). Rural incomes suffered and urban consumers benefited.

During the Seventies, little was done to counteract the damage caused to agricultural production and rural incomes; indeed, most of the revenue derived from oil seems to have been spent on developing production and infrastructure in or serving the larger cities, particularly Lagos and some State capitals. Agriculture and livestock were allocated only six per cent of total planned Federal and State Government expenditure for the 1975-80 Plan, while manufacturing and transport were allocated over 38 per cent (ibid). One of the reasons for the lack of stimulus to urban development in parts of South-West Nigeria (Chapter 6) was the lower return to farmers producing export crops as the naira's exchange rate rose against the currencies of nations to which these crops were exported. Similarly, the fact that the Argentine peso became increasingly strong in the late Seventies against the US dollar and the currencies of other nations to which Argentina exported, seriously affected the income of fruit farmers in the Upper Valley of the Rio Negro, as described in Chapter 2.

In contrast, perhaps the relatively decentralised pattern of industrial development within Taiwan (China), briefly described earlier, owes something to the government's change of its trade policy from import substitution to export promotion in the early Sixties. Labour intensive manufacturing grew rapidly during the Sixties and Seventies and Ho (1979) describes how many of the fastest growing industries set up outside the larger cities to tap the large rural reserve of female labour.

Taxing farmers and subsidising food prices   There is a growing body of literature which describes the various ways in which governments influence the prices of agricultural commodities and the returns farmers receive when selling them. This is linked to an increased interest in analysing the social and economic costs and benefits of government intervention in this area. For instance, Bale and Lutz (1979) look at the effects of agricultural price distortions on output, consumption, trade and rural employment in four Third World nations (Thailand, Egypt, Argentina and Pakistan) and compare them with Japan and various European nations. In each of the four Third World nations, government intervention in setting prices for crops had the effect of taxing the farm sector with large income transfers to urban areas.

Gotsch and Brown (1980) have looked in more detail at prices, subsidies and taxes in Pakistan's agriculture between 1960 and 1976 and come to a similar conclusion. They note how government decisions concerning agricultural prices have to be examined crop by crop since each crop (or agricultural product) involves different interest groups. They also note how the competing interests of agricultural producers, consumers and manufacturers each seek to influence government on policies to serve their interests. In Pakistan, low urban food prices have acted as a way to maintain low wages in industry which, combined with low prices paid for cotton and other raw materials, have sought to enhance industry's competitive position. One reason why cotton prices to farmers have been kept low is the fact that the textile industry was the largest industrial employer and is in the hands of many of Pakistan's most politically powerful families. Farmers receive some compensation for low crop prices through subsidies on such items as fertilisers, improved seeds and tube-well installation. But for the period 1973-1976, the export duties and government profits on just the export of rice, cotton and cotton yarn were greater than the sum of all government subsidies to farmers. For wheat, 'the loss to farmers from receiving less than the world market prices...during 1974 and 1975 was more than ten times as great as the subsidies received from the government' (p. 91). The paper also notes that most of the subsidy payments (and subsidised credit) go to the largest farmers while the impact of lower prices is felt by all farmers who sell some of their output.

Reca (1980) looks in some detail at agricultural prices and subsidies in Argentina, and concludes that high export taxes on grains imply a massive redistribution of income from producers to the benefit of consumers (through lower food prices) and government (through increased revenue). Douglass (1981) describes how national development plans in Thailand between 1961 and 1971 essentially transferred agricultural surpluses to support metropolitan development. A complex revenue collection system known as the 'rice premium' essentially placed the tax burden on rice farmers, keeping domestic rice prices substantially lower than international prices; farm-gate prices were less than 40 per cent of international prices.

One of the major factors put forward to explain agriculture's poor performance in sub-Saharan Africa has been the low prices farmers have received for their products – in addition to such exogenous factors as poor and unpredictable rains. While declining 'real prices' for the most important cash-crop, commodities have been an important factor in this. So too has government intervention – in setting food prices, in taxing certain crops, in providing cheap imported food and in exchange rate controls (World Bank, 1981). Export crop production has been discouraged not only by prevailing exchange rates but by heavy taxes levied on the crops themselves. Producers in many sub-Saharan African nations frequently receive less than half the real value of their crops; for example in Ghana, one of the main reasons for the rapid decline in cocoa prices has been the heavy tax imposed on farmers by the government through the Cocoa Marketing Board's price policies.

Food production for the domestic market has often been discouraged by the low prices set by governments, by policies allowing the import of foodstuffs and their cheap sale at low prices and by the lack of government support for research, for agricultural extension services and for infrastructure to stimulate domestic production. Ellis (1982) describes how the Tanzanian Government's agricultural price policy between 1969 and 1980 effected a large cumulative transfer of resources from peasant producers of export crops to the state. But for most domestic crops, low prices were also paid which discouraged increased production; prices for domestic crops declined sharply in real terms between 1969 and 1974 although for certain crops, prices in real terms improved between 1974 and 1979.

The various ways and means by which agricultural production can be increased and sub-Saharan African nations' economies made less dependent on uncertain rainfall and uncertain supplies of imports are far beyond the scope of this book. But for many nations in sub-Saharan Africa (and indeed other Third World nations) which now face large import bills for food, and have limited possibilities for earning foreign exchange other than through agricultural exports, a more dynamic and more diversified agricultural sector based on smallholder production[9] and on maximising 'value added' in any crop either for domestic consumption or for export has been shown to provide a powerful stimulus to the growth and development of small and intermediate urban centres. It can also considerably expand the scale of national and regional consumer demand and thus boost industrial and commercial development. In addition, the ways in which governments support the provision of inputs into farming and the collection, processing, packing and storing of crop production also affects small and intermediate urban centres – as examples already given demonstrate. Large, hierarchically organised public institutions involved in such operations tend to replace diverse private sector enterprises located in small and intermediate urban centres.

Spatial biases in public investments

Quite apart from the spatial biases in governments' 'non-spatial' policies, like taxation and controls on imports, and in the provision of social and physical services, already discussed, the form and location of all government spending has spatial effects. For instance, improvements or additions to road systems change the spatial pattern of comparative advantage for different economic activities; intra-regional roads and radial roads serving a major city have frequently promoted growth in intermediate urban centres close by. Or they can suddenly provide a fertile agricultural area with access to a major extra-regional market with a consequent growth in population, production and urbanisation. Investments in flood control and irrigation can also provide the basis for rapid growth in agricultural production. Public investment in liquid waste disposal systems and water and electricity supplies enhance certain urban centres' attraction for productive investment. So too do public service provisions in the form of health and education services at different levels. Although we have found few attempts to analyse the spatial implications of national development plans and of public investments, many such plans seem to contain strong spatial biases favouring a concentration of productive investments in larger cities, or of infrastructure to support such investments. Very rarely does agriculture receive a share in investment commensurate with its contribution to GDP, to foreign exchange earnings, to governments' tax base and to employment. Obviously this impinges on many small and intermediate urban centres since their prosperity and growth potential so often depends on rising production and rising incomes for the agricultural population living close by.

It is not uncommon to find governments' sectoral goals – or the goals implicit in the planned sectoral allocation of development funds – which are totally contradictory to expressed spatial aims. For instance, stated social and spatial aims within the 1977/8-1982/3 Plan in the Sudan and the 1975-80 Plan in Nigeria were not visible in the actual sectoral and spatial distribution of investment funds the plans put forward (Hardoy and Satterthwaite, 1981). As Richardson (1977) comments, development planning in the Third World has concentrated on macro-economic and sectoral strategies. But their spatial implications have either been treated separately or simply ignored. The subjugation of spatial policies to sectoral policies is merely a reflection of the subjugation of spatial planning to sectoral planning. Indeed, Harris (1983) comments that spatial goals and policies allow governments to avoid undertaking much needed (and more fundamental) changes. For instance, the lack of piped water and sewers and such public services as garbage disposal, health care and education can be blamed on 'too many people' or 'very rapid population growth' in large cities; the associated policy response is an attempt to control migration to such cities which are usually ineffective and on occasion repressive. This helps to hide the low priority that governments (and international agencies) have given to investments in such services and facilities and governments' reluctance to impose controls on urban land markets as part of a strategy to reduce the cost and increase the supply of low income housing. Similarly, 'spatial policies' to steer industrial investments to poorer regions can be said to be addressing the problem of 'regional imbalance' although as described earlier, such policies can actually bring few benefits and many costs to the lower income majority living in such regions.

One of the clearest illustrations of this conflict between sectoral policies and spatial goals is given by Richardson (1984) in a paper on Lima, Peru. Peru's national capital, with 4.4 million people in its metropolitan area in 1981, had more than 10 times the population of the next largest city, Arequipa. Richardson notes that:

> Lima has received a disproportionately high share of infrastructure and public investments, a response to the more vocal political pressures in the capital and greater awareness of the extent of public service lags in Lima than elsewhere. Utilities such as water and domestic electricity have been subsidised more heavily in Lima. In an attempt to rationalise the invasion process, the government has supplied free lots in many peripheral areas to migrant households; mortgage finance has been heavily subsidised with most of the loans made in Lima. Until very recently, gasoline was priced far below the world price, again benefiting Lima because two-thirds of the country's motor vehicles are concentrated there. Food prices have also been subsidised, shifting the internal terms of trade against the rural areas and resulting in heavy government support to the food import bills for urban consumers. The persistent overvaluation of the currency harmed the agricultural areas and natural resource regions (ie the periphery) by eroding their export potential and subsidising the main focus of import demand, Lima itself. (pp. 123-124)

Richardson goes on to point out that successive governments have included 'slowing down Lima's growth' as one of their objectives, even though the impact of the policies to do so has been outweighed by the effects of these implicit spatial policies that have reinforced primacy. While the Belaunde government took some steps to reduce the spatial biases of policies which helped concentrate developments in Lima, 'modifications to the implicit spatial policies favouring the growth of Lima would have a more powerful impact in slowing its rate of growth than implementation of weak and possibly unsound spatial decentralisation strategies' (p. 136). Existing data suggests that this same recommendation is valid for many other Third World nations.

Spatial biases in subsidising or supporting industrial investment

In most Third World nations, cheap loans for new industrial enterprises, or other forms of subsidy for industrial investments such as some kind of tax incentive will, like many import-substitution policies, tend to subsidise industrial investment in large urban centres.[10] As noted earlier, the attraction of many small and intermediate urban centres in less urbanised regions of the First World for certain industries is due to a mix of factors which are rarely apparent in Third World nations and regions. If subsidies are only given to industries investing in certain regions, then such industries will tend to go to the largest city (or cities) within that region or to the parts of that region closest to existing large cities. It is quite possible that such new industrial investment will have few multiplier links within the region and that profits from the operation are steered out of the region. In effect, the urban centre in the backward region often gains no more than an 'export processing zone' since inputs into the operation come from outside the region and outputs are sold outside it.

Dickenson (1980) noted that initiatives in Brazil to stimulate industrial development in the poor and drought-ridden north-east brought few benefits to the region's population. As noted earlier, special incentives helped attract several hundred new or expanded industries between 1959 and the mid-Seventies. But this created relatively few jobs since the plants were mostly capital intensive and there do not seem to have been many multiplier links from these industries stimulating and supporting other enterprises within the north-east. Most of the new industries were set up in the richer states and the largest cities within the region. Over half the projects approved by 1970 went to Recife, Salvador and Fortaleza (with 2.3 million, 1.8 million and 1.6 million inhabitants in their metropolitan region in 1980, respectively). Gilbert and Goodman (1976) note that the new industries did not bring significant improvements in the living standards even of the urban masses in the cities which benefited most from new industrial investment. Thus, while the government's policy on the northeast might have increased total industrial production and lessened the gap between its per capita GDP compared to other regions, it did little or nothing to address the problems of poverty and malnutrition. Indeed, conditions for the poor masses probably deteriorated during the Sixties.

In a study of economic change between 1960 and 1970 in Tamil Nadu, one of India's more populous, rich, and industrialised states, government incentives to attract new industries succeeded in boosting total industrial production. But much of the expansion in industrial production came from enterprises in or close to the Madras Metropolitan area, the State Capital and India's fourth largest urban centre. This growth in production brought few backward and forward linkages within the State apart from within Madras (the government incentives attracted many industries which simply processed inputs brought into the State and sold final products outside the State). The urban centres which tended to have the most rapid growth in population and economic base were those which were part of larger agglomerations (such as the Madras conurbation).

Meanwhile, most of the urban centres with stagnant economies and slow population growth were those at some distance from the larger urban centres. In spite of many concessions made to stimulate growth and development in backward areas, none of these areas experienced a noticeable boost to very weak industrial bases. The government did not succeed in promoting small-scale industries in smaller towns; indeed it seems that most new small-scale industries set up in the major urban centres, very often with their activities linked to the large-scale industrial sector (Kurien and James, 1979). The promotion of small-scale industries does not necessarily imply that these will develop in small and intermediate urban centres. Indeed, as Moser (1984) points out while reviewing the role of the informal sector in smaller urban centres, 'all the constraints facing small-scale enterprises, particularly finance, raw materials, markets, skill training and legal protection...are exacerbated and more extreme for those with small enterprises in small cities' (pp. 31-32).

Thus, general incentives to encourage industrial investment in loosely defined 'lagging' or 'backward' regions are less likely to benefit regional populations (especially the lower income majority) and the smaller urban centres there, than incentives and public investments designed to make better use of the resource mix particular to each region.

To summarise, note must be taken of the often powerful spatial effects in an enormous range of government policies and expenditures whose explicit aims and goals are not spatial but social, economic or political. Obviously the distribution of power and resources between different levels of government is one. Expenditure on public services and facilities within these different levels is another. So too are the macro-economic and sectoral policies already discussed: import substitution, exchange rates, taxing farmers and subsidising food prices, spatial biases in public investments and in supporting or subsidising industrial investment. This is by no means an exhaustive list. For instance, a government policy to keep interest rates high can lessen the incentive for the private sector to invest in small or intermediate urban centres; conditions, risks and costs are better known in larger urban centres. For taxation, the spatial bias of only one kind of tax – that on export commodities – was mentioned. But other taxes such as those levied on incomes, profits or capital gains or on goods and services, or employers' payroll taxes will also have spatial biases. For instance, if a substantial part of national government tax base is derived from taxes on incomes, profits and capital gains which are known to come mostly from households and enterprises in larger urban centres or more urbanised regions, then there are obvious spatial implications if a proportion of this revenue is used to support agricultural and rural development in backward regions. This, in turn, can support development in small and intermediate urban centres within these regions. Thus, it comes as a little surprise to find Hamer (1984) stating that 'eliminating sectoral distortions may do more for decentralised development than all the myriad spatial efforts conventionally proposed by Third World policy-makers' (pp. 18-19).

The need to improve our understanding of the social and spatial biases within governments' policies, revenue raising and expenditure is crucial to any special policy on small and intermediate urban centres. If the major constraint on such centres' development is the lack of income for most of the surrounding agricultural population, then the redistribution of income or assets redistribution is needed to address this constraint. As Renaud (1981) notes, 'if income redistribution is really the objective, explicit regional policies can be helpful, but they come a very poor second behind other forms of income redistribution (such as land reforms, reform of the fiscal system, pricing policies or education policies)' (p. 124).

Notes

1 The term 'growth centre' is taken to mean a geographic location, chosen by government, where public investment is to be concentrated to promote growth and development of the centre and in many instances of surrounding areas too.

2 The paper also discussed the various ways in which 'polarisation reversal' can be measured.

3 For instance, Bairoch (1982) suggests there are universally valid, population thresholds relating to optimum size for employment and to deteriorations in the general conditions of life.

4 The justification for ambitious plans to slow the growth of population in large urban centres is also often based on an 'effect' – the rapid and uncontrolled physical expansion of the built-up area, as noted for Greater Cairo. The cause is far more the uncontrolled nature of the urban land market and the fact that lower income groups frequently have little alternative but to live on illegally occupied or sub-divided land. Bolaffi (1977) noted that in Sao Paulo, the urbanised area could accommodate a two-thirds increase in population without any further physical expansion by utilising undeveloped land. Sarin (1983) noted that there are thousands of hectares of vacant land in and around cities such as Manila, Bombay, Delhi and Bangkok.

5 In some nations, the sub-regional government and the urban government for the urban centres where the sub-regional government is located are the same.

6 This should not be taken to imply that the lower income groups who usually make up the majority of large city inhabitants in the Third World have necessarily benefited. Indeed, while public investments in hospitals and health care can be highly concentrated in large cities, the lower income groups in large cities often do not have access to such services and are as poorly served as the inhabitants of small urban centres and rural areas.

7 Ruane (1982) points out that the introduction of any policy to foster one or more sectors in an economy relative to others alters the spatial pattern of development unless all factors of production are instantaneously mobile between all sectors and locations of the economy. She also suggests that the actual spatial effect of such policies will be greater, the more location-specific (ie the less footlose) the projects are within the protected sectors.

8 'Over-valued' exchange rates do not necessarily mean cheap imports since they are frequently accompanied by import restrictions.

9 As noted earlier, the crop mix and land tenure system which provide the highest and most equitable distribution of income from the densest agricultural population will tend to provide the largest stimulus to local urban development. Many surveys have shown that a land tenure pattern dominated by small holdings tends to have the highest output and highest employment per hectare.

10 It is also likely to encourage more capital-intensive production and thus make inadequate use of local labour.

References

Abu-Lughod, Janet (1976), chapter on 'Urbanisation in North Africa' in Berry, B.L.J. (editor), *Patterns of Urbanisation and Counter-Urbanisation,* Sage Publications, Beverly Hills.

Agiri, Babatunde (1979), 'The changing socio-economic relationship between Ikorodu and its neighbouring villages, 1950-1977', in Southall Aidan (editor), *Small Urban Centers in Rural Development in Africa,* African Studies Programme, University of Wisconsin.

Apacible M.S. and Yaxley, M. (1979), 'Manila through the eyes of the Malinenos and the Consultant', PTRC Summer Annual Meeting.

Aradeon, David *et al.* (1985), Chapter 6 in this volume.

Bairoch, Paul (1982), 'Employment and large cities: problems and outlook', in *International Labour Review,* Volume 121, Number 5, September-October.

Balan, Jorge (1970), 'Social Classes in a Rural, Non-indigenous Municipality in Mexico', *Revista Mexicana de Sociologia* Vol XXXII, 5, pp 227-249.

Bale, Malcolm D. and Lutz, Ernst (1979), *Price Distortions in Agriculture and their effects: An International Comparison,* World Bank Staff Working Paper No. 359, October.

Becker, Wilhelmus (1969), 'Socio-economic Analysis of the Atyra District', in *Revista Paraguaya de Sociologia,* Sixth Year, No. 16, pp. 116-31.

Beier, George, Churchill, Anthony, Cohen, Michael, and Renaud, Bertrand (1975), *The task ahead for the cities of the developing countries,* International Bank for Reconstruction and Development, Bank Staff Working Paper No. 209.

Bird, Richard (1978), *Intergovernmental Fiscal Relations in Developing Countries,* World Bank Staff Working Paper No. 304, October.

Blitzer, Silvia, Hardoy, Jorge E. and Satterthwaite, David (1983), 'The Sectoral and Spatial Distribution of Multilateral Aid for Human Settlements', in *Habitat International* Volume 7, No. 1/2 pp. 103-27

Bolaffi, Gabriel (1977), lecture given at the Institute of Development Studies, Brighton University, England.

Brebner, Philip and Briggs, John (1982), 'Rural Settlement Planning in Algeria and Tanzania: a Comparative Study' in *Habitat International* Vol 6, No. 5/6, pp. 621-8.

Briscoe, John (1983), *Water Supply and Health in Developing Countries: Selected Primary Health Care Revisited,* paper presented at the International Conference on Oral Rehydration Therapy sponsored by the World Health Organisation, the United States Agency for International Development and the International Centre for Diarrhoeal Disease Research (Bangladesh), Washington DC.

Brutzkus, Eliezer (1975), 'Centralised versus decentralised pattern of urbanisation in developing countries: an attempt to elucidate a guideline principle', in *Economic Development and Cultural Change,* Volume 23, Number 4, July, pp. 633-52.

Bryceson, Deborah (1984), *Urbanisation and Agrarian Development in Tanzania with Special Reference to Secondary Cities,* IIED.

Chambers, R. (1974), *Managing Rural Development: Ideas and Experiences from East Africa,* Scandinavia Institute of African Studies.

Chile, Government of (1983), paper on the political and administrative structure of Chile's system by the Urban Development Division of the Ministry of Housing and Urbanism, September.

Cochrane, Glynn (1983), *Policies for strengthening local government in developing countries,* World Bank Staff Working Papers, Number 582.

Collin Delavaud, Anne (1976), *Uruguay: medium and small cities,* Institut des Hautes Etudes de l'Amerique Latine, Laboratoire Associe du Centre National de la Recherche Scientifique, Paris.

Comay, Yochanan and Kirschenbaum, Alan (1973), 'The Israeli New Town: An Experiment at Population Redistribution', in *Eco-*

nomic Development and Cultural Change Vol 22, No. 1, October, pp. 124-34.

Daly, M. (1977), *Development Planning in Nigeria,* University of Ibadan, Planning Studies Programme.

Davidson, Forbes (1981), 'Ismailia: from master plan to implementation' in *Third World Planning Review,* Volume 3, Number 2, May.

Denis, P. (1976), 'Recent changes in the peripheral villages of Quito: the cases of San Juan de Calderon and San Miquel de Collacoto', *Actas del XLII Congreso Internacional de Americanistas* (Paris), Vol 1.

Dickenson, John (1980), 'Innovation for regional development in Northeast Brazil, a century of failures', in *Third World Planning Review,* Volume 2, Number 1, Spring

Dillman, Daniel C., (1970), Urban Growth Along Mexico's Northern Border and the Mexican National Border Program, *Journal of Developing Areas* No. 4, July.

Douglass, Mike (1981), 'Thailand: territorial dissolution and alternative regional development for the central plains', in *Development from Above or Below?,* John Wiley & Sons, pp. 183-208.

ECLAC/UNCHS (1984) *Middle-rank human settlements in territorial organisation strategies in Latin America and the Caribbean.*

Ecuador, Government of (1980), *National Development Plan 1980-1984,* second part, Volume V, Quito.

Ellis, Frank (1982), 'Agricultural Price Policy in Tanzania', in *World Development* Vol. 10, No. 4, April pp. 263-84.

ESCAP (1979), *Guidelines for Rural Centres Planning.*

ESCAP (1984) *Planning and Management of Human Settlements in the ESCAP region: with emphasis on small and intermediate settlements,* July.

Filani, Michael Olanrewaju (1981), 'Nigeria: the need to modify centre-down development planning', in *Development from Above or Below?,* John Wiley & Sons, pp. 283-304.

Friedmann, John (1972-3), 'The spatial organisation of power in the development of urban systems', in *Development and Change,* Volume IV, Number 3.

Friedmann, John (1981), 'Urban bias in regional development policy, in Misra, R.P. (editor), in *Humanising Development,* Maruzen, Asia.

Friedmann, John and Weaver, Clyde (1979), *Territory and Function,* Edward Arnold, London.

Gaitskell, A. (1959), *Gezira: A Story of Development in the Sudan,* Faber and Faber, London.

Gilbert, Alan G. and Goodman, David E. (1976), 'Regional income disparities and economic development: a critique', in Gilbert,

Alan (editor) *Development Planning and Spatial Structure,* John Wiley & Sons, pp. 113-42.

Gilbert, A. and Gugler, J. (1982), 'Urban and regional systems: a suitable case for treatment?', in *Cities, poverty and development: urbanisation in the Third World,* Oxford University Press.

Gotsch, Carl and Brown, Gilbert (1980), *Prices, Taxes and Subsidies in Pakistan Agriculture 1960-76,* World Bank Staff Working Paper, No. 387, April.

Gugler, J. (1980), 'A Minimum of Urbanism and a Maximum of Ruralism: the Cuban Experience', in *International Journal of Urban and Regional Research,* Volume 4, pp. 516-535.

Gugler, J. (1982), 'Overurbanisation reconsidered', in *Economic Development and Cultural Change,* Volume 31, Number 1, University of Chicago, pp. 173-96.

Hamer, Andrew M. (1984), *Decentralised Urban Development and Industrial Location Behavior in Sao Paulo, Brazil,* in 'A Synthesis of Research Issues and Conclusions', Discussion Paper, Water Supply and Urban Development Department, World Bank.

Hannerz, Ulf (1979), 'Town and country in southern Zaria: a view from Kafanchan', in Southall, Aidan (editor), *Small Urban Centers in Rural Development in Africa,* African Studies Programme, University of Wisconsin.

Hardoy, Jorge E. and Satterthwaite, David (1981), *Shelter: Need and Response,* IIED, John Wiley & Sons.

Hardoy, Jorge E. and Satterthwaite, David (1985), *Third world cities and the environment of poverty,* background paper for the World Resources Institute Global Possible Conference, IIED, to be published with Conference Proceedings by Yale University Press.

Hardoy Jorge E. (1975), 'Two thousand years of Latin American Urbanisation',inHardoy(editor), *Urbanization in Latin America: Approaches and Issues,* Anchor Books, New York.

Harris, Nigel (1983), 'Spatial planning and economic development', in *Habitat International,* Volume 7, Number 5/6.

Hauser, Philip M. and Gardner, Robert W. (1980), 'Urban Future: Trends and Prospects' in *Population and the Urban Future,* UNFPA.

Herbert, Jean Loup (1970), 'A Community Facing the Capitalism of a Social Structure', *Revista Mexicana de Sociologia* Vol XXXII, No. 1, p. 119-45.

Ho, Samuel P.S. (1979), 'Decentralised industrialisation and rural development evidence from Taiwan', in *Economic Development and Cultural Change,* Volume 28, Number 1, October.

Hopkins, Nicholas S. (1979), 'A comparison of the role of the small urban center in rural development: Kita (Mali) and Testour (Tunisia)', in Southall, Aidan (editor), *Small Urban Centers in*

Rural Development in Africa, African Studies Programme, University of Wisconsin.

India, Government of (1983), 'Planning and management of human settlements with emphasis on small and intermediate towns', special theme for discussion in the eighth session of the UNCHS (1984), Gabon, April-May.

Jain, Ashok Kumar (1976), 'Evolution of an urban growth policy for India', in *Ekistics* 249, August, pp. 103-5.

Jenssen, Bernd, Kunzmann, Klaus R. and Saad-El din, Sherif (1979), 'Taming the growth of Cairo: towards a deconcentration of the metropolitan region of Cairo', in *Third World Planning Review,* Volume 3, Number 2, May.

Johnson, E.A.J. (1970), *The Organisation of Space in Developing Countries,* Harvard University Press, Cambridge, Mass.

Johnston, Bruce F. and Clark, William C. (1982), *Redesigning Rural Development,* John Hopkins University Press.

Jones, Richard C., (1982),   'Regional Income   Inequalities and Government Investment in Venezuela', in *Journal of Developing Areas* Volume 16, Number 3, April.

Kalbermatten, John M., Julius, DeAnne S. and Gunnerson, Charles G. (1980), *Appropriate Technology for Water Supply and Sanitation; A Summary of Technical and Economic Options,* World Bank.

Kano, Hiromasa (1978) 'City development and occupational change in Iran: a case study of Hamadan', in *The Developing Economies,* Volume XVI, Number 3, September.

Kenya, Republic of (1975), *National Summary Report for Habitat.*

Kenya, Republic of (1979), *Development Plan 1979-83,* Government Printer, Nairobi.

Kiamba, C.M., Maingi, K., Ng'Ethe, N., and Senga, W.M. (1983), *The role of small and intermediate cities in national development: the case study of Thika, Kenya,* United Nations Centre for Regional Development, Nagoya, Japan.

Knesl, John (1982), 'Town and Country in development from below: the emerging paradigm for the decade', in *Ekistics,* 292, January-February.

Kulaba,S.M. (1982), 'Rural Settlement Strategies in Tanzania', in *Habitat International* Vol. 6, No. 1/2.

Kurien, C.T. and James, Josef (1979), *Economic change in Tamil Nadu,* Allied Publishers, New Delhi.

Kutcher, Gary P. and Scandizzo, Pasquale L. (1981), *The Agricultural Economy of Northeast Brazil,* John Hopkins University Press.

Kwok,R. Yin-Yang (1982), 'The role of small cities in Chinese urban development', in *International Journal for Urban and Regional Research,* Volume 6, Number 4.

Lee, Concepcion E. (1979), 'Medenine: regional capital and small urban center in the Tunisian South', in Southall, Aidan (editor),

Small Urban Centers in Rural Development in Africa, African Studies Programme, University of Wisconsin.

Leichter, Howard M., (1975), 'Political change and policy change: the case of two Philippine cities', in *The Journal of Developing Areas,* Number 10, October.

Lentnek, Barry and Green, Diane Wilner (1983), 'Some Implications of National Income Distribution Policies for National Urban Spatial Policies', Chapter 3 in Lim, Gill-Chin (editor), *Urban Planning and Spatial Strategies in Rapidly Changing Societies,* Consortium on Urban and Regional Policies in Developing Countries, February.

Leonard, John B. (1985), 'Rangoon – City Profile' in *Cities* Vol. 2, No. 1, February.

Linn, Johannes F. (1982), The costs of urbanisation in developing countries, *Economic Development and Cultural Change,* Volume 30(3), University of Chicago.

Linn, Johannes F. (1983), *Cities in the developing world,* World Bank, Oxford University Press.

Malaysia, Government of, (1983), 'The planning and management of human settlements with emphasis on small and intermediate towns and local growth points', an outline paper on the approach taken by Malaysia, paper prepared for the seventh session of the Commission of Human Settlements.

Manzanal, Mabel (1983), *Agro, industria y ciudad en la Patagonia Norte,* Ediciones CEUR.

Mathur, Om Prakash (1982), 'The role of small cities in national development', *Small cities and national development,* United Nations Centre for Regional Development, Nagoya, Japan.

Meissner, Frank (1981), 'Growth without migration: towards a model for integrated regional/rural development planning', in *Ekistics* 291, November-December.

Middleton, John (1985), 'Home Town: a study of an Urban Centre in Southern Ghana', in Southall, Aidan (editor), *Small Urban Centres in Rural Development in Africa,* University of Wisconsin, Madison.

MINVAH (1983), *Politica de ordenamiento y desarrollo de los asentamientos intermedios y rurales en Nicaragua,* Managua, September.

Misra, R.P. (1981), 'Growth centres and rural development', in Misra, R.p. (editor), *Humanising Development,* Maruzen, Asia.

Mohan, Rakesh (1983), 'India: coming to terms with urbanisation', in *Cities,* August.

Morawawetz, David (1978), 'Castro market: slice of economic life in a poor Chilean fishing town', in *World Development,* Volume 6, Number 6, June.

Moser, Caroline O.N. (1984), 'The Role of the Informal Sector in

Small and Intermediate Sized Cities', in *UN Centre for Regional Development,* Nagoya, Japan, September.

Nepal, His Majesty's Government (1974), *Policy Guidelines for the Fifth Plan 1975-1980,* National Planning Commission.

Nwaka, Geoffrey I., 'Owerri: Development of a Nigerian State Capital', in *Third World Planning Review.*

O'Connor, A.M. (1984), *Secondary cities and food production in Nigeria,* IIED, London, February.

Onyemelukwe, J. (1974), 'Some factors in the growth of West African market towns; the example of pre-civil war Onitsha, Nigeria', in *Urban studies,* Volume II, Number 1, February.

Ortuzar, S. (1983), 'Santiago's metro', in *Cities,* Volume 1, Number 2, November.

Panama, Government of (undated), *Planning and Administration of Human Settlements in the Republic of Panama, with special reference to small and intermediate cities and points of local growth,* Ministry of Planning and Economic Policy.

Peru, Government of (1981), *Presidential Message to Congress,* Lima, pp. 376-77.

Reca, Lucio G. (1980), *Argentina: Country Case Study of Agricultural Prices and Subsidies,* World Bank Staff Working Paper No. 386, April.

Renaud, Bertrand (1981), *National urbanisation policy in developing countries,* World Bank, Oxford University Press.

Richardson, Harry W. (1972), 'Optimality in city size, systems of cities and urban policy', in *Ekistics* 205, December.

Richardson, Harry W. (1977), *City size and national spatial strategies in developing countries,* World Bank Staff Working Paper No. 252.

Richardson, Harry W. (1980), 'An urban development strategy for Kenya', in *The Journal of Developing Areas,* Volume 15, Number 1, October.

Richardson, Harry W. (1984), 'Planning strategies and policies for metropolitan Lima,' in *Third World Planning Review,* Volume 6, Number 2, May.

Rivkin Associates (1982), *Approaches to Planning for Secondary Cities in Developing Countries,* US AID, 1982.

Rondinelli, Dennis A., Lombardo, Joseph F. and Yeh, Gar-on Anthony (1979), 'Dispersed urbanisation and population planning in Asia', in *Ekistics* 277, July-August.

Rondinelli, Dennis A. and Ruddle, Kenneth (1978), *Urbanisation and Rural Development; A Spatial Policy for Equitable Growth,* Praeger.

Rondinelli, Dennis A. (1982), 'Intermediate Cities in Developing Countries', in *Third World Planning Review,* Volume 4, Number 4, November.

Rondinelli, Dennis A., Nellis, John R. and Cheema, G. Shabbir (1984), *Decentralisation in developing countries – a review of recent experience,* World Bank Staff Working Papers, No. 581.

Rotblat, Howard (1975), 'Social organisation and development in an Iranian provincial bazaar', in *Economic Development and Cultural Changes,* Volume 23, Number 2, January.

Ruane, Frances P. (1982), *Trade Policies and the Spatial Distribution of Development: A Two Sector Analysis,* Department of Economics, Trinity College, Dublin, Ireland.

Ruane, Frances P. (1982), *Sectoral Policies and the Spatial Concentration of Industrial Activities: A Factor-market Adjustment Approach,* Department of Economics, Trinity College, Dublin, Ireland.

Sabogal Wiesse, Jose (1974), 'The Town of Santiago de Cao, Yesterday: Don Enrique's Narration', in *Anuario Indigenista,* Volume XXXIV, December, pp. 91-151.

Saint, William S. and Goldsmith, William D. (1980), 'Cropping systems structural change and rural-urban migration in Brazil', in *World Development,* Volume 8 (English version) and CEBRAP Number 25 (Spanish version).

Sarin, Mahdu (1983), 'The Rich, the Poor and the Land Question', in Angel, Archer, Tanphiphat and Wegelin, *Land for Housing the Poor,* Select Books, Singapore.

Scott, Ian (1982), *Urban and spatial development in Mexico,* World Bank, The John Hopkins University Press, Baltimore and London.

Simpson, I.G. (1984), *Secondary cities and food security – the Sudan,* IIED, London, February.

Soen, Dan and Kipnis, Baruch (1972), 'The functioning of a cluster of towns in Israel: an analysis of real and expected zones of influence', in *Ekistics* 205, December.

Soiffer, Stephen M., and Howe, Gary N. (1982), 'Patrons, clients, and the articulation of modes of production: an examination of the penetration of capitalism into peripheral agriculture in northeastern Brazil', in *The Journal of Peasant Studies,* No. 9/2, January.

Soja and Weaver (1976), chapter on 'East Africa' in Berry, B.L.J. (editor), *Patterns of Urbanisation and Counter-Urbanisation,* Sage Publications, Beverley Hills.

Song, Byung-Nak (1982), 'The Role of Small and Intermediate Cities in National Development: the Korean Case', in Mathur, Om Prakash (editor), *Small Cities and National Development,* UNCRD, Nagoya.

de Souza, Edgar Bastos (1984), *Urbanisation, urban development policy and the medium size cities project of Brazil,* Ninth Africa

Conference on Housing and Urban Development, Ministry of Interior, Brazil.

Stohr, Walter B. and Taylor, D.R.F. (1981), 'Development from above or below? Some conclusions', in *Development from Above or Below?*, John Wiley & Sons, pp. 453-80.

Stohr, W. and Todtling, F. (1979), 'Spatial Equity: some antitheses to current regional development doctrine', in Folmer H. and Oosterhaven J. (editors), *Spatial Inequalities and Regional Development*, Nijhoff, Boston.

Stuckey, Barbara (1975), 'Spatial Analysis and Economic Development', *Development and Change*, Vol. VI, No. 1.

Suselo, Ir Hendropranoto (1984), *Experiences in providing urban services to secondary cities in Indonesia*, Ninth Africa Conference on Housing and Urban Development, Dakar, Senegal.

Sutton, Keith (1982), 'The Socialist Villages of Algeria', in *Third World Planning Review* Vol. 4, No. 3, August.

Tanzania, Republic of (1975), *National Report on Human Settlements in Tanzania*, report prepared for Habitat Conference.

Tanzania, Republic of (1979), *The Third Five Year Plan for Economic and Social Development*, Dar es Salaam.

Task Force on Human Settlements (1975), *Human Settlements; the Vision of a New Society*.

Townroe, P.M. (1979), 'Employment decentralisation: policy instruments for large cities in less developed countries,' in *Progress in Planning*, Volume 10, Part 2.

Townroe, Peter M. (1982), *The case for adaptive restraint policies in LDC metropolitan areas*, School of Economic and Social Studies, University of East Anglia, UK.

Townroe, Peter M. and Keen, David (1984), 'Polarisation reversal in the state of Sao Paulo, Brazil', in *Regional Studies*, Volume 18.1, pp. 45-54.

Townroe, Peter M. (1984), 'The changing economic environment for spatial policies in the Third World', in *Geoforum* Volume 17, Number 3.

Tyler, William G. (1983), *The Brazilian Sectoral Incentive System and the regional Incidence of Non Spatial Incentive Policies*, Discussion Paper UDD-31, Water Supply and Urban Development Department, The World Bank.

UNCHS (1985a), 'Planning and Management of Human Settlements, with emphasis on Small and Intermediate Towns and Local growth Points', Report of the Executive Director presented to the Commission on Human Settlements, Document No. HS/C/8/3.

UNCHS (1985b) 'Planning and Management of Human Settlements, with Emphasis on Small and Intermediate Towns and Local Growth Points, Review of Past Approaches and Experiences', presented to the Commission on Human Settlements, Document No. HS/C/8/3/Add.3.

UNCHS (1985c), 'Planning and Management of Human Settlements, with Emphasis on Small and Intermediate Towns and Local growth Points, Review of Spatial Biases implicit in Governmental Structure, non-spatial policies and sectoral plans', presented to the Commission on Human Settlements, Document No. HS/C/8/3/Add.4.

United Nations Department of International Economic and Social Affairs (1980), *Patterns of urban and rural population growth,* United Nations, Population Studies Number 68, New York.

Uphoff, N. and Esman, M.J. (1974), *Local Organisation for Rural Development in Asia,* Cornell University Rural Development Committee.

US AID (1977), Office of Housing with Egypt, Arab Republic of, *Urban Land Use in Egypt,* Report of the Joint Policy Team.

US AID (1980), *Haiti Shelter Sector Assessment,* Office of Housing, December.

Vapnarsky, Cesar A. (1983), *Pueblos del norte de la Patagonia, 1779-1957,* Editorial de la Patagonia.

Ward, P.M. (1985), *Welfare Politics in Mexico,* George Allen and Unwin.

World Bank (1981), *Accelerated Development in Sub Saharan Africa.*

World Bank (1984), *World Development Report 1984,* Oxford University Press.

9

Some Tentative Conclusions

Jorge E. Hardoy and David Satterthwaite

Most of the Third World's inhabitants either live in or depend on small or intermediate urban centres for access to goods, services and markets. As noted in Chapter 1, these are the urban centres with which most rural people and rural enterprises interact. In most nations, they also contain a high proportion of the total urban population.

But there seems to have been a certain amount of confusion in many government policies and in the advice given to governments as to the purpose of a special programme for such centres. For such a programme cannot be an end in itself; its purpose is to help achieve social and economic development goals at the least possible cost. The justification for special programmes on small and intermediate urban centres is that they are a crucial component in attaining such social and economic objectives as: increasing the proportion of national population reached by basic services; increasing and diversifying agricultural production; and increasing the influence of sub-national and sub-regional populations both on resource allocation at the national level and on development plans which affect their area. These are not 'spatial goals' although their implementation would have important spatial implications.

Many Third World governments have adopted special programmes for small and intermediate urban centres, as described in previous chapters. But those programmes which have not been designed to serve explicit social and economic goals and to suit each centre's local and regional context have rarely succeeded in achieving the hoped for development objectives. Thus, the identification of specific developmental roles for selected small and intermediate urban centres within broader social and economic development plans should be the first step towards formulating a special programme for such centres. These roles can be divided into four categories: national priorities; local development and resource mobilisation; economic development; and service provision.

With regard to national priorities, national (or regional) urban systems are essentially the 'infrastructure' of development and the backbone on which development projects should be planned. There is a tendency to treat 'Human Settlements' as a sector with its own Ministry or division – just like agriculture or industry or finance. But each nation's 'human settlements' and their various and usually complex interlinkages are the physical context within which all investments are made. Since people, resources and economic activities are distributed in space, it is through the urban system that these are inter-connected. For example, in agriculture, only through the urban system and its links to smaller settlements can farmers be reached by agricultural extension services, inputs, credit, storage, marketing and processsing. Similarly, for service provision, only through the urban system and its links with smaller settlements can governments increase the proportion of the population with access to health care, education, postage and telephones, and other public services. It is through the urban system that both agricultural and non-agricultural enterprises have access to inter-regional and intra-regional transport and communications systems. Finally, it is through the different levels of government (most of which are located in small and intermediate urban centres) that local needs and resources are best assessed and many important development initiatives efficiently implemented.

The role of small and intermediate urban centres within national urban systems and national production is often given little consideration. But it is perhaps a truism to point out that the developmental roles of small and intermediate urban centres cannot be considered in isolation from those of larger urban centres or those of the rural economy. Small or intermediate urban centres – however defined – are merely part of the enormous range of settlements within any nation or region. An understanding of trends in terms of changes in population or in economic structure within small and intermediate urban centres can only be achieved through an understanding of the role of each particular centre within the wider system of production.

Thus, special government programmes for small and intermediate urban centres should be based on the understanding that each such centre will have its own unique mix of resources, development potential, skills, constraints and links with its environs and with the wider regional and national economies. In addition, the potential for, or constraints on, development there will change over time through, for example, changes in the national economy or government macroeconomic policies or the world market. The empirical studies presented and discussed in Chapters 2 to 7 illustrate how small and intermediate urban centres with comparable population sizes cannot be assumed to have similar functions, occupational structures or development potentials. And analyses of the factors which underlie the development of different urban centres (whether small, intermediate or large) point to the phenomenally rich and diverse set of circumstances particular to each. Examples in previous chapters pointed to some centres developing largely because they were chosen to serve as a centre for provincial or state government, or as a centre of military control. Others developed because enterprises located there to benefit from forward and backward linkages with prosperous commercial agriculture or from the demand for goods and services generated by those earning an income in agriculture; others because they came to serve as an important transport centre; others because they became the constituency of a prominent politician who steered public investments and public enterprises there; and others because enterprises developed there to exploit one specialised niche in a regional, national or international market – for instance for tourism or some industry or mining or timber.

While it is possible to identify various factors common to the development of many small and intermediate urban centres such as comparable historical origins, or administrative roles, or links with commercial agriculture, there is a great variation in the relative importance of such factors and their mix and interaction with factors particular to each region and its links with other regions. Certainly, the analyses of inter-census population growth rates in Chapters 2 to 7 do not support the claim that generalisations can be made about population growth rates in small and intermediate urban centres – either within nations or internationally. The fact that possibilities and constraints on development are so specific to each urban centre (and each region) suggests the need for a considerable degree of decentralisation in development planning and implementation; thus, if realistic assessments of development possibilities are so unique to each centre, local governments (most of which are located in small and intermediate urban centres) should be the most effective level of government to articulate local needs (from their area of jurisdiction) to influence resource allocations at higher levels. Only through representative local governments is such an articulation of local needs possible. In addition, assessments of available skills and resources within each locality and the monitoring of changes over time there are also most effectively carried out at the local level. This implies the need for strong and competent local government . But the empirical studies of small and intermediate urban centres showed that generally, government at this level lacks power, resources and trained personnel. Indeed, it frequently has little or no investment capability.

Stronger and more effective local government seems essential for a programme on small and intermediate urban centres; it also brings with it many developmental advantages. One is obviously that it removes from higher levels of government various tasks which are more effectively undertaken at local government level. Central governments frequently seek to vet too thoroughly and this produces slow and cumbersome arrangements as illustrated by examples in Chapter 8. A second is that competent and representative local government can mobilise local resources more effectively than higher levels of government. It is more likely to do so, however, if it benefits directly from such resource mobilisation rather than simply acting as a tax or revenue collector for higher levels of government. But building a stronger and more effective local government demands the reversal of many policies apparent in the last 20–30 years. For instance, it implies the need to reverse the tendency for national government to impose severe limits on local government's revenue raising powers and to take for itself the more lucrative and easily collected taxes. As the official United Nations recommendations on small and intermediate urban centres state, it also demands a clear definition of the constitutional and legal status of local governments (which is often still lacking) and the establishment of clear lines of authority and responsibility (United Nations, 1985).

The most appropriate way for increasing local government revenues will vary greatly from nation to nation (and indeed from centre to centre within a nation). The fact that the employment base and economic trends can differ greatly even for small and intermediate urban centres within the same region suggests a need for considerable flexibility on the part of national governments, in terms of defining which activities local governments can tax. For instance, a small or intermediate urban centre with a prosperous (and growing) market could use market fees or bus-park charges to raise funds to improve services and facilities in the market. A centre with a developing tourist trade could utilise a 'bed tax' for hostels, hotels and boarding houses. A property tax, while relatively complex to collect (since it demands a cadastral survey which needs constant updating) has considerable advantages. First, many local governments have the power to collect these and already derive some income from them – although it is common to find cadastral surveys and tax assessments out of date and total collected revenues far below theoretical yields. Secondly, an up-to-date cadastral survey is needed for physical and land use planning. But it is not only local governments which deserve support from higher levels of governments. In many nations, there are also many local associations or cooperatives which can serve as the organisations in charge of implementing certain local development initiatives. Groups such as an association or cooperative of local farmers can serve as the group responsible for local road or bridge upkeep or electricity supply while local parents and teachers associations might play an essential role in mobilising funds to maintain the school and supply it with books or equipment. The possibility of providing support direct to such groups has perhaps been given too little consideration – especially where local government is particularly weak.

Thus, one of the central justifications for a special policy on small and intermediate urban centres is not so much related to these centres but as to how local levels of government (which tend to be located in such centres) can respond to local needs and mobilise local resources. The kinds of policies suggested above would obviously demand a long-term programme, by national government, to help build the appropriate level of institutional capacity, resource base and skilled personnel at local level. Clearly, there is also a need for better censuses and surveys to provide the information that local government would need if it were to take responsibility for development plans for small and intermediate urban centres which are more geared to local needs, resources and potentials than the 'standard package' so often proposed in special programmes.

Given the general scarcity of resources and the time it will take to build stronger and more competent local governments, national governments could try out innovative approaches to implementing development plans in certain small or intermediate urban centres and their environs. This can allow their effectiveness to be assessed before a commitment is made to a national programme. For instance, national government could support a scheme whereby inhabitants in one particular urban centre could 'pay' local taxes or fees by working for a set number of hours in local development projects; appropriately set exchange rates between the number of hours of labour which had to be contributed in lieu of local taxes could ensure that measures to increase local government revenues would not fall heavily on lower income households. National government might also consider supporting local government schemes to generate employment in slack agricultural periods of the year – to undertake public works with substantial long term paybacks. For instance, activities such as rural feeder road construction or maintenance, bus-park surfacing or maintenance, reforestation plus watershed management, installation of water pipes, construction or maintenance of flood control or irrigation channels can provide seasonal employment and much needed supplements to the incomes of many lower income households. Important social and economic benefits could be achieved at relatively low costs. An annual block grant to each small or intermediate urban centre (or each local government area) based perhaps on population size for use within broad guidelines for projects relating to social and economic development would be another possibility. Pools of skilled personnel and specialised equipment could be made available to a group of local governments or (maybe) local associations; this could lower considerably the cost for each local government in having to purchase and maintain equipment and pay professional salaries which they cannot individually utilise for the whole year. Groups of local governments could also share accountants, engineers and road construction equipment.

While such suggestions might seem a little removed from a discussion on small and intermediate urban centres, in fact it is central to increasing the attraction of such centres to productive investment.

As the quote from Linn (1983) noted in Chapter 8, 'the quality of management by the urban authorities may have an important effect on whether and how a city grows'.

Chapter 1 suggests that many small and intermediate urban centres will (or could) play an important part in helping governments achieve national economic and developmental goals. Such frequently stated national goals as increasing food production for domestic consumption (and cutting down food imports), increasing agricultural exports or enlarging and diversifying the manufacturing sector will need a supporting infrastructure and services located in certain small and intermediate urban centres. This was borne out by the empirical studies discussed in Chapters 2 to 7. But it also became clear that public investments to improve infrastructure and facilities within any particular urban centre have to be based on a careful assessment of each individual centre's potential within wider regional, national and perhaps international production systems. Programmes to attract industries to small or intermediate urban centres by indiscriminately building an infrastructure and special facilities (such as industrial parks) were shown to be ineffective and inexpensive as the many empty or only partially filled industrial estates in such centres around the world will attest. So too will the many factories located in small or intermediate urban centres which have closed down (as noted in Chapter 5) or are working far below capacity (as noted in examples in Chapter 4 and Chapter 7). In addition, the examples given in previous chapters suggest the need for considerable caution, on the part of governments, in seeking to steer productive investment to small and intermediate urban centres within more backward regions with the aim of 'improving regional balance'. Certainly, in market or mixed economies, this has not proved very effective; the links that such industries usually have with the regional economy, and the level of direct and indirect job generation have often been below that anticipated and the direct and indirect cost to government has often been very high.

If governments are concerned about slowing the growth of large cities or about stimulating urban development within backward regions, they should look first at the fundamental causes underlying the backward region's lack of development or the large city's rapid growth. The examples outlined in Chapter 8 suggest that governments' macro-economic and pricing policies and sectoral priorities, combined with weak and ineffective local government, are often a major reason why so much new productive investment concentrates in a few (or indeed just one) large city. As the discussion on the north-east of Brazil in previous chapters suggested, the poverty and lack of development in a great part of the region are due as much to the land owning structure and 100 years of mis-directed government policies as they are to a lack of potential resources.

But inevitably, there are many small and intermediate urban centres where there is little or no possibility that strategic public investments or supports will stimulate development. Many have too poor or depleted a resource base. Others have stagnant or declining economies because enterprises there no longer sell goods or services at a competitive price or because demand for them has declined – and there is little possibility of finding more buoyant alternatives. It is impossible to generalise as to appropriate public actions since these will be so place and case specific. But the widely used policy of steering some public enterprise to a small or intermediate urban centre where it then struggles to survive because of its inappropriate location, poor supporting infrastructure and services, or that of giving a large subsidy to private enterprises to move there are unlikely to tackle the causes of such centres' problems. Indeed, the empirical evidence presented in Chapters 7 and 8 suggests that in many instances they may have little or no effect on alleviating the poverty of such centres' inhabitants, despite the high cost to the government.

As United Nations Recommendations suggest, 'there is no obvious economic or social rationale behind the often recommended policy for governments to create an articulated hierarchy of small and intermediate centres in backward areas' (United Nations, 1985, p. 3). Such an 'articulated hierarchy' (or rather an articulated system) might well develop as a result of social and economic development; certainly within Argentina's Upper Valley, whose development was described in Chapter 2, there is an 'articulated' urban system in terms of different urban centres with multiple inter-linkages between them and a range of services and facilities distributed among them which serve a population larger than their own. But seeking to create or impose an 'articulated hierarchy' as the prime policy intervention can do little or nothing to deal with factors which have been shown to be at the root of the poverty and lack of development in so many regions – poor or depleted soil, inequitable land owning structures (including perhaps many absentee landowners) or lack of investment in flood control, irrigation and other essential infrastructure.

In the analysis of the effect of government policies on small and intermediate urban centres in Chapter 8, it became evident that sectoral policies and policies to redistribute power and resources are often the most effective forms of public intervention to maximise employment and income generation in small and intermediate urban centres. While the relatively equitable distribution of agricultural land and substantial government support for its utilisation were major reasons for growth in production, productivity and urban population in the Upper Valley (Chapter 2), inequitable land owning structures were shown to be a considerable inhibition to local urban development in the two Indian study regions (Chapters 4 and 5). Governments rarely fully appreciate the extent to which a prosperous agriculture and a prosperous agricultural population can underly rapid growth, diversification and development in small and intermediate urban centres; developments in the Upper Valley are one example of this. However, governments should also note the variety of mechanisms by which the potential stimulus provided by prosperous agriculture can be steered away from small and intermediate urban centres located nearby. The first is through inequitable land ownership, as noted above. Vertically integrated, monopolistic organisations responsible for input supply and for marketing certain agricultural crops – whether publicly or privately owned – can also steer much of the potential stimulus to local urban development elsewhere; examples of this were evident in Chapters 3 and 8. So too can heavy government taxation of commercial crops or the fact that government agencies only pay crop prices well below their actual cost of production or current world prices.

The empirical studies presented in Chapters 2 to 7 certainly support the assertion that 'the extent to which intensively cultivated small farms can support increased rural incomes, increased labour absorption in the area and strong and diversified economic bases for nearby small and intermediate centres is much under-rated' (United Nations, 1985, p. 11). Appropriate services and facilities in centres serving such farmers allied to needed watershed management, flood control, irrigation schemes (where appropriate) and controls on land ownership concentration can contribute to such national goals as increasing food production or exports and national spatial goals such as lessening the pressures forcing migrants to the larger cities.

However, the rationale for national governments to discourage productive investment in large urban centres in the hope that this will strengthen small and intermediate urban centres does not seem justified in terms of benefits outweighing costs by the empirical evidence presented in previous chapters. Judgments made as to whether a nation's urban system is 'balanced' or 'primate-city dominated' seem of little value in assessing the actions government should or should not take either to slow large cities' growth or to stimulate smaller urban centres' economies. The relevant question is whether the existing concentration of urban-based activities in the largest city (or cities) and government policies' role in enhancing or counteracting this is serving national economic and social development goals. As noted in Chapter 8, this is a question which can only be addressed firstly by examining the factors particular to each nation or region which are causing or contributing to the largest cities' economic and population growth; secondly, by considering the social and economic costs and benefits of current urban trends; thirdly, by evaluating the role of government policies and structure in contributing to these trends; and fourthly, by evaluating the extent to which changes or innovations in government policies to lessen this concentration would further social and economic development.

Nevertheless, the empirical studies did suggest that stronger local governments and 'removing spatial biases in national macro-economic policies, tax systems, pricing structures and sectoral investment plans will be far more effective at slowing population growth in large urban centres than investment controls and less costly to the national economy' (United Nations, 1985, p. 11-12). While the justification for such national policies and priorities is hardly to do with planning the spatial distribution of development, the social and spatial implications of such national policies have rarely been considered in any depth. Yet such a consideration might well reveal alternative policies which retain their economic goal but lessen what are judged to be undesirable social or spatial impacts.

However, as United Nations Recommendations suggest, in the current recession and with governments lacking resources, capital and a growing economic base, inappropriate public expenditure to steer industries away from large cities can impose 'a hardly needed additional burden on already fragile economies or, contrary to the will of the government, cause productive investment to choose not to invest in that nation...In many of the least populous and least urbanised and industrialised Third World countries, perhaps only the largest city has the location, infrastructure, services, contact with government officials and access to imports and to the main consumer market to allow the efficient operation of many manufacturing enterprises' (United Nations, 1985, p. 12).

One final point with regard to curbing large cities' growth is that controls on migration there, in the hope that these will divert such migration to small or intermediate urban centres, are not justified by the findings from previous chapters. Migration flows in each of the study regions were essentially responses to where economic opportunities (or the possibilities for survival) were better. The tendency to characterise migration flows as only rural to urban obscures the reality; indeed, migration flows are as variable as the changing form and spatial distribution, over time, of economic opportunities. For they are, by and large, responses to these changes. The reasons for rapid in-migration to many large cities become evident in Table 8.3, which reveals the degree to which many large cities concentrate a high proportion of their entire nation's production and trade. Inevitably, the best way to change migration flows is to change their causes, and not to impose artificial and repressive controls on migration to large cities, as has been tried in South Africa. This example, described in Chapter 8, gives an idea of the level of government repression and control, of denial to the majority of inhabitants of basic social, political and economic rights and of forced relocation which is needed to implement such a policy. If governments wish to slow migration flows to large urban centres, then the evidence from Chapters 2 to 8 suggests that they should address the causes of such migration flows. For instance, in rural areas, factors such as the increasing concentration of land ownership, soil erosion, drought and low crop prices are often removing many rural inhabitants' livelihoods. Meanwhile, national government's macro-economic policies, pricing policies, tax system and sectoral plans are often helping concentrate new employment opportunities in the very cities whose rapid population growth is worrying the government.

Thus, it becomes important for governments to consider the social and spatial biases inherent within the policy framework for economic policy. As Chapter 8 noted, virtually every government policy, government action or item of government expenditure has some effect on the spatial distribution of development (and thus of population). And as the examples in Chapter 8 show, many of the most powerful influences on where development takes place within the urban system stem from macro-economic policies, government structure, tax systems, pricing policies and sectoral investment plans. As a recent paper commented, 'eliminating sectoral distortions may do more for decentralised development than all the myriad spatial efforts conventionally proposed by Third World policy makers' (Hamer, 1984, pp. 18-19).

Chapter 8 gave various examples of where the social and spatial impacts of governments' macro-ecomomic or pricing policies or sectoral investment plans were contrary to stated social and spatial goals. But the fact that strong spatial biases within such policies exist is not in itself the issue; the issue is whether such spatial biases are judged to be useful contributions to social and economic development goals. Given the priority that many national governments seem to be attaching to slowing population growth in the largest cities and stimulating development in backward regions, at least in stated goals, spatial biases in such policies rarely coincide with the social and spatial aims of the government which is implementing them.

Certainly, part of the reason is that powerful vested interests benefit from existing policies while special programmes for small and intermediate urban centres (or backward regions), however ineffective, give the impression that government is doing something. So often, special policies for certain urban centres or certain areas are much influenced by the need to gain or retain political support there. Indeed, as was illustrated in Chapter 5, the extent to which a small or intermediate urban centre has received public investments may have been much influenced by the power and status of the politician within whose constituency the centre happens to be located.

The studies reviewed in Chapter 8 suggest not so much an 'urban bias' in government policies and plans, for most small and many intermediate urban centres have been as starved of public investments and as ignored in public programmes as most rural areas. 'Large urban centre' bias would be more accurate for many nations, although this too is a little simplistic for there are also large urban centres which receive little or no public investment. 'Urban bias' or 'large city bias' also implies that the inhabitants of urban areas or large cities benefit more than rural inhabitants from public investments and policies. But this is also not entirely correct. For example, a high proportion of the inhabitants of most large cities have received little or no benefit either from public investments in infrastructure and services or from adequate waged employment from new productive activities. The 'bias' in public policies, investments and provision of services is more in favour of the better off inhabitants and more powerful industrial, commercial and financial concerns. In nations where these are concentrated in or close to large cities, this will become manifest as the 'spatial bias' for large cities, and the form that the spatial bias takes will inevitably change as government policies change to reflect the increasing power of one particular vested interest over others.

If this 'bias' towards major enterprises and richer households in larger cities is apparent in many governments' policies – and too few empirical studies have been undertaken to determine whether this is the case – then it points to the need for changes. In the larger cities, those enterprises and households fortunate enough to have adequate piped water supplies and services to remove household and human wastes may be charged less than the real cost of providing and maintaining such services – and providing the capital needed to extend such services to other households. If a high proportion of national government's investment in water supply is going to provide piped water to middle and upper income groups and to registered enterprises just in large cities, both the social and the spatial biases are obvious. It is not uncommon to find lower income groups who live in houses or shacks constructed on illegally occupied or subdivided land, buying water of dubious quality from private vendors at 10-20 times the price per litre paid by middle or upper income groups in residential areas served by piped water. Similarly, it is not uncommon to find a heavy concentration of publicly financed health care services and facilities in large cities and yet the low income population in that city having little or no access to them.

As the UN Recommendations state (United Nations, 1985), 'only through small and intermediate urban centres can many social and technical services be provided to most of the population of Third World countries' (p. 5). Reaching a higher proportion of the national population with access to health care and options for education and training implies an increase in appropriate services and facilities within many such centres.

Similarly, water supply and sanitation systems for small and intermediate urban centres do not necessarily imply higher per capita costs and lower cost recovery than for larger centres. 'The economies of scale in providing such physical services as protected water supplies and hygienic disposal of household and human wastes have been much over-stated in development literature. If the appropriate technology is chosen, and a suitable organisation is set up for operation and maintenance, per capita costs in small and intermediate urban centres can be lower than in large urban centres. Many options are available to match the wide range of physical conditions, social preferences and economic resources found in different settlements'. (ibid, p. 6) Similarly, there is a wide range of ways of disposing of household wastes, including relatively cheap and simple methods of reusing some components of such waste. In relation to public transport, public authorities have perhaps underestimated the extent to which appropriately designed and managed systems can be largely self-financing. However with these and other public services and facilities, the possibilities for improvement largely depend on a level of skilled personnel and resources at local government level which is rarely apparent.

But just as there is an evident need to give more attention to local needs and resources in formulating plans and programmes, so is there an evident need to lessen the centralisation of school curricula. School programmes are often uniform for entire nations; rarely do they make allowances for local and regional needs and resources. Skill training appropriate to local development possibilities is even rarer, although with the notable exception of the Tiradentes project. As Max Neef (1982) notes, vocational training, as traditionally practised in most countries of Latin America is 'discriminate in the sense that it tends to benefit the large metropolitan areas more than the small cities, towns and villages. Furthermore..the orientation and content of any vocational training curricula has to be determined by – and adapted to – regional and local characteristics, and not by the extrapolation of national and global trends' (p. 121). What distinguishes the Tiradentes project in Brazil from most other programmes for small or intermediate urban centres was the extent to which it was based on locally articulated needs and local skills and resources. The municipality has some 10,000 inhabitants, divided into two urban districts and a rural area of poor soils. In recent decades, its economy stagnated after a period of splendour when gold was mined nearby. The project sought to build on the old traditions of craftsmanship and to allow the craftsmen to pass their skills onto younger apprentices. The project had many other aspects such as the preparation of an exhibition on one hundred years of photographs of Tiradentes, and the formation of a Guild of the Artisans. But the project's relevance is not so much in what it did but how what it sought to do was based on the resources of that particular municipality and on the needs of its inhabitants.

One aspect of small and intermediate urban centres which has gone virtually unmentioned in this volume is the fact that they so often serve as the focus for social life and social contacts in their area. While we found few empirical studies on this, in many areas, there are likely to be friendship, kinship and family links between many rural inhabitants and those in small and intermediate urban centres. Such centres may be the place where young people in the area socialize, where there are important opportunities to meet people of the opposite sex and where there are opportunities for sport, recreation, and for attending religious services and festivals. Certainly it is within many such centres that the culture of the area has its most concentrated expression. Simply because such aspects are less tangible and less researched than, say, the potential of the area for increasing agricultural production, it should not mean that the role they play in making smaller urban centres desirable places to live and work is underestimated.

As noted already, implicit or explicit in the writings of many contemporary urban specialists is the idea that all Third World nations will undergo comparable transformations to those experienced by some of the richer First World nations in terms of the proportion of the population living in urban centres and the spatial distribution of urban population. This is usually based on the assumption that the economies of all Third World nations will undergo similar transformations to those experienced by richer First World nations, as if there were an historically linear development process that all nations should follow. We hope that the case studies in Chapters 2 to 6 have revealed how intimately the urbanisation process and the form it takes are influenced by local, regional and national factors which are very specific to the locality, region and nation, and which in turn also interact with influences from the international economy. Only by a more locality, region and nation specific understanding of how social, economic and political forces influence the social and spatial distribution of the costs and benefits of economic change can development plans and programmes be made more relevant to lower income groups' needs.

References

Hamer, Andrew M. (1984), *Decentralised Urban Development and Industrial Location Behaviour in Sao Paulo, Brazil: A Synthesis of Research Issues and Conclusions,* discussion paper, Water Supply and Urban Development Department, the World Bank.

Linn, Johannes F. (1983), *Cities in the Developing World,* World Bank, Oxford University Press.

Max-Neef, Manfred A. (1982), *From the Outside Looking In,* Dag Hammarskjold Foundation, Uppsala, Sweden.

United Nations (1985), 'Planning and Management of Human Settlements with Emphasis on Small and Intermediate Towns and Local growth Points: Report of the Executive Director', paper HS/C/8/3 presented to the Eighth Session of the UN Commission on Human Settlements, February.

Appendix
The Annotated Bibliographies

Two annotated bibliographies have been published; one in Spanish covering just Latin America and the other in English covering the Third World.

In reviewing published and theoretical work of relevance to the subject of small and intermediate urban centres, we concentrated on those periodicals listed below. Clearly, the annotated bibliographies could have covered more published material, including books and research papers. But the decision was taken to concentrate on these periodicals for two reasons. The first is that with limited time and resources to devote to the annotated bibliographies, we decided to concentrate on journals in which an initial survey found detailed empirical studies. Given the style of the bibliographies – with long and detailed annotations – we had to limit the material they would cover. The second is that we did not want to narrow the choice of papers to those focusing on small and intermediate urban centres. It seemed useful to include, for instance, papers on migratory patterns or rural development or national settlement policies with material of relevance to small and intermediate urban centres. It seemed preferable to limit the amount of publications reviewed but to comprehensively cover the periodicals chosen for review.

The decision to give relatively long and detailed annotations was made because we wish these bibliographies to be widely used in Third World research, training and teaching institutions, where access to many periodicals is difficult. Thus, it is important to give the reader a very clear idea as to what a particular paper contains so that it is easy for the reader to judge whether they wish to go to the trouble (and expense) of obtaining the original.

The English language annotated bibliography covering the whole Third World is divided into two parts. Part I covers papers which focus on one or a group of small and intermediate urban centres; most focus on just one aspect of one centre. The annotations are divided into nine sections under the following headings:

(*a*) economic organisation
(*b*) social organisation
(*c*) political structure
(*d*) social stratification
(*e*) structural change

(*f*) relations between local centre and national society
(*g*) historical studies
(*h*) planning
(*i*) other

Part II is divided into four sections:

(*a*) migration
(*b*) contemporary settlement patterns and trends
(*c*) productive organisation
(*d*) government strategies.

Papers covered in Part II(d) are further broken down under the following headings: 'general', 'national strategies' and 'regional/city' strategies.

The English language annotated bibliography is available from the Human Settlements programme, IIED, 3 Endsleigh Street, London WC1H ODD. The Spanish language annotated bibliography (covering Latin America) is available from CEUR, Piso 7, Cuerpo A, Av. Corrientes 2835, (1193) Buenos Aires, Argentina.

The periodicals covered in the annotated bibliographies are:

Actas de los Congresos de Americanistas, 1966-1976
Africa Development, 1976-1981
America Indigena, 1969-1980
American Anthropologist, 1977-1981
American Sociological Review, 1970-1981
Anuario Indigenista, 1970-1980
Bangladesh Development Studies, 1973-1980
Bulletin of Indonesian Economic Studies, 1970-1982
Boletin de Estudios Latinoamericanos y del Caribe, 1976-1980
Cahiers des Ameriques Latines, 1972-1978
Community Development, 1965-1974
Demografia y Economica, 1970-1981
Desarollo Economico Revista de Ciencias Sociales, 1960-1981
Development and Change, 1970-1982
Development Dialogue, 1975-1981
Developing Economies, 1970-1982
Documentos Internos de la CEPAL
Economic Development and Cultural change, 1970-1982
Ekistics, 1970-1981
Espaces et Societes, 1975-1981
Estudios Andinos, 1970-1981
Estudios CEBRAP, 1973-1980
Estudios Sociales Centroamericanos, 1975-1980
EURE, 1970-1982
Habitat International, 1976-1982

Informes del Istituto Nacional de Antropologia, 1974
International Journal of Urban and Regional Research, 1977-1982
Journal of Modern African Studies, 1970-1982
Journal of Peasant Studies, 1973-1982
Land Economics, 1965-1981
Latin American Research Review, 1967-1980
Latin American Urban Research, 1971
Marga Quarterly Journal, 1971-1982
Pakistan Development Review, 1970-1981
Regional and Urban Economics, 1973-1980
Review of African Political Economy, 1974-1980
Revista Ambiente, 1981-1982
Revista de Administacao Municipal, 1974-1979
Revista de Ciencias Sociales, 1970-1979
Revista CEPAL, 1976-1981
Revista de Indias, 1965
Revista Interamericana de Planificacion, 1972-1982
Revista Latinoamericana de Sociologia, 1969-1980
Revista Mexicana de Sociologia, 1967-1980
Revista Nuestra Architectura
Revista Paraguaya de Sociologia, 1969-1979
Rural Africana, 1978-1980
Tiers Monde, 1968-1975
Third World Planning Review, 1979-1982
Trimestre Economico, 1962-1981
Urban Studies, 1973-1980
Urban Affairs Quarterly, 1969-1981
World Development, 1973-1982

Index